T0152365

Humana Festival 2012
The Complete Plays

About the Humana Foundation

The Humana Foundation was established in 1981 as the philanthropic arm of Humana Inc., one of the nation's leading health care companies. Located in Louisville, Ky., the site of Humana's corporate headquarters, the Foundation's mission is to promote healthy lives and healthy communities. The Foundation's key funding priorities are childhood health, intergenerational health, and active lifestyles. For more information, visit www.humanafoundation.org.

Humana and the Humana Foundation are dedicated to Corporate Social Responsibility. Our goal is to ensure that every business decision we make reflects our commitment to improving the health and well-being of our members, our associates, the communities we serve, and our planet.

Humana Festival 2012
The Complete Plays

Edited by
Amy Wegener and Sarah Lunnie

New York, NY

Copyright © 2013 by Playscripts, Inc.
All rights reserved

Published by Playscripts, Inc.
450 Seventh Avenue, Suite 809
New York, New York, 10123
www.playscripts.com

Cover Design by Andy Perez
Cover Image by Wayne Brezinka
Text Design and Layout by Erin Salvi

First Edition: April 2013
10 9 8 7 6 5 4 3 2 1

CAUTION: Professionals and amateurs are hereby warned that plays represented in this book are subject to a royalty. They are fully protected under the copyright laws of the United States of America and of all countries covered by the International Copyright Union (including the Dominion of Canada and the rest of the British Commonwealth), the Berne Convention, the Pan-American Copyright Convention and the Universal Copyright Convention, as well as all countries with which the United States has reciprocal copyright relations. All rights, including professional and amateur stage rights, motion picture, recitation, lecturing, public reading, radio broadcasting, television, video or sound recording, all other forms of mechanical or electronic reproduction, such as CD-ROM, CD-I, information storage and retrieval systems and photocopying, and the rights of translation into foreign languages, are strictly reserved. Particular emphasis is laid upon the matter of readings, permission for which must be secured in writing. See individual plays for contact information.

LCCN: 95650734
ISSN: 1935-4452

ISBN-13: 978-1-62384-000-6

Contents

Acknowledgments

The editors wish to thank the following persons for their invaluable assistance in compiling this volume:

Jennifer Bielstein
Zach Chotzen-Freund
Molly Clasen
Sean Daniels
Michael Bigelow Dixon
Sara Durham
Dominic Finocchiaro
Meg Fister
Kirsty Gaukel
Kory Kelly
Michael Legg
Danielle Manley
Hannah Rae Montgomery
Andy Perez
Jessica Reese
Jeffrey S. Rodgers
Erin Salvi
Zan Sawyer-Dailey
Naomi Shafer
Stephanie Spalding
Hadi Tabbal
Les Waters
Kathryn Zukaitis

Jessica Amato
William Craver
Val Day
Ron Gwiazda
Corinne Hayoun
Patrick Herold
Mark Orsini
Bruce Ostler
Joseph Rosswog
Chris Till
Derek Zasky

Actors Theatre of Louisville Staff
Humana Festival 2012

ARTISTIC DIRECTOR, Les Waters

MANAGING DIRECTOR, Jennifer Bielstein

ADMINISTRATION

General Manager...Jeffrey S. Rodgers
Human Resources Manager ....Cora Brown
Systems Manager..Dottie Krebs
Executive Assistant...Janelle Baker
Administrative Services Coordinator .... Alan Meyer

Marketing & Communications

Director ....Kory P. Kelly
Public Relations Manager.................................. Kirsty Gaukel
Marketing and Sales Manager...............................Sarah R. Rowan
Audience Development and Special Events Manager .... Stephanie Spalding
Communications Coordinator .... Whitney Miller-Brengle
Graphic Designer .... Andy Perez
Group Sales Manager ....Sarah Peters
Group Sales Associate....................................... Chris O'Leary

Development

Director .... Josef Krebs
Manager of Corporate Relations .... Danielle Manley
Manager of Foundation and Government Relations ....Emily Ruddock
Manager of the Annual Fund........................ Gretchen Abrahamsen
Special Projects ....Kate Chandler
Development Coordinator ....Katie McCandless
Development Fellow..Carrie Cooke

Finance

Finance Director ....Peggy Shake
Accounting Coordinator.................................... Jason Acree
Accounting Assistant....................... Brunhilda Williams-Curington

Operations

Director .... Mike Schüssler-Williams
Operations Manager .... Barry Witt
Maintenance....................................Ricky Baldon, John Voyles
Building Services............................ Gary Baldon, Patricia Duncan,
Hank Hunter, Cindy Woodward
Receptionist .... Griffin Falvey

AUDIENCE SERVICES

Ticket Sales

Director .... Kim McKercher
Senior Box Office Manager .... Saundra Blakeney
Training Manager ....Steve Clark
Season Tickets Manager .... Julie Gallegos
Senior Customer Service Representative.................... Kristy Kannapell
Customer Service Representatives .... Cheryl Anderson, Sera Bonnett-Bredt,
Brady Carnahan, Tony Hammons,
Rachel McKee, Dustin Morris, Kae Thompson

Volunteer and Audience Relations

Director ....Allison Hammons
House Managers .... Dana Cooley, Elizabeth Cooley,
Sara Durham, Jackson C. Haywood,
Amanda Simmons, Rachel Fae Szymanski
Lobby Manager .... Tiffany Walton
Coat Check Supervisor .... Cory Vaughn
Coat Check Attendants .... Tanisha Johnson, Kathleen Kirkpatrick

ARTISTIC

Associate Director..................................... Zan Sawyer-Dailey
Arts Management Executive Assistant .... Meg Fister
Company Manager ....Dot King

Literary

Literary Director .... Amy Wegener
Literary Manager..Sarah Lunnie
Literary Associate .... Hannah Rae Montgomery

Resident Designers

Costume Designer...................................... Lorraine Venberg
Lighting Designer .... Brian J. Lilienthal

Education

Director ....Steven Rahe
Associate Director..Jacob Stoebel
Education Fellow... Jane B. Jones
Teaching Artists................................Liz Fentress, Keith McGill,
Jacqueline Thompson

PRODUCTION

Production Manager ....Kathleen Kronauer
Assistant Production Manager ....Paul Werner
Production Stage Manager ....Paul Mills Holmes
Resident Stage Managers...................... Kathy Preher, Kimberly J. First,
Stephen Horton
Production Assistants ....Jessica Potter, Katie Shade

Scenic

Technical Director. . . . . Jason Grant
Assistant Technical Director . . . . Alexis Tucker
Shop Foreman . . . . Javan Roy-Bachman
Drafter/Rigger. . . . . Braden Blauser
Carpenters . . . . Kathryn Blackburn, Daniel Cutler, Ryan Harvey,
Patrick Jump*, Andrew Patton, Pierre Vendette
Pamela Brown Deck Carpenter . . . . Peter Regalbuto
Bingham Theatre Deck Carpenter. . . . . Mathew Krell
Scenic Charge. . . . . Kieran Wathen
Assistant Scenic Charge . . . . Sabra Crockett

Costumes

Costume Director . . . . Kristopher Castle
Costume Stock & Administrative Coordinator . . . . Lisa Weber
Assistant Costume Designer. . . . . Lindsay Chamberlin
Wig and Makeup Master . . . . Heather Fleming
Crafts Master . . . . Shari Cochran
Draper/Tailor . . . . Bineke Kiernan
First Hand . . . . Christi Johnson
Stitchers . . . . Elizabeth Hahn, Bonnie Jonus
Pamela Brown Wardrobe Supervisor. . . . . Asia Bloemer
Bingham Theatre Wardrobe Supervisor . . . . Julian Arrington
Humana Design Assistant. . . . . Megan Shuey
Journeyman . . . . Danny Chihuahua*
Wig Journeyman . . . . Hannah Wold*

Lighting

Supervisor . . . . Nick Dent
Assistant Supervisor . . . . Christine Ferriter
First Electrician . . . . Erin Teachman
Technicians . . . . Jesse AlFord, Kathleen Dieckmann, Brian Hoehne

Sound

Supervisor/Associate Designer . . . . Benjamin Marcum
Engineer. . . . . Paul Doyle
Technicians . . . . Adam Smith, Mary Stebelton,
Amanda Werre

Properties

Properties Director . . . . Mark Walston
Properties Masters. . . . . Joe Cunningham, Seán McArdle
Carpenter Artisan . . . . Karl Anderson
Soft Goods Artisan . . . . Heather Lindert
General Artisan . . . . Jay Tollefsen
Artisan/Shopper . . . . Jessie Combest
Artisans . . . . Noah Johnson, Nick Passafiume

Video

Media Technologist . . . . Philip Allgeier

APPRENTICE/INTERN COMPANY

Director . . . . Michael Legg
Associate Director . . . . Amy Attaway

Apprentices

Rivka Borek, J. Alexander Coe, Sabrina Conti, Erika Diehl, Lisa Dring, Jonathan Finnegan, Zoë Sophia Garcia, Doug Harris, Kanomé Jones, Alexander Kirby, Daniel Kopystanski, Liz Malarkey, Marianna McClellan, Katie Medford, Sean Mellott, Maggie Raymond, Chris Reid, Keaton Schmidt, Calvin Smith, Trent Stork, Nick Vannoy, Amir Wachterman

Members of the Apprentice Company receive additional training at the Louisville Ballet.

Interns

A/I Administration . . . . Jackson C. Haywood
Arts Administration . . . . Rachel McKee
Directing . . . . Lillian Meredith, Caitlin Ryan O'Connell
Dramaturgy/Literary Management . . . . Molly Clasen,
Dominic Finocchiaro
Education . . . . Betsy Anne Huggins, Dustin C.T. Morris
Festival Management . . . . Laura Durham
Graphic Design . . . . Mary Kate Zihar
Lighting . . . . Alan Pleiman
Marketing . . . . Sara E. Durham
Media Technology . . . . Chris Owens
Production Management . . . . Michael Whatley
Public Relations . . . . Melinda Beck
Stage Management . . . . Kevin Paul Love, Mary Elizabeth Penrose,
Suzanne Elizabeth Spicer, Amelia Vanderbilt

Usher Captains

Dolly Adams, Marie Allen, Libba & Chuck Bonifer, Tanya Briley, Maleva Chamberlain, Donna Conlon, Terry Conway, Doris Elder, Reese Fisher, Joyce French, Tom Gerstle, Marilyn Huffman, Sandy Kissling, Nickie Langdon, Barbara Nichols, Cathy Nooning, Teresa Nusz, Judy Pearson, Nancy Rankin, Nathan Rome, Bob Rosedale, Amanda Simmons, Jenna Thomas, Christopher Thompson, Tim Unruh, David Wallace, Bette Wood

Actors Theatre's company doctors:
Dr. Andrew Mickler, F.A.C.S.
Dr. Edwin Hopson, DC, CSCS
Dr. Bill Breuer, MCH, DC, FAPHP

* Denotes Paul Owen Fellow

Foreword

When I landed in my post as the new Artistic Director at Actors Theatre of Louisville, the 2012 Humana Festival of New American Plays was already going full tilt. I arrived from my previous home in Berkeley, California, set my bags down, and headed into the teeming crowds of producers, literary managers, press, and other theatre addicts who had gathered to take in the marathon of plays during one of the Humana Festival's Industry Weekends—just some of the nearly 40,000 people who attended last year. During this whirlwind celebration of new plays, 14 writers saw their work fully produced, translated from the page to a vibrant, three-dimensional theatrical life that had been shaped every step of the way by their imaginations. There is nothing quite like the energy of an original story captivating an audience for the first time, of actors nailing the unique rhythm of a playwright's language, or of a team of designers making elegant choices that evoke a whole new world.

The journey taken by the plays in the Humana Festival, and the support that they're given along the way, is nothing short of remarkable. I knew this more than a decade before taking the reins as Artistic Director, having worked at the Humana Festival twice before: in 2000, I directed the world premiere of Charles L. Mee's *Big Love*, and in 2004, I returned to direct Naomi Iizuka's *At the Vanishing Point*, a play about Louisville's Butchertown neighborhood that was staged in one of its historic warehouses. So I knew that I was joining an organization that takes good care of new plays and writers, a place where everyone behind the scenes has hearts and minds set on giving this work its best possible launch into the world. The Humana Festival's ability to impact the field—both by introducing these particular plays and playwrights to the American theatre, and by furthering the conversation about the art form—remains unparalleled. Equally importantly, though, there's a spirit of generosity, exchange and adventure surrounding this work from all sides, from the extraordinary writers and their talented collaborators, to the hardworking staff, to our dynamic local and national audiences that come from miles around to experience new plays.

But the Humana Festival doesn't end there, and this book is an important facet of Actors Theatre's effort to champion these plays and their authors. We congratulate the playwrights of the 2012 Humana Festival and hope that this volume continues their journey, reaching new readers and audiences far beyond those lively crowds that I encountered when I touched down in Louisville last spring.

—*Les Waters*
Artistic Director
Actors Theatre of Louisville

Editors' Note

Sometimes it's in the moment when the ground shifts beneath your feet and there's an unfamiliar bend in the road that you take another look at the compass—and remember why you set out walking in the first place. Such was the case with the 2012 Humana Festival of New American Plays, whose lineup was chosen in the midst of a transition in artistic leadership at Actors Theatre of Louisville. Marc Masterson, the theatre's Artistic Director for more than a decade, had departed to head South Coast Repertory in California, and renowned director Les Waters, then at Berkeley Repertory Theatre, would soon be appointed to take his place. But in the meantime, there was an annual Humana Festival to program and produce, which required wide reading, robust conversation, and a roadmap for careful deliberation about the 36th annual incarnation of this national event.

Rather than unmooring the artistic staff at Actors Theatre, the challenge of selecting a Humana Festival without an artistic director awakened us anew to a shared sense of purpose and collaboration. As we prepared for change and began to imagine the theatre's next era, we were inspired to think deeply about what the Humana Festival means—to our staff, to the industry, to the Louisville community, and to playwrights and other artists. Prompted by Jennifer Bielstein, Actors Theatre's Managing Director, we began by defining the values that would guide a small team of literary and artistic staff in choosing the Festival, a set of priorities that could lend clarity to the necessarily subjective curatorial task at hand. So we embarked upon the selection process by thinking not only about why we fall in love with particular plays, but also about how we evaluate the balance and diversity of the lineup. To be sure, these questions had always animated selection conversations with an artistic director, but the absence of this "decider" led to a sharpened and transparent internal articulation of our values.

In other words: this transitional moment in Actors Theatre's evolution forced us to step back and reflect upon how we program this visible and venerable launch pad for new plays. The result was a Humana Festival that we remember with pride, as much for the integrity of the curatorial process as for the breadth, intelligence and power of the selected plays.

The values that we defined during those important initial conversations are very much evident in the diverse mix of voices and styles, cultural perspectives and stories that marked the 2012 Humana Festival of New American Plays. We welcomed multiple writers whose Festival premieres were their first major professional productions, as well as Broadway veterans Lisa Kron and Greg Kotis. The work of female playwrights stood alongside that of men on our stages, and juicy leading roles for women abounded. There were varied cultures and histories represented on stage too: Mona Mansour took us from 1960s Palestine to London with her traveling newlyweds in *The Hour of Feeling*, while in *How We Got On*, rapper-poet-playwright Idris Goodwin spun us back to a Midwestern suburb in 1988, where hip hop takes root in the hearts and identities of three teenagers. Characters hailed from faraway places in Lucas Hnath's tense *Death Tax*, wherein a Haitian nurse strikes a desperate bargain with her wealthy, dying patient, and in Kotis' monstrously funny *Michael von Siebenburg Melts Through the Floorboards*, whose existentially challenged protagonist is a centuries-old undead Austrian baron. There were characters of all appetites and ages in this Festival—from young teenagers to an elderly woman confined to a hospital bed—who inhabited worlds ranging from spare, language-driven dramas to fantastical comedies.

This deliberate diversity was evident not only in terms of landscape, identity and culture, but in the different ways that the plays asked audiences to engage with and reflect upon the world we live in now. Lisa Kron's hilarious and rousing *The Veri**on Play*, which imagines one woman's increasingly absurd battle with her cell phone company, combines madcap comedy with a call to action against corporate malfeasance that echoes the outcry of the Occupy Wall Street movement. Lucas Hnath's incisive *Death Tax* takes a decidedly darker tack, exposing the murky ethics and understandable fears of its characters at the intersection of money, power and medicine. And Courtney Baron's *Eat Your Heart Out* beautifully braids together multiple converging storylines in her powerful (and often painfully funny) drama of parenthood and longing. In vastly varied ways, and very much by design, the mix of plays in the 2012 Festival reverberated with contemporary questions, whether holding up the mirror to our moment or traveling to more remote times and places.

Of course, programming the Humana Festival is not only a matter of curating plays, but also playwrights. The 2012 lineup was shaped with a view toward continuing to support remarkable veterans of Actors Theatre, while also forging new working relationships with writers whom we (and sometimes the field) are just getting to know. Courtney Baron, Greg Kotis, Lisa Kron, and Matt Schatz had seen their work performed in the Humana Festival before, and we eagerly welcomed them back. The ten other playwrights, however, were premiering plays in the Festival for the first time. That embrace of new conversations with artists strengthens Actors Theatre and the American theatre at large. In fact, several annual Humana Festival projects are conceived specifically to allow us to continually widen the circle of voices and stories that we are able to introduce to our audiences. One of them is a bill of ten-minute plays, selected from hundreds of open submissions to Actors Theatre's National Ten-Minute Play Contest. The inclusion of ten-minute plays in the Festival has enabled us to strike up conversations with many wonderful writers; this year, we welcomed the considerable talents and joyful participation of Laura Jacqmin, Nicholas C. Pappas, and Kyle John Schmidt.

Another annual project that multiplies the Festival's mix of voices is a play commissioned to be performed by the 22-member Acting Apprentice Company, the theatre's pre-professional training program. Each year, a seed for exploration is dreamed up by our artistic staff—in this case, a series of questions about the meaning of food in our lives and culture—and a carefully-assembled group of playwrights is invited to create a show, spending time in residence at Actors Theatre for workshops with the Apprentices during the fall and winter. This year's unique recipe resulted in *Oh, Gastronomy!* and brought to the table generous writers Michael Golamco, Carson Kreitzer, Steve Moulds, Tanya Saracho, and playwright-composer Matt Schatz—who created a delicious theatrical feast of scenes and songs. Beyond bringing these imaginative artists into the Humana Festival and engaging young actors in the process of making new work, the project has another creative benefit: it gives writers a rare opportunity to collaborate with one another.

In the end, selecting a Humana Festival is a chance to turn a national spotlight on deserving writers and share must-see new plays with the world. This is a highly visible act of advocacy in the American theatre, so it was with a sense of both responsibility and excitement that a small group of Actors Theatre artistic staffers went about choosing the lineup and throwing ourselves headlong into supporting these world premieres. Alongside the pair of us in the Literary Department, which guided the reading and selection process, a key voice was Zan Sawyer-Dailey, Actors Theatre's Associate Director—who, in addition to advising on play selection, also led the hiring of a wonderful slate of directors and a strong company of actors, and played a large role as a producer. Michael Bigelow Dixon, our Literary Advisor for the summer of 2011, as well as Michael Legg, the Director of the Apprentice/Intern Company, read scripts and provided keen insight at crucial moments in the reading process. Once the plays were selected, Production Manager Kathleen Kronauer and Assistant Production Manager Paul Werner led the hardworking production departments to beautifully support the artistic visions and designs that shaped ten fully-staged events. These are some of the 2012 Festival's architects, but to view the names associated with the countless acts of heroism that brought this celebration of new plays together, one only need turn to the list of Actors Theatre of Louisville staff in the opening pages of this book.

The 2012 Humana Festival of New American Plays was an adventure from start to finish, from early discussions of purpose all the way to the last curtain calls. Thinking back upon our collective process of falling for these plays, our beacon throughout was the initial enthusiasm we felt for these scripts and for their authors' singular imaginations—an admiration which continued to grow as we discussed them with colleagues, watched them evolve in rehearsals, and were finally captivated by seeing them in three dimensions. Revisiting these remarkable plays while editing this volume has been an immense pleasure, as is knowing that this book makes it possible to share with you the experience of discovering these new worlds for the first time—thus completing the circle from page to stage, and once again into readers' hands.

—Amy Wegener and Sarah Lunnie

EAT YOUR HEART OUT
by Courtney Baron

Copyright © 2012 by Courtney Baron. All rights reserved. CAUTION: Professionals and amateurs are hereby warned that *Eat Your Heart Out* is subject to a royalty. It is fully protected under the copyright laws of the United States of America and of all countries covered by the International Copyright Union (including the Dominion of Canada and the rest of the British Commonwealth), the Berne Convention, the Pan-American Copyright Convention and the Universal Copyright Convention, as well as all countries with which the United States has reciprocal copyright relations. All rights, including professional, amateur stage rights, motion picture, recitation, lecturing, public reading, radio broadcasting, television, video or sound recording, all other forms of mechanical or electronic reproduction, such as CD-ROM, CD-I, information storage and retrieval systems and photocopying, and the rights of translation into foreign languages, are strictly reserved. Particular emphasis is laid upon the matter of readings, permission for which must be secured from the Author's agent in writing.

Required royalties must be paid every time this play is performed before any audience, whether or not it is presented for profit and whether or not admission is charged.

All inquiries concerning rights, including amateur rights, should be addressed to: Dramatists Play Service, Inc., 440 Park Avenue South, New York, NY 10016, www.dramatists.com.

ABOUT *EAT YOUR HEART OUT*

This article first ran in the January/February 2012 issue of Inside Actors, Actors Theatre of Louisville's subscriber newsletter, and is based on conversations with the playwright before rehearsals for the Humana Festival production began.

With humor and heartache, Courtney Baron's *Eat Your Heart Out* deftly braids together the intersecting tales of six characters who are consumed by the awkward affliction of longing, trying so hard—sometimes *too* hard—to reach for the missing pieces of their lives. There's Alice and Gabe, a charming and otherwise successful couple unable to have a child of their own, who are facing the uncertain process of international adoption. Meanwhile, the social worker conducting the couple's home study, Nance, is a single mom whose training gives her no aid in handling the teenager she's struggling to raise: her smart, "caustic," and overweight daughter Evie. And Evie has her own yearnings concerning Colin, the good guy who's her best (read: only) friend in the snake pit of ostracism that is high school.

All of these storylines converge on the day of Nance's date with a jovial stranger named Tom, the first time in ages that she's ventured out to try and connect with someone—an encounter that is equal parts desperate and filled with possibility for them both. By weaving these threads into a rich design that emerges as the play unfolds, *Eat Your Heart Out* orchestrates a deeply affecting and often funny examination of the hopes and fears that swirl around parenthood, and of how much we can get in our own way when we're face-to-face with the thing we want most.

Baron began to imagine her characters' predicaments after spotting an article in the *New York Times Magazine*. "It was about a strange medical malady called Broken Heart Syndrome," explains the playwright, "which is brought on by an excess of adrenaline caused by stress, or by grief so overwhelming that your body has a chemical reaction that stimulates a kind of heart attack. There are stories of longtime marriages where one partner dies and the other passes away shortly thereafter, but there have been cases with younger people, too." Fascinated by this physiological phenomenon, Baron decided to mine the idea's metaphorical implications. "I started imagining a group of characters who all have their hearts broken," she recalls. "But I pulled away from the literal expression and started thinking more about what breaks our hearts. How do we live in that state and attempt to recover?"

Each of Baron's constellations of characters adds a specific sort of heartbreak to the mix. In Gabe and Alice's case, "They have this great house and great marriage and then they can't have a kid," says the author, "and their very real parental longing is compounded by their belief that they are people who are *supposed* to have things happen for them." Lacking any ability to sway the outcome of the adoption process (though they certainly try), "They are left with all of this longing and an inability to take control of it, other than putting themselves in the hands of others and being judged." Those hands belong to Nance, a working single mom without a partner to lean on. "Nance and Alice are equal in their judgment of each other," observes Baron, "and, at the same time, both jealous of what the other has."

For both women, in different ways, motherhood is a precarious thing, rife with the possibility of failure. Evie is a handful, and Nance's guilt over her inability to reach her offspring is acute. "There are all these expectations in our culture of what motherhood is supposed to be, and it can never fulfill *all* of those," argues Baron. "You're charged with making a human being, but some of that is not within your control—they're gonna be who they're gonna be." A charismatic wit prone to self-sabotage, Evie lets her size define her in ways that strain not only her relationship with her mom, but with the well-meaning best friend she's crushing on. "Evie is setting herself up to have her heart broken every time she sees Colin," Baron says, "because she is a person who has decided that her weight is her obstacle." Baron keenly observes the complexity of Evie's mindset in a way that makes us fall in love with the teenager even as we see her culpability. In this way, the playwright strives to do Evie's experience justice. "I don't think people really write about what it's like to be an overweight teenager in any *real* way that I've seen," she notes.

Through it all, Nance plays a role in everyone's longings and losses—becoming the nexus of the action as she travels through the play as a mom, a social worker, and a first date gazing toward the possibility of romance. Her fluid movement among the story's threads creates a resonance between them, beautifully bringing the play's form and content full circle as we realize that all these broken hearts beat together in interdependent and surprising ways. And so in spite of their recognizably funny and painful confusion, the denizens of *Eat Your Heart Out* also embody a poignant sense of hope: "They all have the ability to get out of their own way and fulfill what they want," says Baron. "There is the potential that love can consume us."

—Amy Wegener

BIOGRAPHY

Courtney Baron's play *A Very Common Procedure* premiered at the Magic Theatre (dir. Loretta Greco) and then at MCC Theater in New York (dir. Michael Greif). Her play *Consumption* was commissioned and produced by the Guthrie Theater in partnership with the University of Minnesota. Other productions include: *Here I Lie* as part of Rising Phoenix Rep's Cino Nights, New York; *These Three Here* at Actors Theatre of Louisville; *Earlstreetman* and *Confidence Man* as a part of Christine Jones' Theatre For One; *John Brown's Body* with the Keen Company; *In the Widow's Garden* and *Dear Anton* for the ChekhovNOW! Festival, New York City; and *To Know Know Know Me* as part of the Keen Teens, New York City. Her play *Leave,* with music composed by Juliana Nash, was workshopped at Primary Stages. She has had plays read or workshopped at the Cherry Lane Theatre (mentored by David Auburn), Atlantic Theater Company, Manhattan Theatre Club, MCC Theater, The New Group, Famous Door Theatre in Chicago, the Guthrie, Ensemble Studio Theatre, as part of the New Work Now! series at The Public Theater, the Royal Court Theatre in London, and Theatre for the New City, among others. Baron was nominated for the American Theatre Critics Association's Osborn Award and was a winner of the Heideman Award at Actors Theatre of Louisville. She is a part of the Dorothy Strelsin New American Writers Group at Primary Stages. Baron holds an M.F.A. in playwriting from Columbia University.

ACKNOWLEDGMENTS

Eat Your Heart Out premiered at the Humana Festival of New American Plays in March 2012. It was directed by Adam Greenfield with the following cast:

NANCE	Kate Eastwood Norris
TOM	Alex Moggridge
EVIE	Sarah Grodsky
COLIN	Jordan Brodess
ALICE	Kate Arrington
GABE	Mike DiSalvo

and the following production staff:

Scenic Designer	Tom Tutino
Costume Designer	Connie Furr-Soloman
Lighting Designer	Kirk Bookman
Sound Designer	Benjamin Marcum
Properties Designer	Joe Cunningham
Stage Manager	Kimberly J. First
Dramaturg	Amy Wegener
Casting	Kelly Gillespie

Directing Assistant	Michael Whatley
Assistant Costume Designer	Daniel Chihuahua
Production Assistant	Kristen Mun
Assistant Dramaturg	Dominic Finocchiaro

Eat Your Heart Out was developed with The Dorothy Strelsin New American Writers Group. It was also developed at the Perry-Mansfield Performing Arts School New Works Festival, June 2011.

CHARACTERS

NANCE, late 30's. Evie's mom. A social worker.

TOM, mid-30's, incredibly energetic, Nance's date.

EVIE, 17. Overweight, not in the teen movie way, but actually. A size 18/20 is about right.

COLIN, 17. Evie's friend, he's hip and nerdy all at once.

ALICE, late 30's. She's an ivied Texas Jew, all smarts, good looks and charm.

GABE, late 30's, Alice's husband. An entertainment lawyer with an irresistible sense of humor.

SETTING

Pasadena, CA. The present.

NOTE

"/" denotes where the next character begins their interruption.

For Blair

Sarah Grodsky and Kate Eastwood Norris
in *Eat Your Heart Out*

36th Humana Festival of New American Plays
Actors Theatre of Louisville, 2012
Photo by Alan Simons

EAT YOUR HEART OUT

TOM, *mid-30's, sits on a bench in front of a David Hockney painting at the Norton Simon Museum in Pasadena, CA. He reaches into his messenger bag and pulls out a copy of something like* The Girl With the Dragon Tattoo. *He reads, well, he pretends to read. His finger finds a place that he has marked, he taps there until: finally,* NANCE, *late 30's, enters.* TOM *quickly resumes "reading"; he keeps his finger at his marked spot.* NANCE *is keeping it together. She sees* TOM, *offers up a meek wave. He doesn't look up from his book, though of course he's seen her.*

NANCE. Tom?

TOM. Nance? Sorry. Sorry. Just. I've got to finish this one sentence. Sorry. Okay...reading.

(*He slowly says as he reads:*)

"What she had realized was that love was that moment when your heart was about to burst." Wow. Okay. Nance.

NANCE. Sorry I'm late.

TOM. I didn't even—caught up—

NANCE. Exciting book?

TOM. Have you read it?

NANCE. No.

TOM. It's unbelievable. Did you see the movie?

NANCE. No.

TOM. I'm in the small minority that like the American movie better than the Swedish. Don't tell, but: I hate subtitles.

NANCE. Don't tell, but me too.

TOM. Of course, the book is better. Always, don't you think? I'll lend it to you when I'm done. But you have to promise to read it before you see the movie, okay? Promise?

NANCE. Okay.

TOM. You promise?

NANCE. Yes. Promise.

TOM. Good. I'll hold you to it.

NANCE. Okay.

TOM. I hope this is alright.

NANCE. What? The museum? Of course. It's great.

TOM. Do you come to First Fridays? I mean, before?

NANCE. No, I haven't, I—

TOM. (*Like the song "Goody Two Shoes" by Adam Ant.*) No books? No movies? No museums? What do you do?

NANCE. Oh. Well. I garden. A bit. Just a little, but I do.

TOM. My house is a burial ground for ficus trees.

NANCE. Oh. Those are hard to keep.

TOM. Really? The guy at the garden center said they'd be easy. I'm relieved. I thought maybe I'd become the boy with the ficus tattoo.

NANCE. Ficuses are hard.

TOM. Thank goodness. I was getting worried. Thank goodness we met, I feel better.

> (*She smiles. He is thrilled.*)

These First Fridays, people come and they stay in the current exhibitions, nobody comes to the permanent collection. Although this painting is on loan. Not permanent. Still. It's like a private gallery.

NANCE. It's nice.

TOM. Sit down. I've only actually been here once before. But I thought, this is better than coffee. Most people meet for coffee. I like coffee, it's good, but I don't know coffee is the date that says, "I'm not committing to a meal." Whereas, a museum, First Friday, it gives you something to talk about. You don't worry about whether or not you should order a tall or venti. Like if you order a tall, the woman might be insulted, might think you don't want to hang around, a venti might be too much, overeager, I want to sit here for hours kind of message before you even start talking—

NANCE. You could order a grande.

TOM. Good thinking. Land in the middle. That's a good idea. But you get my point. And what did we do, before Starbucks, where did people go?

NANCE. Bars.

TOM. Yeah, bars, the internet of the 90s.

NANCE. That's funny.

TOM. "Sense of humor is important" right? From your profile, one of your requirements.

NANCE. I like funny.

TOM. Do you like art?

NANCE. Sure. Sure.

TOM. Good, me neither.

NANCE. No, come on, I do.

TOM. "Sure" means "not really."

NANCE. I *like* art, I do. I don't go to museums very often.

TOM. Do you have art on your walls at home?

NANCE. Sure, yes, we do. Do you?

TOM. Yes. I have this. This right here, I have a poster of it, framed in the living room over the couch. I don't know, I was just kind of drawn to it.

NANCE. It's nice.

TOM. When I'm drawn to things…people. I react. Like I was drawn to your profile.

NANCE. I was drawn to yours.

TOM. That's why I "winked" at you.

NANCE. That's why I "winked" back.

TOM. We should do that now, wink at each other.

(*She laughs a little nervously.*)

Look, I'm winking at you Nance. Come on, wink back at me. Make it official.

NANCE. It's all so strange, internet dating—

TOM. (*Emphatically.*) Wink at me Nance.

(*She does.*)

There it is! We've now officially winked. Now we should get the profiles out of the way. Tell each other, actually say who we are and then the internet piece of it is erased, because I'm with you. Match dot com. Tell me who is Nance? What's your story?

NANCE. If you'd only asked me three hours ago—I'm sorry. I.

TOM. What? Am I talking too much?

NANCE. I've had a day. I just need two seconds.

TOM. Oh no, is this a tall?

NANCE. What? No. It's me. I just. Two seconds.

TOM. I can do that.

(*They sit and face the painting.* TOM *pats her back, in that awkward comforting way.*)

(EVIE, *17, and* COLIN, *17, are coming into* EVIE's *bedroom.*)

EVIE. I said, "My name is Fat Ass." Are you hearing me?

COLIN. Yeah, I heard you.

EVIE. I said it to—

COLIN. Holly Lynch. Yeah, I heard you.

EVIE. I was literally blindsided— what did she want?

COLIN. What *did* she want?

EVIE. I have no fucking clue. Two years with her, never a word, but I watched her coming across the cafeteria, her thong practically sling-shotting her ass towards me—

COLIN. (*He laughs.*) You're a fucking idiot, Evie.

EVIE. No, no, no, I want to have the afterschool movie moment where you reassure me. Tell me the popular kids are peaking early. They'll never leave Pasadena, hope their own kids are popular too so they can live through it all over again. Say that to me.

COLIN. —

EVIE. Colin, say *that* to me.

COLIN. You're a *stupid* fucking idiot, Evie.

EVIE. I'm not a stupid fucking idiot, in fact, I'm no longer even anonymous outcast senior number 122. No, now, now I'm "fat ass" number one.

COLIN. So everyone will call you "fat ass" for a while.

EVIE. So what?

COLIN. So what, Evie, Holly Lynch is a bitch.

EVIE. Oh really, and if everyone called you—

COLIN. What?

EVIE. I don't know. "Dumb ass."

COLIN. It's not the same. I'm not dumb.

EVIE. But I'm fat, right? So what, Evie, you are a fat ass?

COLIN. You're healthy.

EVIE. Thanks Grandma.

COLIN. I thought you didn't give a crap what people think.

EVIE. I care that when Lynch the Winch asks me my name, I say "Fat Ass." She'll probably fucking tweet about it.

COLIN. Jen Mason is going to love you. She's been trying to downplay that text of her tits for weeks.

EVIE. Did you see it?

COLIN. Yeah.

EVIE. That's like a hard-on "yeah."

COLIN. She's got a good body.

EVIE. Jen Mason has a pig face.

COLIN. I wasn't looking at her face.

EVIE. Oh Jesus, I want to die.

COLIN. You always want to die. Download some Morrissey and write some poetry.

EVIE. I'm a fat ass.

COLIN. So go on a diet.

EVIE. I'm on a diet.

COLIN. You ate a Snickers at lunch.

EVIE. I only ate it because I'm really sad?

COLIN. Are you asking me if you are sad?

EVIE. Are *you?*

COLIN. Nothing to be sad about. Only eight months left.

EVIE. Eight long and lonely months Colin.

COLIN. I have Shauna.

EVIE. A girlfriend in Canada is like the Yeti.

COLIN. Fuck you. New Hampshire.

EVIE. Close enough.

COLIN. Don't be shitty to me.

EVIE. But you love shitty ol' me.

COLIN. You're exhausting.

EVIE. Do you talk to Shauna about me? Will you tell her this? About Holly Lynch? Etcetera?

COLIN. I pretty much tell her everything and etcetera.

EVIE. Yeah. I'm cool with you telling her.

COLIN. We're totally completely honest. I have to tell her everything. Every night I write her a goodnight e-mail. I tell her everything. I haven't missed a single night.

EVIE. She's lucky.

COLIN. Seriously, Evie, I can't see what the point is if you aren't totally fucking honest all the time.

EVIE. You're right.

COLIN. I am.

EVIE. Honestly, Colin, I'm totally miserable about Holly Lynch.

COLIN. I know you are.

EVIE. It happened at lunch and by sixth period someone had put a sign on my locker with my new official title.

COLIN. It's like Jen Mason's tits text, let's fix it, divert attention.

EVIE. Divert attention from my ass? Impossible.

COLIN. Avert attention from your incredibly charming social dysfunction—

EVIE. I really am so charming—

COLIN. You really are so dysfunctional.

EVIE. And you're going to help me?

COLIN. Yeah. Sure.

EVIE. Why?

COLIN. Be-cause-you-are-my-friend.

EVIE. B-F-F.

COLIN. (*With all contempt for the idiots who actually say this word.*) Totes.

(ALICE, *in a pretty wrap dress. She goes to spray the mirror hanging on the wall. She has a bottle of Lemon Pledge. She sprays it and then realizes what she's done. She tries to rub it around, but the spray is greasy and it just makes a smudgy mess. She goes to get Windex, and tries to clean it; it works, but it's streaky.*
ALICE *gets the mirror clean.*)

ALICE. Okay.

(*She puts on her game face. The door opens and* GABE *comes in. He's carrying a giant bouquet, wrapped and stapled so that you can tell it's a big bouquet but you can't see all of the flowers.*)

GABE. Let the games begin!

ALICE. Oh. Wow!

GABE. You said big.

ALICE. I did.

GABE. It's too big?

ALICE. (*Cradling the flowers.*) I feel like Ms. Pasadena.

GABE. I tried.

ALICE. No, really, they're beautiful.

GABE. Wanna get a vase?

ALICE. Maybe two.

(*She starts to go for a vase.*)

GABE. Hey—

ALICE. What?

GABE. You look pretty.

ALICE. I do?

GABE. You do. Very.

ALICE. Too pretty?

GABE. I don't know what that means.

ALICE. Like I'm trying too hard?

GABE. No.

ALICE. Like this is just me?

GABE. Like just you.

ALICE. Because it's important, I mean, to me, that I don't look like I've done something that makes me look like I don't always look like this.

GABE. You always look pretty.

ALICE. We have to make a good first impression—

GABE. Ah-ha, do you think these will make a good first impression?

(*He shows her his hands.*)

ALICE. Wow.

GABE. Manicure. I went to that place you go to, I thought it'd be nice to shake her hand with. To show that we take care of ourselves. Feel it.

(*He runs his hand on her cheek.*)

ALICE. Fantastic. Oh my god, polished?

GABE. What? No. Buffed.

ALICE. So nice. Get that vase, the one up there, from your mother—

GABE. I thought you didn't like it.

ALICE. It's fine. It's big.

GABE. Who does your nails?

ALICE. Who?

GABE. Anne, Jo, Sue? Sue did my nails. But Alice, her name is not Sue. It's Mi-Sook. You can see it on her license up behind her. I mean she should be able to use her real name.

(ALICE *starts to arrange the flowers, she sneezes.*)

They don't think we'll be able to say it?

ALICE. Who?

GABE. The nail girls. Mi-Sook, you can say that, right? Of course you can. It's sad.

(ALICE *sneezes.*)

I wouldn't go to Korea and say my name is Chin, just because Gabe might be hard to pronounce.

ALICE. Are you kidding me?

GABE. What?

ALICE. (*Pulling out roses from the bouquet.*) Oh my fucking god. We've been married for seven years.

GABE. What?

ALICE. I'm allergic to roses Gabe.

(*She sneezes.*)

GABE. You are?

ALICE. My throat is closing up—

GABE. I didn't know—

ALICE. You do!

GABE. Obviously I don't.

ALICE. You *do* know, what about our wedding?

GABE. I forgot.

ALICE. You forgot our wedding?

GABE. No.

ALICE. Oh my god, you had Lizzie buy these flowers.

GABE. What? No I didn't.

ALICE. I asked *you* to do it, not your fucking assistant.

GABE. I did.

ALICE. You didn't.

GABE. So throw them out.

ALICE. You are such an asshole.

GABE. This is why you should do it yourself.

ALICE. Are you serious?

GABE. You always find something wrong with what I do. Always. Always.

    (They yell:)

ALICE. I'm god damned allergic!

GABE. So fucking throw them out Alice!

ALICE. I fucking hate you!

GABE. Jesus Christ Alice! Jesus fucking Christ!

    (GABE takes the flowers from her hands, opens the front door and throws them out.)

ALICE. You aren't really just going to leave those out there are you?

    (GABE goes out and comes back in the house with the flowers; he goes to the kitchen to throw them out.)

    (EVIE, in her room, shoves mini-doughnuts into her mouth. COLIN is standing in her doorway watching her, but she doesn't see him.)

NANCE. *(From offstage.)* Evelyn! Colin's here.

    (EVIE is startled, turns around, sees COLIN there. EVIE spits the doughnuts out.)

EVIE. Hey?

COLIN. You missed school. I brought you your Chemistry homework.

EVIE. Thanks.

    (They both stand there looking at the pile of chewed-up doughnuts on the floor.)

EVIE. Can we hug it out?

COLIN. —

EVIE. You should probably go.

COLIN. Yeah.

> (*He goes.* EVIE *bends down to clean up the doughnuts. She puts one in her mouth and chews it up, swallows.*)

> (GABE *comes back into the living room.*)

GABE. That's a nice spread, I like those black olives—

ALICE. Kalamata.

GABE. Want me to bring it out?

ALICE. No, I'm going to offer it, but not put it out.

GABE. Really?

ALICE. You think I should?

GABE. I don't know.

ALICE. I mean it's not like a cocktail hour or something, it's an interview.

GABE. A home study.

ALICE. Which is essentially an interview. Are you sane, is your house nice enough, can you be trusted to care for a baby?

GABE. Are your hands nicely manicured?

ALICE. I think you should wear a polo.

GABE. Really?

ALICE. You look like an executive.

GABE. I am an executive.

ALICE. You don't look relaxed.

GABE. I'm not.

ALICE. Oh my god, I'm going to cry.

GABE. I'll take off the jacket.

ALICE. Gabe, it's important.

GABE. I'm capable of deciding what to wear.

ALICE. I just. You're right.

GABE. Who wouldn't want to give us a kid?

ALICE. You're right.

GABE. I really am.

> (*They kiss.*)

ALICE. Are you going to talk about your parents' divorce? I mean is that something you've been planning?

GABE. No I'm planning to tell her that I beat you on Fridays.

ALICE. Not funny.

GABE. I'm not going to talk about my parents' divorce, Alice.

ALICE. Good.

GABE. Just don't criticize me in front of this woman.

ALICE. I'm going to sit and breathe.

GABE. Oh that'll be good.

    (*She sneezes. She sneezes again.*)

Bless you.

    (NANCE *and* TOM *in the gallery.*)

NANCE. I do like this painting.

TOM. It's called *Mr. and Mrs. Clark and Percy.* It's David Hockney. It's on loan from another museum.

NANCE. I thought you said you didn't like art.

TOM. I don't. I like this painting. That's all. I saw it and I liked it.

NANCE. You bring all your first dates to the museum?

TOM. What? No.

NANCE. I was kidding.

TOM. Ha. Right. Percy is the cat, I think it's kind of funny.

NANCE. Do you have cats?

TOM. No. Your profile said you didn't have animals.

NANCE. Well, I do have a teenaged daughter.

    (*She laughs. He tries to laugh too.*)

TOM. Teenagers baa-aah scary animals. I'm not scared off by that. My ex-wife didn't want kids.

NANCE. But you do?

TOM. I'm not scared of kids.

NANCE. Oh god, should I have even asked that? I'm not saying that's what I want. Sorry.

TOM. Have you been on a lot of dates?

NANCE. I don't think so.

TOM. No. Me neither.

NANCE. Good.

TOM. But have you had at least one where the person didn't look anything like their picture?

NANCE. You don't think I look like my profile picture?

TOM. No. You do.

NANCE. Good.

TOM. You know the trick is you have to go out with someone who has more than one picture, because nobody has five fantastic pictures, so you can get the real—

NANCE. You've had some bad luck?

TOM. Some women. They post older pictures. And then, they've filled out or something since—

NANCE. Yow. Filled out?

TOM. No. I mean, just changed. Really changed. If I put a picture of 30-year-old me. More hair me. Wouldn't you be disappointed?

NANCE. Only disappointed that you lied.

TOM. Exactly. It isn't about how you look, it's about being honest.

NANCE. It's hard, you know, to put yourself out there.

TOM. I know.

(*Beat.*)

You're pretty Nance, you're better than your picture.

NANCE. Thanks.

(*Beat.*)

TOM. Am I?

NANCE. Oh. Yes, of course.

(COLIN *types.*)

COLIN. Dear Shauna. Day 47. Greetings from the land of perpetual summer. It's boiling my brain. It's why everyone in California is retarded. I'm going to buy you a webcam. I'm dying to see your face. Don't worry I'm not tan. I'm still your pasty white knight. I'm defying the sun. Did you get my package? Pasadena dirt. I couldn't get you sand, there are no beaches here, just strip malls. The death of civilization. We're reading *Inferno* in English. They're two years dumber here, we read it Sophomore, so you're probably reading it now, here they read it Senior. Evie says we should graffiti "Abandon all hope ye who enter here" over the entrance at Woodrow. She's a freak. I think you are my Beatrice and I'm in Hell wishing I was with you. Good night. I love you Shauna. Colin. Send.

(EVIE *sits at the table with her mom,* NANCE.)

NANCE. It's 5:30.

EVIE. Congratulations.

NANCE. This is our talking time.

EVIE. I love talking time.

NANCE. No, I'm serious.

EVIE. Oh, I know you are.

NANCE. Not fighting time, talking time.

EVIE. What's the topic?

NANCE. Good. How about school? How was school?

EVIE. "How was school?" Are you serious.

NANCE. Fine, give me a topic.

EVIE. How about Match dot com?

NANCE. Evelyn.

EVIE. Evie.

NANCE. I named you Evelyn, not Evie.

EVIE. Gotcha Nance.

NANCE. "Mom."

EVIE. You know what? I do want to discuss my education.

NANCE. Great.

EVIE. I want to home school.

NANCE. You want me to teach you?

EVIE. The classes are online.

NANCE. School isn't just a place for academics, it's a social education as well.

EVIE. Really? How interesting.

NANCE. Please, don't deflect.

EVIE. I'm a super deflector.

NANCE. This isn't talking, Evelyn.

EVIE. Really? What is it?

NANCE. It's not talking.

EVIE. So we're done?

NANCE. I want to—maybe *we* should call Susan Shankle. Schedule a session.

EVIE. So call her.

NANCE. You need someone to talk to.

EVIE. Someone like you?

NANCE. Is that so repugnant?

EVIE. I want to see someone with an advanced degree.

NANCE. Evelyn, I have a Masters, Susan Shankle has a Masters.

EVIE. In social work, I want to see someone with a Ph.D. In actual psychology.

NANCE. How about someone who you won't lie to?

EVIE. How about somebody who is interested in my life?

NANCE. Really? That again? I missed one meeting.

EVIE. They only have parent-teacher night once a year.

NANCE. You told me the day before.

EVIE. Really? You don't think you're supposed to look at your daughter's school calendar?

NANCE. I work.

EVIE. Right, save the world, fuck your daughter.

NANCE. Language.

>   (NANCE *takes a breath.*)

I think we can say we both made a mistake. I'm sorry. I think it's time to forgive and move on.

EVIE. Grandma says that forgiveness only works if the person you're forgiving is actually sorry for what they did.

NANCE. Your grandma is clinically depressed, you probably shouldn't take her advice.

EVIE. Maybe I'm clinically depressed, if I saw an actual doctor I could be medicated.

NANCE. You want to be medicated?

EVIE. Numb.

NANCE. Sorry honey, you have to feel things. It's part of the deal.

EVIE. What deal?

NANCE. I'm saying that it's important to acknowledge how you feel so you can process and progress.

EVIE. Every time you say shit like that I know why Daddy left us.

NANCE. He didn't leave you.

EVIE. No? I haven't seen him around for about 10 years, I'm pretty sure that he left me too.

NANCE. I don't want an invitation to your pity party.

EVIE. Don't worry, I'm sure you can't make it, I'm sure you have to work.

NANCE. Evelyn.

EVIE. Nance.

NANCE. "Mom."

EVIE. When you act like one, I'll call you that.

>   (ALICE *hangs up the phone,* GABE *is giving her a stern look.*)

ALICE. It was an accident.

GABE. Oh really, what happened to "There are no accidents Gabe."

ALICE. Oh for god's sake, we USED to live there. I made an honest mistake. I'm sorry. She sounded like it was no big deal.

GABE. "Oh, sure, we don't know where we live, but we are perfectly capable of taking care of a kid."

ALICE. I said I was sorry. I don't know what else you want me to do?

GABE. I want you to look at the form, find the place where our address goes, and put our *current* address.

ALICE. Next time I'll have Lizzie do it. Give me a break, you know I'm meticulous.

GABE. Really? Because I'm pretty sure people who are meticulous don't give social workers/ the wrong address for their home study.

ALICE. You want me to feel bad, I get it. I feel bad. But people make mistakes. It happens.

GABE. Like the roses?

ALICE. Let it go, she's going to be here any minute. We need to seem like we have the ability to laugh at ourselves, to accept our human-ness.

GABE. Oh Jesus, "our human-ness."

ALICE. Don't take the Lord's name in vain.

GABE. The Lord's name?

ALICE. Don't say, "Oh Jesus" when she comes. It's bad enough that we're Jewish.

GABE. What are you talking about?

ALICE. Oh yeah, African countries are so historically accepting of the Jews.

GABE. I'm pretty sure your early-onset dementia will be more of a concern then our Semitism.

ALICE. We lived there! We lived there!

GABE. Three years ago.

ALICE. Oh my fucking God!

GABE. "Oh my fucking God"? And I can't say "Oh Jesus."

ALICE. Maybe we shouldn't talk.

(GABE *sits down next to her. They wait.*)

GABE. You know what Jew is synonymous with? Even in African countries?

ALICE. Gabe.

GABE. Money. Do you know any poor Jews?

ALICE. Gabe you really are naive.

GABE. Really who would you rather give a baby to a poor Christian or a rich—

ALICE. Do you know where the Jews of Africa are? Gone.

GABE. Alright Golda Meir, you didn't even know any other Jews until you moved to LA. You celebrated Christmas.

ALICE. Having a *Star Wars*-themed Bar Mitzvah doesn't exactly make you Super Jew.

GABE. Okay Yentl.

ALICE. (*Singing.*) Papa can you hear me… Papa can you see me…

>(GABE *gets up and takes a menorah off of the shelf. He sits down with it. He puts it on the coffee table.*)

Cute.

GABE. You may be self-hating—

ALICE. Realistic, I'm *realistic*.

>(*She grabs the menorah, he grabs it. They struggle with it. She gets it and he chases her. She opens the kitchen door and throws it. There is a loud crash. He stops short.*)

GABE. You are going to hell.

ALICE. Us devout Jews don't believe in hell.

GABE. They already know we're Jewish. New Horizons knows. It was on our application.

ALICE. There is no point in advertising it/ highlighting it.

GABE. Oh really? Okay.

>(GABE *opens the front door. He Vanna Whites the mezuzah on the door frame.*)

You don't think the mezuzah is a little like lamb's blood?

ALICE. I'm breathing again.

GABE. Should I rip this down?

ALICE. Shut up Gabe.

>(*He starts to rip at it, it's [of course] screwed tightly to the frame.*)

GABE. Wouldn't want anyone to get the wrong idea, I mean, right? Wouldn't want anyone to think we're faithful.

ALICE. Gabe stop.

>(*He doesn't. ALICE goes and pulls his arm from the door frame, they struggle.*)

GABE. (*As they struggle.*) Let's be Christian! Put on a cross!/ Praise Jesus! I love Jesus! Hallelujah! Praise Jesus! Amen! Amen!

ALICE. Great idea! Let's be Christian! Hallelujah! I'm born again! Jesus loves me!

>(*And then, predictably,* NANCE *arrives. She is the social worker.*)

NANCE. Hello?

(ALICE *and* GABE *stop. They stare at* NANCE *for a moment.*)

GABE. Hi.

NANCE. I'm Nance Sanders. From New Horizons.

GABE. Of course you are.

(EVIE *sits on the floor; she is messing with a zit between her eyes.*)

EVIE. Do you believe in karma?

COLIN. I don't know.

EVIE. Karmic retribution. This zit. Me. My whole life.

COLIN. Am I part of your karmic retribution?

EVIE. No, Shauna is.

COLIN. Shut up.

(EVIE *puts her finger between her eyes.*)

EVIE. I'm seeing... Through my third eye: I was the person who invented the electric chair! It's all karmic retribution! My miserable life!

COLIN. You're a freak show.

EVIE. Ladies and germs, I'll be here all week, wakka, wakka!

(COLIN *picks up a* Cosmo *by* EVIE'*s bed.*)

COLIN. You read this? Shauna loves this magazine.

EVIE. There's a good quiz in there. Will let you know if you give good blow jobs. For the record: I do.

COLIN. Evie.

EVIE. Does Shauna?

COLIN. Yeah. She does.

EVIE. Good.

COLIN. She's horoscope-obsessed. Do you know why they don't put horoscopes in guys' magazines?

EVIE. Enlighten me.

COLIN. Because guys don't need to be told how to look at the future.

EVIE. I don't need to be told, I want to be told.

COLIN. Girls like to have a map.

EVIE. And guys like to get lost?

(EVIE *stands on her bed. She lightly bounces on the balls of her feet.*)

Look at me: I'm exercising. I'm an exercising Libra.

COLIN. (*Reading.*) "Libra: See what's possible by trying, rather than worrying, and you may find yourself in a brand new position by next month."

EVIE. Even my horoscope thinks I'm a loser.

COLIN. It's probably good advice.

EVIE. I thought horoscopes were bullshit.

COLIN. It's not saying you're a loser.

EVIE. No?

COLIN. You're not.

EVIE. (*She grabs the magazine.*) What are you? January 17th, right? Capricorn. "Do what you do best, help others this month, focus on giving and you will receive." You know, you could *give* this magazine to Shauna and you could *receive* a better blow job.

COLIN. Slow down Dorothy Parker.

EVIE. Shucks, I was going for Bukowski.

(*Beat.*)

COLIN. You know, I could help you Evie. Shauna says I'm one of those people. I see a problem and I fix it. Like one time, she had this bullshit fight with her best friend and I was the one who got them to smooth it over. I'm good at fixing stuff.

EVIE. Good fix me. What's the plan, Mr. Fix It?

COLIN. We should go out.

EVIE. You want to go out?

COLIN. Get out of your house. In New Hampshire, me and Shauna, we went to the movies, to the lake, actually outside.

EVIE. In Pasadena you can't go out. Air quality.

COLIN. I'm serious we should get out of here—do something.

EVIE. IHOP?

COLIN. You're hungry?

EVIE. Coffee. Never empty coffee pot.

COLIN. Show me why Pasadena doesn't suck.

EVIE. It does suck.

COLIN. There isn't one good thing about it?

EVIE. IHOP.

COLIN. B-b-b-b-bored. Bored. Bored. Bored.

EVIE. I have something for you.

COLIN. For me?

EVIE. Listen.

(*She hands him her headphones and a crappy MP3 player.*)

COLIN. For fuck's sake Evie, you don't even have a stereo or speakers. We can't even listen to music together in your room.

EVIE. We should go out. Hear music. At night./ Do something actually fun, right?

COLIN. Music is good.

EVIE. Me like music.

COLIN. Let's go.

EVIE. Maybe.

COLIN. Are you with me? Because if you aren't with me—

EVIE. I'm against you?

COLIN. B-F-F or fuck you Colin, which is it?

EVIE. Alright, let's go.

COLIN. Really?

EVIE. Aye-aye Captain.

COLIN. I knew you loved me.

EVIE. I do.

COLIN. Where should we go?

EVIE. IHOP.

(NANCE *and* TOM *at the museum.*)

TOM. You know what made me wink at you?

NANCE. What?

TOM. Your nose.

NANCE. Really?

TOM. It makes your face look honest.

NANCE. Thanks?

TOM. Honesty is important. Pretty.

NANCE. Gosh.

TOM. So you're a social worker.

NANCE. I am.

TOM. Do you like it?

NANCE. I do. Your profile said you work in sales, what do you sell?

TOM. Microscopes.

NANCE. Really?

TOM. We import them from China and sell them to schools mostly.

NANCE. That's interesting.

TOM. It pays the bills.

NANCE. That's important.

TOM. Money is important to you?

NANCE. Money? Being able to take care of yourself, that is.

TOM. That's loaded. Loaded.

> (*She laughs a little.*)

That's a courtesy laugh.

NANCE. Sorry.

TOM. Don't be, I appreciate it.

> (*Pause.*)

Do you want to walk around the museum?

NANCE. Do you?

TOM. There is a cafe, do you want something to eat or drink?

NANCE. I'm good.

TOM. So, you're saying this is done?

NANCE. No! I'm just saying. Just to sit here. Right here. I'm not quite ready to go.

TOM. Do you want me to sit too?

NANCE. Only if you want to.

> (*They sit for a moment.*)

TOM. They're newlyweds.

> (*Beat.*)

Are you okay?

NANCE. No. Not really.

> (*Silence.*)

TOM. David Hockney was in their wedding and painted it right afterwards.

NANCE. I don't think I looked like that after I was married.

TOM. How did you look?

NANCE. Pregnant.

> (*He laughs. Then she does too.*)

TOM. I think they look a little pissed, like hey leave us alone it's our honeymoon, or something. But I like that they look the same, in their faces, like they agree.

NANCE. I think it's sweet that you're thinking about this painting of people getting married.

TOM. Hope springs eternal.

NANCE. That's what I— We probably shouldn't talk about marriage.

TOM. Why not?

NANCE. I wasn't very good at it.

TOM. Where is he?

NANCE. Mexico. Yep, he fled the country, beware.

TOM. My ex lives in Santa Monica. She always wanted to live there when we were married, but my job, I couldn't.

NANCE. I like it here in Pasadena.

TOM. Me too.

(COLIN *types.*)

COLIN. Dear Shauna. Day 51. Greetings from the death of civilization. I'm picturing you at Credo Park, sitting in the car. You're drinking beers with Michelle and Sarah. Right? You're playing The Shins. Are you thinking about me? All I do is go to school and hang out with Evie. You'd like her. She's like us. I wish you could picture me here. I'm the same Shauna. Like frozen the day I left you at the airport. I don't think I'm capable of melting until I'm with you again. Still reading *Inferno*, "I come from a place whither I desire to return." New Hampshire is paradise, Beatrice backslash Shauna. Call me. Goodnight. I love you Shauna. Colin. Send.

(NANCE *is standing in the living room,* GABE *closes the door.* ALICE *stands between them.*)

ALICE. I am so sorry you had to goose chase. I think I even have checks left with that address. I mean right Gabe? I don't make mistakes—

NANCE. Please don't worry about it, it happens.

ALICE. Really?

GABE. Can I take your jacket?

ALICE. I'll take it.

NANCE. I'm fine.

ALICE. Is it cold? I could turn down the—

NANCE. Don't worry, I'm fine.

GABE. She's always freezing me out—

ALICE. Ha. My Texas blood—

GABE. Would you like to sit down—

ALICE. I'm sorry, sit down! Please, please.

NANCE. Thanks.

(ALICE *grabs* GABE'*s hand and squeezes it while* NANCE *takes a seat on the couch. They continue to stand.*)

Thank you for having me.

GABE. Thanks for coming.

NANCE. Congratulations. This is an exciting and special journey you are embarking on. I'm sure New Horizons gave you a sense of what the home study process entails?

ALICE. We're ready for you.

NANCE. Good. I always like to say first off: I'm not here to judge you, I'm here—you can sit.

ALICE. We like to sit!

(GABE *sits on the armchair,* ALICE *moves to the loveseat. She pats the spot next to her; she tries to make the gesture surreptitiously.* GABE *stays in the chair.*)

NANCE. This is an opportunity for me to get to know you as a couple and as potential parents—

ALICE. I like the sound of that!

NANCE. Good. I'm going to ask you some questions together and then I will take a little time to speak to you separately. Then I will need a tour of your home, I'll need to see the space you will use for the baby's room and that will be it. The process generally takes about 2 to 3 hours.

ALICE. Our time is yours.

NANCE. Great. Do you have any questions before we get started.

(NANCE *takes out her notebook and papers and pen.*)

ALICE. Can I get you something?

NANCE. I'm good, thanks.

ALICE. Are you sure?

GABE. Are you sure?

NANCE. I'm good.

GABE. Alice made some snacks.

NANCE. No thank you.

GABE. Glass of wine?

ALICE. What?! Oh Gabe… He's kidding. We aren't drinkers.

NANCE. No, thank you.

GABE. I'm kidding.

(NANCE *writes something down.*)

ALICE. He really was kidding.

GABE. Are you writing that down? We don't even have wine in the house.

NANCE. I'm writing the date.

ALICE. Would you rather have a real table? To write?

NANCE. This is fine.

ALICE. Are you sure?

NANCE. I think we're ready to get started. Can you begin by speaking about how you came to the decision to adopt?

ALICE. The big question, huh? The big, big, big question—

GABE. It's simple: We want to have a family.

ALICE. We really do.

GABE. And we can't have a kid of our own.

ALICE. Well, not of our own, on our own.

GABE. That's what I meant.

ALICE. Such a subtle distinction. "Of" and "on." Honey, do you want to come sit here? So it's not a tennis match, ha.

(GABE *sits next to* ALICE, *they hold hands.*)

It's nice of you to come in the evening—

NANCE. People work—

ALICE. How many families do you see a week?

NANCE. It really varies—

GABE. Should I pour waters?

ALICE. He's always thirsty.

NANCE. No thank you.

ALICE. How did you get into this line of work?

NANCE. I like helping families grow.

ALICE. It must be fascinating. Have you always worked in adoption?

NANCE. I have a Masters in Social Work and after I graduated, I thought that I was going to work in addictions.

ALICE. Really? Wow.

NANCE. But then my husband moved us to Seattle, for his job, so I cast my net and found a job working for an adoption agency there.

ALICE. Seattle!

NANCE. Are you familiar—

ALICE. We love Seattle.

GABE. Love it.

ALICE. Just visited. Well, a long time ago. But Pike Place Market.

GABE. Those guys throwing those salmon.

ALICE. Amazing.

(GABE *pours* NANCE *water.*)

NANCE. Thank you.

ALICE. He's always so worried about everyone being hydrated. When did you move from Seattle to Pasadena?

GABE. She'll try to get your complete biography—

ALICE. It's true. I just like to know the whole story. Get to know who people are—

GABE. She does it to waiters, mailmen, strangers at Starbucks.

NANCE. It's alright, I moved here about 10 years ago.

ALICE. For work?

NANCE. No, I was born here. I have family here.

ALICE. Getting back to your family. Roots are important. Gabe has family in Sherman Oaks. It's great to be close. Must be nice for you—

GABE. We don't want to take your whole night—

ALICE. Sorry—

NANCE. No, no. Okay. Your file says you have had some fertility issues.

GABE. Yes.

NANCE. And that's what led you to adoption?

ALICE. It is. It really is. But, I believe, we believe the universe puts you on the right path. When we finally decided International Adoption, we looked at each other and agreed. I feel relieved, excited./ Like it's exactly what we should do.

GABE. Me too.

(NANCE *wraps her jacket tightly.*)

ALICE. Are you cold?

NANCE. I'm comfortable.

ALICE. Just want to be sure.

NANCE. What other options did you look into?

ALICE. Everything.

GABE. It's important to know the whole arena.

ALICE. International, it just felt right. I mean, you can't explain some connections, but we did our research, talked to adoptive parents. And in the end, it just—

GABE. It's right for us.

NANCE. Okay. Good.

GABE. Pasadena is practically LA, where it makes some sense. I mean, if we were in the Deep South.

NANCE. How so?

GABE. Oh, well, to bring an African child/ to rural Texas, it just.

ALICE. He means that we have thought about whether or not we would be good parents in this scenario—

GABE. In LA, Pasadena.

ALICE. It's not just about what's good for us, it's about the kids. The babies, right?

GABE. We've read books about transracial adoption.

NANCE. Have you completed your Hague training?

GABE. Yes.

NANCE. Good.

ALICE. We do think, I mean, we really do think we're the right people/ Maybe I implied that we don't have a choice. I mean on some level that's true, but of course we have a choice. And this is what we're choosing. The right path for us.

GABE. Yes.

NANCE. I want to ask you a little bit more about your fertility issues. When did you discover that you.

ALICE. Four years ago.

NANCE. And what have you done in response?

GABE. IVF.

NANCE. Okay. How many cycles?

ALICE. Four. Well, four and a half.

NANCE. Half?

ALICE. I did the stimulating hormones, but they had to cancel the cycle for hyperstimulation. All those eggs—

GABE. And nary an omelet—

ALICE. Ha. Exactly. Levity.

GABE. We have to laugh.

ALICE. You've got to see us all of the time, we're just a happy couple who thought we'd have some kids and get on with it. You don't *expect* it to be hard.

NANCE. No, of course not. When did you complete your last IVF cycle?

GABE. April.

NANCE. Of this year?

GABE. Yes.

NANCE. Six months—

ALICE. I know what you're asking. We've mourned this. I know we're done. Heck, I'm relieved. I mean finally it's not my fault, you know?

GABE. Alice.

ALICE. I'm just being honest. I know how important that is here.

NANCE. I appreciate your honesty.

ALICE. Do you have kids?

NANCE. I have a daughter.

ALICE. Adopted?

NANCE. No.

ALICE. My second cousin is adopted.

NANCE. It certainly can be helpful to have adoption in your family.

ALICE. And you know, we love our adopted cousin, love her/ She's so pretty. Blonde. Sophia. Prettier than any of us, right Gabe?

NANCE. That's nice.

GABE. (*He pats her back.*) Alice.

ALICE. Yes. Sorry. I'm a chitty-chat-chatter.

NANCE. Don't worry. This is your time. I'm interested in all of your thoughts surrounding adoption.

ALICE. I really like you, Nance.

NANCE. Thanks.

GABE. We've always wanted to be parents.

NANCE. Good. Good. And you've already designated an age preference?

GABE. As young as possible.

ALICE. We know that means up to 12 months old.

NANCE. That's right.

ALICE. Sophia was only one day old when she joined our family.

We have all of this love, in our hearts, we have so much.

GABE. Love.

(GABE *kisses* ALICE's *hand.*)

NANCE. I hear you. Let's talk a little bit about how you plan to incorporate a child into you lives.

ALICE. I'm going to quit my job.

GABE. I'm going to keep mine.

ALICE. We feel strongly that the crucial bonding will happen in that first year a child is here, a baby. With us. I mean you never get those days back, do you? Those first days, months. You have to be there. Give the child a sense of consistency.

GABE. Both of our moms stayed home.

(*A cell phone rings.*)

NANCE. I'm sorry.

(NANCE *digs in her bag, looks at her phone.*)

GABE. If it's important—

NANCE. My daughter.

ALICE. You have to, it's your daughter.

NANCE. I'll call her back. She knows.

(NANCE *fiddles with the phone.*)

(EVIE *and* COLIN *at IHOP.*)

EVIE. Go. Go. Come on Colin. Do it.

COLIN. Slamming coffee with Evie.

EVIE. Damn skippy.

COLIN. This coffee tastes like shit.

EVIE. Nectar of the gods.

COLIN. Crack of the junkies.

EVIE. We're the gods of IHOP, Colin—

COLIN. What time is it? I think I should go home and study.

EVIE. Me too. I think you should go home and study.

COLIN. Yeah?

EVIE. Mmm hmm. I think you should study Galileo? Shakespeare? Jack off to Dante. Do some epic studying. Do it Colin. Do it, do it, do it, do it.

COLIN. You're a freak.

EVIE. I am. You know what we should do?

COLIN. What?

EVIE. We should paper Holly Lynch's house.

COLIN. What are you 12?

EVIE. You're the one who wants to do things—

COLIN. Not what I had in mind.

EVIE. We have to find out where she lives. I think she lives over near Southland.

COLIN. She lives on Kramer.

EVIE. Let's go, maybe she wants to play Barbies or something.

COLIN. She is a Barbie.

EVIE. She's virgin cheerleading Pasadena bitch Barbie.

COLIN. I don't think she's a virgin.

EVIE. Oh my god Colin, how do you know Holly Lynch lives on Kramer?

COLIN. I don't know—

EVIE. What do you mean, you don't—

COLIN. Evie, I don't know.

EVIE. You hang out with her?

COLIN. You weren't the first person I met—

EVIE. Are you serious?

COLIN. Come on Osama, let's devise our evil plan, right?

EVIE. I need a real plan. A high school plan. A get it right plan. You're going to help me. An homage to teen flicks plan. In eight months, you'll fall into Shauna's arms, right? And me? I'll just be sitting here.

COLIN. You love IHOP.

EVIE. Maybe someday they'll let me wear an apron.

COLIN. You'll graduate too.

EVIE. In the girls' bathroom today, Carla Swenson said, "Hey fat ass, don't break the seat."

COLIN. So?

EVIE. Carla Swenson has a harelip.

COLIN. Don't pour that. I don't want it.

EVIE. Come on. Never empty. Never fucking empty Colin. And the entire soccer team, they went "Beep, beep." Like a truck backing out.

COLIN. That's fucked up.

EVIE. So. What's the plan?

COLIN. Give into the undeniable fact that the public school system has failed you. Fuck high school.

EVIE. Fuck high school? Drop out? Get my GED? Become a dental assistant. Wear scrubs with puppies on them? I go to school every day Colin. Every day. I can't fuck high school.

COLIN. Don't you love teeth?

EVIE. I'm serious.

COLIN. Shoving your hands in rotting mouths.

EVIE. Euthanize me.

COLIN. You'd look good in puppy scrubs.

> (EVIE *makes* COLIN's *hand into a gun and then uses it to shoot herself under the chin with a nice little "kapow" sound.*)

Okay. Okay Evie. I have a plan.

EVIE. Oh my god, you're serious.

COLIN. Yes.

EVIE. Let's hear it.

COLIN. Okay. My mom said—

EVIE. Your mom? You told your mom?

COLIN. Yeah, she's cool.

EVIE. "She's cool." Seriously?

COLIN. Homecoming.

EVIE. What about it?

COLIN. We should go.

EVIE. To Homecoming?

COLIN. Yeah.

EVIE. That wouldn't offend your nonconformist sensibilities?

COLIN. I'm not a nonconformist, I'm a survivalist.

EVIE. The Thoreau of Woodrow.

COLIN. Thoreau was a transcendentalist.

EVIE. You want to go to Homecoming?

COLIN. Yeah. We'll go. My mom says you just have to show people you are normal.

EVIE. I am. I am so normal. I'm like Brady Bunch normal.

COLIN. Like Manson Family normal.

EVIE. What about the Yeti?

COLIN. Don't be an asshole.

EVIE. We'll go to Homecoming.

COLIN. Do it up. Dance. In the middle of the dance floor. A royal kind of fuck you.

EVIE. My teen flick moment.

COLIN. Yeah, but directed by Hitchcock.

(*A genuine girly smile spreads across* EVIE's *face.*)

(TOM *and* NANCE, *still at the museum.*)

NANCE. Pasadena's a good place to raise kids.

TOM. How old is your daughter?

NANCE. Seventeen. A senior. Tonight's her Homecoming dance.

TOM. Where does she go to school?

NANCE. Woodrow.

TOM. Look at that, I supply their microscopes.

NANCE. Small world.

TOM. You should get me some feedback from her. It'd be great.

NANCE. I will. She's great.

TOM. Takes after her mom?

NANCE. That's sweet.

TOM. Do you know what science she takes?

NANCE. Oh. Chemistry. No, maybe Biology—

TOM. Biology uses them the most—

NANCE. Tom, how is this going?

TOM. Cut to the chase? I like it.

NANCE. Listen Tom, you are interested in a long-term committed relationship, right?

TOM. Whoa Nellie.

NANCE. I'm sorry, I'm sorry. I don't mean with me, necessarily. I just mean is that what you're after—

TOM. —I'm not after anything—

NANCE. —Because, I've had this crap-filled day and I don't think I have any choice but to sort of lay my cards on the table.

TOM. There's no bluff to call.

NANCE. You know what I was thinking on my way here? Why do I have to be the lonely one? Why do you have to be lonely?

TOM. I'm not lonely.

NANCE. Really? Then what are you doing here?

TOM. I'm having a first date.

NANCE. Date? Because your profile said you're looking for a long-term committed relationship—

TOM. I'm making a new friend.

NANCE. Oh. Okay. Well, Tom, I am not looking for a friend. I don't have the energy for a friend.

TOM. Nance—

NANCE. I'm scaring you off.

TOM. I'm not scared.

NANCE. I'm just trying to be truthful, to look like my profile picture.

TOM. It's refreshing.

NANCE. Liar.

TOM. It is.

NANCE. Have you ever dated a woman with a teenaged daughter?

TOM. No.

NANCE. I may look like my profile picture Tom, but that's the surface. The stuff I come with doesn't look like me at all.

TOM. What does it look like?

NANCE. Here's what my profile should say: lonely divorcee with caustic teenager seeks refuge from sorry life. What about you Tom?

TOM. Nobody's perfect.

NANCE. Oh my god, you are too nice. You should run screaming.

TOM. You aren't nice?

NANCE. No.

TOM. I bet you are. I'm attracted to nice people.

NANCE. Was your ex-wife nice?

TOM. Not as nice as you are.

NANCE. Oh my god, I'm not nice.

TOM. What's so not nice about you Nance?

NANCE. You think I've been nice to you?

TOM. I think you're testing me.

NANCE. I'm not. This is just how I am.

TOM. And this is how I am.

NANCE. Do you want to come home with me?

TOM. Now?

NANCE. Yes.

TOM. Yes.

NANCE. Let's go.

(*They go.*)

(ALICE *gets up and moves closer to* GABE *which makes him feel a little crammed.* NANCE *is writing.*)

ALICE. We've talked about it a lot. Birth parents. A child's origin story. We'll gather as much information as we can. Have it ready.

GABE. We'll be ready.

NANCE. I think it's important to try not to have any built-in expectations about what you might discover.

ALICE. The truth is we don't have any expectations, we are making this real effort to live in each moment.

GABE. Exactly.

ALICE. I mean, we plan: for the future. But the route. It changes. We aren't naive. You have to plan for the future, but you can't let it control you—I'm sorry, can I tell you I love your bag?

NANCE. Thanks.

ALICE. Gabe, make a mental picture, next holiday, that's what I want.

GABE. Bag noted.

ALICE. I love it.

GABE. I'm sorry, do you care if I eat something.

ALICE. What?

NANCE. No, of course—

GABE. Starving.

ALICE. Really? Honey, are you sure?

GABE. Yeah—

ALICE. Should I get it?

GABE. I got it—

(*He goes to the kitchen.*)

ALICE. Sorry.

NANCE. It is dinner time.

ALICE. I could order Chinese.

NANCE. It's not necessary.

ALICE. Don't think I don't cook, I love to cook, but I could order—

NANCE. No, no. I'm just saying that of course, he's hungry.

ALICE. He's got a tapeworm.

(*Beat.*)

How old is your daughter?

NANCE. Seventeen.

ALICE. Really? Wow, you look fantastic.

NANCE. Thanks.

ALICE. What did you have her when you were 12?

NANCE. I was young, 19.

ALICE. That's smart. I wish I had done that. I mean, what's with all of us waiting? Like we can defy the nature of our bodies or something? Do you know how many women I know who are having fertility problems? Tons. I mean tons.

NANCE. You can't beat yourself up.

ALICE. No, I know. Although, when I was 19. Ha! I mean what did you do, drag her to Pearl Jam concerts and debate feminist theory in the labor room? And when I think about who I was dating at 19. How did you do it?

NANCE. You do what you have to do—

ALICE. Darren Reeves! He was a comp lit German major. I met him in the laundromat. I swear I saw him folding his Lynyrd Skynyrd T-shirt. Oh god! Darren Reeves. He had a terrible goatee, scraggly—

(*Yelling to* GABE *in the kitchen.*)

Gabe: Darren Reeves.

GABE. (*Yelling from the kitchen.*) Pubic chin.

(GABE *enters from the kitchen carrying a platter of dips that* ALICE *made for* NANCE.)

ALICE. Gabe! Gross!

GABE. Your grunge boyfriend.

NANCE. Alright, let's see—

ALICE. You are lucky. You must have really known yourself to get married and have a kid at 19. How long have you been married?

NANCE. Divorced.

> (COLIN *types*.)

COLIN. (*Typing*.) Dear Shauna. Why didn't you call back. Delete. Dear Shauna. Day 53. You didn't call me back. Delete. Dear Shauna. Day 53. Greetings from Vapidville. What's up? How was your Spanish quiz? Listen, I'm going to go with Evie to Homecoming. Not like a date, just friends. She has been getting a lot of crap for being fat, so I'm being nice. You know me, I always like to fix stuff. Did your dad let you start driver's ed? Remember when I let you drive the Brown Machine? Too fast, too furious. Watch out highways of New Hampshire. I miss you. Call me back. Or e-mail. Or text. Good night. I love you Shauna. Colin. Send.

> (EVIE *is in the bathroom washing her face,* NANCE *stands in the doorway.*)

NANCE. Come on now, I was 17. It's like you think I just appeared at age 19 and birthed you.

EVIE. Twenty-two. You were 22.

NANCE. The point is I was young.

EVIE. You want me to be a teen pregnancy you overcame, but you were 22 not 19.

NANCE. It's just acne.

EVIE. It's never just something.

NANCE. But it isn't the end of the world.

EVIE. You're wrong, high school is the apocalypse.

NANCE. Sit down, let me.

> (EVIE *sits on the closed toilet. Throughout the following* NANCE *washes* EVIE'*s face.*)

Rubbing it with a washcloth, it's bad. You are just a girl with acne. Take the washcloth, soak it in the hottest water you can run out of the tap, use it as a compress, it will draw all of the oil to the surface. Like this.

EVIE. Ouch!

NANCE. Your grandmother said God gave me zits to keep me humble. That I was too pretty. Drink a lot of water. Every kid at Woodrow gets them. You aren't special. Zits are zits. But if you didn't eat so much junk. If you—

EVIE. There it is.

NANCE. I care about your health.

EVIE. You were too pretty. And I'm too fat.

NANCE. Your word.

EVIE. What's yours?

NANCE. Evelyn, come on.

EVIE. I want Lap-Band surgery.

NANCE. You have it in you to do it yourself.

EVIE. I don't think so.

NANCE. You know, Evelyn, I think it would be easier for you if that were true. But you have to own your piece of it, take responsibility.

EVIE. I fantasize about breaking my jaw so it will have to be wired shut.

NANCE. Don't say that.

EVIE. Don't say true things?

NANCE. You can be okay.

EVIE. Just okay?

NANCE. You're like a bomb, a ticking time bomb, I'm sick of walking on eggshells.

EVIE. Do you even hear yourself. Bombs and eggshells?

NANCE. What do you want me to say? There's clearly something you think I should be saying.

EVIE. Say the truth.

NANCE. What's the truth?

EVIE. Get thinner, get a boyfriend.

NANCE. Don't you think your relationship with Colin would change?

EVIE. You're thin, where's your boyfriend?

NANCE. Oh yes, men just love women in their late 30's with teenaged daughters.

EVIE. All my fault, right?

NANCE. Evelyn, I want you to be happy.

EVIE. So you can be?

NANCE. What about your dad? Wouldn't you say losing the weight made him happier?

EVIE. Are we going to ignore the fact that he stayed fat until he left you?

(ALICE *is sitting cross-legged,* GABE *eats pita.* NANCE *is taking notes.*)

NANCE. Let's talk a little bit about how you deal with crises in your relationship. Can you give me an example and then talk about how you dealt with it?

GABE. What kind of crisis?

NANCE. A hardship, something that you had to deal with as a couple. It's a good way for us to explore how you will react in the face of the inevitable challenges with your adopted child.

ALICE. Like fertility?

NANCE. Of course. But here, let's talk about a different hardship—

GABE. A different hardship.

ALICE. Like a death in the family?

NANCE. Yes.

ALICE. Well. My mother died.

GABE. Good, your mother died.

ALICE. Good.

NANCE. I'm sorry for your loss.

ALICE. Thank you.

NANCE. A death in the family can certainly challenge the mettle of a couple. It can be a real shock.

GABE. It wasn't exactly a surprise.

NANCE. She had been sick?

ALICE. She discovered cancer.

GABE. Like climbing Everest: The chemo, radiation.

NANCE. And as a couple?

ALICE. I would say we leaned on each other.

GABE. Her mom lived in Dallas. We racked up the frequent flier miles.

ALICE. Gabe was really there for me.

GABE. Really there.

NANCE. And can you talk a little bit about how you dealt with the grief.

ALICE. Well, we talked about it. Right Gabe?

GABE. Yes. We talked.

ALICE. And, of course, there is still sadness.

NANCE. You're still grieving her death?

ALICE. Yes. Well, no. I mean I'm okay. Good. Happy. I'm really happy.

NANCE. When did she pass?

ALICE. In June.

NANCE. This past June?

GABE. They weren't very close.

ALICE. What? Ha! Yes, of course, I was close to my mom. But, she was not very good at communicating, she lived in Dallas, it was hard to get together—

But I loved my mom. We did.

GABE. We loved her.

NANCE. Good.

ALICE. Are both of your parents living?

NANCE. Yes. Both of my parents.

ALICE. So are Gabe's.

NANCE. Let me go ahead and ask you about how your families and loved ones have reacted to the news of your adoption.

GABE. Really well.

ALICE. Yes, everyone has been so supportive.

NANCE. Good.

ALICE. Everyone has always said I should be a mom. Right, honey?

GABE. She mothers me.

ALICE. Ha! Stop.

GABE. In the best way, I feel safe.

(NANCE*'s purse vibrates.*)

NANCE. Good. Let's talk about how you plan to incorporate your child's culture of origin into your—

(NANCE*'s purse vibrates again.*)

GABE. Is that your phone?

NANCE. Is that my— You know what, I'm not available when I'm doing a home study. If there is an emergency, New Horizons will call me here.

(*In a dressing room,* EVIE *in her bra and panties.* COLIN *stands outside the door.*)

EVIE. I lied.

COLIN. What?

EVIE. I lied.

COLIN. About what?

EVIE. I can't shop here.

COLIN. What?

EVIE. Why are you shopping with me? Are you gay?

COLIN. Fuck you.

EVIE. Sorry.

COLIN. You dress for shit.

EVIE. I know.

COLIN. You begged me to come.

EVIE. I know. Sorry. Sorry. I'm sorry.

(EVIE *is quiet.* COLIN *leans against the door.* EVIE *just stands there.*)

COLIN. Who else is going shopping with you?

EVIE. —

COLIN. All your girlfriends?

EVIE. —

COLIN. No? No freakishly robotic pep squad entourage to cheer stupid girl shit over dresses?

EVIE. —

COLIN. How about your mom? You think she's going to come?

EVIE. —

COLIN. Get a fucking dress, Evie.

(*She opens the door to the dressing room. She is still in bra and panties.*)

EVIE. We have to go to the fat department.

COLIN. Am I supposed to gasp or something?

EVIE. I'm not good at this—

COLIN. I don't care.

EVIE. Because you have a girlfriend.

COLIN. Because I don't care.

EVIE. I'm scared you're lying.

COLIN. You know when you do this kind of shit, you aren't pathetic, you're kind of a bitch.

EVIE. What you just said makes you an asshole.

COLIN. Then I guess we belong together.

EVIE. Yeah, a bitch and an asshole sitting in a tree.

COLIN. You can't freak me out.

EVIE. I can.

COLIN. Don't try. I'm nice.

EVIE. You are nice, really.

(COLIN *hands* EVIE *her jeans and T-shirt.*)

(GABE *and* NANCE *sit on the couch.* ALICE *leans over to kiss* GABE *on the top his head before exiting.*)

ALICE. Alright, Gabe play nice. Ha.

NANCE. It will only take about 15 minutes.

ALICE. Take your time.

(ALICE *goes.*)

NANCE. Okay.

GABE. Alrighty.

NANCE. Let's talk a little bit about your upbringing.

GABE. Dig out the skeletons.

NANCE. Can you talk a little bit about your parents?

GABE. Vivian and Benjamin.

NANCE. I love the name Vivian.

GABE. She went by Viv.

NANCE. My daughter is the same, has a beautiful name, shortens it.

GABE. My mom feels the same, Gabe, Gabriel. Aren't you a "Nancy"?

NANCE. No. It's just Nance. It's a family name. A Hebrew name.

GABE. You're Jewish?

NANCE. Hebrew, Biblical, but not Jewish.

GABE. But people must always assume it's short for Nancy?

NANCE. Yes. They do. So, tell me about what kind of parents yours were.

GABE. Nice.

NANCE. Nice?

GABE. Loving. Fair.

NANCE. Can you be more specific?

GABE. They love me and my sister. They support me. My parents have a near-perfect marriage. They are role models.

NANCE. It's good to have a strong family base.

GABE. They'll make great grandparents.

NANCE. Can you describe a happy memory from your childhood?

GABE. A happy memory.

NANCE. Yes.

GABE. Well, what would your daughter say?

NANCE. My daughter?

GABE. Yes, what would your daughter say is a happy memory?

NANCE. I'm sorry Gabe, what are you asking?

GABE. I'm just trying to get a sense of what you're looking for.

NANCE. Oh, just how your past might inform your parenting.

GABE. —I see—

NANCE. There is no right answer.

GABE. Playing ball. Car trips to Yosemite. The usual. Just a normal, run-of-the-mill childhood. Boring really. I mean, boring to tell you about, I had a perfectly good time.

NANCE. Good. Can you tell me how you are like your parents?

GABE. I'm nice.

NANCE. Okay, and different?

GABE. Well, they don't like foreign films and won't eat sushi—

NANCE. You're saying you're adventurous?

GABE. No, I was kidding—sorry. Different—I'm ambitious.

NANCE. Your parents aren't ambitious.

GABE. Nope. Content, but not exactly driven to succeed.

NANCE. Okay. Can you tell me what was missing from your childhood?

GABE. Nothing.

NANCE. Really?

GABE. Yeah, really.

NANCE. Good.

GABE. Nance, I'm an open book. I'm happy. I love my life. I like my job. Love my wife. My house. I love my parents. I like where I came from. I am just a simple person. We want to have a baby. We tried the old fashioned way. It didn't work. So here we are.

NANCE. Can you tell me who was or is the most influential person in your life?

GABE. Do these questions come directly from the agency?

NANCE. These are standard home study questions.

GABE. There's a form?

NANCE. Yes. There is a form. The questions are compiled by experienced social workers, we work with New Horizons. They are carefully developed to be comprehensive.

GABE. The person who has been most influential in my life is my father.

NANCE. That's great.

> (*Beat.*)

In what ways?

GABE. My father. He was. I mean, he is— My father was a good breadwinner, loves his wife and cared for his children like he was lucky to have us. It is because of him. My father is the reason I want to have a family. He is. He is the, um, the standard for. I have. He is an excellent role model.

NANCE. Gabe, you seem a little uncomfortable. I don't want you to be.

GABE. I'm actually okay being uncomfortable. I said to Alice, this should be hard. That every aspect of this process should be grueling. We should rip our hearts out and have them examined while we watch. I mean it's not like we're adopting a puppy.

NANCE. No.

GABE. But you have to admit, I mean, it would be good, right? It would be a good idea for everyone to be pre-screened, not just adoptive parents. Just because we have a biological issue, a physical problem here, we get scrutinized. But I mean, there is no magic bean to make the world fair. You can't always just throw your hands up in the air and yell: "We want a baby!" "Mr. Stork BRING US A BABY!" This is our challenge, our hurdle.

(ALICE *peeks her head in.*)

ALICE. I'm so sorry, but I left my book.

GABE. We were just talking about the process.

ALICE. He's very passionate about it.

NANCE. I see that.

ALICE. Really?

GABE. Do you see your book dear?

ALICE. Oh. Huh. Yeppers. Here. Here it is.

(ALICE *picks up the Bible from the side table.*)

The good book.

(EVIE *in another dressing room with* NANCE*, she is in a fairly substantial formal dress. She looks almost nice.* NANCE *looks at the price tag on the dress.*)

(COLIN *types.*)

COLIN. (*Typing.*) Shauna. Day 56. Are you seriously still pissed? I didn't *do* anything. It was the first day of school. A month and a half ago. So you are clear 1. Holly Lynch's mom and my mom met at a PTA meeting. 2. We went to dinner at Holly Lynch's house. 3. She made me go into her room to listen to music. 4. She tried to kiss me, I didn't kiss her back. 5. I told her I am in a *committed* relationship. 6. Holly Lynch called me cocksucker. 7. It was no big deal, that's why I didn't tell you until last week. Holly Lynch is just a stupid bitch. Shauna, you are my life. I love you. Please Shauna, don't do this. We've been together 16 months. The best 16 months of my life. I'm sorry, don't be pissed. Only 131 days until I come visit Spring Break. Good night. Shauna I love you. Colin. Send.

(NANCE *in the dressing room with* EVIE.)

EVIE. It's purple.

NANCE. It's more eggplant than purple. You could wear your hair up. Wear flats so you're not too tall. You like it?

EVIE. Do you?

NANCE. If you do.

EVIE. You don't?

(EVIE *goes to her.* NANCE *pulls the straps.*)

NANCE. Maybe it's too big.

EVIE. Too big?

(EVIE *smoothes the fabric over her tummy.*)

NANCE. Stand up straight.

(EVIE *tries.*)

Do you like the color?

EVIE. You don't?

NANCE. (*Playfully.*) Is this the first time in your life you don't have an opinion?

(NANCE *stands behind* EVIE *and pulls and tugs the dress.*)

You know what I think? I think you should get the next size down.

EVIE. Really?

NANCE. I do.

EVIE. But this isn't that big.

NANCE. But look at the straps.

EVIE. Yeah?

NANCE. Absolutely.

EVIE. Seriously.

NANCE. I'll pay for it. The whole thing. I'll pay for the whole thing.

EVIE. Really?

NANCE. Get it in a size smaller.

EVIE. Homecoming is in two weeks.

NANCE. This is your first dance. Show Colin.

EVIE. Show him what?

NANCE. What you're made of.

EVIE. What am I made of?

NANCE. Willpower.

EVIE. I'm made of willpower.

NANCE. This is a pretty dress. Look at you. Love yourself Evelyn, love yourself.

EVIE. Do you love yourself?

NANCE. Yes.

EVIE. I know you love *your*self.

NANCE. You know Evelyn, your contempt for me, it isn't just par for the mother-daughter course.

EVIE. I'm sorry.

(NANCE *grabs* EVIE*'s shoulders and pushes her to face the mirror.*)

NANCE. You are my daughter. I want it to be easier. I do. I am not out to get you. I am not interested in you being unhappy. I want you to have a moment where you like yourself. You know what I want: I want you to look here and say, "I'm beautiful."
Come on. Say it.
Do this for you.
Do it for me.
Do this for Colin.

EVIE. I'll do it. I want to.

NANCE. You can. The difference is only maybe five pounds away. I'll buy it. It's expensive, but I'll buy it. I want to. The dress, shoes. Maybe earrings.

EVIE. I want the dress.

NANCE. Alright. Good girl. I'll get the next size smaller and go pay for it. You can do this.

EVIE. I can.

(NANCE *exits.* EVIE *looks at herself in the mirror. She throws back her shoulders.*)

(ALICE *is sitting with* NANCE *on the couch.* NANCE *is loving* ALICE*'s story.*)

ALICE. —and my parents had to chase after me, I had jumped over the fence and was sitting with the little piglets. Feeding them this little promotional loaf of Wonder Bread that they hand out when you first enter the state fair. It was hilarious. I guess I was fast. But you know, they got it, my parents jumped the fence and fed the piglets with me. We all loved animals. It was so sweet. One of my favorite pictures is of the three of us sitting in that pigpen.

NANCE. I bet it's cute. Okay. That was my last question for just you. Let's call Gabe back in.

ALICE. Can I ask you something?

NANCE. Of course.

ALICE. About Gabe.

NANCE. Yes. Okay.

ALICE. I know he's learned a lot from the mistakes of his parents. I mean, we have.

NANCE. It's good to learn both good and bad from our parents.

ALICE. Exactly. And their divorce. It was a cautionary tale.

NANCE. Gabe's parents' divorce?

ALICE. Yes, what we learned, because they never talked. Gabe and I talk. All of the time. I just want to be clear, I think sometimes, people think that if you come from divorce you may not, you may not be able to truly appreciate the sanctity of marriage. Gabe and I have been through a lot together. We are committed.

NANCE. Should we call Gabe back in?

ALICE. I just want to say: Marriage is sacred. You have to be in it for the long haul right?

NANCE. I think we all hope that's true, but just like anything, like adoption, you can't predict where you are headed.

ALICE. Oh my god, Nance, you said before you were divorced. I'm—

NANCE. Don't worry about it.

ALICE. Gabe!

      (GABE *enters.*)

GABE. You're done?

ALICE. Yes. I was just about to try and remove the foot from my mouth—

GABE. Uh-oh.

NANCE. Don't worry about it.

ALICE. Nervous. I just want you to know what I know about us.

NANCE. No. Don't worry.

ALICE. That everyone has different backgrounds. I know that. I have this tendency to say things as absolute truths/ Gabe always chides me for it. I know no two trees grow the same way.

NANCE. Seriously, Alice/ It's fine. It's fine.

GABE. Alice, Alice: she's saying that you should stop talking.

ALICE. Right.

NANCE. Okay, there's something we need to address.

GABE. Shoot.

      (NANCE*'s phone vibrates.* ALICE *and* GABE *watch her purse.*)

NANCE. I'm sorry. It's a new phone.

ALICE. Don't worry about it.

      (NANCE *is a little flustered, she pulls out the phone.*)

GABE. Want me to turn it off?

NANCE. I thought I did. Sorry, no, they all work a little differently—

GABE. Let me.

(GABE *takes the phone.*)

NANCE. Oh.

ALICE. He's been through a gazillion phones. Like toys for him.

(GABE *shuts it off, hands it back.*)

GABE. There you go.

NANCE. Thanks.

ALICE. See?

GABE. "Evelyn."

NANCE. What?

GABE. Your caller ID. That's who called.

NANCE. Thank you.
Okay. We need to address Gabe's background.

GABE. My background?

NANCE. Yes, there seems to be a discrepancy.

GABE. Discrepancy.

NANCE. In speaking with Alice, it came to light that you possibly neglected to tell me about your parents' divorce.

(*There is a moment.*)

ALICE. I'm— Honey?

NANCE. I need you both to fully understand, this process requires me to take a full and honest family history from each potential parent.

(GABE *stands up.*)

ALICE. Gabe?

(*He goes to the kitchen.*)

Gabe?

(*She gets up.*)

Gabe? I don't. Sorry Nance, I think maybe he misunderstood—

(GABE *comes back in with a glass and bottle of wine.*)

Gabe? What's that?

GABE. I told her my parents were married.

ALICE. What?

GABE. (*As if she were deaf.*) I-told-her-my-parents-were-still-married.

(ALICE *sits back down.* GABE *uncorks the bottle.*)

(COLIN *types.*)

COLIN. Shauna. Day 59. Please. Please. Please. Please. Please. Please. Please. Please. Please. Please. Please. Send.

(On the porch to NANCE*'s house,* TOM *walks up behind* NANCE *who stands on the porch. She looks at him.)*

NANCE. That's it.

TOM. It's a nice neighborhood.

NANCE. I grew up in this neighborhood.

TOM. I like that.

NANCE. My daughter's car is here.

TOM. Oh.

NANCE. I think she's out.

TOM. Do you want to check?

NANCE. She's supposed to be gone.

TOM. Want me to leave you?

NANCE. That seems to be the trend in my life.

TOM. Help me out here. I'm a gamer. I just need a little guidance.

NANCE. What's wrong with you Tom?

TOM. As in: what's wrong with me, if I'm so great why am I single? Is that your question? Because that question is always the question. You're waiting for the curtain to come down, right?

NANCE. I think I'm being pretty up-front, giving you a front-row seat as to why I'm single.

TOM. She's 17, right? Surely she knows you date.

NANCE. She's supposed to be gone. I wouldn't have.

TOM. I'm not afraid to come in and meet your daughter.

NANCE. That's not the problem.

TOM. Then what's the problem?

NANCE. I don't know.

TOM. Maybe there isn't one.

NANCE. Oh god I'm afraid the problem is that we are both desperate enough to still be here.

(COLIN and EVIE are sitting on a bench watching people go by. EVIE is eating a salad.)

EVIE. Oh my god!

COLIN. Don't stare.

EVIE. You know what I call a skirt like that?

COLIN. What?

EVIE. A cunt duster.

COLIN. Jesus, Evie.

EVIE. Hey Colin, are you sure you still want to go?

COLIN. Friday night. You and me and Homecoming.

EVIE. I've got the salad to prove it.

COLIN. Fulfilling our adolescent obligation to engage in the expected rituals—

EVIE. I was going to make it through without a single dance.

COLIN. Killing your dream.

EVIE. Oh, I can't wait to see your ass dance.

COLIN. Fuck you, I've got moves.

EVIE. Yeah?

COLIN. Last year at Homecoming, Shauna wore this hot black dress. I swear to god she looked 21. She didn't get carded. We mixed vodka with lime slushees. I got sick. Puke all over the back of the limo. Green like a fucking alien.

EVIE. How romantic.

COLIN. It was. We got a room at the Embassy Suites. It was.

EVIE. We should get a limo.

COLIN. We should definitely get wasted.

EVIE. Totally. Score some X.

COLIN. We'll get beer.

EVIE. Beer in a limo, perfect.

COLIN. We can't afford a limo.

EVIE. Beer in a Ford Taurus, even better—

COLIN. I actually *need* to have some fun.

EVIE. For sure.

COLIN. Everything else is fucked. You're now obligated to make sure that this is fun.

EVIE. Consider it fun.

COLIN. Fucking shit, I miss New Hampshire.

EVIE. You miss Shauna.

COLIN. Not just her. It's Fall. It's supposed to be cold. Pasadena is unnatural. I'm not even who I was in Manchester. I'm this guy.

EVIE. Who is this guy?

COLIN. I don't fucking know— I swear to God, ever since I left New Hampshire I'm disappearing— Like I'm real but not important— Not— I don't fucking know Evie.

EVIE. You're feeling bad.

COLIN. Yeah. I am.

EVIE. I feel bad too.

COLIN. Are you fucking kidding me, it's not a competition.

EVIE. No, I know, I'm commiserating.

COLIN. Our misery isn't the same.

EVIE. Really. I think we're both broken-hearted.

COLIN. Bullshit.

EVIE. Okay, you're right it's bullshit. You want to know why I'm fat? *My damage?*

COLIN. No.

EVIE. Yeah, you do.

COLIN. —No, I don't—

EVIE. (*Blurting.*) I'm fat because I used to be really fucked up about a bunch of shit, but now I'm not and I'm still fat. Like I can't stop it even though the reason is done, my dad was fat, but look at me, I'm eating salads this week. I'm trying this week. You know why, right? By the end of the year I think by the end of the year, I'm sorry that Shauna isn't calling you back. Colin, I can do this, I'm ready, I know I'm not supposed to talk to guys about this shit. But you're it Colin. The right friend to tell. I'm shutting up. But I'm glad I said it. I just need you to know how important you are to me. You're a badass. You know and if you could just fall in love with me. Ha! I'm kidding. If I could just shut up. Shauna's a stupid fucking idiot Colin.

COLIN. Shit.

EVIE. She is.

(*Beat.*)

When do you think you'll stop being my friend.

COLIN. Jesus Evie. Can't you just be a little less desperate.

EVIE. Yes. I really can.

COLIN. I'm your friend.

EVIE. Fall in love with me.

COLIN. Evie shut up.

(GABE *drinks.* ALICE *is up and pacing.* NANCE *is in control.*)

NANCE. We need to take a moment to try and sort out this, well, miscommunication. Gabe, when were your parents divorced?

GABE. What difference does it make?

ALICE. He was 11. And it was very hard on him, I think that's why he didn't tell you.

GABE. No, Alice you, *you* told me not to—

ALICE. Please Gabe.

GABE. I'm just being honest.

ALICE. I said, "Don't talk about it." I did not say lie. I didn't say lie.

GABE. "Don't talk about it."

ALICE. We are just so nervous, you understand Nance, don't you?

NANCE. I do.

(NANCE *closes her notebook.*)

ALICE. Why did you close your notebook?

NANCE. Please let's just—

ALICE. Open your notebook, Gabe tell her about your parents Gabe.

GABE. Well, Nance, my parents are divorced.

ALICE. Like so many people.

GABE. Like you Nance.

NANCE. Oh boy. Okay. Of course you know the issue isn't the divorce. It's the dishonesty.

ALICE. We are honest people. Gabe's intention—

GABE. She knows what my intentions were, to show her how utterly, amazingly, outstandingly perfect we are Alice.

ALICE. Open your notebook Nance, we'll tell you the entire story. You can just give us a second chance. We are just trying too hard. We can all relax. Let us just start over. We'll order take-out. Let us buy you dinner.

NANCE. There are guidelines and we have to deal with this piece of the interview. But we'll see. Let's just finish up. You can give me a tour of your home, and I'll get in touch with your case worker and we'll see.

GABE. See if you'll give a baby to liars?

ALICE. Please Gabe.

(He *pours another glass of wine.*)

GABE. Lying alcoholics?

ALICE. Gabe.

GABE. (*Raising his glass.*) Lying *Jewish* alcoholics, L'Chaim.

ALICE. Shut up. Gabe is just upset.

NANCE. Please. This isn't necessary.

ALICE. Really? I mean, you're saying that if we tell you that we just made a mistake, you'll leave it out of the report?

NANCE. I can't do that.

ALICE. You can. You have to.

GABE. Won't. She won't do that.

ALICE. Just this one thing. Look at our house, our life. A child would be lucky.

GABE. She doesn't give a shit. Do you, Nance?

NANCE. Gabe, Alice. Emotions are high.

ALICE. Yes. We are emotional.

NANCE. I know you are—

ALICE. No, no, no Nance. Please, please—lives, this baby is the last thing I think about at night, first thing I think about in the morning. We are not taking this lightly.

NANCE. Alice, neither am I.

ALICE. I'm begging—woman to woman—

NANCE. We'll speak with your case worker at New Horizons and regroup.

GABE. Regroup and release. Cast us back into the barren waters?

ALICE. Shut up!

(NANCE *gathers her things.*)

Please don't go home, please don't judge us?

GABE. I don't think she needs to go home to judge us.

ALICE. I didn't tell him to lie.

GABE. Really, I'm pretty sure that's exactly what you told me to do—

NANCE. Okay, I hear you.

ALICE. No, I said don't go on and on about it, don't tell your stupid stories, don't talk about how your mom made you take over the master bedroom. How she moved into your room. How on Sundays she made you wear the suits your father left behind to go with her to the country club. Don't talk about how you almost couldn't get married, how you thought that if you got married you'd be repeating their sad sorry story. That's what I meant when I said don't talk about the divorce.

(GABE *drinks.*)

(*In the foyer:* COLIN *is there in his Homecoming outfit: jeans, a button-down and a skinny tie. The effect is very charming, Homecoming cool. He has a point-and-shoot camera and a corsage.* NANCE *is rushing to get out the door.*)

NANCE. The big event.

COLIN. Yeah.

NANCE. Okay, I've got to get going, I think she is almost ready. EVELYN!!

COLIN. I'm good, thanks Mrs. Sanders.

NANCE. What time does the dance start?

COLIN. Seven. We're going to get dinner first.

NANCE. Thanks for taking Evelyn, Colin.

COLIN. Oh yeah, sure.

NANCE. (*Getting close, earnestly.*) Thank you, she really needs this.

COLIN. Yeah. You got it.

NANCE. Have fun. I've got to go.

COLIN. Don't you want to take a picture?

NANCE. Oh! Take one for me? I've got a 5 o'clock appointment, work.

COLIN. Right.

NANCE. EVELYN, COLIN IS HERE!

(NANCE *is almost at the door.*)

ALICE. Wait. This will kill us.

NANCE. Everyone is upset. I'm going to just go/ and let you two. Just.

ALICE. You've never made a mistake?

GABE. Oh no Alice/ she's the Solomon of Pasadena.

NANCE. Of course I have, but I take responsibility.

ALICE. I do take responsibility.

NANCE. I'm not sure you do.

ALICE. What do you mean?

GABE. (*Singing.*) The party's over…it's time to call it a day…

ALICE. We aren't wrong. We aren't suddenly wrong.

NANCE. Well this is hardly right— Good night.

ALICE. Argghh. Bitch.

(COLIN *sits on the bed in* EVIE*'s room. He has the point-and-shoot camera.* EVIE *is in the bathroom, door closed.*)

COLIN. (*Pissed.*) Evie!

(*He falls back on the bed. He snaps a picture of himself. Tosses the camera aside.*)

Fuck.

(*He sits up. Flops back. Sits up. Flops back. He opens up the corsage.*)

Don't do this Evie. Don't be such a little girl. I paid for this stuff. It's almost six. I've been sitting here an hour Evie. We have to go. Evie. For fuck's sake. Come on, please. Please, let's just go. Be kick-ass Evie.

(*Now we can see* EVIE *in the bathroom, she is in the Homecoming dress, but it won't zip up. She has her phone and keeps dialing, waiting for her mom to pick up and then hanging up when she doesn't. She redials.*)

I'm done with your bullshit Evie. I'm going. I went to a shitload of trouble. You know what? I don't give a shit. You are not worth this bullshit. You want to be miserable. You want people to hate you. Go for it. You can't handle people being nice to you.

EVIE. (*From the bathroom.*) Please don't say that. Please Colin. I'm sorry.

COLIN. You're always sorry.

EVIE. (*From the bathroom.*) Please don't be mean.

COLIN. Then come out.

EVIE. (*From the bathroom.*) I can't go.

COLIN. You're fucking selfish.

EVIE. (*From the bathroom.*) I love you Colin.

COLIN. You love me? Bullshit. You wouldn't know how. I fucking hate this place. You said you wanted me to help you. I am a nice guy. I should have fucked Holly Lynch. Fucked her brains out. At least then. It's like you think everything in the whole fucking world is about you. You are supposed to be my friend. You suck as a friend. Fuck shit up. It's bullshit. I'm going.

> (*He exits.*)

EVIE. (*Calling after him.*) I'm sorry!

> (*He's gone.*)

THE DRESS DOESN'T FUCKING FIT!

> (EVIE *opens the door, walks into her room. Her dress unzipped. She sits on the edge of the bed. She dials her mom again.*)

Come on, pick up, Mom, pick up.

> (*No answer. She hangs up.*)

> (NANCE *is at the door,* GABE *and* ALICE *in the living room.*)

NANCE. Did you just call me a bitch?

ALICE. What gives you the right to decide—

NANCE. It's my job.

ALICE. You think a paycheck qualifies you. How many fucking times did you ignore your kid tonight? How many times did your phone ring? How about that? How could you possibly/ be qualified to tell me if I would be a good mom.

NANCE. My child/ is none of your fucking business.

GABE. Atta girl.

NANCE. Do you even hear yourself?! When you wake up tomorrow, you're going to be embarrassed.

ALICE. Oh finally, finally she's going to openly ride that high horse.

NANCE. High horse? Really?

ALICE. A woman like you won't be the reason that we don't get what we want.

NANCE. Wanting and deserving are two entirely different things.

ALICE. I deserve a baby!

NANCE. Oh okay, great. Let me get out the baby catalog. You've already picked color, right?/ You've specified gender? Age? Oh wait, you want to pick eye color too?

ALICE. You're disgusting./ You have no idea what we've been through.

NANCE. What you've been through in your nice house where you feel entitled to have children. And then when it doesn't happen you have to figure out something else. So you think, oh, getting a baby from Africa will be cool. But it isn't your first choice./ Whatever child you bring home wouldn't be your first choice.

ALICE. Screw you Nance, we know what we're getting into, just because you had the luck, because that's what it is: luck. The luck to have a child of your own you're more entitled than I am?

NANCE. And you think your liberal intellectualism, your bank account, the fact that you took an African Studies course at Yale makes you qualified? It doesn't. It makes you pathetic.

ALICE. Pathetic! Who the hell are you? You could never know, never feel, you with your daughter, people like you. With your notebooks and stupid questions.

NANCE. Your condescension is exactly your problem! Your pillows. This image you have of you as a mother, you have no idea./ A child coming to your home with the inevitable issues. When the baby doesn't attach, what are you going to do then?

ALICE. Don't tell me what I don't know. I know. I am going to be the best mother, write it in your notebook/ put in your bag, I am going to be the best mother.

NANCE. Oh my god! You are so naive. It isn't easy. It isn't a pretty accessory, it's a child. It's hard. It's so much harder than you'll ever know.

ALICE. You know what's hard: is someone like you can be a mother and I can't.

NANCE. Someone like me? The world isn't fair! Let that be your take away here.

ALICE. I feel sorry for your daughter.

NANCE. Well, I hope to god no child ever lives here.

(GABE *is making sure that* NANCE *is leaving, but just before she's gone, he calmly says:*)

GABE. We may be embarrassed when we wake up tomorrow, but you'll be unemployed.

(NANCE *slams the door behind her. The mezuzah falls off.*)

(EVIE's *still in her room. She cries. She is having a hard time breathing. She is taking short, hard breaths. Her chest hurts. She dials again.*)

EVIE. (*Repeating as much as necessary to get the full panic attack going.*) Why am I such a fucking loser. I'm a fucking loser. I'm a fucking loser. I'm a fucking loser.

(*She can't breathe. She crumples on the floor. She dials again.*)

(COLIN *typing.*)

COLIN. Dear Shauna. Fuck you. Fuck your now single Facebook status. Fuck your blonde hair. Fuck your laughing. Fuck you living in New Hampshire. Fuck you for being such a bitch and not ever calling. Fuck you for telling Michelle to call me and tell me that you are dating Henry Overman. Fuck Henry Overman. Fucking illiterate twat wad Overman. Fuck you, you probably have fucked him. Fuck you for being a slut. Fuck me for being so stupid and thinking that if I loved you that you would love me back. Fuck love. Fuck Dante. Fuck you for ruining my life. Fuck you for breathing. Fuck me for breathing. We're dead. If it wasn't clear: fuck you. P.S. FUCK YOU! Send.

(TOM *and* NANCE *on the porch.*)

NANCE. We can't go in. Not for the reason you think. My daughter hates me.

TOM. She's a teenager.

NANCE. I don't think she's going to turn 20 and suddenly like me.

TOM. I really want to go inside with you.

NANCE. I really want it to be alright for you to stay.

TOM. I really think it is.

(*Beat.*)

NANCE. She's fat.

TOM. Okay.

NANCE. Her dad was fat. Every time I look at her I see my failure. She's fat Tom. That's the part of me you don't see in my profile. It'll make you uncomfortable. And she hates me. She hates the world. Oh my god. I can't do it. You should leave Tom. I'm toxic. Save yourself.

TOM. Stop it.

NANCE. I don't love my daughter in the right way.

TOM. There's no right way.

NANCE. I do it the wrong way, I look in myself and I say, "Feel the love." Like I could conjure it from deep inside of me. I think that I am actually deficient. That I'm incapable of unconditional love.

TOM. Nance.

NANCE. Oh my god, I don't love my daughter. Oh my god. Oh my fucking god.

> (*They kiss.*)

> (GABE *and* ALICE *stand at the door,* NANCE *has just left.*)

GABE. I'm sorry.

> (*Pause.*)

We'll call that lawyer. The one that Martin and Shelly used.

> (*Pause.*)

I'll call New Horizons. I'm sure.

> (*Pause.*)

This isn't done, we need to regroup.

> (*Pause.*)

Or an egg donor. Dr. Levine said it was still on the table.

> (*Pause.*)

We'll make a family.

> (*Pause.*)

For the love of god, say something. You can't hate me Alice. I won't let you hate me.

ALICE. I don't.

> (ALICE *goes to pour herself a glass of wine, she sees* NANCE's *phone on the table. She picks it up.*)

Great. Her phone.

> (*She hands it to* GABE. *He turns it on.* ALICE *starts for the kitchen.* NANCE's *phone rings.* GABE *looks at it.*)

GABE. "Evelyn."

> (ALICE *grabs the phone. She looks at it. Then:*)

ALICE. Hello?

(COLIN *climbs through* EVIE*'s bedroom window. He's still dressed for Homecoming, but he's disheveled.*)

COLIN. Evie! Evie? Evie!

(*He's carrying a six-pack missing four beers. He drinks. He lies back on* EVIE*'s bed.*)

(*In the* ER, EVIE *is in a bed, in a hospital gown, she is hooked up to an IV.* ALICE *and* GABE *have just arrived.*)

ALICE. Evelyn?

(EVIE *looks at* ALICE.)

Are you Evelyn Sanders?

EVIE. Yeah.

ALICE. Hi. I'm Alice. I answered when you called. Your mom left her phone—

EVIE. Where's my mom?

ALICE. She's coming. Are you okay? Do you need anything? This is Gabe, my husband.

GABE. Hi.

(*Pause.*)

EVIE. I had a heart attack.

ALICE. No. You didn't.

EVIE. I did.

ALICE. The doctor said it was like a heart attack.

GABE. But not one. You're okay.

(*There is a long moment.*)

ALICE. You're okay.

EVIE. I really want my mom.

ALICE. You called 911. You're okay.

EVIE. Can you please find my mom?

ALICE. New Horizons, where your mom works, they said, right Gabe?

GABE. They're trying to locate her.

ALICE. They'll find her.

EVIE. I really need her.

GABE. What about your dad?

EVIE. He lives in Mexico.

GABE. Do you know where your mom might be? I'll go find her.

EVIE. I don't know where she is.

GABE. Give me your address, I could go to your house and see if she's there. She doesn't have her phone, so she doesn't—

ALICE. Gabe will find her.

(TOM *and* NANCE *on the porch.*)

NANCE. This feels like a complicated first date.

TOM. I like complicated stories. Like *The Girl with the Dragon Tattoo.*

NANCE. Are you kidding me? I'm not complicated. I just told you that I don't think I'm capable of loving my daughter.

TOM. Well, at the museum, when I said I wasn't lonely. I lied.

NANCE. I think I'm going to be fired on Monday.

TOM. My wife left me because she was bored.

NANCE. My fat husband left me because I wasn't sexually attracted to him.

TOM. Since my divorce three years ago I've only had one *second* date.

NANCE. Every time I look at my daughter, my heart breaks.

TOM. See you do love her.

NANCE. You know about love.

TOM. I know your heart can't break if it doesn't love.

NANCE. You know what I would appreciate? I would really appreciate it if you would pat my back, like you did at the museum. Will you do that?

TOM. Yes.

(TOM *pats her back, she leans into him.*)

(ALICE *is still standing next to* EVIE's *hospital bed. The curtains are drawn all around them.*)

ALICE. Evelyn, listen, don't worry. You are going to be fine. I am good at helping people.

(EVIE *is crying.*)

Don't. You are going to be okay.

EVIE. I don't think so.

ALICE. Your mom said some pretty great things about you. Yep. How smart. How pretty you are.

EVIE. You're lying.

ALICE. I'll just sit here with you. Okay?

EVIE. I really just need my mom, I really just need her to be here now, I really just want her to be here now.

ALICE. She is coming. Don't worry. Your mom is definitely coming. I promise. You need your mom.

(ALICE *smoothes part of the rumpled sheet on* EVIE's *hospital bed.* EVIE *closes her eyes.*

COLIN *is sitting in* EVIE's *bedroom on the bed, he drinks his beer, he pulls back the covers and then tucks himself in, hugs* EVIE's *teddy bear.*

TOM *and* NANCE *are still sitting on the porch,* TOM *has arm draped over* NANCE's *shoulder.* GABE *walks towards them.*

ALICE *sits in a chair by* EVIE's *bed.* EVIE *opens her eyes.* ALICE *gives her a small smile.*)

End of Play

HOW WE GOT ON
by Idris Goodwin

Copyright © 2012 by Idris Goodwin. All rights reserved. CAUTION: Professionals and amateurs are hereby warned that *How We Got On* is subject to a royalty. It is fully protected under the copyright laws of the United States of America and of all countries covered by the International Copyright Union (including the Dominion of Canada and the rest of the British Commonwealth), the Berne Convention, the Pan-American Copyright Convention and the Universal Copyright Convention, as well as all countries with which the United States has reciprocal copyright relations. All rights, including professional, amateur stage rights, motion picture, recitation, lecturing, public reading, radio broadcasting, television, video or sound recording, all other forms of mechanical or electronic reproduction, such as CD-ROM, CD-I, information storage and retrieval systems and photocopying, and the rights of translation into foreign languages, are strictly reserved. Particular emphasis is laid upon the matter of readings, permission for which must be secured from the Author's agent in writing.

Required royalties must be paid every time this play is performed before any audience, whether or not it is presented for profit and whether or not admission is charged.

All inquiries concerning rights, including amateur rights, should be addressed to: Jessica Amato, The Gersh Agency, 41 Madison Avenue, 33rd Floor, New York, NY 10010. 212-997-1818.

ABOUT *HOW WE GOT ON*

This article first ran in the January/February 2012 issue of Inside Actors, *Actors Theatre of Louisville's subscriber newsletter, and is based on conversations with the playwright before rehearsals for the Humana Festival production began.*

Remember the days of old school DJs? The ones who got you into the groove with turntables, hands dancing from record to record, fingers sliding across vinyl to mix, remix, and funk up the beat? In Idris Goodwin's *How We Got On*, one such DJ—the smooth-talkin' Selector—spins us back to 1988. Thanks to *YO! MTV Raps*, hip hop is spreading from gritty streets on the urban coasts to TV screens across Middle America. Watching Big Daddy Kane rock the mic inspires Hank and Julian, suburban boys with dreams beyond homework and basketball camp, to spit their own rhymes.

At first, they're enemies; can't have two rappin' dudes occupying the same territory. (Particularly if that territory is a predominantly white—and white-collar—neighborhood where black kids stand out.) Following a lyrical battle in a mall parking lot, however, the dueling MCs form an uneasy alliance. Hank's a wizard with words, while Julian's got charismatic cool; together, they could be the dopest rap duo in the Hill. But from their fathers berating them to "get serious" to their struggles to create a great new sound, Hank and Julian still have a lot to learn...sometimes from unlikely sources. Like Luann, the seemingly stuck-up rich girl who schools the boys in the ways of freestyling. Because hip hop is also about spitting your soul, without fear; it's about having the confidence to "plug in your open mind" and be okay with taking a loss. And hey, so is growing up.

How We Got On is playwright and spoken word poet Idris Goodwin's attempt to lay fresh beats over a familiar story. "I wanted to take a coming-of-age story about these kids who live in a small town and want to do big things, but tell it in an unfamiliar way," he explains, "which was to use a hip hop mixed tape format." (Think of the compilation albums you've seen in CD stores.) A funk or soul track—evoking hip hop's roots—accompanies each scene, introduced by the Selector. The Selector doesn't just control the music, but also loops and re-loops segments of dialogue, creating distinctive rhythms and refrains, so that our heroes become like records revolving under the needle of the narrative. Goodwin isn't the first to riff on the mixed tape structure, but he's unique in stringing the songs/scenes together into one story. "What others have done is bring together unrelated pieces and blend them to create more of a collage effect," he says. *How We Got On* emerges as the collaboration between a deepening dramatic arc and spontaneous hip hop swagger; classic narrative remixed.

But this remix isn't just about the boys. Though we may associate hip hop with tough-talking masculinity, Goodwin points out, "When I started listening to rap music in the '80s, there were just as many female voices." So we're seduced into the world of sound manipulation by a female DJ, and given the lowdown on lyrical improv by a teenage girl. While prim Luann might be the last person we'd expect to have hip hop know-how (she hangs out with the "stuck-up black kids" who think rap is "ghetto"), she illustrates Goodwin's awareness that "there are kids right now in the last place you'd imagine, messing with their recording equipment, throwing their computers against the wall and trying to figure out how to make them do things they're not supposed to do."

Set in the Midwestern 'burbs instead of the Bronx (hip hop's birthplace), *How We Got On* happens in the last place we'd imagine cool beats reverberating. Not that Goodwin doesn't think it's important to remember the music's origins: "The challenge for my generation of hip hoppers is making sure we're reminding folks where this comes from," he says. But Goodwin also understands that although "we romanticize the Bronx in the '70s and '80s, street aspects of the culture, for most hip hop fans the experience is in your room." Hip hop reminds Hank and Julian of their roots in "the City," and reinforces their sense of racial identity. But hip hop also allows them to express new identities, shaped by their circumstances; they rhyme about "cereal breakfast" and "Tree Lined/Streets wide and empty." And the possibility that they could actually "get on" (make a name for themselves as MCs) in the Hill points to why hip hop has gotten on in the popular consciousness. It can give voice to the tones of our ordinary lives, because it hinges on words, tools that we all use to express emotions, make memories, and thus compose the poem of who we are and who we want to be.

So you don't need to know how to beatbox to nod your head to the beats in *How We Got On*. You don't need to know anything about hip hop for this "break beat play" to get your heart pumping like thumping bass. As Luann breaks it down for Hank and Julian, hip hop isn't about looking or acting a certain way. It's about unlocking the head and heart, releasing your true self with joy.

—Hannah Rae Montgomery

BIOGRAPHY

Idris Goodwin is a playwright who performs, a rapper who writes essays, and a teacher who makes albums. He's been recognized for his work across mediums by the National Endowment for the Arts, the Ford and Mellon Foundations, the *New York Times* and National Public Radio. His plays include *Blackademics* and *How We Got On*, developed at the Eugene O'Neill Theater Center and featured in the 2012 Humana Festival of New American Plays. Other stage works have been commissioned or produced by Steppenwolf Theatre Company, American Theater Company, Pillsbury House Theatre, and the Los Angeles Theatre Center. He's appeared on HBO's *Def Poetry*, The Discovery Channel, and *Sesame Street*. *These Are The Breaks*, his debut collection of essays, was nominated for a Pushcart Prize. An award-winning educator, he's taught at the University of Iowa and Northwestern University. He is currently a performance writing professor at Colorado College.

ACKNOWLEDGMENTS

How We Got On premiered at the Humana Festival of New American Plays in March 2012. It was directed by Wendy C. Goldberg with the following cast:

HANK	Terrell Donnell Sledge
JULIAN	Brian Quijada
LUANN	Deonna Bouye
SELECTOR	Crystal Fox

and the following production staff:

Scenic Designer	Tom Tutino
Costume Designer	Connie Furr-Soloman
Lighting Designer	Kirk Bookman
Sound Designer	Matt Hubbs
Properties Designer	Seán McArdle
Stage Manager	Bret Torbeck
Dramaturg	Hannah Rae Montgomery
Casting	Harriet Bass

Directing Assistant	Jane B. Jones
Assistant Costume Designer	Daniel Chihuahua
Production Assistant	Caitlin O'Rourke
Fight Supervisor	Nick Vannoy
Assistant Dramaturg	Molly Clasen

The development of *How We Got On* was supported by New Leaf Theatre's Treehouse Reading Series 2011, and the Eugene O'Neill Theater Center.

CHARACTERS

HANK, 15, black boy

JULIAN, 15, bi/poly-racial boy

LUANN, 15, black girl

SELECTOR, female, late 30s-40s, a woman of color with a voice for underground radio

How they sound?

The teenagers' speaking voices differ from those they adopt when they rap. Their rap voices should reflect the '88 East Coast sounds but with a suburban tinge. Hank idolizes Big Daddy Kane, Luann idolizes MC Lyte, Julian can sound like anyone.

Selector's voice is magnetic, there is a hive of honey bees in her throat, a rhythmic bounce.

She speaks to the audience, to the characters—she controls the world.

She provides narration, tangential information, and plays a variety of music from a record player. Selector will also provide the voices of offstage characters referenced throughout, like Hank's and Julian's fathers, the coach, the Battle of the Bands host, the contest spokesman, various teenagers, etc.

How they look?

Hank and Julian could have high top fades. However, the height of these fades should never reach Christopher "Kid" Reid absurdity. No wigs either. (Trust me, you'll thank me later.) Julian probably has three cuts in one of his eyebrows. Fashion-wise—T-shirts and tank tops with Nike Swooshes, Adidas, Detroit Pistons, Chicago Bulls, Cleveland Cavs are also likely. Izod and Rugby shirts. High-top sneakers, Julian probably has the first edition Air Jordans, Hank most likely has a generic rip-off. Baseball caps with the lids flipped up. Julian always looks maybe 10 degrees hipper than Hank.

Luann dresses much more conservatively and modest. She should look like the last person to ever listen to rap music, let alone create it.

SETTING

Time: 1988.

Offstage Setting: Suburban, Midwest America—maybe Michigan, Indiana or Ohio.

Onstage Setting: A DJ booth with a mic, an easel, a few pieces to suggest locations.

> The Studio: In the present, Selector speaking to the "listeners" (the audience) from a microphone.
>
> Scene: A moment from the past, performed as if it's happening now—a fourth wall moment.
>
> Dads: the remix: Hank and Julian talking with their fathers' voices (provided by the Selector). This is a hyper-reality in which scenes are crossfaded together.
>
> In Concert: Any time Hank, Julian or Luann perform their raps. This is a manifestation of how they feel/what they imagine.

NOTES

Concerning the Repetition: Lines that repeat should be performed with the same inflection and tone each time—these are not characters repeating the same lines because other characters are not understanding them, these lines are being spun back and replayed, spun back and replayed, spun back and replayed, spun back, spun back, spun, spun, spun and replayed by Selector.

Words that Echo: Either manipulated by the sound designer or created by the actor on stage; they look like this (this this this this—)

Crystal Fox
in *How We Got On*

36th Humana Festival of New American Plays
Actors Theatre of Louisville, 2012
Photo by Alan Simons

HOW WE GOT ON

Lights up on SELECTOR *in her studio. She is drinking something colorful, dressed comfortably.*

She wears headphones. She puts a record on. We hear "Sufferer's Dub" by The Upsetters.

SELECTOR *speaks into the mic to us—her listeners for the evening.*

SELECTOR. *Listeners. Tonight I bring you tones*

Grooves, friction. Vibes and Vibrations off the wax melted.
Mother and father. Yin, yang. The Dub side.

Yeah. I bring you tones.

The flip to the A—I bring you the B side

I'll be toasting.
I'll be selecting.

The Waves. Steerin' the wheel.

Welcome
I am Selector (Selector Selector Selector Selector——)
          (The music plays.)
Perhaps you are here to take a little trip through memory

Maybe you "remember when"

Well, "remember whens"
—and there is nothing wrong with that
the wax artifact is memory—tangible

and here we use these wax artifacts
to take us back one time

Perhaps some of you are lost
thought you'd signed up—different

Well, there are no intermissions
so time to plug in
your open mind
          (The music plays.)
What I'm doin' right now called—toasting
you know, riffin'
signifyin'
representing who I be over the groove

art of toasting blew life into Hip Hop

and Hip Hop spared a rib
to mold rap—which is the voice

Hip Hop is the body
toasting is the spirit
but I digress

We going back to '88, ya'll (ya'll ya'll ya'll ya'll—)

Hip Hop culture is 15 years old.
Rap music—younger—but it's on the move

Now, this is not an uptown boogie down story
about the urban loins from which Hip Hop was squeezed

and no doubt
that story is beautiful

But tonight's selection brings us to The Hill

Somewhere round Motown, just up from Chitown,
not far from Ohio, but not quite Indiana
the middle, the land in between, America's bread basket.

there are no b-boys, DJs or taggers
but best believe
Hip Hop lived in The Hill

The summer of '88.
the premiere of YO! (YO! YO! YO! YO!) MTV Raps

    (SELECTOR *holds an unlabeled record in her hand.*)

SELECTOR. *We gonna start things off with Henry Charles. Fifteen. Or as he calls himself: John Henry. Freshman. Or as he is called by everyone else: Hank!*

    (*She puts the record on.*

    We hear:)

VOICE OF HANK. What up! Yeah, this the microphone Mafioso comin' straight out The Hill. Got that new album coming real soon. Dope lyrics, fresh beats—Yeah!

    (*This* PRE-RECORDED HANK *crossfades into the actual* HANK *onstage talking into a cheap mic attached to the back of his boombox.*)

HANK. (*Trying his best to sound authentic.*) Glad to finally be on *YO! MTV Raps!* I watch it all the time. I know usually you got rappers from New York and Compton, but I do my thing too. I mean, I got the skills to pay the bills—I'm fresher than anybody. Where I come from doesn't matter! It's about how I get busy on the mic. That's all that matter, right?

SELECTOR. *Yes and No.*
No but yes.

For Henry Charles and others like him.
In the land in between. In the middle.

Nowhere.

It was born in the mall. Station. Station. Station. Born on the radio.
Born by TV. Born in the mouth. Word of…that is.

HANK. (*His real voice slowly revealing itself.*) My parents' music is all R&B, "*Baby come close! Let me do this! Why you leave me? Why won't you come back?*" Sometimes that's how you feel. I guess. Sometimes you feel like:

(HANK *recites a few lines from his favorite 1986 LL Cool J song.*)

Because everybody, well, most people in real life. They take an "L." Rich People. Poor. Handsome people. Ugly. Citizens. Immigrants. Everybody takes a loss. But in a rap song—you're the winner, even if you're small, you're fat, even if you're black and you live in The Hill.

SELECTOR. *Hank—Henry Charles lives 35 miles outside The Urban Epicenter, we call*

The City (City. City. City. City)

Henry Charles and his family were part of that first wave of African Americans who left The City during Ronald Reagan's first term.

HANK. No. Not a lot of black kids in The Hill. I stand out, sure. But not just cuz of that. Because I can rap. Oh yeah, they like rap out here, sure.

Not really though. As a joke I think. Even the other black kids say it's ghetto. They're all so stuck up. Everybody out here listens to like Rick Astley, INXS, Debbie Gibson.

But they know. Even if they don't like rap, they love rap. Or at least they will. Everybody will.

Anybody else?

There is NO competition. All the real good MCs live back in The City. But as far as The Hill. I am the fresh prince.

SELECTOR. *Or is he?*

during the second wave—As Bush Sr. readied his campaign posters
came another crop of the upwardly mobile.

So as Hank-Henry Charles boasts into his boombox about being
the best and ONLY MC in The Hill

Just down the road at a different school there was another

(SELECTOR *holds up another unlabeled record and puts it on the plate.*)

VOICE OF JULIAN. The rhyme villain. The lyrical criminal. The smooth soul technician.

HANK. Oh, yeah—I heard of him.

VOICE OF JULIAN. I go by Vic Vicious! See, I'm part Latino.

> (PRE-RECORDED JULIAN *fades into actual* JULIAN *onstage, gesturing and posturing to an unseen listener.*)

JULIAN. Julian Mark Hayes doesn't sound very, you know, so I thought a name like Vic was more, you know? Plus it's kinda sharp. Like a blade. Not trying to stereotype that Latinos carry knives or whatever. Anyway, I'm flipping it. I'm sharp with the rhymes. Cut you…lyrically.

HANK. Some of the kids from school said a couple things about him.

SELECTOR. (*As a teen.*) He's real good and I don't even like rap.

HANK. Little rumors. Probably not true.

SELECTOR. (*Teen.*) I heard Vic Vicious had a record deal back when he lived in The City.

JULIAN. The *Vicious* is like the old school. Everybody was treacherous, furious…Vic Vicious. Somebody might get hurt.

HANK. (*Authentic rapper voice returning.*) Threatened? Nope. Why would I be? There can be two rappin' dudes in The Hill.

SELECTOR. (*Teen.*) I heard he's LL Cool J's cousin.

HANK. There can be two rappin' dudes in The Hill.

SELECTOR. (*Teen.*) Oh, I heard—

HANK. But there can't! Yo! Tomorrow I'm gonna send word: "Vic Vicious, I want to square off!"

> (*Pause.*)

You know, verbally.

SELECTOR. *The battle was set.*
First Friday of that December.
parking lot of the new mall on Fischer Road.
Noon.

HANK. What's my strategy? Everything I listen to right now, most of it anyway, is a battle rap. Or about a girl. Sometimes it's about Africa. But usually, "*I'm this. I'm that. You're not.*" A good battle rap has something personal, specific, about the opponent like*, "Your shoes are wack* or *your rhymes are wack* or *your family is wack* or *you…you're just wack*"…but, you know…even more specific. So you gotta do research—that's what my dad always says, not about battle rap, but whenever I have to do a paper or something. He always says,

SELECTOR. (*As HANK'S DAD.*) There is a science to everything.

HANK. So I start to do my research on this Vic Vicious guy. Realize. I met this dude before.

SELECTOR. *In 1988—if you are in The Hill or The City—you want to be Michael Jordan.*

HANK. Summer before we started our different high schools, we're at the same basketball camp.

SELECTOR. *Basketball camp!*

> (*Shift*—HANK *and* JULIAN *in scene—they are side-by-side, doing defensive slides.*)

JULIAN. These kids can't ball

HANK. The same basketball camp.

JULIAN. These kids can't ball

HANK. The same basketball camp.

SELECTOR. *Basketball camp!*

JULIAN. These kids can't ball

HANK. The same basketball camp.

JULIAN. These kids can't ball

HANK. We're at the same basketball camp.

JULIAN. These kids can't ball

SELECTOR. *Basketball camp!*

HANK. Huh.

JULIAN. Yeah, man. They suck.

> (*They move silently for a moment.*)

HANK. I really don't even like basketball.

JULIAN. Your D is alright.

HANK. Thanks.

JULIAN. Can't shoot for shit.

> (*They move.*)

Bunch of rich punks. Everybody has new shoes on.

> (*Beat.*)

Just cuz you got on new Jordans don't make you Jordan.

HANK. (*Peers down.*) Those Reeboks you got on look pretty new.

JULIAN. I like Reeboks.

> (*Beat.*)

In my old neighborhood, these guys would be…man, they'd be crying.

HANK. Where are you from?

JULIAN. City.

HANK. Me too.

JULIAN. What side?

HANK. North, you?

JULIAN. West.

> (*They keep going.*)

You don't like ball. What do you do then?

HANK. Rap.

JULIAN. Oh yeah?

HANK. You like rap too?

> (JULIAN *stops shuffling.* HANK *stops as well.*)

JULIAN. Yo, check this out…

SELECTOR. (*As the coach.*) Guys! Did I blow my whistle?! Hustle! Hustle! Hustle!

> (*Shift*—HANK *with the boombox.*)

HANK. Coach took him off the blue team and put him on the red team so we didn't really talk again after that. But now—I'm gonna do more than just talk. I'm gonna—What?

First battle? Where'd you get that from? You gotta check your sources. No, no, no, I been in a million battles. I've never been taken out. First battle.

SELECTOR. *And now for something completely funky*

> (SELECTOR *puts on "Pungee" by The Meters. Over "Pungee":*)

Battle rhymes.
When you start—drop a lot of popular nouns—words people will know but be surprised to hear—they'll be like

Oooooohhhh snap!!

say the other guy is not actually a guy at all
say you got intimate with his mother. Or his sister

Use techniques like metaphor

HANK. *If rap was a shoe, you'd be a sandal*

SELECTOR. *Simile*

HANK. *Black and heavy, just like an anvil*

SELECTOR. *Hyperbole*

HANK. *Ice Mr. Freeze MCs to a Standstill*

SELECTOR. *Alliteration*

HANK. *compete with this casual*
confident cool kid
you get cancelled

SELECTOR. *Never ever cry. No crying. Ever.*

 (*"Pungee" fades out.*)

HANK. (*In authentic rapper voice.*) First battle? Where'd you get that from? You gotta check your sources. No, no, no, I been in a million battles. I've never been taken out. First battle.

SELECTOR. *Not that it isn't obvious—painfully*

but the battle
first Friday of that December
parking lot
new mall on Fischer Road
noon

was Hank's first battle
not counting of course the times he'd
verbally demolished his flip side
in the mirror

It would be his first and last

 (HANK *speaking into the boombox.*)

HANK. So I guess you wanna know what happened?

The parking lot of the new mall on Fischer Road was packed—even some of the stuck-up black kids who say rap is ghetto. I never knew so many people liked rap.

I got there before him. He came like fifteen minutes late. He had on the new Jordans. He was actin' like he didn't remember me from basketball camp. I caught him eyeballing my bike. Which is nice, but his is even nicer. So I start thinking:

I am gonna crush this kid, lyrically, and take his bike as my prize.

 (*Shift*—JULIAN *and* HANK *in scene, preparing to battle!*)

JULIAN. You go first.

HANK. No. You.

JULIAN. No. We're closer to my high school. So you're a guest in my kingdom. You go first.

HANK. I moved here before you. You're a guest in my kingdom. You go first.

 (*Shift*—SELECTOR *in studio.*)

SELECTOR. *In a battle a rapper should go second*
the memory of the first can get hazy
second rapper can flip what first rapper said

flat on its back

Bend the lines into daggers
strike the audience
make 'em say
"Oooooohhhh snap!!"

    (*Shift*—JULIAN *in scene.*)

JULIAN. Don't cry. I'll go first.

    (HANK *at the boombox.*)

HANK. And off he went. He didn't say anything about how bad I was at basketball last summer. Nothing about my shoes. And they were lookin' busted. He was just rippin' it. Line after line—crystal clean like a recording. On top of that…he looked very cool the whole time—like *it ain't no thing.* My mouth was like (*Opens mouth.*) when he drops the last line. The crowd, even the stuck-up black kids who say rap is ghetto—they erupt!

Now, most people would be like, "How am I supposed to follow that?" But I thought: Yo, my verse is solid.

    (*Shift*—HANK *in scene.*)

HANK. (*A little flat, not fully confident.*)
Ain't nuthin' Vicious bout this villain
his vowels ain't vibrant

his vocals don't hit
he's softer than violets

I break him apart

Resort to violence
Show up at his funeral

Black clothes
And violins

SELECTOR. (*The crowd.*) Booooooooooooo. Booooooooooooo.

    (*Shift*—HANK *into the boombox.*)

HANK. I kept on. I was gonna say my rap. They couldn't hear me.

They were already patting Vic on the back. Even people from my own school! And then he took off on my bike!

    (*Shift*—Dads: the remix.*)

SELECTOR. (*As* HANK'S DAD.) A loss is an opportunity. It will take you twice as long to walk to school than to bike, therefore, you have twice as much time to reflect on what went wrong.

HANK. It's rap, Dad, not science.

SELECTOR. (HANK'S DAD.) It's not the end of the world.

HANK. I'm supposed to be the rapper. And now *he's* the rapper.

SELECTOR. (HANK'S DAD.) What you both are—students. That's your first priority.

HANK. It's like the Pauli exclusion principle.

SELECTOR. (HANK'S DAD.) How so?

HANK. No two rappers can occupy the same space at the same time.

SELECTOR. (HANK'S DAD.) Well, that's not an exact comparison. I have a great book on the exclusion principle.

HANK. Dad.

SELECTOR. (HANK'S DAD.) Yes.

HANK. It was like someone sucked all the air out my lungs. I can write the rhymes, but when I start to say 'em…I *got* the words, but when I say 'em—I hear them booing at me. That's all I hear.

SELECTOR. (HANK'S DAD.) Maybe it's time to try something different. Like studying.

HANK. Yes sir.

SELECTOR. *And Hank did just that*
Electronics, time, music theory.

He studied via the seminal Hip Hop albums of '87 of '88

  (SELECTOR *plays the instrumental from BDP's* Criminal Minded.)

SELECTOR. *Public Enemy*—It Takes a Nation of Millions to Hold Us Back
Soundtrack to Colors
Too Short—Born to Mack
Kid 'n Play—2 Hype
Boogie Down Productions—By All Means Necessary
EPMD—Strictly Business
MC Lyte—Lyte as a Rock
Slick Rick—The Great Adventures of Slick Rick

  (HANK *talks into his boombox.*)

HANK. (*Authentic DJ voice.*) Yes yes y'all! This is DJ John Henry with the *"No Mistakes in '88"* mixtape!

  (SELECTOR *plays "Set It Off" by Big Daddy Kane.* HANK *revels in the wordplay unleashed in the first 25 seconds—until something clicks.*
  Transition to scene.)

SELECTOR. Hank spots his bike in front of Pizza Pete's.

HANK. You're a biter!

JULIAN. Shhhhh. I'm working

HANK. You're a biter

JULIAN. Shhhhh. I'm working

HANK. You're a biter

JULIAN. Shhhhh. I'm working

SELECTOR. Hank spots his bike at Pizza Pete's.

> (HANK *and* JULIAN *in scene.*)

HANK. You're a biter

JULIAN. Shhhhh. I'm working

HANK. You're biting.

JULIAN. You want your bike back? Take it. Kinda sucks.

HANK. Doesn't suck. Shut up.

JULIAN. I'm working, so...

> (HANK *flawlessly raps parts of "Set It Off."*)

So?

HANK. That's not yours. That's Big Daddy Kane's verse from "Set it Off."

JULIAN. Yeah.

HANK. Come on. It's my rap versus your rap. Not karaoke.

JULIAN. Where are the rules?

HANK. I can't believe I didn't realize that!

JULIAN. Yeah, I used Big Daddy Kane rhymes. He's the best.

HANK. Yeah, I know.

JULIAN. Those kids in choir, they go all over the country singing old-assed songs. Over and over. Who cares?

HANK. This ain't choir.

JULIAN. So, what? Those rhymes you said were yours?

HANK. Yes.

JULIAN. Oh.

> (*Beat.*)

HANK. Yeah, I write a rhyme a day.

JULIAN. How?

HANK. One word, then another.

JULIAN. Sarcastic.

HANK. No. That's being a smart aleck.

JULIAN. It's ass. Smart ass.

Smart aleck? Are you a Christian or something?

HANK. Shut up.

> (*Beat.*)

JULIAN. I gotta break here in a few minutes.

HANK. So?

JULIAN. I got some Schnapps.

HANK. What?

JULIAN. Yeah. Peach.

HANK. Um. I gotta go.

JULIAN. You should write me some rhymes.

HANK. Why would I write rhymes for you?

JULIAN. So when I battle, kids like you won't go home. Listen to all their rap tapes, come back and call me a biter.

HANK. You gotta ride? Cuz I'm going to take my bike.

JULIAN. I rap better than you.

HANK. No.

JULIAN. That's why you should write me rhymes. I perform better. That's why I won. I can do anybody's style. Kane, Eazy-E, Too Short. Anybody. You're not...big enough...so let me do 'em.

HANK. Big enough?

    (*Shift*—SELECTOR *in studio.*)

SELECTOR. *People like their rappers brash*
People like their rappers
to project projectiles

People like their rappers
to be new money
to be smoother than
s-m-double o-smooth

People like their rappers big
and Hank knew it

he didn't like it

but he knew

    (*Shift*—HANK *and* JULIAN *in scene.*)

HANK. And what do I get to do?

JULIAN. You get to hang out and say, See that smooth, dope, fresh MC? I wrote those rhymes that guy is saying.

    (HANK *considers.*)

At my school they got this Battle of the Bands.

HANK. Yeah, I heard about that. I'm jealous.

JULIAN. Yeah, your school is wack.

HANK. Shut up.

JULIAN. I'm trying to win that.

HANK. You play any instrument?

JULIAN. What? Hells no. I'm gonna rap what you write me.

HANK. Rap in Battle of the Bands? No. No. You gotta do something people know. Maybe, just maybe, you could get away with like, Run-DMC. Do "Mary, Mary" or that Aerosmith song.

JULIAN. That song is wack.

HANK. The Beastie Boys?

JULIAN. Hells no!

HANK. You gotta have something with some rock if you're trying to win Battle of the Bands in The Hill.

JULIAN. I win. That's what I do. I don't know about you, but I win things.

HANK. I don't know.

JULIAN. So you're one of those "I don't know" types, huh? Losers, I think they're called.

(*Beat.*)

HANK. What's the prize?

JULIAN. Twenty dollar gift certificate. Any store in the new mall on Fischer Road. Free frozen coke at the movie theater.

HANK. I want a free pizza.

JULIAN. Better be some smoking rhymes.

HANK. I like ham and pineapple.

JULIAN. Uggghhhh.

HANK. The better the pizza, the better the pen work.

JULIAN. Alright.

(*They give each other five.*)

HANK. So first we gotta figure out the sorts of things you would say.

JULIAN. You know how the guys on *YO! MTV Raps,* like, how they are. They're just like, you know—I'm the shit!

HANK. You can't just *say* that. You have to like, *show* it.

JULIAN. But I'm showing it, because I am.

(HANK *sits down with pad and pen.*

JULIAN *looks over* HANK's *shoulder as he works.* HANK *feels the hovering presence, gives* JULIAN *a look.* JULIAN *steps back, fronts like he's got something else to do.*)

HANK. (*Holding the new rhymes.*) Okay, um…

might of won this time but next time I kill

(*Pause.* HANK *hears them boo.*)

JULIAN. It's just one line?

HANK. No.

JULIAN. Why'd you stop?

HANK. (*Handing over the rhymes.*) Here.

    (*Shift*—SELECTOR *in studio.*)

SELECTOR. *Ghostwriting—one of Hip Hop's best-kept secrets*

For Hank, it was easier than he thought. Finally, somebody who could say his boasts with full confidence.

*Sure, Julian—Vic Vicious—would get the applause—but this way
Hank wouldn't hear them boo again.*

    (*Shift*—HANK *and* JULIAN *in scene.*)

JULIAN. Yeah, that's dope…I mean, you know, for your first time.

HANK. It's not.

JULIAN. Writing for me. It's your first time. But it's not really…for me. I mean, "might of won this time," no. I always win, so I wouldn't say that. Maybe you would.

HANK. Yeah.

JULIAN. (*Crumpling the rhymes.*) I was thinking we could do something like with the letters of my name. Wouldn't that be fresh?

    (JULIAN *tosses* HANK *the notepad.*)

HANK. (*Starting a new page.*) Yes. It would.

    (*Shift*—*transition to* JULIAN *in concert.*)

SELECTOR. Battle of the Bands!

JULIAN. Hill Foster High

SELECTOR. Vic Vicious Live!

JULIAN. Hill Foster High

SELECTOR. Battle of the Bands!

    (*Shift*—JULIAN *in concert.*)

JULIAN. Make some noise!

That was kinda weak—lemme hear you?

We'll work on it.

So Yo, Yo, Yo, Check it out
Vic Vicious in the place to be
So yo check it

Just throw your hands in the air!
And wave 'em like ya just don't care

and if you got on clean underwear
lemme hear you say "Oh Yeeeeah"
SELECTOR. *Oh YEAH!*
JULIAN. And it don't stop

Check my rhyme…

V is for victory
Listen and get with me
Straight out The City
Givin' competition misery
It ain't a mystery. The place be jumpin'
"is he some kinda rappin angel or something"
V is for Vic—letters they stand for
Vocals I Contain/ put you on the dance floor

You betta clap
That's what you got hands for
I'm the answer to the question
"who was that can-tor?"

Back and forth and
Forth and back and
Rap packed excitin'
your heart's attackin'

Vicious this villain
vowels are vibrant

vocals straight hit
rappers softer than violets

I break them apart
Resort to violence

Show up at they funeral
Black clothes
And violins

Yeah!

My name is Vic Vicious, y'all
peace!
SELECTOR. (*As Battle of the Bands host.*) We have tallied the votes. Ladies
and Gentlemen, your third place winner—Trojan Horse! Give it up for 'em.
In second place, put your hands together for The Mass Debaters! Now,
drumroll please…your first place winner of the Hill Foster High Battle of
the Bands…put your hands together for…Steel and Dan!!!

(The agony of defeat is felt.)

Steel and Dan's version of "Patience" brought the house down.

(SELECTOR *plays an acoustic version of "Patience."*)

HANK. *(Placing a comforting hand on* JULIAN*'s shoulder.)* Everybody takes an "L."

JULIAN. *(Shoving* HANK*'s hand off.)* I don't take L's, I hand 'em out!

HANK. Oh.

JULIAN. I should've won that. Those were some weird rhymes you gave me.

HANK. No they weren't.

JULIAN. What the hell is a "Can-tor." Nobody knows what a "Can-tor" is.

HANK. I do. You don't.

JULIAN. Losing? Hells no. Not to no Steel and Dan.

HANK. It's okay.

JULIAN. It's NOT okay. Losing is not allowed in my house!

HANK. It's just Battle of the Bands.

JULIAN. What's your father do, Hank?

HANK. Well, he's…

JULIAN. My father was like, All-American in football, basketball, track. He was the number one sales rep for the whole Midwest for like 5 years in a row. All my half-brothers are top-ranked in whatever they do. Nobody loses in my family, Hank! You might be satisfied to just be okay. But not me—not me!

HANK. Yeah.

JULIAN. Steel and Dan? Hells no. That rock stuff is wack. A lot of that stuff—that heavy metal, you can't even understand what they say. Not like you're missing anything. *(Imitating a metal lead singer.)* "Bat heads, swords, the end of the world!" And they say rap is bad. Least it ain't a horror movie.

HANK. They got instruments. People in The Hill. They go crazy for that.

JULIAN. Well I'm gonna get me an instrument.

You'll write me some fresher rhymes. I'm gonna come back and show The Hill what's up. Show everybody.

(*Shift*—SELECTOR *in studio.*)

SELECTOR. *There is an art to taking an "L"*
Swallowing pride
Struggling to accept defeat
when the memory won't die

(JULIAN *stops.* SELECTOR *lets her last statement sink in.*)

I get deep on you sometimes, huh? But don't worry—we don't stop rockin'!

(SELECTOR *holds up an unlabeled record.*)

Luann Finnis. Like Hank, she was part of that first wave.

> (SELECTOR *plays the record.*)

VOICE OF LUANN. How come you didn't have any beats?

SELECTOR. *To Hank and Julian*
she is one of the stuck-up
black kids that thinks rap is ghetto.

> (*Shift*—LUANN *and* JULIAN *in scene.*)

JULIAN. Pete don't let us play rap in here.

> (LUANN *fades in/appears onstage.*)

LUANN. At the Battle of the Bands. You could've won if you had beats.

> (JULIAN *doesn't respond. He turns his head around.*)

JULIAN. Pizza for Finnis!

LUANN. Sore loser, huh?

> (*Silence.*)

You can flow alright, but you need more to make it unique.

JULIAN. Finnis!

> (SELECTOR *puts an image of a pizza on the easel.*)

SELECTOR. (*As offstage Pizza Pete's employee.*) Pizza for Finnis!

JULIAN. That'll be twelve fifty-eight.

LUANN. My dad has a tab.

JULIAN. (*Snarkiest tone imaginable.*) Yeah, yeah, I know who your dad is.

SELECTOR. *You probably heard of her dad too. Nat Finnis. NBA. Center.*
Lot of pro athletes play for The City, but live in The Hill. Football. Hockey. Baseball.

Luann is one of five, all girls. Nat is determined to father a boy. People like to joke and say that he's already got a starting lineup.

Luann don't like sports. But she can be competitive.

> (*Shift*—Dads: the remix.)

JULIAN. Dad, I want to learn an instrument.

SELECTOR. (*As* JULIAN'S DAD.) Saxophone.

JULIAN. No.

SELECTOR. (JULIAN'S DAD.) That's where it's at. I played in the school band. We were state champs.
Did you know that?

JULIAN. I know that, Dad, yeah, but I was thinking the drums.

SELECTOR. (JULIAN'S DAD.) Drums, huh?

JULIAN. Now *that's* where it's at. If I woulda been rappin' and drummin' at the same time, I woulda won that Battle of the Bands for sure.

SELECTOR. (JULIAN'S DAD.) Rappin' and drummin' simultaneous? Don't nobody wanna hear that. Get you a saxophone. Smooth, play some of that Jazz, get you all the ladies. You got a girl yet?

JULIAN. Not yet.

SELECTOR. (JULIAN'S DAD.) What's wrong with you? You are *my* son, right? Huh? Huh?

HANK. Yeah, Dad?

SELECTOR. (HANK'S DAD.) Are there any extracurricular activities at the school that you're interested in?

HANK. Not at school.

SELECTOR. (HANK'S DAD.) None? My school had all sorts of interesting pursuits for us to challenge ourselves.

HANK. I'm not interested in what they offer at school.

SELECTOR. (HANK'S DAD.) You seem to be an expert on what you DON'T want to do.

JULIAN. I don't understand.

SELECTOR. (JULIAN'S DAD.) Pick something you have to *stand up* to play. Where people can see you. That's key.

HANK. I *know* what I'm interested in. It's just not offered at my school.

SELECTOR. (HANK'S DAD.) Poetry?

HANK. Rap, Dad.

JULIAN. Drums, Dad. I will. Be seen.

SELECTOR. (JULIAN'S DAD.) I'm going out. Somebody around here has to get laid, right?! Huh? Right!?

JULIAN. Gross.

SELECTOR. (HANK'S DAD.) Will rap help you get into a top-ranked institution?

HANK. I don't know.

SELECTOR. (HANK'S DAD.) My query was rhetorical, son.

HANK. I got to study, Dad.

JULIAN. I will. Be seen.

> (JULIAN *emulates the sound of a kick drum—then a hi hat—a snare—a cymbal. Can I beatbox?*)

SELECTOR. (*Interwoven with* JULIAN'*s discovery.*)
That moment of spark.
Recognition that music lives in the body.
Knows no zip code
is not beholden to any brass, woodwind, strings

reeds

Recognition that the funk—It lives in the DNA.

>(JULIAN *finally brings it all together.*

>*We see* LUANN, *presumably in her room, it's late.*)

LUANN. (*Over* JULIAN's *beatbox, rapping as if these are brand new.*)
pardon me/scuse me/ let me introduce me/ L to the U to the A
double N/ known all around town/ but my mic my best friend
paper and pen/ let me begin/ I'm the freshest girl out there/ no need to pretend

>(*She stops, checks to see if she heard something.*)

highly academic/ creative/ stylish/
wild with the words I compile/ not childish/
mature for my

>(*Stops again. Yeah, definitely heard something. Lights out abrupt.*

>*Shift*—JULIAN *and* HANK *in scene.*)

JULIAN. You see *YO! MTV Raps* last night?

HANK. Yep.

JULIAN. You ever think "That should be me on there"?!

HANK. All the time!

JULIAN. Have some truck jewels, track suit, fresh kicks, four-finger ring, three cuts in the eyebrow, "Fades fresh cut every day!"

HANK. What kinda song?

JULIAN. Be some girls too, big earrings.

HANK. A battle song or like a dance song?

JULIAN. Nah, wouldn't do none of that. No dance-type R&B.

HANK. No, that's wack.

JULIAN. Just chillin'. Leaning against the car like, "I'm just here." You know?

HANK. Yeah. "I'm just here." It'd be amazing.

JULIAN. Just chilled, man, nobody stressing. Just…living like, "fuck it."

HANK. Yeah.

JULIAN. Be all like "fuck it." Like, "I got this car, I got these girls, these jewels, these skills, but you know…ain't no thing."

HANK. Yeah. "Fuck it. Ain't no thing."

JULIAN. We gotta get on, man. I got talent. You write the rhymes, let me say 'em. Boom!
Let's do this, man. We gotta get on. LL Cool J was only 15 when he got on. I'm 15.

HANK. Get on? Man, you're not LL Cool J from Queens.

JULIAN. Yeah, well, I am who I am, from right here, so…

HANK. Yeah. Okay.

JULIAN. How do we do it?

HANK. We'd need a demo.

JULIAN. Word.

HANK. Well, the only recording studio in The Hill makes advertising jingles. Kyle Jorgen's dad owns it. But Kyle's dad is a racist so that's out. I'm not just saying that either.

JULIAN. I know. I heard that.

SELECTOR. *It's true.*

HANK. Man, if we had us an AKAI MPC, we'd make a dope demo.

JULIAN. What's an AKAI MPC?

>   (SELECTOR *places a diagram of the AKAI MPC on an easel and uses a pointer.*)

SELECTOR. *1988 the AKAI electronic company*
unleashed the MPC.
This was not the first drum machine
There was the Roland TR-808. The SP-1200
But MPC can sample longer

those sampled sounds end up on these pads

they get played by tapping

At your command, quite possibly, the entire history of sound.

HANK. It's real expensive though.

JULIAN. How much?

HANK. Like, a thousand dollars or something.

>   (*Oh…well I guess…*)

JULIAN. Well, yo! Look what I can do.

>   (JULIAN *kicks a little beatbox routine he's been working on.*)

HANK. (*Jokingly.*) This is because of Battle of the Bands?

JULIAN. Man, shut up.

HANK. Come on, I was just…because the whole thing about playin' an instrument and…

JULIAN. Shut up!

>   (*Pause.*
>
>   JULIAN *punches* HANK *in the shoulder.*)

HANK. Ow.

>   (JULIAN *hits him again.*)

Stop!

> (JULIAN *bounces on his toes like a boxer.*)

JULIAN. Come on!

HANK. Stop, man. Quit.

JULIAN. You gonna cry. Come on!

> (JULIAN *slaps* HANK, *and chuckles.*)

HANK. Julian! Stop!

> (JULIAN *stops, and forces a laugh.*)

JULIAN. You got any brothers?

HANK. No.

JULIAN. Yeah. I could tell.

> (*Beat.*)

Yeah. We're gonna do it. Even from out here in the middle of this nothing.

> (*Beat.*)

You'll figure it out.

SELECTOR. *You see cardboard box, I see dance floor.*
You see train, I see canvas.
You see record player, I see instrument.
Hip Hoppers have always figured it out.

> (SELECTOR *puts on "The Grunt" by The JB's.*)
>
> (*Over "The Grunt," which fades out slowly.*)

The breakdown.
only about 7 seconds
When you get that rhythm section

Rolling around in dirt and toe jam.

Funk! You feel unbeatable!

Your neck snaps harder
Hips pop sharper

But it's so short
How can you make it last
longer?

> (SELECTOR *places an image of two turntables and a crossfader on the easel.*)

If you're Grandmaster Flash, you invent The Quick Mix Theory
two of the same record, played at the same time

7 seconds ends on turntable right, you crossfade to 7 seconds on turntable left

7 seconds left, 7 seconds right, 7 seconds left, 7 seconds right in a circle—extended until you got tired

so for example let's say

JULIAN. Have some truck jewels, track suit, fresh kicks, four-finger ring, three cuts in the eyebrow, "Fades fresh cut every day!"

SELECTOR. *is an entire song. But I just want:*

JULIAN. track suit, fresh kicks, four-finger ring

SELECTOR. *(Pointing on the diagram.) On turntable right I have Julian's song*

JULIAN. Have some truck jewels, track suit, fresh kicks, four-finger ring, three cuts in the eyebrow, "Fades fresh cut every day!"

SELECTOR. *(Pointing on the diagram.) On turntable left I have Julian's song, but I start it right at*

JULIAN. Track suit, fresh kicks, four-finger ring

SELECTOR. *(Pointing on the diagram.) Then I crossfade to the other Julian break, which I've cued up at*

JULIAN. Track suit, fresh kicks, four-finger ring

SELECTOR. *I repeat it.*

JULIAN. track suit, fresh kicks, four-finger ring
track suit, fresh kicks, four-finger ring
track suit, fresh kicks, four-finger ring
track suit, fresh kicks, four-finger ring

SELECTOR. *(Over JULIAN repeating his phrase.) It's crude, but you get the idea*

But Hank. Henry Charles. John Henry
didn't have turntables or a crossfader.

What he did have was his boombox
and a record button.

(SELECTOR *replaces the diagram of the turntables and crossfader with the diagram of the boombox.)*

Shift—HANK and JULIAN with the boombox.

JULIAN *takes the mic.*

The SELECTOR puts the needle on a record. We hear the crackle, then the drums of "Impeach the President" by The Honey Drippers.)

HANK. Can you do something like that?

(*The SELECTOR starts the record over. JULIAN beatboxes along with the record until the singing begins.)*

Okay. Let's play it back.

(SELECTOR *plays the beatbox loop JULIAN created.)*

Alright, now we lay your rhymes over that. I was thinking we come up with some kind of chorus, you know? A hook.

JULIAN. Why?

HANK. Because it's a song.

JULIAN. All the MCs I listen to—they just rhyme for a while, then they have scratching like "Aw yeah!" and some other voices in there. You scratch?

HANK. No.

JULIAN. You just get the record and…scratch it, right…like …*wicka, wicka, wicka.*

HANK. I don't think so.

JULIAN. Yeah, that's how.

HANK. Maybe we can just take one of the lines from the verse I wrote.

JULIAN. Co-wrote.

HANK. Um, how bout, *"I'm fly like Mighty Mouse"?*

JULIAN. How 'bout just, *"I'm Mighty Mouse"?*

HANK. No way. Simile over metaphor every time. If you say, *"I'm Mighty Mouse,"* then I'm saying—

JULIAN. I'm saying.

HANK. You're saying you're a mouse, which is dumb, but *"fly like Mighty Mouse"* is—

JULIAN. Just cuz you write rhymes doesn't make you the boss.

HANK. And the beats.

JULIAN. Like hell. That's my beatbox there, buddy.

HANK. But I record it—on *my…*

JULIAN. Why you being such a…

HANK. You'll say the rhymes. I'll do the chorus, okay?

JULIAN. What do you mean, you'll do it? I'm the rapper.

HANK. I know. You rap and I'll do the hook, like TJ Swan.

JULIAN. Ugggghhh, like singing?

HANK. Like when he's on Biz Markie's songs. He only does the hooks and Biz does the rhymes.

JULIAN. I don't like Biz Markie.

>   (HANK *takes an exasperated breath.*)

HANK. Let's just record the verses, okay?

JULIAN. Whatever you want.

>   (HANK *hands him the rhymes and puts on their homemade beatbox beat.*
>   JULIAN *picks up the cheap mic.*)

I'm tryin' to have a hottie
hot wheels and a tidy house

I got from raps that're fly
like Mighty Mouse

HANK. Why'd you stop?

JULIAN. I think I need to say it:

Tryin' to have a hottie
hot wheels and a tidy house
I'm fly/ my raps is Mighty Mouse

HANK. That makes no sense.

JULIAN. Makes sense to me. Oh, even better… *"my raps is Mighty Mouse/ they'll knock you out!"*

HANK. Hmmm…I don't—

JULIAN. We're doing this together, right?

HANK. Um.

JULIAN. Let me have the pen so I can change it.

(HANK *doesn't budge.*)

You gotta learn how to make rhymes for me like how I would say 'em. Not you.

(HANK *tries to take the rhymes back.* JULIAN *won't let him.*)

Matter of fact, I want to change all these, too. I wouldn't say stuff like this.

(HANK *tries again—no luck.*)

JULIAN. And this right here—sounds kinda—I don't know—soft.

HANK. Stop!

(HANK *tries again, more aggressive.*)

JULIAN. Chill out.

(HANK *won't let up.* JULIAN *keeps him away with forearms and elbows, laughing the whole time.* HANK's *frustration escalates until he finally punches* JULIAN *somewhere on his back, harder than he's hit anyone in his entire life.*

JULIAN *lets out a painful wince and falls to one knee.* HANK *picks up the rhymes, crumples and tears them up.*

After a few moments of breath-catching, JULIAN *looks up at* HANK.

HANK *starts to exit.*)

Aye! Hank. See you later, man. Come back with something better next time.

(*Shift*—SELECTOR *in studio, puts on "Funky Drummer Reprise."*)

SELECTOR. *Violence in the rap game (game game game game—)*

but not just rap
musicians abuse each other
even when what they make
is so damn beautiful

like this right here—that's Brother Clyde Stubblefield on the skins

Most sampled drummer in history—y'all know that?
Y'all ain't know that!

James Brown just told him (Imitates James Brown.) "Let's lay out and let this funky drummer take it out."

Clyde hasn't been paid nearly what he's owed
not from James Brown or the laundry list of rappers
who toast over his magic

Hell I ain't no better—I'm toasting on it too!
        ("Funky Drummer" continues to underscore.)

HANK. Tonight, I waited until the house was sleeping. I tiptoed down the steps. Got my bike. Needed a little fresh air. Some inspiration.

SELECTOR. (JULIAN'S DAD. *A little tipsy.*) Julian.

HANK. See, there is this water tower—probably the highest point really in The Hill. I remember when we moved out here from The City—I could see it from the freeway. I'd never seen anything like it.

SELECTOR. (JULIAN'S DAD.) You got anything to drink?

JULIAN. I got school tomorrow, Dad.

        (LUANN *appears, in her room again.*)

LUANN. (*With a greater confidence and intention.*)
pardon me/scuse me/ let me introduce me/ L to the U to the A
double N/ known all around town/ but my mic my best friend
paper and pen/ let me begin/ I'm the freshest girl out there/ no need to pretend

HANK. I always imagined that on the top you could probably see the whole town, that you could get in touch, channel all the creativity flowing. But every time I go there, I look at how high to the top and realize—I'm not as brave as I think.
And then it started to rain, but I stayed. I sat underneath the water tower. Listened to the rain.

SELECTOR. (JULIAN'S DAD.) You don't got anything stashed? Little girly-man Schnapps?

JULIAN. No.

LUANN. (*With growing fierceness and attitude.*)
highly academic/ creative/ stylish/
wild with the words I compile/ not childish/
mature for my age/ get up on the stage/
beat come on/ I go off on a rampage

HANK. I knew there was something better. I just had to wait for it.

SELECTOR. (JULIAN'S DAD.) So serious. Not serious about your basketball anymore. But when it comes to me—

HANK. Shut my eyes tight, waited.

JULIAN. Did you lose a client today?

LUANN. *MCs try and dis/ talking trash to this Miss*
get dis-missed/ can I get a witness?
No prin-cess—but I'm royal
shine like a diamond—smooth like oil

SELECTOR. (JULIAN'S DAD.) Go to bed. You got school tomorrow.

LUANN. (*At an apex of lady dopeness.*)
not trying to kiss you on the cheek/
hangin' all on your shoulder

the era of the brain-dead rap girl is over!

> (*"Funky Drummer" out.*)

SELECTOR. (LUANN'S DAD.) Luann!! Go to bed.

HANK. And then something better came.

> (*Shift*—SELECTOR *in studio.*
> SELECTOR *puts on the beatbox loop* JULIAN *and* HANK *made earlier.*
> *Transition to* JULIAN *and* HANK *in concert.*)

JULIAN. *Straight off the interstate/ no skyscrapers*
Far from the street talk and sky pagers

SELECTOR. Winter break.

JULIAN. *Far from the corners/ graffiti/ street lights*
car speakers bumpin' jams that we like

SELECTOR. Hank came back with something.

JULIAN. *Straight off the interstate/ no skyscrapers*
Far from the street talk and sky pagers

SELECTOR. "Riot in The Hill."

> (JULIAN *and* HANK *in concert.*)

JULIAN. *Straight off the interstate/ no skyscrapers*
Far from the street talk and sky pagers
Far from the corners/ graffiti/ street lights
car speakers bumpin' jams that we like

HANK. *The Hill/ we straight from The Hill*
But this is where we chill/ yeah right here
Green in The Hill
quiet in The Hill
But listen right here
There's a riot in The Hill

JULIAN. *Malls and Maître D's*
May I take your order please
No forget that
We get disorderly
parents supporting me
But think I'm crazy
I'd rather kick a rhyme
Then act how they raised me
Drama don't phase me

I ain't an actor
My motivation
Motivating crowds
To answer

We in The Hill
No crowds to move
We got a lot to show
Even more to prove

HANK. *Green in The Hill*
quiet in The Hill
But listen right here
There's a riot in The Hill

The Hill/ we straight from The Hill/
this is where we chill/ yeah right here

JULIAN. *We young we restless*
Cereal breakfast
No gold rings
No gold necklace
Five-day school week
work on my technique
breakin' up English
you can't extinguish

my fire/
find me on the
basketball court/
lyrical snowballs
smash your whole fort

no violent tendencies
lyrical symphonies
drop gems that shine
give people epiphanies

I am a simile
Just like metaphor
Me to this rap/ Ric Flair to figure four

HANK. *Green in The Hill*
quiet in The Hill
But listen right here
There's a riot in The Hill

JULIAN. *Tree-lined*
Streets wide and empty
Reindeer sweaters
And lawns don't tempt me

HANK. *The Hill/ we straight from The Hill*
this is where we chill/ yeah right here

Green in The Hill
quiet in The Hill
But listen right here
There's a riot in The Hill

The Hill/ we straight from The Hill
this is where we chill/ yeah right here

HANK AND JULIAN. *Green in The Hill*
quiet in The Hill
But listen right here
There's a riot in The Hill

> (*The beat fades out.* HANK *and* JULIAN *slowly back away from the mics.*
> *Shift*—JULIAN *and* HANK *in scene. They look at one another.*)

JULIAN. I'm not sure what it means.

> ("*Really?*")

BUT…I like how I feel when I'm saying it.

HANK. So?

JULIAN. Let's do another one.

> (*Shift*—HANK *into the boombox,*
> JULIAN *speaks to someone unseen.*)

HANK. We had "Riot in The Hill."

JULIAN. We had "Class Clown," "Breakin' Beats and Curfews."

HANK. We had "Shut Up! (Yeah, I'm talking to you)."

> (*Shift*—HANK *and* JULIAN *in concert.*)

JULIAN. *Shut up! Yeah, I'm talking to you*

HANK. *Cuz you keep running ya lip*
running ya lip

runnin'/runnin'/ runnin'/runnin'
runnin' ya lip

JULIAN. *I see you in the halls flappin' ya jaws*
rich kid, think you fresh, but you got flaws
but me I'm dope/ even though I'm broke
I'ma get paid from makin' words that smoke
so shut up!
Yeah, I'm talking to you.

HANK. *Cuz you keep runnin' ya lip*
runnin' ya lip
runnin'/runnin'/ runnin'/runnin'
runnin' ya lip

So shut up!

JULIAN. *Yeah, I'm talking to you.*

> (*Shift*—HANK *at the boombox,*
> JULIAN *speaks to someone unseen.*)

HANK. I dub at least 10 before bed every night, give 'em out the next day. Bus Driver. Lunch Lady. Coach. I swear to God. Mrs. Lynum let me hand in my demo instead of a paper.

SELECTOR. (*As* MRS. LYNUM, *condescending.*) I feel the spirit of Gospel. The deep howl. It's reminiscent of LeRoi Jones. Such soulful texture. Negro Spirituals. James Baldwin. *Invisible Man.* February. "We shall overcome." A-minus.

HANK. At my job, bagging groceries. If I see somebody that looks like a rap fan—

SELECTOR. *any and all black people*

HANK. —if I see somebody that looks like a rap fan, I slip the demo in the bag.

JULIAN.	HANK.
Hank is more in charge of the distribution and marketing. Yeah, you know, *he* writes the rhymes and makes the beats. I mean, I lay the box down and, you know, say *his rhymes,* but yeah, it's pretty much his baby.	Basketball team
	Football team
	Baseball team
	Track
	Chess team
	A/V club
Yeah, it's—You know, Hank has a lot of energy. He gets real excited.	D&D Society
	Tennis club
	Varsity cheer
	Field
	Janitorial staff

Track Team
Debate team
Student Council

HANK. Rich people. Poor. Handsome people. Ugly. Everybody is playin' our tape. Everybody.

(*Shift—Dads: the remix.*)

SELECTOR. (JULIAN'S DAD.) I'm watchin' my program.

JULIAN. It's a commercial.

SELECTOR. (JULIAN'S DAD.) I like this commercial.

JULIAN. Come on, Dad.

SELECTOR. (JULIAN'S DAD.) So sensitive. What's up?

JULIAN. Did you get a chance to, um—

SELECTOR. (JULIAN'S DAD.) What?

JULIAN. Did you um—

SELECTOR. (JULIAN'S DAD.) You get somebody pregnant?

JULIAN. No.

SELECTOR. (JULIAN'S DAD.) Huh?

JULIAN. Listen—to—my tape?

(*A long moment.*)

SELECTOR. (JULIAN'S DAD.) Oop. My show is back on. Grab me whatever's cold in the fridge, huh?

(SELECTOR *places an image of* HANK *and* JULIAN*'s demo on the easel. Shift—*HANK *and* LUANN *in scene.*)

LUANN. You drop this in our grocery bag? My dad is famous, but he's not Jimmy Jam or Terry Lewis.

HANK. I'm just trying to get our name out there.

LUANN. John Henry? That's your—*nom de plume?*

HANK. Yeah.

LUANN. That's a weird rap name.

HANK. Don't you know the story of John Henry?

LUANN. My father doesn't like rap. He was gonna throw it out.

HANK. No rap?

LUANN. I listened to it.

HANK. Oh really, thank you, wow, thank you.

LUANN. Not too…professional.

HANK. You should see the equipment we have.

LUANN. Is that why it sounds like this?

HANK. Oh yeah. We're using pretty simple equipment. My boombox, a cheap mic.

The guys on, do you watch *YO! MTV Raps*?

LUANN. Yeah.

HANK. Well, those guys go to…

LUANN. Guys? S'not just "guys," you know.

HANK. No, I mean "guys" like when you say "hey you guys," like when you just mean "y'all."

LUANN. "Y'all" could mean "All y'all boys *and* girls."

HANK. Oh. Sorry.

    (*Pause.*)

LUANN. I rap too.

HANK. Yeah?

    (*She nods. A quiet moment.*)

Could I hear something?

    (*Quick shift*—HANK *and* JULIAN *in scene.*)

Then she rapped and she was dope! Then she asked if she could be in our crew.

JULIAN. Man, hells no! She said it didn't sound professional.

HANK. That's what *you* said.

JULIAN. Hank. You're like…my DJ…it's okay for *me* to say that.

HANK. Listen, she could flow—I mean, why not?

JULIAN. Just stop talking!

    (*Awkward silence.*)

You just take all this stuff so serious.

HANK. Everybody is playin' our tape right now! We got on!

JULIAN. Did we?

HANK. If you wanna be all negative, you be negative, but don't go bringing me down with your negativity.

JULIAN. I'm just hearing what everybody else is saying.

HANK. Who's sayin'? Everybody thinks it's fresh. Rich people, poor, han—

JULIAN. Not in The City. When I went to visit my mom, I played it for some of the guys in my old neighborhood.

HANK. Oh yeah? In The City? What'd they say?

SELECTOR. (*As guys from* JULIAN*'s old neighborhood.*) "S'aight." "S'okay."

"Yeah, you know, you're doing your thing."

"Oh, they got rap out in The Hill now?"

HANK. Well, they're just jealous. Dissin', because we rep for the suburbs.

    (JULIAN *is unconvinced.*)

You're just dissin' it cuz they were dissin' it.

JULIAN. Gotta go to work.

HANK. We're dope, Julian! I know we're dope! We just need better equipment.

    (JULIAN *is mildly curious—mildly.*)

LL Cool J has Rick Rubin making his beats. Those are dope, right? Well, he has great equipment. If we had great equipment, I could make you sound like LL Cool J. Doper! Because I am just as dope—doper—than Rick Rubin.

JULIAN. (*Like, "Negro please."*) Oh yeah? Doper than Rick Rubin? Right.

HANK. Yeah, all I need is better equipment.

SELECTOR. (*As the* CONTEST SPOKESPERSON.) Are you fresh! Do you keep it funky! Send us your illest, dopest beats and rhymes to the Rapper's Delight Contest! Grand Prize…the AKAI MPC.

HANK. If I had an AKAI MPC, I could make a beat out of anything.

JULIAN. A what?

    (SELECTOR *places a diagram of the AKAI MPC on an easel and uses a pointer.*)

SELECTOR. *Okay, I know this the second time it's come up. But it's pretty dope. For those who don't know—Let me demonstrate.*

    (*Pointing to a pad.*)

I sampled Hank.

    (*Taps the pad.*)

HANK. Out of anything.

    (*Taps it again.*)

Out of anything.

    (*Taps it quicker, repeatedly.*)

Out of. Out of.

    (*Again.*)

Out.

    (*Rapid succession.*)

Out. Out. Out. Out. Out. Out.

SELECTOR. *Now.*

    (*Lights up on* JULIAN.)

I'll put a different sound on this one.

    (SELECTOR *points to a different pad, then presses it.*)

JULIAN. Right.

(SELECTOR *taps back and forth between* HANK'*s pad and* JULIAN'*s pad.*)

HANK. Out.

JULIAN. Right.

HANK. Out.

JULIAN. Right.

HANK. Out. Out.

JULIAN. Right. Right.

SELECTOR. *Now, you loop it.*

(SELECTOR *taps a syncopated pattern of "Out" and "Right" for a few loops.*

HANK *and* JULIAN *demonstrate.*)

That's your drum loop. Now, on top of our drum loop I can blend another element. So let's say…

(*Lights up on* LUANN.)

LUANN. You need more to make it

SELECTOR. is our bassline.

(SELECTOR *taps a different pad.*)

LUANN. You need more to make it

SELECTOR. Bring it all together.

(JULIAN *and* HANK *create a percussive loop using the words "Out" and "Right," with* LUANN *saying the entire phrase "You need more to make it" over it, in sync… This should loop a few times.*

HANK, JULIAN, *and* LUANN *demonstrate—their beat should fade into* JULIAN *repeating his next line, "It's a lottery, man."*)

JULIAN. It's a lottery, man. I bet there's an entry fee.

SELECTOR. (*As* CONTEST SPOKESPERSON.) Fifteen dollars. Make checks payable to…

HANK. I'll make the greatest suburban rap song ever made and we will win and get the MPC. We'd have an edge if we put Luann on a song. I'm telling you. Guy and Girl. Back and forth. Be fresh! Can't you just hear it already? It's like:

(HANK *does a loose, improvised version of what a* VIC VICIOUS *and* LUANN *collaboration might sound like.*

He slows to a quiet when he realizes that JULIAN *is just not buying it.*)

You afraid she might be better than you?

(*Ouch.*)

JULIAN. I gotta go.

(*Shift*—LUANN *and* HANK *in scene.*)

LUANN. Sometimes when I'm bored at church I try to rhyme things in my head. Whatever is in the room. *Chair, people, hair, steeple, light, bench, white, inch.* Then challenge myself. Two-word rhymes. *Hymn-maker, thin wafer.* I always loved rhymes. You know. Ever since I heard Melle Mel's "The Message."

(LUANN *starts to rhyme a bit of "The Message." HANK joins in.*)

My sisters used to love it. Have me do it when their friends were around. But they'd shush me whenever my mom or dad would come in. Especially my dad. He'd say,

SELECTOR. (*As* LUANN'S DAD.) I'm not trying to hear that. That's excuse music.

LUANN. But I couldn't stop. Rhymes are made to stick in your mind. He'd say,

SELECTOR. (LUANN'S DAD.) There is no training. I couldn't get in the NBA without training.

LUANN. But I couldn't stop. Rhymes are made to stick in your mind. Rhymes have so much power, right? You can come up with something that takes over somebody's…brain! One time he heard me singing "The Message" and man, *woooo,* he just went upside my head. I stopped singing that song. But I couldn't stop rhyming. I came up with my own rhymes instead.

SELECTOR. (LUANN'S DAD.) I don't want to see this or hear this in my house.

LUANN. He'd find 'em and rip 'em up! So I just stopped writing. On paper. But now, I want them recorded. I want everybody to hear 'em—to get *my* rhymes stuck. You know?

So what's up, Hank? When you gonna let me rip the mic?

HANK. Soon. I gotta finish this. Other thing.

LUANN. What kinda thing?

HANK. Project.

LUANN. What, for you and Julian?

HANK. Yeah.

LUANN. What's the project?

HANK. I don't like to talk about my projects before they're done.

LUANN. Well, whatever it is—*I'll* make it fresh.

(HANK *is unsure.*)

You know, groups break up. New Edition broke up.

HANK. Didn't they just put out a new album?

LUANN. But *eventually* they're gonna break up.

(*Beat.*)

You know, I was at that battle. Parking lot. The mall on Fischer Road.
I mean, okay, he beat you, but with Kane's rhymes. That's wack.

HANK. He's a good rapper.

LUANN. We'll see.

HANK. What's that mean?

LUANN. He can't even write his own rhymes.

HANK. Well, I heard that Kane writes for everybody. Biz Markie, MC Lyte.

LUANN. No way!

HANK. Yeah. Ice Cube writes for Eazy-E.

LUANN. Everybody knows that.

HANK. Just...never mind, okay?

   (*Silence.*)

LUANN. Look, Julian just needs to really get to know me. I'll talk to him.

HANK. Yeah?

LUANN. It's pizza night anyway.

SELECTOR. *Pizza for Finnis!*

JULIAN. That'll be twelve fifty-eight.

SELECTOR. *Pizza for Finnis!*

LUANN. My dad has a tab.

SELECTOR. *Pizza for Finnis!*

JULIAN. That'll be twelve fifty-eight.

SELECTOR. *Pizza for Finnis!*

JULIAN. That'll be twelve fifty-eight.

SELECTOR. *Pizza for Finnis!*

LUANN. My dad has a tab.

SELECTOR. *Pizza for Finnis!*

   (*Shift*—LUANN *and* JULIAN *in scene.*
   Long, awkward silence.)

LUANN. You're not as dope as people say you are.

JULIAN. Huh?

LUANN. You ever had a real challenge?

   (JULIAN *smirks the comment off.*)

LUANN. I'm gon' count to three

JULIAN. And then what?

LUANN. We're gonna see who's dope.

JULIAN. This is my job. Don't come in my job.

LUANN. 1

JULIAN. I'm serious.

LUANN. 2

> (*Pause.*)

JULIAN. 3

LUANN. *4 to the 5/*
6, 7 beyond/
the queen has arrived
to school you—peon
eons/centuries
from now they'll mention me
my feminine energy
my rappin' ability

JULIAN. S'okay.

LUANN. That was fly.

JULIAN. Wasn't awful.

LUANN. Just jealous.

JULIAN. HA!

LUANN. Cuz I can rhyme better than you.

JULIAN. HA!

LUANN. What you got?

JULIAN. *Dynamite/ excite/ explode/ expose*
Fake MCs/ crack they code
Hold mic/ pose/
Foes get flatten
toss like a salad/
Crush with a mallet/
Crack they whole cabbage
Do 'nuff damage
You ain't a challenge
You bologna I'm Manwich

LUANN. *Please, you bout as hard as water*
fragile like ya mama's china saucers
this super dope daughter
Super fresh rhymes/ super fresh style
I…

JULIAN. *Fresher better/ hella fresh to the letter*
you wilted, moldy, spinach/ you'll get finished
strong like Popeye…

LUANN. *not fly/ you not/ I transform Megatron/*
you bootleg Gobot

I stop the rhyme

> (LUANN *does a few robot moves.*)

Then, bust out the robot

> (JULIAN *can't help himself, his whole body lights up in delight. He laughs.*)

Even got the devil sayin', that MC is so hot/ blew up yo spot
With the fresh raps I got/ you laughin' / but it ain't funny
how I flow like snot/ don't need a beat/ I rap unique
right here in Pizza Pete's

JULIAN. Wait, wait, wait! Hold up. Were you makin' it up?

LUANN. Yeah.

JULIAN. Like, just on the spot?

LUANN. What? You've never done that?

JULIAN. Huh? Yeah.

> (*Beat.*)

Yeah…I done that before. I done it before.

LUANN. Do it now.

JULIAN. What?

LUANN. Come on.

JULIAN. Nah, nah…

LUANN. Do it.

JULIAN. What?

LUANN. You scared?

> (*Quiet.*)

I don't roll with scared babies. I take back my offer.

> (LUANN *starts to exit.*)

JULIAN. What offer?

LUANN. I thought maybe I could be in your crew. Cuz every crew has a rapper, a DJ, a human beat box, and a girl.

JULIAN. What crew has a girl?

LUANN. They all do.

JULIAN. Who? Girls are just girls. Salt-N-Pepa, MC Lyte, no girl-guy. Just girl acts and guy acts.

LUANN. Doesn't matter. Even if they don't have a girl, they want one. I take back my offer.

> (*Starts to exit again.*)

JULIAN. Hold up.

LUANN. Yes?

(JULIAN *takes a deep breath.*)

(*Surprisingly sincere.*) Want me to show you how?

(*Long moment.*)

You ain't no MC—you're a poser.

(SELECTOR *puts on "Apache" by The Incredible Bongo Band.*)

SELECTOR. *Respect, Luann. Massive.*

Damn! I love that Robot line.

Rap got to have that improvisation.
to let go is to let go. Intellect and naiveté hand in hand.
No parachute. Toasting is intuitive.
comes from the bowels.

Gotta follow the road the break lays out for ya.

You're like Dorothy. Everything just got color. Got funky. You get loose. You get loose.
Invent. You let your whole life twirl you around. Let your whole life and your tomorrow
spin around. Bring it back. One-time toast. Tell 'em how it's done.

(*Shift*—HANK *and* LUANN *in scene.*)

HANK. How do you come up with rhymes with no paper?

LUANN. It's easy.

HANK. For you, maybe.

LUANN. I can show you how to make up rhymes without paper. But only if you record some of my raps.

HANK. Yeah. Show me.

(*Shift*—Dads: *the remix.*)

JULIAN. Dad. You listen to my tape or what?

SELECTOR. (JULIAN'S DAD.) Uh huh.

JULIAN. Well?

SELECTOR. (JULIAN'S DAD.) That you makin' them fartin' noises on there?

JULIAN. What?

SELECTOR. (JULIAN'S DAD.) You know—

(*Sloppy imitation of* JULIAN'*s beatboxing, before chuckling at himself.*)

JULIAN. Come on, really, what'd you think?

(*The laughter fades.*)

SELECTOR. (JULIAN'S DAD.) You need to stick with basketball.

(*Shift*—HANK *talking into his boombox.*)

HANK. I did like before. Waited 'til everybody went to sleep. Hopped on my bike. Rode over there. I look around. Don't see Luann. She told me to meet her at the water tower. I couldn't believe it. She knew about it too. But she's not here. Was this a prank? But then I hear something. Far. I look left, I look right—then I look up. She's at the top.

(SELECTOR *puts on "Holy Thursday" by David Axelrod. Over "Holy Thursday".*)

She motioned for me to come up there. I was scared, I ain't gonna lie—but I wanted to learn. I mean, no paper? Unstoppable—no paper!

High...I climbed...and...I kept climbing...I got to the top.

(LUANN *in scene.*)

LUANN. First thing you gotta do is accept that there will be mistakes.

HANK. There will be mistakes. I repeat it like some kind of religious thing.

LUANN. The surroundings. Everything you can see, smell, hear—whatever you're interacting with.

HANK. I hear the crickets. Every now and then a car goes by. A car door slams. A dog barks. Another dog barks back. A plane soars above. Where is it going? Who's in it? What're they listening to?

LUANN. And don't forget the joy. Cuz that's what it is. You're creating. Even if what you're saying is messed up, wrong, a little ignorant...I mean, just saying stupid stuff. You're dumping everything out. But your tongue, lips, teeth all gotta have joy.

HANK. I breathe in joy, I blow out joy.

LUANN. You breathe in joy, blow out joy. And that's it. Then you just go.

HANK. And it all comes back. Confidence fills your throat. All the words flood my mouth and then...I just go.

(*The music fades.*)

I still need paper. What can I say—perfectionist. But now when I rap I don't hear them boo. I don't hear them booing any more. Not at all. It's just quiet. I don't hear them boo.

(*Shift—HANK and* JULIAN *in scene.*)

JULIAN. That show is stupid. I stopped watching *YO! MTV Raps.* I don't like that everybody is so confident. I mean, yeah, okay, I get it. It's a video. But like, I know it's not like that.

There is a camera. There is a cameraman. There is a director. Probably some white guy from someplace like The Hill. Telling all these guys, acting all badass—telling 'em where to stand and to take it from the top. It's a lie. I know it is. How can anybody be that...sure? Nah. Nobody is. Nobody can be sure of anything.

HANK. Are you serious?

(JULIAN *continues.*)

JULIAN. Let's play.

HANK. I don't have…

JULIAN. Your shoes? We'll just shoot around. Come on. I could use some comp. I'm trying out next year.

HANK. For basketball?

JULIAN. No, for lacrosse.

HANK. Smart ass.

JULIAN. From now on, I'm out here every day.

HANK. Every day?

JULIAN. Yeah. I been wasting all this time. Messing around.

(JULIAN *picks up his pace.*)

What you been doing? Working on the world's greatest suburban rap song?

HANK. Yeah, it's done. I mean, written. I been calling so we can set up a time to…

JULIAN. Well, I'm gonna double up. Practice twice as much. Yeah. Twice as much, so what's up?

(JULIAN *tries to start a slap-boxing match with* HANK, *but it's a no-go.*)

Why do we only do the stuff you want to do?!

HANK. It's not stuff, man!

JULIAN. It's just *stuff,* man. Basketball is way fresher.

HANK. I gotta go.

JULIAN. Good. I'm busy too.

HANK. I got important stuff to do.

JULIAN. Hanging out writin' rhymes with girls. What're you now, Jazzy Joyce and the fresh princess?

HANK. Least I can write my own rhymes.

JULIAN. Nobody wants to listen to us, Hank. We're not the real thing— we're a couple posers.

HANK. Maybe you are, but—

JULIAN. No. You.

HANK. You.

JULIAN. No. You.

HANK. You.

JULIAN. No. You.

SELECTOR. (HANK'S DAD.) Hank!

JULIAN. No. You.

HANK. You.

SELECTOR. (HANK'S DAD.) Hank! Where did you go last night?

JULIAN. No. You.

HANK. You.

JULIAN. No. You.

    (*Shift—Dads: the remix.*)

SELECTOR. (HANK'S DAD.) Hank! Where did you go last night?

HANK. What are you talking about?

SELECTOR. (HANK'S DAD.) Don't lie.

HANK. I'm kinda busy right now, Dad.

SELECTOR. (HANK'S DAD.) Well, you might as well get comfortable in here. You're grounded. I'm taking your stereo.

HANK. But I need it!

SELECTOR. (HANK'S DAD.) What you need is to focus. The things that you need to focus on, Son, have nothing to do with this device.

HANK. No, Dad, you *can't* take it!

SELECTOR. (HANK'S DAD.) Your mother and I walk by your room. We hear these repetitive phrases.

HANK. I'm working.

SELECTOR. (HANK'S DAD.) Not on what you need to be.

HANK. Wait!

SELECTOR. (HANK'S DAD.) Good night, Hank.

HANK. I have an assignment! It's for school and I need it!

SELECTOR. (HANK'S DAD.) What sort of assignment?

HANK. (*Lying his butt off.*) I need to um…create an original…poem for my English class…we're studying

um…the technique of rhyme…

SELECTOR. (HANK'S DAD.) Assonance?

HANK. (*A bit surprised.*) Yeah. Assonance. I'm gonna make a song. One that uses assonance.

SELECTOR. (HANK'S DAD.) You make songs on this?

HANK. Yes. I'm trying to figure out how to make a song that's…um…

SELECTOR. (HANK'S DAD.) Perfect?

HANK. Yes. I been conducting experiments—using words and rhythm.

    (*Beat.*)

SELECTOR. (HANK'S DAD.) Did you know that I studied poetry with Robert Hayden at University of Michigan? Do you even know who that is? There were black poets before Big Daddy Kane, you know.

HANK. Could I hear something?

SELECTOR. (HANK'S DAD.) This is one of my favorite poems by Hayden.

> (SELECTOR, *as* HANK'S DAD, *recites "Those Winter Sundays" by Robert Hayden.*)

HANK. That was fresh!

SELECTOR. (JULIAN'S DAD.) Where you been?

JULIAN. At the court. "Gotta get serious," right?

SELECTOR. (JULIAN'S DAD.) I said that? "Gotta get serious"?

> (JULIAN *nods.*)

Hard work. Always hard work. But...you're not promised anything.

> (*Long pause.*)

JULIAN. Did you get fired again?

SELECTOR. (JULIAN'S DAD.) When the semester ends you'll go be with your mom. I need you to do that.

> (*As* HANK'S DAD.)

Okay, now it's your turn.

HANK. Uhhhhh.

SELECTOR. (HANK'S DAD.) If you want this boombox back, you'd better start rapping.

HANK. Okay. Um. It has two parts, like for a guy and a girl.

SELECTOR. (HANK'S DAD.) A duet?

HANK. No, Dad. In rap we don't call 'em "duets." It's just a guy rapping and a girl rapping. So, just imagine.

> (*Shift*—HANK, *in concert, steps to the mic. He takes a deep breath.*)

We goin' off
Every time we get it on
Turn your speakers up
So you can listen to our song
We goin' off
Every time we get it on
Bout to burn the mic
until the early break of dawn

> (LUANN *appears and joins him on the second mic, slowly a backing track is audible.*)

LUANN. *We goin' off*

HANK. *Every time we get it on*

LUANN. *Turn your speakers up*

So you can listen to our song

HANK. *We goin' off*

LUANN. *Every time we get it on*

HANK. *Bout to burn the mic til the early break of dawn*

John Henry
Never stop/ rock/ till I fall out
If I was a car, I would never stall out

LUANN. *"We tried to find your tape*
but the guy said they were all out"

HANK. *I know this/ we focused/ in The Hill*
Trying to crawl out

LUANN. *The sound is original*
The music is criminal
We should be arrested
For this dope that we're bringin' you
Supplying you/ trying to
Get the name known round
Chi town to Motown
my town to yo' town

HANK. *Only 15 already feel like a vet*
Even though you ain't seen me yet on your TV set

Arrow through an apple I ain't no teacher's pet
I'm here to teach you rappers how to freak the alphabet

LUANN. *futuristic styles*
you can call me Boba Fett

HANK. *Rock the mic in a sec/ it ain't no sweat*
'Cause we be goin' off

LUANN. *Every time we get it on*

HANK. *Turn your speakers up*
So you can listen to our song

LUANN. *We goin' off*

HANK. *Every time we get it on*

LUANN. *Bout to burn the mic until the early break of dawn*

HANK. *And we been on since day one.*
The moment we first wrote
The very first rhymes that escaped from our throats

LUANN. *The very first time we made a person say*

TOGETHER. *"Daaaaaaaaaaamn!! That was so fresh can you do it again!"*

LUANN. *On is not off.*

HANK. *Off is not on*

LUANN. *You're on when you're awake*

HANK. *On is when you're strong*

LUANN. *On is always on.*

HANK. *On is never off.*

LUANN. *On is universal*

HANK. *On is never lost*

LUANN. *And it doesn't cost*

HANK. *Not even one cent*

LUANN. *On is when you're goin' off*
Over drum kicks

HANK. *Cuz we be goin' off*

LUANN. *Every time we get it on*

HANK. *Turn your speakers up*
So you can listen to our song

LUANN. *We goin' off*

HANK. *Every time we get it on*

LUANN. *Bout to burn the mic*
until the early break of dawn

TOGETHER. *Until the break of dawn*
Until the break of dawn
Until the break of dawn
Until the break of dawn

      (LUANN *fades away.*

      HANK *steps away from the mic.*)

HANK. So, what'd you think?

      (*Shift*—HANK *and* JULIAN *in scene.*

      There is silence between them for an uncomfortable amount of time.)

Where you been at, man? I been calling. I know you're doubling up and I know we were—y'know—but you're not gonna believe it. I got it! I got it, man!

JULIAN. What'd you get, Hank?

HANK. The AKAI! I got the MPC!

      (*Nothing.*)

Maybe you didn't hear me?

JULIAN. No. I heard you. You won the contest?

HANK. No. I missed the deadline.

JULIAN. Yeah?

HANK. I rapped for him—and then I saw him scratch his head. When my dad scratches his head, means his brain is itching. When his brain is itching that means he's interested. When he's interested that means the things you want to do, he wants to help you do. I need to keep at least a B average, but he's down for the rap thing.

(*Beat.*)

This is a big deal!

(HANK *punches* JULIAN *in the arm.*)

It's coming in the mail next week. I'll probably need some time to figure out how to work it. But maybe over the summer.

JULIAN. I won't be here.

(*Beat.*)

Gonna stay with my mom.

HANK. You're going back to The City?

JULIAN. Yeah.

HANK. Damn…that's…well, cool, man. The Hill is wack anyway.

JULIAN. Yeah. It is.

HANK. So…hey, maybe we could get together over the summer…we could make some songs?

JULIAN. I'm not really…

HANK. We gotta make dope songs. That is how we get on.

(JULIAN *shrugs.*)

I know you and Luann don't get along. I didn't make the world's greatest suburban rap song, but I can. It'd be great…It'd be dope if you were on it.

JULIAN. Come on, Hank. You can make beats, you can write rhymes, you can say 'em. You *can.* You got stuff to say, you know. Like a rapper. I just… I'm not like that.

HANK. You have *nothing* to say? The rhyme villain, the lyrical criminal, the smooth soul technician?

(JULIAN *shrugs.*)

Nothing?

(*Long moment.*)

Get your bike.

JULIAN. Where we goin'?

HANK. Just come on.

(*Shift*—SELECTOR *in studio.*)

SELECTOR. *Yes yes*
Best believe. The water tower

Of course when they get there
Julian looks at it

Julian says he ain't goin' up there

Hank asks if he is scared
Julian climbs to the top in record speed
They look out

Hank shares the gospel according to Luann

Julian is skeptical
cracking jokes

Hank stays on it
Patient
he keeps on cuz he knows

Julian deeply wants to breathe in joy, but can't until he blows out everything
that's not joy
All that's come before
Push it all away
Julian deeply wants to breathe in joy

       (Shift—HANK and JULIAN in scene.)

HANK. Everything that ain't joy.

       (Beat.)

Go 'head, man. Invent the beat.

       (A few moments, fighting through trepidation.)

JULIAN. *Push out—spit out—chew*
chew up—scream—lean
stand—flex—dream
Extreme—intense—bit—fangs
anger—strange—shuffle—move
Hustle—lose
L—W—draw—nothing
loving—fighting—punching
Crunching—singeing—burning—learning—leaving—breathing—huffing-puffing

choking—drinking—sinking—blinking—lights—blinding—tapes

Rewinding—grinding—pulling—shoving—screaming—hollering—knives—razors
Bullets—pagers—engravers—coffins—graves—dig deep—slaves—
black sheep—whites—browns—grays—haze—mazes—break—stages

Ashes—dirty floors Thirty—more chores
Pour me—another Fuck you—my brother
Fuck you—other

       (Teary-eyed now.)

I can't be bothered

I can't be found
Face in the ground
A face in the crowd
a face for the screen
a line up
a haircut
a line up
a high-top
fade
a fade
a fade
a fade
a fade
a fade
a—a—a—

> (JULIAN *stops—wipes tears.*)

HANK. You okay?

JULIAN. Can we stay? I got more.

> (*Shift*—SELECTOR *in studio.*)

SELECTOR. *And it don't stop.*

He's probably still up there
And Hank is still listening

Hank is loading the pads in his mind
Like a good beat-builder
A walking recorder

A beat-maker ain't no instrument
a builder. Words. Numbers. Loops. Memory.
Change. Daggers. Bend. Memory. Shift. Slice.
A beat-maker treats sound like artifact to take you on a trip back

Let me demonstrate.

> (*The* SELECTOR *places the MPC diagram back on the easel. She turns and surveys the audience. The cast appears.*)

HANK.	JULIAN.	LUANN.	SELECTOR.
Rich People. Poor. Handsome people. Ugly. Citizens. Immigrants. Everybody			
Rich People. Poor. Handsome people. Ugly. Citizens. Immigrants. Everybody	An L An L An L An L An L An L An L	You could've won if you had beats	
Rich People. Poor. Handsome people. Ugly. Citizens. Immigrants. Everybody		You could've won if you had beats	*bring the Beatbox in!*
Rich People. Poor. Handsome people. Ugly. Citizens. Immigrants. Everybody	BEATBOX | | | | |	beats beats beats beats if you had beats you could've won	
Rich People. Poor. Handsome people. Ugly. Citizens. Immigrants. Everybody	| | | |	You could've won if you had beats if you had beats	
Rich People. Poor. Handsome people. Ugly. Citizens. Immigrants. Everybody	| | |	beats beats beats beats	
		beats	*Switch it up one time!*

HANK.	**JULIAN.**	**LUANN.**
7 seconds left,	7 seconds left,	7 seconds left,
7 seconds right,	7 seconds right,	7 seconds right,
7 seconds left,	7 seconds left,	7 seconds left,
7 seconds right	7 seconds right	7 seconds right
		pardon me
7 seconds left,	Those rhymes you said	scuse me
7 seconds right,		pardon me
7 seconds left,	those rhymes you said	scuse me
7 seconds right		pardon me scuse me
	those rhymes you said	let me introduce
7 seconds left,	were yours?	7 seconds left,
7 seconds right,		7 seconds right,
7 seconds left,	7 seconds left	7 seconds left,
7 seconds right	7 seconds right	7 seconds right
	7	pardon me
7 seconds left,	7	scuse me
7 seconds right,	7	pardon me
7 seconds left,	7	scuse me
7 seconds right		pardon me scuse me
	(Beatbox.)	let me introduce me
7 seconds left,		L to the U to the A
7 seconds right,		double N
7 seconds left,		known around the
7 seconds right		world but my mic my
		best friend
7 seconds left,		paper and pen
7 seconds right,		let me begin
7 seconds left,		freshest girl out
7 seconds right		

HANK.	JULIAN.	LUANN.	SELECTOR.
			Now speed it up one time!
amazing	BEATBOX (*Quicker tempo.*)	paper and pen let me begin	
it'd be amazing		paper	
it'd be amazing		paper and pen let me begin	
it'd be amazing It'd be amazing it'd be amazing		paper paper and pen let me begin	
it'd be amazing			
it'd be amazing living like it'd be amazing	(*Should reach the apex here.*)	I'm fly you not bust out robot	*Come on Luann!*
living like it'd be amazing		let me begin let me begin	
That Was Fresh Fresh Dope		I'm fly you not bust out robot let me begin	*Whooo!!*
		let me begin paper paper	
That Was Fresh Fresh Dope		let me begin begin begin	
Show me			

HANK.	JULIAN.	LUANN.	SELECTOR.
	(Beatbox slows down gradually.)		
I repeat		first thing	*Let's cool it out y'all.*
	|	you gotta accept	
I repeat	|	is that there	
	|	will be mistakes	
I repeat	|		
	|	mistakes	
Yeah, show me	|	first thing	
	|	you gotta accept	
I repeat	|	is that there	
	|	will be mistakes	
I repeat	|		
	|	mistakes	
I repeat	|	first thing	
	|	you gotta accept	
Yeah, show me		is that there	
	(Continue to slow and	will be mistakes	
(Repeat repeat	*fade beatbox out.)*		
fading out slowly.)		*(Repeat* mistakes	
		fading out slowly.)	*Remember whens newcomers*

these be the multiple sounds, crossfaded to one—brought back one time woven to one sound

toast, Hip Hop and rap spirit, body and voice

alive and spitting in The Hill

The flip side to the A story just one rap… out …of many

*(Everything visible begins to fade away very slowly.
Last thing we see onstage is the red light on* SELECTOR*'s record player,
which, after a few moments of dark, vanishes.)*

End of Play

DEATH TAX
by Lucas Hnath

Copyright © 2012 by Lucas Hnath. All rights reserved. CAUTION: Professionals and amateurs are hereby warned that *Death Tax* is subject to a royalty. It is fully protected under the copyright laws of the United States of America and of all countries covered by the International Copyright Union (including the Dominion of Canada and the rest of the British Commonwealth), the Berne Convention, the Pan-American Copyright Convention and the Universal Copyright Convention, as well as all countries with which the United States has reciprocal copyright relations. All rights, including professional, amateur stage rights, motion picture, recitation, lecturing, public reading, radio broadcasting, television, video or sound recording, all other forms of mechanical or electronic reproduction, such as CD-ROM, CD-I, information storage and retrieval systems and photocopying, and the rights of translation into foreign languages, are strictly reserved. Particular emphasis is laid upon the matter of readings, permission for which must be secured from the Author's agent in writing.

Required royalties must be paid every time this play is performed before any audience, whether or not it is presented for profit and whether or not admission is charged.

All inquiries concerning rights, including amateur rights, should be addressed to: Dramatists Play Service, Inc., 440 Park Avenue South, New York, NY 10016. 212-683-8960. www.dramatists.com

ABOUT *DEATH TAX*

This article first ran in the January/February 2012 issue of Inside Actors, *Actors Theatre of Louisville's subscriber newsletter, and is based on conversations with the playwright before rehearsals for the Humana Festival production began.*

People who have money are preserved.
They get old, they have money, they are preserved.
People who do not have money, they are not preserved.
If one does not get preserved, things get messy.

Death Tax opens on a seemingly unremarkable tableau in a quiet nursing home: as patient Maxine Judson lies in a hospital bed, nurse Tina Deluna goes about her evening routine. It's almost Christmas, and the soft strains of "Jesu, Joy of Man's Desiring" pipe through a tabletop radio. Glossing crisply over Maxine's fatalistic reflections, Tina checks the patient's vital signs. But when the nurse begins to take her blood pressure, Maxine's brooding gives way to a startling accusation. "Nurse Tina?" she says, "I know that you are killing me."

Maxine is sick. Maxine is dying. Maxine has money, lots of it. And she can feel herself getting worse. She does not consider this a mere matter of chance. It's December, 2010, and the tax code is about to change. Maxine's estranged daughter stands to inherit a great deal more money if Maxine passes in December than if she lives past the New Year. "It wouldn't be much for my daughter to pay you off," says Maxine, daring Tina to contradict her. "You wouldn't cost much." As Tina's actions come under increased scrutiny by her supervisor, Todd, and as Maxine's daughter shows up demanding information, the walls begin to close in on the nurse, whose mind is further clouded with worry for a son back in Haiti. What unfurls is a spellbinding thriller about money, power and the value of a human life.

According to playwright Lucas Hnath, the first narrative impulse for *Death Tax* sprang from real-life stories from his mother, a Florida hospital chaplain. "A few years ago she told me she'd been hearing rumors about family members of elderly patients who were sort of lingering, just barely holding onto life," explains Hnath. "The ongoing medical care would slowly eat into their family's savings account until—this was the fear—there would be nothing left." In such cases, the rumors went, someone eventually would offer to pay off a nurse to help things along. Nothing brutal, no pillow over the face, "just a little extra morphine here and there so that their dying relative would finally tip over," says Hnath. Fascinated, he began making notes for a play. When proposals for changes to the estate tax came up for debate in Washington a few years later, Hnath incorporated some of the attending alarmist prophecies of sudden hospital deaths into the premise of his developing story. But *Death Tax* is not primarily political or "topical" in its aspirations. Instead, Hnath focuses the plot on ordinary people grappling with extraordinary ethical and existential dilemmas, transforming a Washington tax-code controversy-of-the-week into something transcendent.

Reflecting on the murky ethical terrain his characters occupy in *Death Tax*, the playwright admits an interest in generating contradictory emotional responses in his audiences. "When I write I'm always going after a moment in which the audience laughs, while experiencing simultaneous affection and revulsion. An '*aww*' and a '*ha*' and an '*eww*,' all at once," he says. Such dissonance abounds in *Death Tax*, as distinctions between right and wrong, the just and the self-serving, become increasingly blurry. The questionable actions taken by the play's characters are counterbalanced—or, at least, complicated—by motives with which the audience can empathize. Tina is fighting to regain custody of her young son. Supervisor Todd is in love with Tina. Maxine's daughter says she wants to reconcile with her mother. "Wrestling with conflicting reactions in a theatre can make us more accepting, in the long run, by making us more comfortable with complex emotion," Hnath explains. "It's a kind of emotional-slash-intellectual workout that makes our brains a little more limber."

Refracted through Hnath's particular aesthetic sensibility, this arresting narrative transforms into an elegant and oddly poetic experience. Carefully calibrated repetitions and silences are scored in the script like music. "My plays are very composed," says Hnath. "There's a really specific rhythm that I'm after, and I often use it to communicate elements of character: what they want, their hesitations." *Death Tax* concerns itself with the difficulty of accurately assessing experience and discerning the truth among conflicting accounts of history. In a play so keenly attuned to how one's judgment can be distorted by the intrusion of desire, says Hnath, "I want the audience to rely on the words, what they're being told—and then, at a certain point, to realize they can't necessarily trust all the information they've been given."

Indeed, as the characters leverage information for control and attempt to manipulate the situation to their own advantages, the play spins into an ever-tighter vortex of power games and mounting anxiety. But at its core, says Hnath, *Death Tax* is really about people who are all, in their way, afraid of abandonment. "In a sense, that is the more real death, the more immediate threat facing these characters—or at least, the threat each one thinks she can do something about," he reflects. "Unfortunately, the steps they take to avoid that fate are not always so very admirable."

—Sarah Lunnie

BIOGRAPHY

A resident playwright at New Dramatists since 2011, Hnath's work has been produced at Actors Theatre of Louisville, University of Miami, The Culture Project, Target Margin and Ontological-Hysteric Theater. Additionally, his plays have been developed at Ensemble Studio Theatre, Rattlestick Playwrights Theater, and Cleveland Public Theatre. He has enjoyed playwriting residencies with The Royal Court Theatre and 24Seven Lab. He is a two-time winner of the Alfred P. Sloan Foundation Grant for his feature-length screenplays, *The Painting, the Machine, and the Apple* and *Still Life*. He is also a recipient of an EST/Sloan Project commission for his play, *Isaac's Eye*. Hnath received both his B.F.A. and M.F.A. from New York University's Department of Dramatic Writing and is a lecturer in NYU's Expository Writing Program.

ACKNOWLEDGMENTS

Death Tax premiered at the Humana Festival of New American Plays in March 2012. It was directed by Ken Rus Schmoll with the following cast:

TINA ....Quincy Tyler Bernstine
TODD ....Paul Niebanck
MAXINE..Judith Roberts
DAUGHTER ....Danielle Skraastad

and the following production staff:

Scenic Designer.. Philip Witcomb
Costume Designer .... Kristopher Castle
Lighting Designer...Brian H. Scott
Sound Designer... Matt Hubbs
Properties Designer..Joe Cunningham
Stage Manager .... Christine Lomaka
Dramaturg...Sarah Lunnie
Casting ....Judy Bowman

Directing Assistant ....Caitlin O'Connell
Assistant Costume Designer.....................................Lisa Weber
Assistant Lighting Designer................................. Kevin Frazier
Production Assistant .... Leslie Cobb
Assistant Dramaturg...............................Dominic Finocchiaro

CHARACTERS

TINA, a nurse, Haitian, speaks with an accent, 30s

MAXINE, wealthy, near death, elderly

TODD, nurse supervisor, 30s

DAUGHTER, Maxine's daughter, 30s

PLAYWRIGHT'S NOTES

In *Death Tax*, less is always more. The play requires only a bed, a couple of ordinary props, and perhaps a chair and an end table. Avoid having to have complicated scene transitions, incidental music, and blackouts. Let the play move swiftly. The ellipses show you where you can have a beat or take a breath or give the characters a chance to exchange silent glances. Otherwise, keep the pacing tight. This is a play about the actions people take when they're caught up in a whirlwind. If the play runs much longer than 85 minutes, you're probably missing the whirlwind.

Keep the blocking simple. The text is extremely dense; it requires the audience's undivided attention. Give the play too much business and the audience won't be able to parse the language.

Lastly, resist the temptation to give Scene Five a "futuristic" look. Again, less is more. Yes, Tina and Todd should change their costumes to reflect their new "roles," but the clothes should look no different from the clothes folks wear today. Also, in production, we decided that Maxine should wear an elegant robe in Scene One, but in Scene Five, she should appear unkempt and wear a plain white patient's gown. If you make the scene look too different from the rest of the play, you will raise irrelevant questions about the world of the play and its logic, distracting the audience from the characters' problems.

SPECIAL THANKS

I would like to thank Dana Higginbotham (for giving me the idea for this play and keeping me accurate in the parts where accuracy matters), Marisa Viola (for reading draft after draft, giving me feedback and advice), Sarah Lunnie (for championing the play and for being my compass and for Scene Four), and Ken Rus Schmoll (for his questions and for knowing what to add and, most importantly, what to take away).

I am also enormously indebted to the actors—Quincy Tyler Bernstine, Paul Niebanck, Judith Roberts, and Danielle Skraastad—for their input and patience and blind faith.

NOTE

The acting edition of *Death Tax* is published by Dramatists Play Service, Inc. Companies producing the play should acquire that version of the script, as it includes updates the playwright made following the Humana Festival production.

This play is dedicated to Rev. Dana Higginbotham.

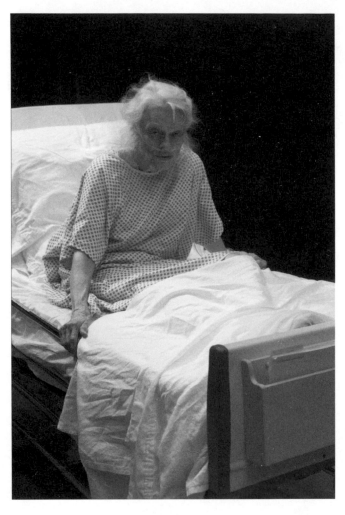

Judith Roberts
in *Death Tax*

36ᵗʰ Humana Festival of New American Plays
Actors Theatre of Louisville, 2012
Photo by Alan Simons

DEATH TAX

For a will takes effect only at death, since it is not in force as long as the one who made it is alive.
—Hebrews 9:17

A bed.
An old woman in the bed.
Old woman in bed wearing a nasal cannula.
A nurse.
A radio. On a table. It plays "Jesu, Joy of Man's Desiring." A late night Christmastime broadcast.
The nurse slips the blood pressure cuff on the old woman's arm.
As she takes the woman's blood pressure, the nurse speaks to the audience—

1.

TINA. This play has five scenes. This is scene 1.
Scene 1: It's December, 2010.
I am a nurse.
This is a room in a nursing home.
This is a patient.
I am taking her vitals.
The patient is looking at me.
She says to me…
MAXINE. People who have money are preserved.
They get old, they have money, they are preserved.
People who do not have money, they are not preserved.
If one does not get preserved, things get messy.
TINA. …
MAXINE. …
TINA. …I turn to her and say:
I am going to take your blood pressure now.
MAXINE. Okay.
TINA. …

(TINA *takes* MAXINE's *blood pressure.*)

MAXINE. …

TINA. How are you feeling today, Ms. Judson.

MAXINE. Terrible.

TINA. Have you been feeling any pain or discomfort?

MAXINE. Yes.

TINA. Where?

MAXINE. All over.

TINA. …Can you be more specific.

MAXINE. Specific?

TINA. Yes.

MAXINE. …No.

TINA. …

MAXINE. …

TINA. I will tell the doctor.

MAXINE. What will you tell the doctor?

TINA. That you are having general discomfort.

MAXINE. And pain.

TINA. And pain.

> (TINA *finishes taking the blood pressure, she removes the cuff, she writes down what she writes down…*)

I am going to check your ankles for swelling.
I am going to pull back your sheets.

> (TINA *lifts the bedsheets covering* MAXINE*'s legs.*)

Are you cold?

> (*Shakes her head no.*)

My hands are warm so you should not feel any discomfort.
I am going to check the ankles for swelling.

> (*Beat.*)

Alright.
There is some swelling, Ms. Judson.
Not much. Nothing to worry about.
I will let the doctor know.
I am writing it down for him.

MAXINE. …Uh-huh.

TINA. …

MAXINE. …

TINA. I am checking your catheter now.

MAXINE. Go for it.

TINA. I am making sure the point of insertion is clean,
no infections…

MAXINE. …

TINA. …

MAXINE. …

(TINA *is done checking the catheter.*)

TINA. All of that looks fine.

MAXINE. It does –

TINA. I see no problems.

(TINA *finishes her notes.*)

MAXINE. Nurse Tina?

TINA. …Yes?

MAXINE. I know that you are killing me.

TINA. …

MAXINE. …

TINA. …

MAXINE. I know.

TINA. …

MAXINE. Didn't know I knew – did you know that I knew?

TINA. I don't know.

MAXINE. Don't know what?

TINA. That I am killing you. I did not know this.
I am not aware of this.

MAXINE. Uh-huh.

TINA. Killing?

MAXINE. Murder.

TINA. …Why are you saying that, Ms. Judson?
Ms. Judson, that is not something to joke about.

MAXINE. …I'm not joking.

TINA. You are joking.
You are joking.
I am not killing you, do not say things like that.
It is dangerous, you understand, to say things like

MAXINE. Turn off the radio, please.

(TINA *does so.*)

Shut the door.

TINA. …

MAXINE. Shut the door. So no one will hear us talk when we talk.

TINA. No.

MAXINE. Shut the door and we will

TINA. We cannot talk, you are not

MAXINE. We *will* talk,
door shut or not.

TINA. ...

> (TINA *shuts the door.*)

MAXINE. Lock the door.

> (TINA *locks the door.*)

...Do you know about taxes?

TINA. Taxes?

MAXINE. Yes, taxes.

TINA. Yes. I know about taxes.

MAXINE. What do you know about taxes?

TINA. ...People pay them.

MAXINE. And when you've paid them?
Then what?

TINA. ...

MAXINE. Then what?

TINA. We pay them again.

MAXINE. Yes. You pay the taxes and what happens to the money that you
have?

TINA. It is gone.

MAXINE. It is gone, yes, it is gone.
You have money, and then after the taxes, you have less money.
And the bigger the pile of money, the more money that goes away.
Sometimes. Sometimes that's how it works.
Today, that is not how it works.
Today, if I were to die today, my daughter,
my only daughter, my only family,
my daughter would get all the money that I have left.
This much.

> (*Shows with her hands.*)

If I were to die after the first of January,
the tax laws change.
And because these tax laws change,
my daughter will only get this much money.

> (*Shows with her hands a much smaller amount.*)

That is, if I die after the new year.
This much is much less than this much.
You see?
And I know what happens.
I have heard what happens.
People hear about what happens.
I know of women like myself
who have died in the past couple of months.
And they did not need to die.
And I know that nurses, like you,
nurses like you make very little.
You make…

> (*Shows with her fingers.*)

…this much.

TINA. …

MAXINE. So it's not hard for a family member to come along
and offer you some money
and say, "Well, if there's anything you can do to speed things along,
there's more where that came from."
And I know, I know there are…things you can do,
small things, to speed things along.
Small adjustments in my care.
Or small steps taken or not taken.
You lie a patient on her side,
her left side,
just at the right moment, the patient will die.
Yes?
Yes.
See, I know about that trick, I know about it.
I've heard.
Or maybe better yet:
a little extra morphine here and there,
over the course of a month,
a little extra morphine relaxes the patient,
relaxes the body,
makes the body fight just a little less.
And when the body stops fighting,
the body starts dying.
You see?
…You see.
You know.
And I know, I know my body.

I know the feeling of my body fighting,
and I know, or I think I know,
or am starting to know the feeling of what I think I think
is the feeling of my body stopping.

TINA. Ms. Judson.
You are in decline.
This is what the doctor has told you.
You are in decline.

MAXINE. Yes, but this is different.
This is…
It's like the difference between a plane coming in for a nice easy landing,
and a plane—

> (*With her hand, gestures a nose-dive.*)

There is a difference.

TINA. …

MAXINE. And I know my daughter wants that money.
She's already asked me to give it to her, all of it,
before I'm dead, before I die,
as though I'm already dead,
she's already asked for this,
and when I said no, she said, you're going to regret this,
that's exactly, *exactly*, what she said,
and she hung up the phone.
Slammed it. Slammed down the phone.

TINA. …

MAXINE. And if I were to try to do something about it,
change my will, right now, if I were to write her out,
then she'd challenge it. She'd challenge it, and there's a good chance she'd win.
This close to death, this close to death,
too easy to just say, well, Maxine was so close to death,
Maxine didn't know what she was doing,
Maxine was crazy,
someone coaxed her, she was under an influence.
And my daughter would challenge the will and she'd win and I'd be dead.
What good would that do?
Change the will, keep the will the same—both options leave me dead.

TINA. …

MAXINE. …

TINA. …

MAXINE. ...

TINA. Okay.

MAXINE. ...

TINA. Alright, Ms. Judson...

MAXINE. ...

TINA. (*Diffusing a bomb.*) I understand
where you are coming from.

MAXINE. *Uh-huh.*

TINA. I understand.
It is scary.
All of this is very frightening
I am sure.
I cannot imagine
what it is like to be you.
But please,
let's just think about
what you have seen.
Not
what is happening
up inside of your head.
Just think
about
what you have seen...
Have you seen me *do* anything?
Anything "not right"?

MAXINE. If you were doing something,
something you shouldn't be doing,
would I see it?
Wouldn't you be very careful to hide what you were doing if
you shouldn't be doing what you were doing?

TINA. ...

MAXINE. ...

TINA. ...Alright. Say you are dying.

MAXINE. ...

TINA. Say that you are dying and say that it is because of something outside
of you—

MAXINE. An outside influence

TINA. An outside influence, yes.
...Why me? I'm not the only nurse.
Not the only one who works with you.

There's Nurse Toad.
The overnight nurse.
Why not her?

MAXINE. Nurse Toad?

TINA. Nurse Toad.
Why not Nurse Toad?

MAXINE. I already talked to Toad.

TINA. And?

MAXINE. And based on what she said and how she said what she said,
I don't think she's

TINA. No?

MAXINE. No.

TINA. And what am I doing that makes you think she should be trusted
and not me?

MAXINE. (*Shrugs.*) Things I've heard

TINA. What things?

MAXINE. …

TINA. What things?

MAXINE. I eavesdrop.
I ask around.
I know that you have some legal trouble.

TINA. No, it's not

MAXINE. Problems back home,
back in Haiti.

TINA. Is that *all* you've heard?

MAXINE. You have a kid.

TINA. I have a kid. Yes. I have a kid.

MAXINE. You have a kid who was taken away from you.

TINA. No

MAXINE. Oh, so he is with you?
He's back at home?
You got a sitter back at your place watching him right now?
Yes or no.
Yes or

TINA. No.

MAXINE. Where is he?

TINA. …In Haiti.

MAXINE. That's the type of thing that makes one wonder.

You're here, and he's back in Haiti.

It's peculiar is all.

TINA. I do have a kid. Yes.

And he is in Haiti.

And I am here.

But that's all you know.

Is that all you know?

MAXINE. ...

TINA. That is all you know.

And you've made up, in your head, a whole story about it.

But whatever I tell you, you'll tell yourself is a lie.

My word against – who knows what.

Well. Here.

Here's something that I can show you.

(TINA *takes her badge, flips it around, takes out a laminated photo.*)

That's him.

That's John Paul.

Alright.

You see he's real.

He's 8 years old.

And he's real.

And

I dunno, what can I tell you –

He likes to swim.

He swims fast.

And...he also likes diving.

He wants to be on a diving team.

He does well in school.

He's one of the smartest in his class.

He is maybe number 2 or 3 in his class – he's very smart.

He reads lots of books.

He's read the entire Bible.

He memorizes whole pieces from the Bible.

And someday, he wants to be either a doctor

or a preacher.

And he acts like a little adult sometimes.

He has very serious eyes.

My husband and I, we would fight.

And he would try to talk to us.

He would try to make the fight stop,

he would try to work it out.
That's the type of kid he is.
Wise beyond his years. Kind of weird.
And I look at him,
and I ask myself how did I make that?
How did that come from me?
He is the best thing I ever made.
There is no reason,
no reason, I should have made him.
Because I *was*,
I *was* bad.
When I was young.
I'm different now.
I've changed.
But when I was young,
I was a bad girl.
I did a lot of drugs.
I did a lot of partying.
I did a lot of things I should not have done.
I got with men, men who were the dangerous kind,
I liked a bit of danger.
If there was no danger there was no spark.
My husband was one of those types.
Nasty.
Mean.
Type that would kick you when you're down
and keep on kicking.
And I was not better, when I was young,
I was not better than him.
And together, we were a nasty pair.
And I did stuff, I did all sorts of stuff with him,
before we had our kid,
a lot of stuff that could get me in a lot of trouble,
stuff I had to keep a secret,
stuff I will never talk about for the rest of my life.
I swear I will never –
And it is like I am always being punished for it.
And maybe I deserve to be punished, but I am trying,
trying to be good.

MAXINE. …

TINA. I tried. When my son was born,
I got scared,

I got scared for him,
and I stopped that old life,
I became a Christian,
I took my son to church,
and we moved here,
we moved away from the,
from the shit,
the shit of our past,
we moved away from it,
but my husband, he stayed the same.
And I knew, I could not let my son be exposed to that.
And I left him, we got divorced.
But we had to share custody.
And one weekend, he had my son,
and my son did not come back.
He took my son back to Haiti.
And I called the police,
and they said there was nothing they could do.
I called the senator.
Nothing.
Governor.
Nothing.
Anyone I could call I called.
Nothing.
They say, oh the laws are different there than here.
They say, oh we can't get involved.
They say, we don't have any power.
They say, you need a special type of lawyer for that.
They say, you need to go there,
go back to Haiti and fight in their courts,
not our courts.
And my husband, my *ex*-husband,
he says, you come back here,
I'm gonna dig up all that shit from your past.
You'll never get him.
You'll never get anything.
I'll dig up all that stuff,
they'll arrest you for even coming back here.
You'll pay, he says.
MAXINE. ...

TINA. And my son,
he is the best thing I ever made,

he is the best thing I ever made,
and I cannot live without him.
I am here for one reason.
I am here to get my son back.
I am here, just trying to work hard,
make a nice home, buy a house,
a house with a pool,
a diving board for John Paul,
so he can practice his diving,
and a yard for a dog,
because he always wanted a dog.
And John Paul will come here and he will go to school here,
and he'll play on the diving team,
and he'll have his dog,
and he'll go to college and become a doctor or a preacher.
And I will make a nice home here,
and the courts will see that he is better with me than his father,
and I will save up money, and I will get a lawyer,
and my lawyer will fight this,
and I will win.
Because John Paul is the best thing I ever made.
And I made him.
And he is mine.

MAXINE. ...

TINA. Do you understand?
Do you see where *I* am coming from?

MAXINE. ...I do.

TINA. Ms. Judson.
I am begging you.

           (*Down on her knees.*)

I am begging you.
I don't want any trouble.
That's all.
I've had enough trouble.
I don't need trouble from the police.
I don't need anything on my record,
anything that could hurt my chances of getting my boy back.
Please. Please think of that.
Please consider
that when you say stuff like the stuff you are saying,
you are hurting me

and my son.

You are hurting my son.

Look.

(TINA *holds out the picture.*)

This is my son.

You need to understand that.

This is who you are hurting.

TINA. …

MAXINE. So that's the reason.

TINA. Yes…

MAXINE. That's your reason

for taking money from my daughter to have me die.

TINA. Oh sweet Jesus

MAXINE. You need the money to get your new house and get your lawyer.

You're desperate. That's what you're telling me.

That's what I'm hearing.

TINA. You're going to report me to the police.

MAXINE. No.

TINA. No?

MAXINE. No. Of course not.

TINA. …

MAXINE. I don't have any proof.

I don't have any proof that would mean anything to a cop.

I say murder, they say dementia.

TINA. You're going to tell my boss then.

MAXINE. What good would that do?

It's not in their interest to acknowledge that such a thing could happen.

If it gets out that one of their nurses is killing patients,

then it looks bad and it hurts them.

…No, Tina. This is something that I have to deal with myself.

That *we're* going to deal with, right now.

TINA. …

MAXINE. …How much is my daughter paying you?

TINA. …

MAXINE. I'll give you more than she's giving you.

How much is she paying you?

TINA. …

MAXINE. How much.

TINA. …

MAXINE. Tell me how much, Nurse Tina.

TINA. ...

MAXINE. ...

TINA. ...A thousand dollars.

MAXINE. (*Making a decision...*)
Good.

TINA. ...A thousand up front.
And when it's done,
another thousand.

MAXINE. Alright.

TINA. ...

MAXINE. For each week I stay alive, I will also give you a thousand dollars.

TINA. ...

MAXINE. And if I make it to January first, then I'll give you $200,000.

TINA. ...

MAXINE. You get two hundred thousand. If, and only if, I'm alive on January first.
How does that sound? Do we have a deal?

2.

TINA. Scene 2.
I walk into Todd's office.

TODD. ...

TINA. (*Points to a man, who sits in a chair.*) Todd. In his office.

TODD. ...

TINA. Todd?

TODD. Yeah?

TINA. ...I need a leave of absence.

TODD. ...Um. Okay.

TINA. Is that possible?

TODD. ...When?

TINA. After January first.

TODD. How soon after?

TINA. As soon as possible.

TODD. Oh.

Uh.

For how long?

TINA. I don't know.

TODD. What do you mean – ?

TINA. What do you mean, what do I mean?

TODD. You don't know how long – ?

TINA. People do this type of thing all the time.

TODD. ...Can I ask why?

TINA. Family business.

TODD. Something with your son

TINA. Yes.

TODD. (*Genuine.*) Is he okay?

TINA. It's family business, Todd.

You are not

TODD. I was just, I don't mean to, sorry. I was just wondering if you'd heard from him.

TINA. No.

Nothing's changed. Same situation.

TODD. I'm sorry.

TINA. ...

TODD. So you really don't know how long you'll be gone?

TINA. I do not.

TODD. You aren't *leaving* leaving are you?

You aren't...running off

TINA. I am not running off.

TODD. I didn't mean – I mean –

You'd tell me if you were leaving for good.

TINA. Yes.

TODD. I wouldn't want you just disappearing.

I'd, well, you

TINA. I'm not

TODD. can't hold your position indefinitely.

TINA. Then just say a month.

TODD. ...

TINA. ...

TODD. You sure this is just family business? That's

TINA. Yes.

TODD. Nothing else.

TINA. No.

TODD. Doesn't have anything to do with

TINA. what

TODD. me?

TINA. No, it's not

TODD. because I

TINA. not about you.

TODD. And you're not in some sort of trouble.

TINA. No.

TODD. Family business.

TINA. Family business, with my son.

TODD. In Haiti.

TODD. …

TINA. …

TODD. Fill out the paperwork, and I'll send it in to HR.

TINA. Okay.

TODD. Tina.

TINA. Yeah?

TODD. …

TINA. …

TODD. I need to ask you about something.

TINA. …What.

TODD. One of the other nurses says she saw you taking a check from Ms. Judson.

TINA. …I did not do that.

TODD. It's just what Nurse Toad said.

TINA. …

TODD. …

TINA. Toad's a liar.

TODD. You can get in a lot of trouble for that.

TINA. For what? For saying that she's a lying bitch cunt?

TODD. You can get into trouble for that too, no, what I meant was that you can get into trouble for taking money from patients.

TINA. I'm not

TODD. Okay

TINA. but I am calling Nurse Toad a lying bitch cunt.

TODD. Alright

TINA. That part's true.

TODD. Just don't say that outside of this office.

TINA. You know she's a liar.

TODD. No, I know.

TINA. You know she has it in for me.

TODD. I'm just letting you know that taking money from a patient,
regardless of whether or not the money is being given voluntarily,
is something that you can into a lot of trouble for.
But if there was some way in which you were not entirely clear on the policy,
or the way it's written in the employee manual, then we can give you a pass
this time,
provided…you give the money back to Ms. Judson.

TINA. I understand the policy.

TODD. Good

TINA. That's why I didn't do it.
I don't break policies

TODD. because I'm really just trying to give you an out if you made a mistake.
We all make mistakes.
I make mistakes all the time, and if policies were applied to me as strictly as
they're written,
you know, I wouldn't still be around here. I'd –
No one's perfect. I mean

TINA. (*A look.*) …

TODD. I mean, yes. You are right.
Nurse Toad, she does have a habit of lying.

TINA. It's documented.

TODD. Yes. And she's been warned for making false accusations.
Which is why, which is why when she came to me with this accusation,
I had to ask her,
"Sheila, do you have proof of this?"
And she said, "Yes"

TINA. and she's a lying bitch cunt

TODD. and that's when she took out her cell phone
and showed me a picture.
And the picture shows you
in Maxine's room,
and Maxine handing you what appears to be a check.

TINA. Appears.

TODD. Appears, yes, appears a lot like a check.

TINA. …

TODD. It's a check, Tina.
It's clearly a check.

TINA. …

TODD. So what do I do? What do I do now?

TINA. She must've Photoshopped it or something on her computer,
you can Photoshop things, all sorts of

TODD. No. Tina. It's

TINA. The check wasn't money.

TODD. No, a check is money, that's what a check is

TINA. the check wasn't for me.

TODD. Even if it wasn't for you, it's a violation to even

TINA. I know.
I know, Todd.

TODD. …

TINA. …

TODD. I'm supposed to report this to my

TINA. you wouldn't do that.
Todd, I know you wouldn't, and –
Report *me?*
Really?

TODD. If I don't, Nurse Toad will go over my head.

TINA. …

TODD. I need to know your side of this story.
If I know your story, if I understand what was really happening,
we can come up with a solution. Like I said, you can return the money and…

TINA. …

TODD. …

TINA. …

TODD. Come on. Talk to me.

TINA. What is there to talk about?

TODD. Why is she giving you money?

TINA. …

TODD. What, is it like a little Christmas tip,
a little Christmas gift? I mean, that's fine.
Happens all the time. We just need to

TINA. She thinks her daughter is paying me money to have her die before the first,
so that the daughter doesn't have to pay a lot of tax money to the government.
I could not convince her that I was not doing this.
She then said she would pay me to ensure that she lives until the first.

TODD. ...

TINA. ...

TODD. ...

TINA. ...

TODD. ...

TINA. ...

TODD. Oh God, Tina

TINA. Todd, don't

TODD. That's really bad

TINA. you're over-reacting

TODD. No, I'm not, I'm –
How much is she paying you?

TINA. Who?

TODD. Maxine

TINA. A thousand each week until the first.

TODD. A thousand

TINA. each week

TODD. Okay

TINA. and then if she's alive on the first, she'll give me 200,000

TODD. Oh for fuck's sake –

TINA. ...

TODD. Aw, Jesus –

TINA. ...

TODD. This is like a federal offense or something,
I mean

TINA. I doubt that

TODD. I think it's extortion

TINA. no

TODD. yeah, I think...

TINA. Todd

TODD. yeah

TINA. I can use the money to get back my son.
I'm going to get him back.

I met with a lawyer, and the lawyer is very confident

TODD. This is why you need the leave

TINA. I have a court date, and there's still some stuff I need to get,
papers and letters, I'll need some stuff from you,
character reference

TODD. sure

TINA. I can get him,
I can get John Paul,
the money will help me get

TODD. yeah

TINA. you see

TODD. I mean,
that's great. It's really...

TINA. ...

TODD. But you don't have to do it this way. You

TINA. It's very expensive

TODD. I know but there are

TINA. are not other options.

TODD. But there are.
I mean
...what about me.

TINA. ...

TODD. I can help.
I've offered to help.
Several times. I've –

TINA. ...

TODD. This, what you're doing here, this can land you in jail.
Taking money from me – that will not land you in jail.
One option is clearly better than the other.

TINA. But taking money from you

TODD. yeah

TINA. is

TODD. what

TINA. complicated.

TODD. ...Only if you want it to be.

TINA. No

TODD. yeah

TINA. No, Todd. It's complicated.

TODD. And this other plan isn't?
Really?

TINA. Different kind of complicated.

TODD. …

TINA. It doesn't feel right to take money from you.

TODD. You don't have to take money.
I mean you could also just move into my place –
make it so you don't have to pay rent

TINA. That is not better. What you're describing is

TODD. I have a nice place. A lot of space

TINA. That is sexual harassment.

TODD. Wha – huh? What?!? No. No, it's,
it's not sexual harassment if there's
already been sex.

TINA. I don't think that makes sense.

TODD. No, I mean, if there's, you know what I mean

TINA. It's sexual harassment if it's unwanted.

TODD. Is it unwanted? Is this unwanted?

TINA. …Yes.

TODD. A person presents himself.
A person says, I'm here. I care.

TINA. No one cares for free.

TODD. Well that's what I'm offering.

TINA. not what you're offering.
You have feelings for me.
I can tell.
You still have feelings for me.
You've said stuff. You've said stuff before.
Stuff about me and about how much you care.
That's what you want.
Admit it.

TODD. So?
I can want that.

TINA. I'm not saying you can't.
I'm just saying you probably wouldn't care as much if you weren't interested in something more
than us being co-workers.

TODD. We already have been

TINA. Have been what?

TODD. More than co-workers.

TINA. And then we went back.
Just co-workers.

TODD. Yeah.

TINA. So

TODD. we're on a break, just taking some time off.
Right? We're
Just

TINA. ...

TODD. Right?

TINA. ...

TODD. (*Drops his head.*) ...I really like you.

TINA. I know.

TODD. I think you're

TINA. I know

TODD. And I think we're

TINA. I know

TODD. And I think,
I think you think I'm weak.

TINA. No.

TODD. I think you think I'm weak.
I think you're used to the type of guys
who push people around
and I'm not that type of person.

TINA. that's why I liked you

TODD. But I think I bore you.
I think you miss the other type of guy.
I think you don't want to be with someone like me.
I think I embarrass you.
You'd rather be with someone who, I dunno,
who wore leather jackets –

TINA. ...(?)

TODD. Yeah, you know what I mean

TINA. no

TODD. Leather jackets.
Rides a motorcycle.
I have cardigans. Polo shirts.
Khaki pants.

TINA. I

TODD. the time when we went out and had dinner,
and I saw you looking at the guy at the bar wearing a leather jacket,
I saw you looking at him,
and I could see you seeing in your eye
that you'd rather be with him.
And that was just a week before we decided to take a break.
That was just a week before, but when I saw you seeing him,
in his leather jacket, I could tell you were
And I wish I were that person.
I wish I were a leather jacket guy, Tina.
I try.
I want to be that guy.
I think that's why I want to be with you, I think,
I think, because I think that being with you
would help maybe make me more the type of guy that I want to be.
But you just don't have patience for me I guess.

TINA. That has nothing to do with leather jackets, Todd.
I

TODD. No, I know.

TINA. ...I do like you, Todd. A lot.
And I do think we
But I got a lotta shit I gotta deal with.
And it's just the wrong time for me.
I just need to stay focused.

> (TINA *moves in closer.*
> *Strokes his head.*)

TODD. ...

TINA. ...

TODD. ...

TINA. So Todd...

TODD. ...Yeah?

TINA. ...Where's the phone?

TODD. What phone?

TINA. The phone with the photo.
Toad's phone.

TODD. I have it.

TINA. Where?

TODD. In my desk.

TINA. Can I see it?

TODD. No.

TINA. You *could* delete it.

TODD. I know.

TINA. You could delete it –

TODD. And then what?

What do I tell her?

I tell Toad that the photo isn't on her phone anymore.

And then she accuses me of deleting it.

Or she accuses me of siding with you.

And then she goes to my supervisor

TINA. and you tell your supervisor that she has a history of lying,

and you show your supervisor her file.

And then that's that.

She'll go to your supervisor and they'll just shrug it off.

TODD. …

TINA. You said you don't want to be a pushover anymore. Right?

TODD. This is different. This has nothing to do with being a pushover.

TINA. …

TODD. You're asking me to help you scam a woman who thinks you're murdering

TINA. I'm not scamming anyone.

I just need you to keep Toad quiet,

and I need you to help me keep Maxine alive until the first.

The swelling in her ankles is getting worse.

Blood pressure's going up.

And I'm worried about complications, and the doctor's not doing anything.

He thinks she's a lost cause.

So I need you to step in and order more around-the-clock.

I need you to get the *good* doctor. Doctor Morris.

Get Dr. Morris to come down from Orlando to see her,

maybe two times a week.

I need your help keeping her alive until the first.

TODD. …I don't know.

TINA. A person can live a long time, if you help them live a long time.

There's a lot that can be done to keep someone going on and

TODD. Sure, but it's

TINA. what

TODD. expensive.

TINA. She can pay.

TODD. …

TINA. She can pay

TODD. And what about me?
What do I get?
What do I get in return?

TINA. ...Half.

TODD. Half?

TINA. (*Nods.*) ...

TODD. ...Half of...?

TINA. Everything.
Everything she gives me. You get half.
$100,000. If she lives until

TODD. I don't care about that.
I don't need

TINA. what

TODD. money

TINA. it's a lot of money

TODD. I need to not be alone in the world.
I am so alone

TINA. You're not alone. You have your mother.
You like spending time with her.

TODD. ...

TINA. You and I are just taking some time off. That's all.

TODD. ...

TINA. ...

TODD. You know I want to help you, in any way I can, you know

TINA. I know, Todd.
I know.

TODD. ...

TINA. So that means yes,
yes?

TODD. ...

TINA. Yes.

3.

TINA. Scene 3.
Christmas Eve.
The daughter comes to visit.

> (DAUGHTER *enters. She wears a T-shirt. Slightly ripped jeans. Earrings and rings and an anklet—all probably cheap. She's not trashy* per se, *but she doesn't immediately appear to be the daughter of a very wealthy woman.*)

She walks up to me and says

DAUGHTER. Are you Tina?

TINA. ...

DAUGHTER. Tina. Are you Nurse Tina?

TINA. ...Yes.

DAUGHTER. You are the nurse who works with my mother

TINA. Your mother is

DAUGHTER. Maxine.

TINA. ...

DAUGHTER. I asked at the front desk,
I said I was here to see my mother,
and they said that I needed to speak with you.

TINA. ...

DAUGHTER. So where is she? Am I in the right place

TINA. Yes

DAUGHTER. and

TINA. and?

DAUGHTER. I'm here to see her.

TINA. ...okay.

DAUGHTER. Where is she?

TINA. ...You can't see her.

DAUGHTER. Why not?

TINA. She asked for no visitors.

DAUGHTER. my mother?

TINA. yes

DAUGHTER. said

TINA. no visitors.

DAUGHTER. I'm her daughter.
I'm not a visitor.

TINA. You are a visitor.

DAUGHTER. She might have said no visitors but she probably meant people who are not family.

TINA. No visitors means no visitors.

DAUGHTER. …

TINA. I can call a chaplain.
You can talk to the chaplain.
Chaplains are good at dealing with problems like this.

DAUGHTER. What problems?

TINA. uh

DAUGHTER. This is bullshit.

TINA. Patients have a right to request no visitors.
She has requested no visitors.

DAUGHTER. …Do you know why?

TINA. …

DAUGHTER. …

TINA. No.

DAUGHTER. You don't.

TINA. No.

DAUGHTER. She said nothing to

TINA. No.

DAUGHTER. …You must know something.

TINA. No.

DAUGHTER. She must have said something, she's always saying something, she never stops saying something.

TINA. …

DAUGHTER. You're saying she said nothing.

TINA. If I knew something, I would not be allowed to say.

DAUGHTER. Why?

TINA. Confidentiality.

DAUGHTER. Patients' rights.

TINA. Yes, patients' rights.

DAUGHTER. Right. So what about me?
Where are my rights?

TINA. …I'm sorry.

DAUGHTER. Okay. Listen. I know that you have a way you're supposed to handle situations.
I know that this place has its rules

TINA. I could lose my job

DAUGHTER. Yeah, you could lose your job if you don't follow them.
Yeah, I get that.
But …
I mean.

TINA. …

DAUGHTER. Okay.

TINA. …

DAUGHTER. …Person to person – are you a mother – ?

TINA. …Yes.

DAUGHTER. Okay, mother to mother.
I got my kid here.
He's here. He's
back there in the waiting room.

TINA. …

DAUGHTER. It's Christmas Eve.
He wants to see her.
He knows that this is probably the last chance he'll get. I mean,
I told him that she's not well,
I told him that this is probably her last Christmas.
I had to prepare him, cuz of course I didn't want it coming out of the blue.
And the whole thing kinda freaks him out, the whole thing is giving him
nightmares.
…He'd really like to see her,
he knows it's his last chance,
I think it would be good for him to see her.

TINA. …

DAUGHTER. I mean, what am I supposed to tell him?
We make the trip out here, he knows he's here to see his grandmother,
he knows this is his last chance to see her.
So do I go out there and tell him, "no"?
He'll ask, "why?"
He'll ask why his grandmother doesn't want to see him.
Do I tell him – what do I tell him – do I tell him – ?

TINA. Actually, ma'am –

DAUGHTER. Yeah

TINA. He *is* allowed.

DAUGHTER. …Charley?

TINA. Your son –

DAUGHTER. His name is Charley –

TINA. Charley is allowed.

DAUGHTER. She said that.

TINA. (*Nods.*)

…

DAUGHTER. But not me.
He's allowed to see her, but not her own daughter.

TINA. When she said "no visitors,"
she meant…certain people

DAUGHTER. certain people

TINA. yes

DAUGHTER. meaning me.

TINA. Yes.
You.
She said, "you."

DAUGHTER. Anyone other than me?

TINA. …No.

DAUGHTER. Alright.

TINA. …

DAUGHTER. What's your supervisor's name?

TINA. Todd.

DAUGHTER. Todd what?

TINA. Kapinsky.

DAUGHTER. C-a-p –

TINA. *K*-a-p…
i-n-s-k-y.
– you can talk with him if you want.
I have no problem with that.
He'll tell you exactly what I just told you.

DAUGHTER. …

TINA. Your son can see her.

DAUGHTER. …

TINA. Your son can see her.
I can bring him in.
It will be okay.
He'll be okay.

DAUGHTER. …

TINA. Do you want to do that?

DAUGHTER. …

TINA. …

DAUGHTER. No

TINA. but, your son, Charley, he did want to see her, you said

DAUGHTER. I don't want him to see her alone.

TINA. …

DAUGHTER. No, I can't do that.
I don't know what she'll say.
Charley's young.
She might say something to him.
I don't trust her.
She's like that.
You know she's like that.

TINA. I don't know.

DAUGHTER. …Uh-huh.

TINA. …

DAUGHTER. …

TINA. …

DAUGHTER. So what has she said about me?

TINA. …I can't

DAUGHTER. right, you can't say.
"You can't say" means "she did say."
If she didn't say, then you'd say she didn't say.
But I can tell, she's said something.

TINA. …

DAUGHTER. Did she say that I'm evil.
She says that.
She says from Day 1, I was a bad seed.
Did she say that?

TINA. …

DAUGHTER. She likes to say that to people.
That I was evil from the start.
She says that she looked into my eyes,
and saw something in my eyes,
and could just tell that I was evil,
and there was nothing she could do about it except to treat me like an evil child,
because that's what you do to children who have the evil look in their eyes.

TINA. …

DAUGHTER. Or did she say I'm after her money.
I'm sure she said that.
I'm sure she said I'm after her money.

TINA. …

DAUGHTER. Here's the thing. Okay, so that you see my side,
because I know you've only seen her side,
I can tell, I can tell the way you are,
the way you look at me, the way you're silent at moments,
the way you're judging me,
I can tell – I'm really good at this by now –
telling when my mother's said something about me,
it's happened enough, I can tell.
And so, I know you've heard her side,
but now I want you to hear my side,
so that you can know both sides:

TINA. …

DAUGHTER. She says I want her money.
She has so much money, just sitting there.
And what do I have?
What do Charley and I live on?

TINA. …

DAUGHTER. We use food stamps.
…How is that right?
Is that right?
Do you think that's

TINA. using food stamps?

DAUGHTER. Yeah

TINA. I've used them.
I don't think there's anything wrong with using food stamps.

DAUGHTER. Okay.
I get what you're saying.
Okay.
I'm just saying, alright, food stamps, was maybe the wrong example,
I'm sorry if I offended you

TINA. should I be – ?

DAUGHTER. sorry.
I just think it's not right, I think –
How is it right that she has so much money just sitting there in the bank,
and her daughter and grandson have to struggle as hard as they struggle.

TINA. It sucks that anyone struggles.

DAUGHTER. I agree. And –
It's not like I'm not trying.
I'm trying.

I'm doing some work as a substitute teacher,
but they're only able to give me like two shifts a month,
and two shifts a month means about, what, like, 200 bucks.
And also I'm in a real estate course, an online thing,
but even once I get that,
I mean, that's commission based work. That isn't even –
And I thought of becoming a nurse too. Or maybe a CNA.
I forget which one requires less school, or they're both –
both don't require much, like two years,
is that right? – it's pretty quick, right?
I mean, I'm sure that's part of why you became a nurse.
I'm sure that this isn't where you meant to wind up.
Is it?
It's something you did because you were trying to support your kid,
because you needed the money, because it was there.
Not because it's easy, I'm sure it's not easy, but because there was work there
for you.
So I'm saying, I'm saying I'm like you in this way.
You and I, we're kind of on the same page here, right?

TINA. …

DAUGHTER. And anyway, I mean, is it so wrong for me to want some of
the money?
Isn't that what parents do? They help. They help their children.
Their children are children, which means they aren't as far along in life as
the parent.
They're a couple of steps behind.
Shouldn't a parent *want* to help?
I understand that. I understand that now.
Now that I have Charley, I'd do anything I can to help Charley.
I want his life to be easier. Easier than mine.
If I had the power to make his life a lot better…
And she has all this money. And it's not even hers. It was my dad's.
If she didn't have him, she'd have nothing.
So I think it's pretty hypocritical what she's doing.
So I'm not gonna hide it.
I think about money a lot.
I think about money a lot, because I'm having a really shitty time right now,
making things just "okay."
I think about money a lot because I don't have money.
I think about money because it's not okay to not have money.
I think about money because I think about what happens when you don't
have money.

I think about money because I think about my kid getting sick or getting hurt

or if he like fell down the stairs and broke something,

and we don't have the money to deal with something like that.

Or what if the landlord next month decides that he's gonna jack up the rent.

Or what if I get into a car accident and I need to get car repairs and the insurance goes up.

Or what if Charley needs new shoes for school, or there's some school trip I have to pay for,

and I don't want him to be left out.

Or what if, what if my husband doesn't pay child support,

or what if the judge reduces the child support, what if suddenly we get less,

or what if, you know, and –

TINA. …

DAUGHTER. But I don't bring it up. I shut up. I say nothing.

I don't complain. I don't tell my mother.

I don't make a big deal of it.

But then I think, that's bullshit.

Why shouldn't I bring it up?

Why shouldn't I stand up for myself, for my kid?

Why should I, and I – and I'm like, well, fuck it,

fuck it, you know,

and so I call her up about a month ago,

and I call her up, and I tell her everything,

everything I just told you, I tell her that.

I tell her about how things are tight.

I tell her what I'm scared of.

I say, "I'm having a hard time and I'm scared."

And I say, "I need you."

And I ask her, "Can I have some money?"

And she tells me something like you'll get what you get when I'm gone.

And I'm like, "Well, you know, these problems I'm having, I'm having them like now.

Like today. I need some money now."

And something about that just really rubbed her the wrong way.

And she starts yelling.

And she's like, "That's all I am to you, just a checkbook,

and you just use me for my money."

And I was like, alright, okay, I'm not going to deal with this.

This is kinda like abuse, and I'm not –

And –

And before I hang up the phone – I'm gonna hang up on her –

and, I say:
"You know,
you're gonna regret this,
when you're in your final moments,
when you're there, and you know you're going,
you know death is coming for you,
when you're in pain,
when you're gasping for breath,
when your heart is stopping and your lungs stop working:
the last thoughts you'll ever have,
you're gonna sit there and think about how you didn't help your family when
you could have.
When you realize that you left your grandson out to dry,
then you're going to really feel like shit.
And you're not gonna be able to justify it.
And you're gonna feel like shit.
In your final moments, you will feel like shit."
And I hung up the phone.
I mean, I might have said some other things,
but that was like basically it.
But I'm not wrong…
…right? It's true, isn't it?
She will feel like shit.
You hear about this type of thing all the time,
parents, when they die, if they're still fighting with the kids,
then when they die, it's like a really awful death.
It's true, right? Isn't it true?

TINA. I've seen all sorts of things.
Everyone is different.

DAUGHTER. …Right.

TINA. …

DAUGHTER. So…
I got a call from her accountant.
Three, four days ago.

TINA. …

DAUGHTER. …

TINA. …

DAUGHTER. And he told me
that she's been writing some checks,
she's been giving someone, someone we don't know,
every week, some…sizable checks.

It seemed a little weird,

and he said he wondered if she was trying to get rid of money.

He said he wondered if by the time she dies there might not be money left.

He said he's seen it happen before.

He said he couldn't say more.

He said he couldn't give me names or specifics or dollar amounts.

He just said, "Watch out."

He just said he thought I should know.

TINA. ...

DAUGHTER. And I said,

I said, "Are you kidding? – I kinda have to know."

And he said, you can't know.

And I said, you need to tell me,

And he said, no I don't.

He said he *couldn't* tell me who it was.

Confidentiality. Client rights and stuff.

And I said, well, what about my rights.

And I said – well I just kinda lost it,

I don't remember what I said, I,

And

And he says,

He says he shouldn't say, but he's going to say so long as I don't say –

TINA. ...

DAUGHTER. sooooo...

I know,

Tina,

I know

TINA. ...

DAUGHTER. I know who you are, and I know that my mother is giving you money.

TINA. ...

DAUGHTER. Are you going to deny it?

TINA. ...No.

DAUGHTER. ...

TINA. ...

DAUGHTER. ...Why?

TINA. Why what?

DAUGHTER. ...

TINA. ...

DAUGHTER. Why is she doing it?
To hurt me?

TINA. …

DAUGHTER. …Does she like you?

TINA. Maybe.

DAUGHTER. She likes you.

TINA. Yes.

DAUGHTER. Why?

TINA. …

DAUGHTER. …

TINA. I touch her.
You know. I touch her body.
I feed her.
I clean her.
I help her breathe.
When you touch someone, feed them, when you clean them, when you help them breathe,
that does something.

DAUGHTER. I'm her daughter.

TINA. And what does that mean?
Yes. You are her daughter.
But I help her live.
It's different, different from you.
I help her live.
…What do you do?

DAUGHTER. …

TINA. What do you do? See, I clean her shit.
I've disimpacted her bowels. Do you know what that is?
Do you

DAUGHTER. I can guess

TINA. Would you do that?
Would you go in there and
do that? Right now?
I doubt you would

DAUGHTER. You're paid to do that

TINA. You're right. I am.
But still. Still.
No disrespect, I'm sorry, but
what do you do?

DAUGHTER. ...

TINA. ...

DAUGHTER. ...

TINA. I am not being mean.
It's just...
And she talks.
And I listen.

DAUGHTER. What does she talk about?

TINA. ...

DAUGHTER. ...

TINA. (*Shrugs, pause, then:*) The weather.
The news.
Sometimes her husband, your father.
How she misses him.
How she wishes he were here. Sometimes.
Sometimes not. Sometimes she curses him.

DAUGHTER. ...What else?

TINA. Dogs.
She talks about dogs.
She likes to talk about dogs.
How she used to breed dogs.
Raise them. Train them.
Attack dogs.
She likes dogs.
And she talks about training them to
attack, and how they wouldn't attack her.
They would never attack her.
They liked her. But they would attack others.
And she seems to like that.
And she talked about how
when she was pregnant with you,
how her husband, your father,
said she had to give up the dogs,
get rid of the dogs,
because the dogs were dangerous,
and that it wasn't safe to have the attack dogs around,
if there was going to be a kid around.
So she got rid of the dogs, sold them all

DAUGHTER. She would have preferred to keep the dogs.

TINA. No.

DAUGHTER. Yes.

TINA. I...

DAUGHTER. See she doesn't talk about me,
or if she does talk about me, it's bad,
or if she does talk about me, it's about how much better everything was before
I was born.

TINA. ...

DAUGHTER. ...

TINA. Once...

DAUGHTER. ...

TINA. One time she talked about you, having you, trying to have you.
She talked about how many times she tried to have a baby
before she had you,
and how you were her last chance,
and how all the others didn't make it,
and how there were a lot of miscarriages

DAUGHTER. ...

TINA. and she was getting older,
and she figured she had one last chance,
and you were her last chance,
and you made it
...and she was happy.
I could tell.
I could tell she was happy.

DAUGHTER. ...

TINA. And you were born.
And you grew up.
And
And she said,
she said to me,
you were the best thing she ever made,
she said, you were the best thing she ever –
she never made anything like you,
you were the

DAUGHTER. ...

TINA. no idea how she made something so wonderful,
no idea, she said that,
she said that to me.

DAUGHTER. ...

TINA. ...

DAUGHTER. (*Skeptical.*) uh-huh

TINA. that's what she, and I dunno,
maybe she was on some morphine at the time

DAUGHTER. …

TINA. …but that's what she said.
I swear.
It's true.
Yeah…

DAUGHTER. …

TINA. …

DAUGHTER. …

TINA. Are you here to get money from me?

DAUGHTER. No.

TINA. Are you sure? I can give you some.
I'd give you a little money. Some of what she gave me,
for you and your kid

DAUGHTER. Keep it.
Keep it, I'm sure you've earned it, whatever you're getting from her,
you've earned it.
You keep the money,
but in return,
there's something I need you to do for me.

TINA. …

DAUGHTER. I came here today,
because I wanted to tell her that I'm sorry,
I wanted to apologize, take some of the blame,
but clearly she won't even let me do that.
I'm blocked from
even, and –
and when we talked on the phone last month,
I know I said some
really bad things,
some really bad things that,
and I can't take them back,
and she's going to die thinking those things I said,
and that's just not right, not for her, and not for me.
I think I fucked up.
And I think I'm an asshole.
I know I'm an asshole – well, so is she, but –
You know, you're right: what have I done? What have I actually done?

Nothing.

And so I need to convince her, show her,

do something to show her that I'm not after her money.

She needs to understand the reason why I said what I said,

but she also needs to understand that it's not about the money,

that it's not really about that.

I don't want her to die feeling shitty,

because if she dies feeling shitty,

I'll feel shitty. And I'll feel the type of shitty feeling that doesn't ever go away.

(DAUGHTER *takes out a sealed manila envelope from her purse.*)

DAUGHTER. …

TINA. …

DAUGHTER. …

TINA. …What's that?

DAUGHTER. It's a letter, a document, something some lawyer drew up, and it's signed, and it's notarized,

and it's all legal and stuff.

TINA. …

DAUGHTER. And it says that I give up all rights to her money.

It says that I give up my inheritance.

I've taken myself out of the will, completely.

TINA. …

DAUGHTER. You'll give her this, and then maybe she'll not see me like she sees me.

TINA. …

DAUGHTER. Will you do this for me?

TINA. …Okay.

DAUGHTER. You promise. You promise you'll do this. Exactly as I

TINA. Yes.

4.

TINA. Scene 4.

In Todd's office.

December 31ˢᵗ.

(TINA *hands* TODD *a wrapped gift.*)

TODD. …What's this?

TINA. …Christmas present.

TODD. ...Oh.

TINA. ...

TODD. I didn't know we were doing that.

TINA. Doing what?

TODD. Giving gifts.

TINA. (*Shrugs.*)

...It's just a Christmas present.

TODD. ...I don't have anything for you.

TINA. That's okay.

I know. I don't –

You've given me a lot already.

You've helped with Maxine.

You've helped me get my character references together, all those papers for the courts.

And I just want to thank you.

TODD. ...

TINA. (*Gestures for* TODD *to open the gift.*)

...

(TODD *opens the gift.*

It's a leather jacket.)

TODD. ...

TINA. ...Try it on.

(TODD *tries it on.*

His demeanor changes, slightly. A little more strut.

He checks himself out.)

Looks good.

TODD. Is it too big?

TINA. Uh-uh.

TODD. ...

TINA. Looks hot, Todd.

TODD. ...

TINA. Bad boy.

TODD. ...

TINA. ...

TODD. Um.

TINA. ...

TODD. Thank you. (*Gesturing to the jacket.*) For this.

TINA. It's nothing

TODD. No, it's

TINA. not even real leather

TODD. oh

TINA. but it looks real, doesn't it. Feels real

TODD. yeah, um,
oh, no, yeah it's definitely nice

TINA. And also

(TINA *takes out an envelope—the letter from the* DAUGHTER.)

TODD. …what's that?

TINA. Maxine's daughter visited on Christmas Eve.

TODD. …Did she see Maxine?

TINA. No. I told her that she didn't want visitors, because I didn't want

TODD. right

TINA. and she was upset about it, at first,
but

TODD. no, but yeah, that was probably smart

TINA. and you know, she's doing that thing

TODD. what thing – ?

TINA. the thing that the kids do when their parents are dying,
where they get all spooked,
and they start regretting everything,
and they get scared that the parent is going to die,
and they haven't made up –
you know: that thing they do.

TODD. …

TINA. The daughter. She wants me to help her and her mother to, uh, reconcile

TODD. Oh.

TINA. because Maxine thinks the daughter just wants her money,
and the daughter knows that Maxine thinks that,
so the daughter went to a lawyer and had him write up something
that says she won't take any of the inheritance.

TODD. *Oh.*

TINA. See.

TODD. I see.
And she

TINA. wants me to give this to Maxine

TODD. she hasn't seen it?

TINA. No.

TODD. You're not going to show it to her, are you?

TINA. I think we should, actually.

I think after we get the 200,000 dollars,

we should give Maxine this letter,

we should give the daughter a chance to reconcile,

This is the right thing to do.

TODD. …

TINA. We're helping Maxine feel like her daughter is killing her

TODD. she already thought that before we got involved

TINA. She did, but

TODD. and you told me that there was no way to convince her otherwise

TINA. Yes, but still, I mean,

what if there was a way that we could

give her what she wants,

be paid for it, and also, take this problem she has with her daughter,

and fix that too

TINA. Will you help me do this?

I will need your help to do this—

to do this right. I will need your help.

Will you help?

TODD. …

TINA. …

TODD. …I don't think this idea is a good idea.

…I think this idea could backfire.

…I think this idea will backfire.

Maxine thinks she's giving you money,

because she thinks that the daughter is trying to kill her,

so if she finds out that the daughter *isn't* trying to kill her,

then she's going to wonder why she gave you the money in the first place.

And she will get upset.

I think this idea of yours could backfire, and if it backfires, it's gonna backfire bad.

TINA. Just listen, Todd, if we

TODD. I see you think that this is the right thing to do.

I understand what you mean,

I think this is all very kind of you,

I admire your, uh –

but I think –

I think you should not let anybody see those papers.

I think you should rip up those papers.

TINA. …

TODD. You should rip up those

TINA. Todd, I can't, it wouldn't be right,

If I don't do this this way,

I'll have a kind of shitty feeling,

a kind of shitty feeling that doesn't go away

TODD. because if this plan backfires,

we might not get the money

TINA. no, we'll give her the papers *after* we've cashed the check

TODD. But if this plan backfires, Maxine might call the police.

She might report you,

there could be an investigation,

we could get into a lot of trouble, if Maxine gets upset,

if Maxine feels betrayed

TINA. she won't

She likes me. A lot.

So much that she refuses to let any of the other nurses see her,

she will only see me.

You see she thinks I'm an angel

TODD. She won't if she finds out you've been lying to her

TINA. no, you don't know her like I know her,

you really don't,

you have to trust me.

Do you trust me?

Do you trust me?

TODD. We've been so careful so far.

We've put a lot of work into

TINA. I know

TODD. I've put a lot of work into this.

I've put a lot money into this.

A lot of my own money.

I paid for Doctor Morris, the good doctor, the one from Orlando,

I've paid for Doctor Morris to come here

two times a week.

And I paid for it out of my own pocket.

And the meds he ordered for her.

I paid for those too.

Toad, we had to pay off Toad to keep Toad quiet about what she saw,

I paid for that. I dealt with that.
And for the past four weeks,
this is all I've been doing,
this is all I've been thinking about,
for the past four weeks –
forget the holidays,
forget Christmas,
forget spending time with my mother on Christmas Day,
because I was here, I was dealing with this.
And I'm happy to do it.
I'm happy to do things for you.
I'm happy to do it, but

TINA. ...

TODD. But if this plan backfires,
everything we've worked for could just go away.
And if this plan backfires,
we could get into a lot of trouble.
You could get into a lot of trouble.
The police could get involved,
there would be an investigation,
the nursing home might even get shut down,
it's true, this is what happens when stuff like this happens,
and you could get into a lot of trouble.
Serious trouble.
And if you get into serious trouble,
you might not be able to return.
You might not be able to come back to the country.
Then I'm left to deal with the fallout alone,
by myself,
and with you gone, the investigators will come to me,
and they'll have a lot of questions for me,
and I'll have to deal with it all on my own.

TINA. ...

TODD. You understand

TINA. it won't backfire, I promise

TODD. but if it does, if on the off-chance it does

TINA. then I won't come back.
I'll get my John Paul,
and John Paul and I, we'll start a new life somewhere else.

TODD. and, what about us?

TINA. us?

TODD. us

TINA. what about "us"?

TODD. You were going to bring John Paul back,
and we were

TINA. we?

TODD. I was going to use some of the money to get a swimming pool and a diving board,
you know, so John Paul can practice his diving and

TINA. ...

TODD. Do you understand?
I had

TINA. ...

TODD. I want you to tear up those papers.
Tear them up.
If you care about me,
you will tear up those papers.

TINA. ...

TODD. I am asking you to tear up those papers.
If you care about me, then

TINA. ...

TODD. ...

TINA. ...

TODD. Please tear up those papers, Tina.
...Please?

TINA. ...

TODD. ...

TINA. ...

TODD. You're not tearing up those papers.

TINA. ...

TODD. I see.
I understand.
You don't care

TINA. Todd, I do care, but in a different way from the way you want me to care.
I keep hearing you talk about "us,"
you keep saying us this and us that,
it's always about this "us" that isn't.
That wasn't. That won't be.
There is no "us."

TODD. yeah, well, you sure act like there is

TINA. no, I

TODD. it's you leading me on.
It's you lying to me.
Is everything you say a lie?
I have to wonder how much of what you've told me is true?
I have to wonder about everything:
what you've told me about Maxine,
what you've told me about her daughter.
I mean, this business with the daughter,
I don't buy it. It doesn't make sense.
I don't even think it's legally possible to relinquish your own inheritance,
I don't think

TINA. I don't know, I'm not a lawyer, Todd

TODD. and even what you've told me about your son,
about your ex-husband, about –
how do I know

TINA. I don't lie about my son

TODD. When *was* the last time you had any contact with John Paul?

TINA. …

TODD. When was the last time – ?

TINA. It's not like he can just pick up a phone

TODD. email

TINA. no, he doesn't have email Todd,
in Haiti, it isn't like it is over here,
in Haiti, it is a big shithole, it's

TODD. A letter? Even just a regular letter?

TINA. He's just a kid.

TODD. A letter—he's a kid, okay—but a letter? He can't send a letter?
To his mother?

TINA. what are – ?

TODD. You make it sound like he's suffering down there,
you make it sound like he's so desperate to be rescued,
but has he even asked you to bring him back?
If he's so unhappy there

TINA. He is, I know

TODD. then why hasn't he gotten in touch with you,
if he misses you so much, why haven't you heard from him.
Have you considered the possibility that he's okay.

That he doesn't need you to come and save him.

That there's nothing to save, that he's actually perfectly happy where he is.

Have you? No. And so here you are, wrecking people's lives,

interfering, making a giant mess,

and it makes me think, it makes me think that

maybe

the *father's* not the bad guy here.

> (TINA *spits in* TODD*'s face. For real, she spits in his face.*)

TINA. Fuck

you.

> (TODD *doesn't wipe. He keeps going.*)

TODD. I think I'm right.

TINA. You little bitch.

TODD. You're irresponsible.

You're manipulative.

You use everyone.

Maxine, me, her daughter,

her daughter, you're using her to make yourself feel better about –

And you use me.

All the time.

There's always something you need from me.

You need me to keep our relationship a secret.

You need me to help you with the Maxine situation.

You need me to get you an indefinite leave.

You need me to be your reference for the custody hearings.

And what do I get? What do I get?

I get nothing. And the moment I ask for something,

you're gone, you're out,

and that's what you're doing now.

You're gonna get what you want from Maxine,

and you're gonna do whatever you need to do to feel like you're an okay person,

and you're off,

you're off to Haiti, and you're leaving me to deal with the mess.

You're leaving me to deal with a mess that might get me fired,

that might even get me arrested.

Yeah go ahead and spit in my face again,

I don't care.

You don't care. I don't care.

You don't care that I've spent money, out of my own pocket,

money I don't have,

And I haven't gotten my cut of the money. Not yet.

For all I know you're just going to take the money and run.

TINA. …

TODD. You treat me like shit.

TINA. …

TODD. You treat me like shit.

> (*Maybe tearing up a little.*)

You treat me like a pile of shit.

TINA. …I do.

TODD. You treat me like shit.

TINA. I do, I'm sorry, I do.

I don't know why, but I do.

TODD. …You called me *a little bitch.*

TINA. I know.

I'm sorry.

I won't ever call you a little bitch again.

I promise.

TODD. …

TINA. …I'm sorry that my heart is not open to you.

It's not.

It's not.

I'm sorry that my heart is not open to you.

I'm sorry

TODD. …

TINA. …but Todd, you knew that.

You knew that.

You knew that my heart was not open to you,

but you just kept on – and I – and you –

> (TODD *wipes away the tears that were maybe there.*
> TINA *takes part of her shirt, and tries to help, tries to wipe the spit away.*
> He *adjusts himself.*
> He *takes a breath.*)

TODD. Okay.

TINA. …

TODD. Here's what it is, this is, this is what's happening:

I'm not going to sign off on your leave.

It's too dangerous, I can't have you just running off like that,

leaving the country, it will raise questions

TINA. If I don't get the leave then

TODD. Then what

TINA. The case will default.

TODD. So it defaults.

TINA. It defaults, I lose.

TODD. Sorry, you'll just have to reschedule

TINA. I'll quit this job before I lose

TODD. No, you're not quitting.
You're staying here.
You're giving me those documents.
We're destroying them.
I'm not gonna let you foul this up.
I'm getting my half.
I'm getting what's due to me.
And if you don't do what I say,
I will notify the Haitian courts of both your employment and character status,
I will tell them what you're like,
that you assaulted me,
I will tell them the truth,
whether you want me to or not —
If you don't do what I say,
I'll make sure you never get your kid back.

TINA. ...

TODD. As it stands, Maxine is dangerous.
She knows too much, too much she could say,
too much that would hurt *both* of us very badly.
It's not safe to leave until Maxine has passed on,
until everything Maxine knows dies with her.
So until then, we keep everything like it is,
you will continue to be Maxine's nurse,
that's how she likes it, that's what she wants,
like you said, she loves you, she adores you,
and that's how we'll keep it.
And you will keep an eye on her,
and I will keep an eye on you.
And when Maxine is gone, then,
I don't care, you can go, you can leave forever,
I don't care. I don't care. But until then.

      (Beat.)

This is it, Tina.
No more.
No more sympathy.

5.

TINA. Scene 5.

20 years later.

December 27, 2030.

Maxine in her bed.

I am a social worker named Candice.

Maxine says

MAXINE. People who have money are preserved.

They get old, they have money, they are preserved.

People who do not have money, they are not preserved.

If one does not get preserved, things get messy.

> (*The actress playing* TINA *plays* CANDICE. *As* CANDICE, *she has no accent.*)

TINA/CANDICE. We want to avoid that.

We want to do this in a way that isn't messy.

MAXINE. ...

CANDICE. I think we can do this in a way that isn't messy.

MAXINE. ...

CANDICE. ...

MAXINE. We'll see.

Things that are firmly rooted are not easily ripped out.

I am firmly rooted.

I have been here for 20 years.

I have grown into this place, and this place has, in turn,

grown around me. We are one.

We are an organism.

Now you,

you don't want me here,

is that right, is that

CANDICE. No

MAXINE. Well you won't say it, but it's true, and I don't mind that it's true –

I heard, I can hear, I can hear into the hallways,

nurses and staff members passing by,

whispering, I can hear them making plans for the party that will happen next week,

when I'm out of here, I know that the entire staff is planning,

a party to which everyone is invited except for me,

a party that will last all night long,

because people are so happy and so relieved that I am finally gone.
But I don't mind not being wanted,
because what matters isn't whether or not you are wanted,
but whether or not you are needed.
And you need me, *needed* me,
needed me for my money. I *had* money.
I had a lot of money, and if I was going to pay to be here,
then you needed me here.
And I cost a lot, but I pay a lot,
and as long as I paid a lot, you didn't care that I cost a lot,
because I paid more than I cost,
and when I paid, you had a place for me.
But with the money gone,
you want me gone.

CANDICE. You're paid through to the 31st, and unfortunately,
you simply don't have the funds to carry you into the next year.

MAXINE. …

CANDICE. But there are

MAXINE. other options
Will they keep me alive?

CANDICE. You can get medical care. Free

MAXINE. Free what

CANDICE. Medical care

MAXINE. For free?

CANDICE. Yes

MAXINE. What—Band-Aids and bedpans?

CANDICE. …

MAXINE. Don't sugarcoat it, sweetie. I was supposed to die a long time ago.
I had a date. They gave me a departure date.
And that date came and I kept on going.
And they said, "Well, it's a miracle."
"You weren't supposed to live. But you're living."
And I kept on going on.
And as time passed, the medicine, the technology,
the machines, they got better, so as I got worse, the machines got better,
which meant, if I was hooked up to the machine, I got better.

CANDICE. …Well. Miracles can still happen

MAXINE. The days of miracles are over.
It's now machines.
As long as you can afford the machine,

you can afford to keep on going on.
When you can't, you don't.
You don't and that's it.

CANDICE. …

MAXINE. Don't fucking sugarcoat it.
You're giving me a death sentence.
You're kicking me out,
and when I'm out, I'm as good as dead.

CANDICE. …

MAXINE. Admit it.

CANDICE. It's expensive to keep someone alive.
You cannot pay for it.
What do you want me to say?

MAXINE. I want you to say
that you're murdering me.

CANDICE. Maxine, at some point everyone passes on.

MAXINE. Tell me something a little less obvious

CANDICE. fact of life, everyone who lives

MAXINE. Here's one, when a dog farts it smells like shit

CANDICE. When you are released

MAXINE. Yes.

CANDICE. You need somewhere to go

MAXINE. Sure, why not

CANDICE. Your house

MAXINE. Sold it.

CANDICE. Yes.

MAXINE. Years ago. Sold it.

CANDICE. So that's not an option

MAXINE. Nope.

CANDICE. But there are other options. The senior living facilities

MAXINE. Homeless shelters.

CANDICE. They're not homeless shelters.

MAXINE. How exactly are they not homeless shelters?
Explain.

CANDICE. …I'm giving you a packet. It has information on the different
senior living

MAXINE. Dying.
Senior dying

CANDICE. living facilities

MAXINE. not going to a facility.

CANDICE. …

MAXINE. We're not talking about this, I'm not looking at anything, I'm not signing anything until I have my family

CANDICE. Your grandson.

MAXINE. My family.

CANDICE. Charley

MAXINE. Yes.

CANDICE. Unfortunately he's

MAXINE. Not here.

CANDICE. Yes.

MAXINE. I'm aware of that.

CANDICE. He was supposed to be here at

MAXINE. Four.

CANDICE. It's already five.

MAXINE. …

CANDICE. He seems to be running late

MAXINE. Again thank you for pointing out the obvious

CANDICE. have another appointment soon

MAXINE. You do

CANDICE. I do

MAXINE. Then go. I don't need you here.

CANDICE. We need to know what's happening to you.

MAXINE. You told me. I'm going to die.
You know what's going to

CANDICE. What do you think is the likelihood
that your grandson will take you in?

MAXINE. …

CANDICE. What do you think is the

MAXINE. (*Shrugs.*)
How should I know?

CANDICE. …

MAXINE. He's not here, is he?
What does that tell us?
I don't know.
That there's traffic?

That my family has abandoned me?

That there's both traffic and that my family has abandoned me?

CANDICE. ...

MAXINE. ...

CANDICE. I'll make the call to the living facility.

We'll get you a spot there.

If anything changes

MAXINE. I do not approve

CANDICE. Maxine.

MAXINE. ...

CANDICE. We don't need your approval.

You understand that.

We don't need your approval.

MAXINE. ...

CANDICE. If anything changes,

we can always cancel the arrangements

(CHARLEY, *played by the actor who played* TODD, *enters.*)

CHARLEY. ...

(MAXINE *notices him.*)

MAXINE. ...

CHARLEY. ...

MAXINE. Well there he is.

There's Charley.

Hello Charley.

CHARLEY. (*A little out of breath.*) Hi Maxine. (*He walks over to her bed, gives her a kiss on the cheek.*)

MAXINE. (*To* CANDICE.) This is Charley.

He is my grandson.

CANDICE. (*Shakes his hand.*) I'm Candice. I'm the social worker working with Maxine.

CHARLEY. Hi.

MAXINE. We were worried you weren't going to show, Charley.

CHARLEY. I got a little lost.

I thought this place was on the other side of I-95

MAXINE. That's fine.

It's understandable.

You don't make it down here all that much

CHARLEY. just had a memory lapse is all.

MAXINE. No, of course, you have so much on your mind.

> (*To* CANDICE.)

He has so much on his mind. He's such a busy person.

> (*To* CHARLEY.)

I saw them mention you on that show

CHARLEY. The

MAXINE. That show on television

CHARLEY. Which one – there were a couple recently that

MAXINE. Oh I don't know –

> (*To* CANDICE.)

They talk about him on the television, he's an important person

CANDICE. What sort of business are you

CHARLEY. Tech, development, that sort of

MAXINE. He's smart.

He's done well.

And at a young age.

And the girlfriend

CHARLEY. Wife

MAXINE. Wife?

CHARLEY. You know about that.

You should know about that.

We sent you a card

MAXINE. The invitation, I don't think I got

CHARLEY. Well it was a card,

because I wasn't sure,

I didn't think you'd be able to

MAXINE. Oh, I see. That's why I was confused: I wasn't invited.

CHARLEY. I mean, seeing as

MAXINE. I'm all hooked up to stuff

CHARLEY. Yes.

MAXINE. Not very mobile

CHARLEY. Right

MAXINE. No, yes, that's considerate of you.

> (*Beat.*)

Although soon I will be a little more mobile

CANDICE. Let me just step in here

MAXINE. Go right ahead

CANDICE. Charley

CHARLEY. Yes?

CANDICE. The situation

MAXINE. He knows the situation, I told him on the phone

CANDICE. just want to make sure we're on the same page

MAXINE. kicking me out next week

CANDICE. We need to know where to transfer her

MAXINE. want to send me to some facility to die

CANDICE. She has either the option of going to a senior living facility

MAXINE. With no medical treatment

CANDICE. They actually do provide basic care

MAXINE. "Basic" means bedpans and Band-Aids.

CANDICE. Or she has the option of going home with you.

CHARLEY. ...

MAXINE. They need us to make a decision.

CHARLEY. Okay

CANDICE. And Charley?

CHARLEY. Yes.

CANDICE. I should also let you know that if she goes home with you, you need to be prepared for the challenges that might arise, and I want to make sure that you're able to handle that.

MAXINE. She means that when I go home with you my whole body is just going to fall apart.

CANDICE. There are certain services she's being provided now that you'll unlikely be able to provide

MAXINE. Shit is going to hit the fan

CANDICE. Family members find it challenging – can find it challenging

MAXINE. It's grotesque

CANDICE. We can help find you support.

MAXINE. I have these tumors along my sides, sides of my torso, along here, on my skin, they're like long bristles, dozens of them, clusters

CANDICE. We can put you in touch with home care providers.

CHARLEY. ...uh-huh.

MAXINE. Of course, Charley...

CHARLEY. ...

MAXINE. There is another option.

CHARLEY. …

MAXINE. I stay.

CHARLEY. You stay.

MAXINE. I stay.

CHARLEY. You stay where?

MAXINE. Here.

CHARLEY. In the nursing home.

MAXINE. If you
were to help me,
stay a little longer.

CHARLEY. …I see.

MAXINE. There is that option.

    (*To* CANDICE.)

Isn't there? There is that option,
course it would mean Friday's party is canceled, but

CANDICE. There is, yes. But that option costs money,
you need to understand, her care is expensive.

MAXINE. But he has money.
You have money.
You're doing well.
You have money.
You did well.
It runs in the family.
He's like his grandfather.
The people in our family do well,
they tend to do well,
most of them…
It skips a generation.

CHARLEY. …

MAXINE. …

CHARLEY. …

CANDICE. Charley.

CHARLEY. Yeah

CANDICE. I want to get an idea of what you're thinking.

CHARLEY. I, uh

CANDICE. You're processing it

CHARLEY. Yeah.

CANDICE. We can take this one step at a time.

MAXINE. (*To* CANDICE.) I thought you had another appointment to get to.

CHARLEY. I just

CANDICE. Yes?

CHARLEY. did not anticipate that this was about arranging for her to have more time here

CANDICE. Right

CHARLEY. was prepared to just discuss the option of

CANDICE. Maxine coming to live with you

CHARLEY. Yes

CANDICE. Right, I had not anticipated this either.
The option of her staying here longer, it seems, is a new option.

MAXINE. Hey, I just figured while we're talking options, might as well

CANDICE. Yes, sure

CHARLEY. I just want to get this straight.

CANDICE. Okay

CHARLEY. (*To* MAXINE.) You're asking me for –
you're asking me to spend, an extremely large sum of money,
to keep you living,
indefinitely.

MAXINE. …Well, I'm not sure I

CHARLEY. Because, that's the thing,

     (*To* CANDICE.)

correct me if I'm wrong,
the way they have it now,
they can just keep people going,
keep them going as long as there's the money to keep them going.
This isn't,
this isn't like it used to be,
where, you know, you get someone specialized care, a good doctor,
and it'll extend their life another six months, a year at most,
or take someone who's in a lot of pain,
and make those final months easier to bear. This is different.
People can live a long time.

MAXINE. …

CHARLEY. So I mean, just being realistic, I could start paying for your care,
and this could be another 10, 15 years, and that's everything.
That's everything I have

MAXINE. You're very concerned with your money.

CHARLEY. I have to be

MAXINE. you're doing well

CHARLEY. That's why I'm doing well.

MAXINE. ...

CHARLEY. I'm thinking about my ability to pay for the things I need, that my wife needs, that our child is going to need, I need to

MAXINE. So it's really just about the money

CHARLEY. It's about my life.

MAXINE. ...And *my* life?

CHARLEY. ...

MAXINE. ...

CHARLEY. Your life is your life.

MAXINE. ...No. No, it's not.
That's the situation we're dealing with,
my life is getting taken away from me.

CHARLEY. ...I understand that you feel that way

MAXINE. Who said anything about feelings. These are facts, grandson

CHARLEY. This is difficult.

CANDICE. This *is* difficult, Maxine, you need to understand

CHARLEY. the thing is that

CANDICE. many people's lives are being affected here

MAXINE. so my life doesn't matter now.
At a certain point, a person's life doesn't matter.

CHARLEY. ...

MAXINE. I'm shocked.
I'm truly shocked.
I'm shocked that you're even thinking of

CHARLEY. Thinking of what?

MAXINE. I paid for your school,
I paid for your college,
I paid so that

CANDICE. Maybe we can table the discussion of continued care,
maybe that's a longer discussion,
maybe we can table that and look at, for the moment,
what's going to happen on the first of the month.

     (*To* CHARLEY.)

In the meantime,

until it's decided whether she'll go on extended care,
you'll be able to take her in? Is that correct?

CHARLEY. That's what I wanted to talk about.

CANDICE. Okay, are there – ?

CHARLEY. I don't …

MAXINE. …

CHARLEY. I don't know if it's a good idea.

MAXINE. …

CANDICE. …

MAXINE. So you're saying "no" to everything.

CHARLEY. You said yourself, you're in bad shape.
Maybe it's better that you be somewhere
where there's a professional

MAXINE. Bullshit.

CANDICE. Maxine

MAXINE. (*To* CANDICE.) You just said that professional home care can
be arranged –
You said this, didn't you. I'm not making things up am I?

CANDICE. …Yes.
You are correct. A visiting nurse can be arranged.

MAXINE. So I don't see what the

CHARLEY. just not sure it's the best idea.

MAXINE. …

CHARLEY. …

MAXINE. …Is this punishment?

CANDICE. Maxine, I don't think anybody here

MAXINE. (To CANDICE.) Fuck off

CANDICE. okay

MAXINE. (*To* CHARLEY.) Is this punishment?
Is this punishment for something?
This feels like punishment.
The way you – this feels like punishment,
something in this feels like –

CHARLEY. It's not punishment.

MAXINE. You're not angry with me?

CHARLEY. No.

MAXINE. …It's just that it feels like it's not you that's talking, feels like
someone else

CHARLEY. Who?

MAXINE. very hostile

CHARLEY. My mother?

MAXINE. Did you tell her you were coming to see me?

CHARLEY. …

MAXINE. I see.

CHARLEY. I don't keep secrets from my mother if that's what you're asking

MAXINE. I wasn't asking, but that's good to know.

CHARLEY. …

MAXINE. Are you scared – ?

CHARLEY. Of what?

MAXINE. Of what your mother's going to say if you take me in.
She doesn't want you to take me in.
She doesn't want you to help me.

CHARLEY. I don't want to be in the middle here

MAXINE. Well you are. You are in the middle.
You were born—you're in the middle.
Now you need to be a grown up. Be an adult.
Time to grow up, Charley.
This is your responsibility now.
You're not your mother's child anymore.
You're an adult.
Besides, it looks like you're already taking sides.

CHARLEY. No sides are being taken.

MAXINE. You don't take me in, that means you're siding with her, I don't know what else could

CHARLEY. This is my choice, based on

MAXINE. what

CHARLEY. my needs, my family's needs

MAXINE. I'm family

CHARLEY. based on

MAXINE. I don't want to hear it.
No.
I don't want to hear it.
You can go.
Go. Please.
Go now.
Candice. Social worker lady.

Take him out.

I don't want his help

CANDICE. We should try to

MAXINE. or have I lost that right too?

Do I have to be subjected to any person who decides to come here and

CHARLEY. Okay. That's fine.

I'll go. You want me to go, I'll go.

Is that really what you want?

MAXINE. …

CHARLEY. Is that really what you want?

MAXINE. I want you to be direct with me.

I want you to tell me what's really going on here.

CHARLEY. You're

MAXINE. what

CHARLEY. just so

MAXINE. what

CHARLEY. *awful* to my mother.

It's true. You were. You still are

MAXINE. and that's why I deserve to die?

CHARLEY. That's why you don't deserve my help.

MAXINE. What have I done?

What have I done? Name one thing – one concrete –

other than maybe saying that she tried to kill me

CHARLEY. that's a good example

MAXINE. I only repeated what the nurse told me

CHARLEY. you can't possibly believe

MAXINE. I was being threatened, I was being extorted,

this nurse told me that your mother was paying her to

CHARLEY. don't want to hear it

MAXINE. I was deceived, I was deceived by a horrible person,

it was the nurse, she deceived me, she tried to kill me,

she did, it's true, and they arrested her, and they deported her,

or something, I don't know, it doesn't matter

CHARLEY. My mother tried to be good to you

MAXINE. when

CHARLEY. we would come to visit you here

MAXINE. never visited

CHARLEY. refused to see us

MAXINE. no, I never

CHARLEY. Maxine, I know you were awful to my mother,
because of the way she feels, because I *see* the effect you had on her.
I say your name, and I can see it in her eyes.
I say your name, and she cries.
I say your name, and

MAXINE. Charley.

CHARLEY. …

MAXINE. You know how your mother is.
You know she has a way of exaggerating.
She sees only what she wants to see,
and when you see only what you want to see,
you have a way of making it so.
And so you know she's like that, you know.
You've seen it happen.
You don't need to say anything: you know.

CHARLEY. …

MAXINE. But Charley, let me be clear, let me be very clear:
She wasn't a bad person.
Of course not. She was my daughter and I loved her.
Of course I did.
I loved her.
I loved her, but she made it so difficult.
She just couldn't accept how much I cared for her,
how much I sacrificed for her.
She twisted it all around, in her head,
she twisted it around, so that neither one of us knew which way was up,
and maybe I'm to blame.
Maybe it's my fault.
I raised her wrong.
I was too lenient. Too nice.
Too permissive.
It's just not good, not a good way to raise a child,
but I wanted her to like me so much,
a mother wants to be loved,
a father wants to be loved,
you'll learn. When you have your kid,
you'll learn, and there's nothing that hurts more,
than to have a child and have that child think that everything you do is wrong,

and that every single thing you do to show that you care,
the child interprets it exactly the opposite way.
Exactly the opposite of how you mean it.
And it just, just makes your head spin.
You have to remember that she rejected *me*.
You have to remember that. It wasn't the other way around.
I did not want to come here.
I had nowhere to go.
Your mother lived halfway across the country.
I asked her to come help me. I was all on my own.
I had no one. I asked her to come help.
She said she had you and she was busy and she had her job to worry about.
She said she couldn't just uproot everything.
She said she needed to take care of you.
I said, we could've worked it out. We could have found a way to work things out.
I could help her and she could help me.
And she said no.
And I said okay. I'll fend for myself.
Forget that I cared for her, her whole life.
And then I got sick.
And I wasn't able to care for myself.
And I had nowhere to go,
so I said, well, fuck it, send me to the place where they send abandoned old farts,
and so they sent me here,
like someone who doesn't have a family.

CHARLEY. …

MAXINE. …I don't think what she did was right.

CHARLEY. …

MAXINE. Do you agree? Do you agree that it was the right decision?

CHARLEY. …

MAXINE. Do you? – I really want to know.
I want to know, so I know.
Because maybe I'm wrong.
And if I'm wrong, then I want to know that I'm wrong.
If you were in the position, if your mother needed you –
Now imagine deciding you didn't care, imagine seeing your mother in need,
imagine seeing your mother sick and not even bothering to visit her.
Imagine that.
Would you do that?

CHARLEY. …

MAXINE. Would you?

Could you do that?

I know what you're thinking.

I know you. I know you that well.

No, you couldn't do that, you couldn't do that to your mother?

Answer me. Tell me, could you

CHARLEY. No

MAXINE. Then I know, I know you agree with me

that she should not have done what she did.

I know that you know

what is right

and what is wrong.

CHARLEY. …I

MAXINE. You know that what she did is wrong.

You know, you agree, you see

CHARLEY. in some ways

MAXINE. Yes, in some ways.

Possibly. She was wrong.

CHARLEY. …

MAXINE. But let's forget that. That's the past and what's past is past.

Right now. I want to have the chance to make it right.

To show, to do a better job of showing her that I do care about her,

that I do love her.

Can you see that?

Can you see that I do really love your mother?

I want to see my grandson.

Live long enough to see my great-grandson or granddaughter born.

Just long enough to sit in a room,

at Christmas,

next Christmas,

to make it to next Christmas,

with you and your wife—I've never even met her—

and your new child, my great-grandchild,

and your mother, all of us together,

one last time.

CHARLEY. …

MAXINE. Please, Charley.

Please.

Please help me.

CHARLEY. …

MAXINE. …

CHARLEY. …

MAXINE. Please.

CHARLEY. I'll see what I can do.

I'll talk to my wife.

I'll talk to my mother.

We'll talk.

We'll all talk.

We'll figure this out.

We'll figure something out.

MAXINE. You promise?

CHARLEY. …I promise.

MAXINE. Thank you.

Thank you.

CHARLEY. I should go, I have a plane to catch.

MAXINE. Yes, go catch your plane.

CHARLEY. Okay

MAXINE. Thank you.

CHARLEY. Okay.

MAXINE. Thank you, Charley.

And please, tell your mother I love her.

I miss her.

And I want to make things right.

CHARLEY. Okay.

MAXINE. …

CHARLEY. Goodbye.

(*To* CANDICE.)

Thank you for your help.

I'll be in touch.

CANDICE. Alright.

I'll walk you out.

CHARLEY. (*To* MAXINE.) Goodbye.

(CHARLEY *and* CANDICE *exit.*
Beat.
MAXINE *looks at the side table. Looks at the radio sitting on it.*
The side table is just close enough, if she just reaches…
From her bed, MAXINE *reaches, she reaches for the radio, it's* precarious…
…and just barely switches on the radio.

"Jesu, Joy of Man's Desiring" begins to play.
A period of silence. MAXINE *alone. Alone with music.*
MAXINE *alone. Music.*
CANDICE *re-enters.*)

MAXINE. ...

CANDICE. He'll be in touch with me.

MAXINE. ...

CANDICE. I'll let you know what gets worked out and we'll

MAXINE. Just a pile of lies.

CANDICE. I'm sorry, what?

MAXINE. That

CANDICE. What

MAXINE. This

CANDICE. I'm not sure I

MAXINE. follow me

CANDICE. No, I'm

MAXINE. It's okay.
You don't need to follow me.
I hardly follow me.

CANDICE. You seem upset.

MAXINE. ...

CANDICE. I don't understand, that seemed to go well

MAXINE. No

CANDICE. He said

MAXINE. What

CANDICE. he's going to

MAXINE. What

CANDICE. consider

MAXINE. Nothing. He said nothing.

CANDICE. ...

MAXINE. No one does something for nothing.

CANDICE. ...

MAXINE. I know.
I know I'm never going to hear from him again.
Charley. I know he's not going to help me.
I know.
I know it.
No one does something for nothing.

He was just letting me down easy.
I know.
I think I know.
I don't know.
CANDICE. ...
MAXINE. Just a pile of lies.
And maybe you're right and I'm wrong,
and I didn't see what I just saw,
who knows. I don't know.
I don't know who's telling the truth.
I don't know.
Everyone lies.
I don't know, I know.
Can't know, who knows.
I'm scared to die.
CANDICE. ...
MAXINE. ...
CANDICE. ...
MAXINE. ...
CANDICE. ...
MAXINE. ...
CANDICE. ...

> (*Music keeps playing.*
> *Blackout.*)

End of Play

HERO DAD
by Laura Jacqmin

Copyright © 2012 by Laura Jacqmin. All rights reserved. CAUTION: Professionals and amateurs are hereby warned that *Hero Dad* is subject to a royalty. It is fully protected under the copyright laws of the United States of America and of all countries covered by the International Copyright Union (including the Dominion of Canada and the rest of the British Commonwealth), the Berne Convention, the Pan-American Copyright Convention and the Universal Copyright Convention, as well as all countries with which the United States has reciprocal copyright relations. All rights, including professional, amateur stage rights, motion picture, recitation, lecturing, public reading, radio broadcasting, television, video or sound recording, all other forms of mechanical or electronic reproduction, such as CD-ROM, CD-I, information storage and retrieval systems and photocopying, and the rights of translation into foreign languages, are strictly reserved. Particular emphasis is laid upon the matter of readings, permission for which must be secured from the Author's agent in writing.

Required royalties must be paid every time this play is performed before any audience, whether or not it is presented for profit and whether or not admission is charged.

All inquiries concerning rights, including amateur rights, should be addressed to: William Morris Endeavor Entertainment, 1325 Avenue of the Americas, New York, NY 10019, ATTN: Derek Zasky. 212-903-1396.

BIOGRAPHY

Laura Jacqmin was the winner of the 2008 Wendy Wasserstein Prize, a $25,000 award to recognize an emerging female playwright. Her play *January Joiner* premiered in Long Wharf Theatre's 2012-2013 season, dir. Eric Ting. *Two Lakes, Two Rivers* was workshopped at the 2012 O'Neill National Playwrights Conference (commissioned by the Goodman Theatre; further developed during the Royal Court Theatre's 2011 International Residency). She was the Faith Broome Playwright-in-Residence at University of Oklahoma in Fall 2012.

Other plays include *Ski Dubai* (Steppenwolf Theatre Company), *Look, We Are Breathing* (Sundance Theatre Lab), and *Dental Society Midwinter Meeting* (which enjoyed a sold-out run with Chicago Dramatists/At Play in 2010, and was remounted at 16th Street Theater and Theater on the Lake in 2011). Her short play *Hero Dad* (a finalist for the 2012 Heideman Award) premiered in the 2012 Humana Festival of New American Plays at Actors Theatre of Louisville.

Her work has been produced and developed by LCT3, Atlantic Theater Company, Roundabout Underground, Vineyard Theatre, Cape Cod Theatre Project, Ars Nova, Second Stage, Lark Theatre, Chicago Dramatists (where she is a Resident Playwright), and more. From 2007 to 2008, she was a contributing writer for *The Onion A.V. Club* and *A.V. Club Chicago*. Jacqmin was a member of the inaugural 2010-2011 Playwrights' Unit at the Goodman Theatre. She has been commissioned by South Coast Repertory, the Goodman Theatre, Arden Theater Company, InterAct Theatre, Victory Gardens Theater/National New Play Network (NNPN), and the Ensemble Studio Theatre/Alfred P. Sloan Foundation Science and Technology Project. B.A. Yale University; M.F.A. Ohio University.

ACKNOWLEDGMENTS

Hero Dad premiered at the Humana Festival of New American Plays in March 2012. It was directed by Sarah Rasmussen with the following cast:

FEMALE TENANT/FEMALE JOGGER/
SEATED FEMALE .... Marianna McClellan
VINCENT .... William Connell
BILLY ....Alex Moggridge
MIKE.. Mike DiSalvo

and the following production staff:

Scenic Designer..Tom Burch
Costume Designer.................................... Lindsay Chamberlin

Lighting Designer..Nick Dent
Sound Designer.. Paul Doyle
Properties Designer..Mark Walston
Wig Designer...Hannah Wold
Production Stage Manager.....................................Kathy Preher
Dramaturg..Hannah Rae Montgomery
Casting..Zan Sawyer-Dailey

Production Manager...Michael Whatley
Production Assistant .... Katie Shade

CHARACTERS

FEMALE TENANT (Michelle) / FEMALE JOGGER (Sarah) /
    SEATED FEMALE (Daisy)
VINCENT
BILLY
MIKE

A NOTE ABOUT THE PLAYING OF THE PLAY

MICHELLE, SARAH and DAISY are separate characters. Whatever you think will help in the differentiation is fine. Maybe one prop to switch to, or one costume piece for each different vignette, but nothing overly fussy. None of these snap into realistic, naturalistic scenes—when one of the men has an interaction with the woman, they face out and speak out. Though one of these interactions is a phone conversation, don't use actual cell phones, or mime phones. The audience will get it.

When BILLY and FEMALE JOGGER refer to the "kid," just plant him somewhere in the audience. Let him be a little far away, but still present.

None of the men can come across as overtly awful. None hit on her in a gross way: just let the language communicate their intentions. Don't play the jokes in an overly broad way—just let them happen in as honest a way as possible.

Marianna McClellan and Mike DiSalvo
in *Hero Dad*

36th Humana Festival of New American Plays
Actors Theatre of Louisville, 2012
Photo by Alan Simons

HERO DAD

BILLY, MIKE, *and* VINCENT *enter. They stand in a line, apart from each other: one in the middle, one on either side, at the opposite ends of the stage. They face out.*

VINCENT. (*Not angry; he just doesn't get it:*)
Okay, yes, I got your note
But it was sort of incoherent
Like:
"There are little footsteps there is nothing but the sound of little footsteps all the time the noise coming from above and into my apartment, it is the sound of little footsteps" and just so you know
That's my *daughter.*
That's my *daughter.*
That sound of little footsteps.
I get her two weeks a year.
And in case you wanted to know, her name is Veronica.
And I only get her two weeks a year because her mother lives in South Carolina and you're leaving me notes about *footsteps?*

(FEMALE TENANT *enters. She speaks out, but she's speaking to* VINCENT. VINCENT *is sort of semi almost flirtatious,* FEMALE TENANT *is on the verge of – something potentially dangerous.*)

FEMALE TENANT. I wouldn't do this except I have the bar exam tomorrow. I'm taking the bar exam tomorrow.

VINCENT. So you're a lawyer?

FEMALE TENANT. *After I take the bar exam,* yeah, maybe.

VINCENT. It's Michelle, right?

FEMALE TENANT. Yeah, Michelle. It's just, maybe if she wasn't wearing her shoes?

VINCENT. She's learning to walk Michelle
(Wow, that's a pretty name)
So
The shoes make it easier. They provide structure. Support.

FEMALE TENANT. Or maybe if you had a rubber mat? The kind that goes under rolling office chairs? Like a mat?
Made of plastic.
And she could practice walking on the mat.

VINCENT. I'm so sorry, but I don't have a mat like that.

FEMALE TENANT. I wouldn't – I'm sorry – I'm honestly really sorry I'm freaking out like this

But

I have to be up at four-thirty in the morning? Or I have to leave the house at four-thirty in the morning, actually? And it's ten o'clock at night? And your daughter, who is a toddler, is up at ten o'clock at night?

And it's just that there's a really strict noise policy in our lease and that's probably fifty percent of the reason I moved into this building, right there, that noise policy, and it *especially* applies after ten o'clock and *please* can you just take her shoes off?

I don't think it's a big deal for me to ask you to take her shoes off.

VINCENT. (*Still not angry:*) See: I only have her two weeks a year. So if we wanna stay up past ten o'clock at night, and really make the most of every second of every minute of every day during those two weeks: we're going to. You know?

Her mom lives in *South Carolina.*

FEMALE TENANT. So why don't you live in South Carolina?

> (VINCENT *is struck dumb for a moment.* FEMALE TENANT *turns, is gone.*)

BILLY. Oh shit, we totally did not mean to bounce that ball in your direction. He's just so – so *boisterous,* you know?

He takes after his dad.

> (*Woman turns, becomes* FEMALE JOGGER. *She jogs in place. She speaks out.*)

FEMALE JOGGER. Sorry, were you saying something? I had my earbuds in.

BILLY. My kid totally threw that ball at you. It was a complete accident.

FEMALE JOGGER. Well. Not if he threw it at me, it wasn't.

So was it?

BILLY. He's just kiddin' around. He's such a kidder. He takes after his dad.

FEMALE JOGGER. He doesn't actually look like he's

Um

Yeah, now he's crying.

BILLY. She knows it was an accident, buddy! She knows! Hey, what's your name? C'mon, what's your name?

FEMALE JOGGER. Sarah.

BILLY. Please, Sarah, tell him you know it was an accident.

> (*Beat.*)

See, Sarah knows it was an accident!

FEMALE JOGGER. He's saying "mommy."
Where's his mommy?

BILLY. Don't get me started.
She lives in Hoboken. She's *so* Hoboken, you know? And I'm so *not*.
We don't really – you know. We didn't really, you know.
Nah, I've just got this little guy on weekends.
On some weekends.
Maybe if his mom didn't live out in *Hoboken* –
Her choice is, you know, totally her choice. Her decision. As per yoozh.

FEMALE JOGGER. Yeah.
Well, I'm happy to bring his ball back. But my heart rate is dropping, actually –

BILLY. God, this is embarrassing, but –
Could you like
Hold him?
For a little?
It's just, he likes the ladies.
He likes women. A woman's touch. A woman's soft caress.
He takes after his dad.
No but seriously don't go yet, it's just that he's been so fussy and who knows
what kids want, you know?
Like who knows?

FEMALE JOGGER. I think he wants his mommy.

BILLY. *Well*, his mommy doesn't come and get him until Sunday at noon, so
he's stuck with me until then, you know?

FEMALE JOGGER. Yeah.
He's stuck.

BILLY. (*This will hang there ever-so-briefly, like a fart.*) He takes after his dad.
I mean.
Anyway.

     (*They both flinch.*)

Wow, that's loud. Yeah, he screams like that sometimes.

FEMALE JOGGER. How do you get him to stop?

BILLY. I mean…usually I just wait.
And he gets tired.
And then he stops.
He has to get tired first.

FEMALE JOGGER. He's a really good-looking boy.

BILLY. (*Beams.*) Yeah. Thanks!
Wow. Thank you.

     (*Looking harder at her.*)

Listen – I don't know if you maybe feel like getting a beer or something? Not now, obviously, because I'm with this little champ, but maybe Sunday brunch? Like 12:30? I should be totally free and clear by 12:30.

FEMALE JOGGER. I don't think so.

BILLY. No?

FEMALE JOGGER. I don't think so.
Good luck.

BILLY. Yeah.

(FEMALE JOGGER *"jogs" off, turns away*.)

Fuckin' bitch.

(*To the "kid:"*)

Shhhhhhh. Shhhhhhhhhh. Shhhhhhhhhh.

MIKE. Okay, Daisy, this is the fifth message I'm leaving.
I don't know if you're not getting reception, or just –
I'd really appreciate it if you'd call me.
Oh shit, you're on the other line. Um. Hold on.

(FEMALE JOGGER *turns out, becomes* SEATED FEMALE.)

Are you in the office?

SEATED FEMALE. Yeah.

MIKE. You're waiting in the office?

SEATED FEMALE. Yeah.

MIKE. Like, you're about to go in?

SEATED FEMALE. I mean, I paid. I paid and first I sat in one waiting room and now I'm in a different waiting room but there's like a line.
So I'm not in yet, but I'm in line to go in.

MIKE. How much was it?

SEATED FEMALE. Like $450. Plus I paid fifteen for Valium. They charge a hundred-fifty for general anesthesia but I can't take the subway after general anesthesia and I'm here by myself
So.

MIKE. I thought you said it was like seven hundred.

SEATED FEMALE. That's for the pills. They can like insert one pill here and then you put in more at home and then it just happens like in the toilet.

MIKE. Four hundred fifty.

SEATED FEMALE. Plus fifteen for Valium.

MIKE. So that's not a lot of money to lose, really.
I mean, it's real money, but it's not –
Could you ask for your money back?

SEATED FEMALE. Um.

> (*Beat.*)

Um.

I already took the Valium.

MIKE. No, but if you just told them you'd changed your mind, could they void the transaction or whatever?

SEATED FEMALE. Um...probably not?

MIKE. Okay.

The thing is. Daisy.

I disagree with this. With what you're doing.

> (SEATED FEMALE *stares, straight ahead. A sort of quiet rage. But out of control. But it isn't coming out just yet.*)

SEATED FEMALE. Okay.

Okay.

MIKE. So what if we're not in love? With each other?

SEATED FEMALE. I mean, the thing is I'm not in love with you.

I'm sorry for that.

We talked about all this, I'm sorry for that.

MIKE. Just because we don't love each other doesn't mean we can't have a kid together.

SEATED FEMALE. I think it does mean that, actually.

MIKE. I mean, the vision I have of myself? As a dad?

I mean

I have this vision

I have *always* had this vision

I mean

Going to the park and we'd mess around in those tire swings or in those rings of tires they have on the ground like an obstacle course and I could push the stroller and go in to get coffee and we could walk around me pushing the stroller and drinking the coffee and he the kid or she whichever it turned out to be the kid would be smiling at me and I would have nicknames for him I would have a dozen nicknames for him and we would have nicknames for each other and there would be teaching him about how to serve a volleyball and swimming at the pool the ways kids swim with pool noodles and screaming all over the place and running and me telling him not to run and that baby food cooker thing we saw in a store window once and we both said how cool it would be to have that baby food cooker thing even if there was no baby around and miniature Nikes or miniature any kind of shoes and how cool that would be and why won't you give me a chance to do those things?

If you gave me a chance.

You could give me a chance and we'd work it out, I know we would.

SEATED FEMALE. How would we work it out? Would we live together, would we –

MIKE. I'm saying this is all stuff we can figure out if you leave that waiting room and go back through that other waiting room and get it voided and maybe come meet me and we can figure it out.

SEATED FEMALE. I just think that the vision you have of what you could be, that's hard, that's really hard, and those things you just said, those things were really wonderful but Mike, when I told you, you didn't say those things, when I told you –

MIKE. That's not even fair, that's not even fair –

SEATED FEMALE. No, Mike, when I told you, you said "Fuck that."

And you left the room and you threw up.

And you left.

You left.

You left.

I think? If you were to be honest? With me? And yourself? You'd look at that vision of yourself? Of yourself as a dad? And in the actual version of that picture you'd actually just spend most of the time leaving. And I'd spend most of the time staying. And being left. And our –

And the kid? The kid? Would also stay. And therefore be left.

It would be left.

You would have left.

And that's? And honestly? And that's?

No. Okay? I feel *very* strongly, I feel *very* strongly that that is what it would *actually* be versus what you *think* it would be, or *hope* it would be, or *dream* it could be, and right now we can't think about dreams, we have to think about me and my debit card transaction and I'm here and you said "Fuck that" and I'm here now and you're wherever you are now and we're not in love and we'll never be in love, we never were to begin with and I don't think we ever would have, and it isn't fair, it's not fair, this whole thing is the exact fucking opposite of fair, but please don't make it unfair for somebody else, please don't spread this disease of unfairness any further, especially not to some helpless innocent thing, and please just think about the fact that this is forever, this is forever, and really this lack of foreverness that I am about to give you is a gift.

It is a gift.

That I present to you.

And it is a very expensive gift.

And it is one I will always remember.

And let that be enough.

(Beat.)

They're calling my name.

MIKE. C'mon.

Just –

I just think we could figure it out!

SEATED FEMALE. I'm not even supposed to be on my phone in here.

(SEATED FEMALE *stands, exits.*)

VINCENT. I mean ...

How could I even *be* in South Carolina?

I couldn't.

My daughter's mom can, and great for her, you know.

But not me.

That is not for me.

South Carolina is just not for me.

It was never meant to be, you know?

BILLY. I'm gonna count to five, and then you've gotta stop screaming.

One.

Two.

Three.

Four.

One more. Just one more. Just one more and then you've gotta stop screaming.

(Beat.)

Five.

See? Look at us. Nobody's screaming here, right? Which means everything's fine.

If nobody's screaming, everything's a-okay.

MIKE. Okay, so this is like the sixth message at this point.

I guess you went in. I mean, you said they called you, so I guess you went in.

Let me know if you need – anything.

Um –

Cab fare or anything. I mean, if you take a cab, I'll pay for it. I don't mind doing that. Not at all.

I'm just gonna be hanging out at home tonight if you wanna talk. Watching a movie or something. We could totally – hang out! I know it's been a while, but.

Cool.

Let me know.

Okay?

Okay.

Bye.

(MIKE *breathes a sigh of relief. A small one. But still.*
MIKE, BILLY *and* VINCENT *look out. Beat.*
Blackout.)

End of Play

MICHAEL VON SIEBENBURG MELTS THROUGH THE FLOORBOARDS
by Greg Kotis

Copyright © 2012 by Greg Kotis. All rights reserved. CAUTION: Professionals and amateurs are hereby warned that *Michael von Siebenburg Melts Through the Floorboards* is subject to a royalty. It is fully protected under the copyright laws of the United States of America and of all countries covered by the International Copyright Union (including the Dominion of Canada and the rest of the British Commonwealth), the Berne Convention, the Pan-American Copyright Convention and the Universal Copyright Convention, as well as all countries with which the United States has reciprocal copyright relations. All rights, including professional, amateur stage rights, motion picture, recitation, lecturing, public reading, radio broadcasting, television, video or sound recording, all other forms of mechanical or electronic reproduction, such as CD-ROM, CD-I, information storage and retrieval systems and photocopying, and the rights of translation into foreign languages, are strictly reserved. Particular emphasis is laid upon the matter of readings, permission for which must be secured from the Author's agent in writing.

Required royalties must be paid every time this play is performed before any audience, whether or not it is presented for profit and whether or not admission is charged.

All inquiries concerning rights, including amateur rights, should be addressed to: Paradigm Talent Agency, 360 Park Avenue South, 16th Floor, New York, NY 10010, ATTN: William Craver. 212-897-6400.

ABOUT *MICHAEL VON SIEBENBURG MELTS THROUGH THE FLOORBOARDS*

This article first ran in the January/February 2012 issue of Inside Actors, *Actors Theatre of Louisville's subscriber newsletter, and is based on conversations with the playwright before rehearsals for the Humana Festival production began.*

Greg Kotis has a bone to pick with conventional vampire wisdom. "It's based on the idea that you have these teeth and you drink a couple of tablespoons of blood and suddenly you've sucked out someone's life essence," he explains. "You know what? That's not enough. You have to *eat*." Welcome to the glorious and terrible world of Michael von Siebenburg, a dashing Austrian baron who has been indulging his epicurean proclivity for human flesh for the last, oh, five hundred years.

A well-honed cannibalistic instinct isn't the only quality that distinguishes the title character of *Michael von Siebenburg Melts Through the Floorboards* from his vampiric colleagues who inhabit literature, lore, and pop culture. Kotis' play dispenses with Gothic romantic intrigue and opts instead for silly, irreverent comedy that evokes the existential dilemmas of modern-day living. Sure, we all struggle to reconcile our daily routines with our larger sense of purpose, Kotis suggests, but most of us haven't been on the same strict diet for five centuries. Contemporary urban living can be a grind, and when there's literally no end in sight—well, those big questions just loom even larger.

The idea came to Kotis during a 1995 visit to Romania, just a few years after dictator Nicolae Ceausescu had been overthrown. Next door, a war was raging in the former Yugoslavia. To Kotis, the whole Balkan region felt mired in violence in a way that was more pervasive and immediate than anything he had ever experienced. It got him thinking about the long history of bloodshed that has been woven into the legacy of every world empire: from the Romans and Ottomans, who once dominated the same ground on which he stood, to his own United States of America. "I started to wonder— is there a brutal nature at the core of everybody? Is there a thin line between the civility of how we live during times of prosperity and the brutality that we associate with the past?" He wondered what medieval warriors might make of the contemporary world. How would they fit in? How would they stand out? And so Michael von Siebenburg was born.

Michael is a wealthy baron in 15th century Austria who joins his countrymen and warriors throughout Christendom in their volunteer effort to defend Constantinople from Turkish attack. The city falls to the Muslim hordes, but the Austrian warriors who survive stumble upon a very important discovery: human meat, specially prepared, might just be the unlikely elixir of life. Add a little paprika and some cardamom, and eternal life really isn't so hard to stomach.

Centuries later, Michael and his old friend Sammy are still kicking around, and they've settled down in an unnamed American city. Their predatory practice is now a well-oiled routine: Sammy, the wingman, coaxes attractive young women into romantic dinners with his handsome friend, and Michael wines and dines the ladies before turning them into the next day's sustenance. It's an endless smorgasbord of first dates with especially high stakes (no pun intended). But after a half-millennium of thriving teamwork, Michael and Sammy suddenly find themselves struggling to stave off the ominous threat of famine. Modern women, it seems, are more savvy and less exploitable than their predecessors, Michael's nosy landlady is growing increasingly suspicious, and a pair of ethereal visitors from Michael's past— each with their own agenda—have him suddenly wondering if immortality is as sustainable as it's cracked up to be.

As Kotis explores contemporary America through the eyes of his hungry, old-world protagonist, he also winks slyly at the antiquated beliefs to which 21st century inhabitants sometimes cling. He emphasizes feminism and changing gender roles as one of the "sharpest expressions of modernity in the West," and he suggests that Michael may not be the only man who finds himself stymied by his own medieval ideas about gender. "There are plenty of men who feel at a loss," he says. "Women are catching up and surpassing them. There are privileges and positions that they take for granted...but they still have to make their way in this modern world." The provocative relationship between violence and religious fundamentalism is another point of interest, and Kotis offers us a pair of cannibals who ply their trade in the name of Christendom. "They have no problem reconciling their Christianity with killing other people," he says. All that violence, he suggests, is "just a way—I hope a fun way—to remind us that our Judeo-Christian culture can't really point fingers at other religions (like Islam)."

When the past and present collide in *Michael von Siebenburg Melts Through the Floorboards*, they do so with devastatingly comedic consequences. Michael's efforts to reconcile his age-old hunger and his brand-new conscience are funny, winsome, and alarmingly poignant. "I think it's about exploring the idea that the past lives with us always, and there's no freedom from it, ever," Kotis muses. His play is many things: a meditation on obsolescence, a bloody valentine to American progress, and a hilarious elegy for the glory days of vampire cannibalism. Mostly, though, it's about the struggle to stay hungry and relevant—a pursuit that might feel familiar to anyone who belongs to the delicious human race.

—Zach Chotzen-Freund

BIOGRAPHY

Greg Kotis is the author of many plays and musicals including *Michael von Siebenburg Melts Through the Floorboards, Yeast Nation* (Book/Lyrics), *The Boringest Poem in the World, The Truth About Santa, Pig Farm, Eat the Taste, Urinetown* (Book/Lyrics, for which he won an Obie Award and two Tony® Awards), and *Jobey and Katherine*. His work has been produced and developed in theatres across the country and around the world, including Actors Theatre of Louisville, American Conservatory Theater, American Theater Company, the Eugene O'Neill National Playwrights Conference (Writer in Residence 2012), Henry Miller's Theatre (Broadway), Manhattan Theatre Club, New York Stage and Film, Perseverance Theatre, Roundabout Theatre Company, Soho Rep, South Coast Repertory, and The Old Globe, among others. Kotis is a member of the Neo-Futurists, the Cardiff Giant Theater Company, the American Society of Composers, Authors, and Publishers (ASCAP), and the Dramatists Guild, and was a 2010-2011 Lark Play Development Center Playwrights Workshop Fellow. He grew up in Wellfleet, Massachusetts and now lives in Brooklyn with his wife Ayun Halliday, his daughter India, and his son Milo.

ACKNOWLEDGMENTS

Michael von Siebenburg Melts Through the Floorboards premiered at the Humana Festival of New American Plays in March 2012. It was directed by Kip Fagan with the following cast:

OTTO..John Ahlin
MICHAEL VON SIEBENBURG.....................Rufus Collins
JANE/OFFICER LEE* ....Ariana Venturi
SAMMY ....Micah Stock
APRIL/OFFICER CLAIRE* ....Laura Heisler
MARIA/ANGELA.....................................Caralyn Kozlowski
MRS. ROSEMARY..Rita Gardner

and the following production staff:

Scenic Designer..Michael B. Raiford
Costume Designer ....Lorraine Venberg
Lighting Designer...Brian J. Lilienthal
Sound Designer.. Matt Callahan
Properties Designer.. Seán McArdle
Wig Designer .... Heather Fleming
Fight Director..Joe Isenberg
Dialect Coach ....Rinda Frye
Production Stage Manager...........................Paul Mills Holmes
Dramaturg..Zach Chotzen-Freund
Casting ....Laura Stanczyk

Directing Assistant ....Lillian Meredith
Assistant Costume Designer.................................. Megan Shuey
Assistant Lighting Designer.......................................Kyle Grant
Production Assistant .... Lizzy Lee
Assistant Dramaturg................................Dominic Finocchiaro

Michael von Siebenburg Melts Through the Floorboards was developed at The Lark Play Development Center, New York City.

* The roles of OFFICER CLAIRE and OFFICER LEE have since been cut from the script and two new roles, HELGA and ANNA, have been added.

CHARACTERS

OTTO, 40s/50s, a hulking, brutal warrior from a dark, dark age. Hoping to reclaim Constantinople from the Ottoman Turks.

MICHAEL VON SIEBENBURG, 30s/40s, a retired crusader. A little lost at the moment.

JANE, 20s/30s, a sophisticated, urban woman. Ready for anything.

TURKISH SOLDIER, A hulking, brutal warrior from the dark ages. Overconfident.

MARIA, 20s/30s. A haunting beauty from a dark, dark age. Worried about Michael's spiritual well-being.

SAMMY, 20s/30s. A retired crusader. Doing what he can to get by.

APRIL, 30s. An overworked, urban woman. Tired of looking for Mr. Right.

MRS. ROSEMARY, 70s/80s. A landlady, physically frail but nobody's fool.

HELGA, a Himmelmaiden.

ANNA, another Himmelmaiden.

ANGELA, 20s/30s. A lost soul.

DOUBLE CASTING

SAMMY/VOICE OF TURKISH SOLDIER

MARIA/ANGELA

JANE/HELGA

APRIL/ANNA

SETTING

The play takes place over several weeks in a major American city. The locations include:
A once elegant, now faded pre-war apartment living room
A bedroom in that same elegantly faded pre-war apartment
The loading dock of a big office building
A battlefield circa 1452, just outside Constantinople
Purgatory

THANKS TO

Sean Daniels, an early crusader for this odd crusader tale; everyone at The Lark and Actors Theatre of Louisville; India and Milo for flying out to Kentucky; and Ayun for seeing this show on Ayun Halliday Day.

Rufus Collins and John Ahlin
in *Michael von Siebenburg Melts Through the Floorboards*

36th Humana Festival of New American Plays
Actors Theatre of Louisville, 2012
Photo by Alan Simons

MICHAEL VON SIEBENBURG
MELTS THROUGH THE
FLOORBOARDS

Scene 1

In the darkness we hear the sound of medieval battle—swords clanking, horses neighing, the whole bit. As the battle sounds roar then fade, OTTO, *a brutish, chain-mailed specter from the dark ages enters and plants himself in the light. He speaks with an accent.*

OTTO. In years past the men would dig the chain mail suits from out their earthen hiding places and hang them in the sun to dry, rust flaking off them like ashes from a fire. They would take the swords of their fathers and their fathers' fathers to the river stones and scrape them clean and sharp. They would gather in the villages and the towns to hear the old songs, eat meat from the forests and the farms, and clasp hands like brothers would. Banners would fly. Metal would glint and sparkle in the morning sunlight and all thoughts would whisper of battle. In years past we fought the infidel, to save our souls, and to feel the strength of being men at the end of a sharpened blade. In years past we lived. We shall live again.

(Romantic music plays. OTTO, *defiant, looks for his exit and leaves. Lights shift, and we find ourselves in...)*

Scene 2

A once grand, now faded pre-war apartment. MICHAEL, *40s, elegant, mysterious, and* JANE, *late 20s, sultry, sophisticated, have just finished eating a wonderful meal. Romantic music plays softly in the background.* MICHAEL *speaks with a slight accent.*

JANE. Well. That was a wonderful meal.

MICHAEL. Thank you.

JANE. Sammy was right, you really can cook.

MICHAEL. I know one or two dishes.

JANE. Oh, I'm sure you know more than that.

(An exchange of glances. They drink.)

Little sausages. I don't think I've ever known a man to serve me little sausages before.

MICHAEL. No?

JANE. Not for dinner, at least.

MICHAEL. Cevapcici.

JANE. Che-vap…?

MICHAEL. The sausages, their name. Che-vap-tsi-tsi.

JANE. Cevapcici.

MICHAEL. Travel inland from the Adriatic, north of Ragusa, east of Diocletian's Tomb. This is the land of these sausages.

JANE. Ah.

MICHAEL. Many influences.

JANE. Oh?

MICHAEL. Magyar. Turk. Gypsy. Jew. All these people, they are in these sausages. You understand?

JANE. I do. Culture-wise, you mean.

MICHAEL. Oh, yes. More wine?

JANE. Please.

MICHAEL. I'll get another bottle.

> (MICHAEL *exits to the kitchen to retrieve another bottle of wine.* JANE *calls to him from the dining area.*)

JANE. So tender!

MICHAEL. (*Offstage.*) Hmmm?!

JANE. The sausage meat! So juicy! Like a—I want to say like a potato pancake!

MICHAEL. (*O.S.*) Yes! Well, that's the tenderizer for you!

JANE. The tenderizer?!

> (MICHAEL *returns with a fresh bottle.*)

MICHAEL. The meat tenderizer. You know, one of those little hammers with the knobbly ends.

JANE. Oh, I know what a meat tenderizer is. But for sausage meat?

MICHAEL. For any meat. It's fallen out of fashion, but I must confess: I tenderize all my meats.

JANE. (*Suggestively.*) As do I.

> (MICHAEL *sets about opening the bottle.*)

MICHAEL. You know, the thing about the meat tenderizer is the design was actually based on a weapon.

JANE. Is that right?

MICHAEL. A mace, or something like a mace. A great big hammer with knobs and spikes and things like that. A Turkish weapon.

JANE. You seem to know a lot about Turkey.

MICHAEL. It is a—preoccupation.

JANE. So I gathered.

MICHAEL. But I'm sure you know the stories, The Turks, their crimes against Christendom and so forth.

JANE. No.

MICHAEL. No?

JANE. Not really. But I must say, I like a man with a—preoccupation.

MICHAEL. Oh?

JANE. Most of the "men" I know are into video games or the latest app or whatever. Not very meaty preoccupations if you ask me. Not compared to crimes against Christendom.

(MICHAEL *pops the cork.*)

MICHAEL. Ja. Well, it was during the final Siege of Constantinople—1453, The Big One—that the Turks really put their hammers to use.

JANE. Just a splash.

(MICHAEL *pours.*)

MICHAEL. There were these troops—Austrian troops—stationed on a bluff overlooking the city, keeping an eye out for the Ottomans.

JANE. Austrian?

MICHAEL. Volunteers. As the Turks marched on the city, men from throughout Christendom came to Constantinople—or Istanbul, as it's known today—to fight the Ottomans, to make what they thought would be a last stand before the Muslims overran Europe. Italian, Spanish, even Swiss. They all considered it God's work to shove a pike into a Muslim belly, not just in the name of self-defense but as a good in its own right.

JANE. Oo, this is very strong, isn't it.

MICHAEL. The story?

JANE. The wine.

MICHAEL. It's old, this wine. Very rare. Very, mm, flavorful.

JANE. I'm enjoying it very much.

MICHAEL. I'm glad. Anyway, the soldiers, something like 20 Austrian volunteers, went out onto this bluff, they made camp, waited waited waited, no Turks. Night comes, they go to sleep, sun rises, Turks everywhere.

JANE. No.

MICHAEL. Yes. Drinking their coffee, cooking their kebobs. Lamb. A little Turkish city out of nothing.

JANE. They snuck in in the middle of the night.

MICHAEL. That's right. That was the Turkish way.

JANE. Like thieves.

MICHAEL. Well, like Turks, anyway. So, here are these volunteers, stuck out on this bluff with a sea of Turks between them and their city walls.

JANE. What did they do?

MICHAEL. What could they do? They dug in, or whatever medieval soldiers do, and the siege began. The Turks would come in the morning, they'd fight fight fight, the Turks would retreat, that would be their day. Another—"splash"?

JANE. Please.

(MICHAEL *pours.*)

MICHAEL. So, these soldiers spend week after week on this bluff, fighting Turks, living in their own filth, that sort of stuff. Eventually they run out of food. The siege was going on and on, the Turks were attacking every day, the volunteers were living in their own feces, and one day the sergeant or whoever sticks his head up and says "Guess what? We're out of gruel!"

JANE. No shit.

MICHAEL. Cross my heart.

JANE. So what did they do then?

MICHAEL. What do you think they did?

JANE. I don't know.

MICHAEL. Guess.

JANE. I don't know. They ate bodies.

MICHAEL. That's absolutely right, they ate bodies. Like in that movie. Bodies all over the place, I mean all over the place, and they not eating for weeks, so what were they supposed to do?

JANE. Eat bodies.

MICHAEL. That's right. First they started with the Turks, because they didn't want to eat their chums. But when they ran out of Turks they had to eat their chums. And you know what?

JANE. No, what?

MICHAEL. Their chums tasted so much better than the Turks they couldn't believe it. The meat was juicy, it was tasty, you could eat it rare, medium rare, it was better. So at first they said "well, of course our men taste better. They're Austrians. We eat right, live right, pray to the right God, why shouldn't our meat taste better than the coffee-drinking Turks?" And then one of the men turned to the others and said "but this one here, this wasn't an Austrian, it was a Turk who had defected to our side. Abdul, or something like that. Why was Abdul's meat as delicious as, say, Otto's?" And they looked at the defector's body, and they looked at the Austrians, and they looked at the Turks, and they tasted a little bit from each, and they agreed "Ja, Abdul tasted just as good." Then one of them noticed how Abdul and the Austrians were all beat to Hell and the Turks were mostly punctured once or twice, because the Austrians used swords—and crossbows and primitive firearms, but mostly swords—and the Turks used these massive war hammers. Then they noticed how truly pulverized the meat from their chums was and how relatively untouched the Turk meat was. Because when the Turks went to war they would just wail on these schwächlinge until they were just a bloody mess. I mean they would hold these guys down and just start wailing on their legs or some such schmus until they passed out. Then they would SEASON the meat, can you believe that? Secret, ancient, Asiatic seasonings. And THEN they would deliver the death blow. Because they were Turks, that was their way, they loved inflicting pain. That's why they loved war so much—massive opportunities to create new pain situations. Which is also why they were ultimately so terrible at war. At least compared to the Austrians. I mean, these Turkish arschgesichter would be wailing on some poor bastard's shins, squeezing out a final few squeals before applying the paprika, or cardamom, or whatever-the-fuck, and then WHAM! A bolt from a crossbow, right through the armor, right through the heart. The Turks lost thousands that way.

JANE. God, I have such a headache all of a sudden.

MICHAEL. So, the city eventually falls, the inhabitants are slaughtered, Constantinople becomes Istanbul, but somehow the Austrians escaped, eventually making their way back to Vienna, saving themselves to fight another day. The strange thing, however, was how well these soldiers looked upon their return. Men of forty had about them the buttery glow of teenagers. Men of sixty looked ripe and virile. You see, what these Christian volunteers didn't share with the historians of Europe was their discovery that the eating of human flesh was the secret to life everlasting.

JANE. What?

MICHAEL. That a steady diet of specially tenderized, specially seasoned human meat was—is—the secret to immortality. They could feel it, feel the power it gave them after a meal. Like sushi, just much, much more. They didn't tell this to anyone, of course, because they reasoned if they did they would be burned at the stake.

(*Beat.*)

And that is the story of the meat tenderizer.

(*Beat.*)

More wine?

JANE. I think I need to leave now.

> (MICHAEL *pours.*)

MICHAEL. The past still lives with us, you see. Sometimes in the most unexpected of places.

JANE. I said I think I need to leave, now, Michael.

MICHAEL. We can't escape it. We can't escape who we are. I can't, anyway.

JANE. What have I been drinking?

MICHAEL. As I said, an old vintage. Centuries old. Old as me.

JANE. You're joking.

MICHAEL. I'm not.

JANE. I'm going.

> (*She tries to stand. A gentle tap from* MICHAEL *sits her back down.*)

MICHAEL. You're staying.

JANE. What are you going to do to me?

MICHAEL. Go to sleep.

> (JANE *lowers her head and is soon fast asleep. Lights and romantic music fade as medieval battle sounds grow to a sword-clanking roar.*)

Scene 3

> *In the darkness we hear battle sounds and the smack of a Turkish mallet. The stage remains dark throughout the following dialogue.*

OTTO. Eeeyyaahh!! You bastard! You bloody Turkish bastard!!

> (*Smack!*)

EeeeeyyyyaaaaaaAAAAAHHHHHHHH!!!

TURK VOICE. Mmm, et! Kuzu gibi! Kuzu kebabi gibi!!

OTTO. Give me back my sword you thieving heathen! Fight me like a man—like a CHRISTIAN! Then we'll see about your so-called kebabi gibi!

TURK VOICE. "Hristiyan"?!

> (*Smack!*)

OTTO. Eeeyyaaoooo!! My shins!!

TURK VOICE. Hristiyan*iyi!* Is lamb kebab, evet?! Hristiyan *is* lamb!!

OTTO. Do what you want to me you bloody, coffee drinking Ottoman Turk! But you'll never take Constantinople! Do you hear me?! Never!!

> (*Smack!*)

Eeeyyaaahhh!!

TURK VOICE. "Never"? "NEVER"?!!

(*Suddenly, the hiss of a bolt from a crossbow: sssssssssssssSSSSSWA-PANK!*)

TURK VOICE. Kuzu…kebabi…gibi…

(*The sound of a body collapsing. Lights come up just a bit, enough for us to barely see the action. OTTO, badly mutilated, lies center stage. MICHAEL, carrying a crossbow and dressed in medieval soldier garb, rushes to OTTO's side.*)

OTTO. Who goes there?!

MICHAEL. Otto, it's me.

OTTO. Michael, thank Gott!

MICHAEL. Come on, then, Otto. The others will be done with their coffees soon enough. We have to get you out of here.

OTTO. Nein, Michael. I can't. Go on without me.

MICHAEL. What are you talking about, let's go!

OTTO. He's gotten to my shins, Michael. I can't move.

MICHAEL. Dear Christian Gott im Himmel, what has he done to you?!

OTTO. He's pulverized them, Michael. My shins. Dear Gott, Michael, my shins!

MICHAEL. Here, put your arm around my neck, I'll carry you back.

OTTO. Nein, Michael. It's too late for that.

MICHAEL. But Otto—

OTTO. Too late! Just stay with me a moment.

MICHAEL. Easy, Otto.

OTTO. I saw a patch of moss out here by the rocks, Michael. I thought I could dig it out and bring it back before anyone saw me. You know. For variety's sake.

MICHAEL. Don't worry about the moss, Otto. I'll make sure it gets back to the outpost.

OTTO. For a nice salad or something. Something nice for the men. Or a side or something. Steamed. You know, like spinach.

MICHAEL. We'll make something delicious with it.

OTTO. Don't let them take Constantinople, Michael. Don't let them take it!

MICHAEL. We won't, Otto.

OTTO. Think of your soul, if nothing else! Whatever crimes we may or may not have committed, all will be forgiven if we push back the infidel! So push them back, Michael!

MICHAEL. I will, Otto.

OTTO. To Antioch! To Jerusalem! Take your blade and—ACH! This is it! I'm going to Jesus!

MICHAEL. I'm here with you, Otto.

OTTO. I can see the light, now, Michael! It's blinding me!

MICHAEL. It won't be long now, Otto!

OTTO. Steam it, Michael! Use some of the paprika we found on Abdul! Or some ground cumin, that's also nice!

MICHAEL. I will, Otto.

OTTO. And Michael?

MICHAEL. Yes, Otto?

OTTO. Don't let them eat my body.

MICHAEL. What?

OTTO. Don't let them eat my body, Michael! Promise me! On your word as a Christian. I want to meet my maker whole.

MICHAEL. I promise you, Otto.

OTTO. Say it, Michael! On your word as a Christian!

MICHAEL. On my word as a Christian.

OTTO. You won't let them eat me!

MICHAEL. You won't let them eat me!

OTTO. Nein! You won't let them eat me!

MICHAEL. Right, sorry. I won't let—"them" eat you.

OTTO. Wait a minute! Who is "them"? In your mind how are you defining —uh… Jesus?! Is that you?!

MICHAEL. Otto!

OTTO. I'm going, Michael. Farewell, my friend. I'll be watching you from Himmel. Forever. And remember, Michael… remember… Michael… remember…

> (*Lights fade as* OTTO*'s voice becomes fainter, then disappears altogether. In the dark we hear the voice of a woman who, like* OTTO, *speaks with an accent.*)

MARIA. (*O.S.*) Michael.

> (*Beat, no response.*)

Michael.

> (*Beat, still no response.*)

It's me, Michael, wake up.

> (*Silence, then.*)

Hello?

Turn on the light, Michael, I'm tired of sitting here in the dark.

> (*Beat.*)

MICHAEL. (*O.S.*) Maria?

MARIA. (*O.S.*) Don't be afraid, Michael. I haven't come to hurt you. I've come to take you home.

(*MICHAEL turns on the light by his bed and listens.*)

MICHAEL. Hello?

(*He listens some more, peering into the darkness of his apartment.*)

Maria?

(*No response. After a moment,* MICHAEL *turns the light back off. Battle sounds rise then fall, replaced by the murmur of a busy city street.*)

Scene 4

SAMMY, *wiry, strangely charismatic, sits on a loading dock beside* APRIL, *a cosmopolitan woman.* SAMMY *holds a milkshake from which he slurps from time to time. Like* MICHAEL, *he speaks with an accent.* APRIL *smokes.*

SAMMY. Loneliness is a hunger, a hunger of the soul. It creeps into the sinews, into the bones. It becomes a part of you.

APRIL. You see a lot.

SAMMY. I see what I see.

(SAMMY *slurps, taking a moment to take* APRIL's *measure.*)

I look at you and I see a woman who spends too much time in health clubs, in night clubs. I see a woman who dances in expensive clothes.

APRIL. I like expensive clothes.

SAMMY. Of course you do, but who are they for, these clothes? That's my question to you. Who do you expect to meet by wearing them?

APRIL. I don't know. Someone nice.

SAMMY. Nice?

APRIL. Someone to talk to, to trust.

SAMMY. You don't want nice.

APRIL. No?

SAMMY. No.

APRIL. Who, then?

SAMMY. I will tell you, but you have to open your mind to hear me, to hear what I'm saying.

APRIL. My mind is open.

SAMMY. No, my dear, it is not.

APRIL. It is.

SAMMY. I don't believe so, no.

(*She takes a few breaths.*)

APRIL. It is. Now it is.

(He moves closer, transfixing her just the slightest bit with his gaze.)

SAMMY. Yes?

APRIL. Yes.

SAMMY. Open?

APRIL. Open.

(He moves closer still, peering deeply into her eyes.)

SAMMY. Yes. Yes, I see that now.

APRIL. So? Who do I want?

SAMMY. What everyone wants. Someone to give yourself to. Completely. Perhaps even—literally.

APRIL. Literally?

(He takes another sip from his milkshake.)

SAMMY. Let me tell you something, something true. Once upon a time there were men—not very nice men—who would stand tall before a sea of troubles, and they would do it all for you—for women like you. Once upon a time, women like you—beautiful women, fierce and resourceful women— would spend their days tilling the fields and their nights dancing barefoot before the kettle fires. When called, the men—your men—would reclaim their pikes long hidden within cottage walls, they would form ranks and march out to meet the bloody Turk on the field of battle. You think you are strong now because you wear a power suit to work, you make long distance calls for free, and your secretary nearly always does as you command. But you are not strong. Not as you used to be.

APRIL. No?

SAMMY. Of course not, no. You are hungry, that's why. Hungry for a man—and I'm going to delve a little deeper here—for a man who would kill for you, who would burn for you, who would strip the baubles from off the Turken corpses and present them as gifts to you. You may not mention it at the office parties, at the Thanksgiving dinners, but you ache for a man such as this. You hunger for him. And you know what?

APRIL. No. What?

SAMMY. He hungers for you. He hungers for you very, very much.

(APRIL blinks, emerging from her barely perceptible transfixation. SAMMY sips his milkshake.)

APRIL. What did you say your friend's name was?

SAMMY. Michael. Siebenburg. The greatest guy you'll ever want to meet. And a baron, to boot.

APRIL. A baron?

SAMMY. Like I say, a really special guy. Easy to talk to, a great cook. Text me. I'll set it up.

> (*She gets herself ready to go.*)

APRIL. Listen, it was really nice talking to you, um…

SAMMY. Sammy.

APRIL. Sammy. I'm surprised we never met before.

SAMMY. The mailroom is a world away, especially from your floor.

APRIL. The fourteenth floor.

SAMMY. A most unhappy floor. For you. But not for long.

> (APRIL *turns to go.*)

And April.

> (APRIL *stops.*)

APRIL. Yeah?

SAMMY. I trust I can rely on your, mm, discretion. If the baron is to be your prize, no one can know of our conversation.

APRIL. Mum's the word.

> (APRIL *exits as* MICHAEL *enters carrying something wrapped in butcher paper. He hands it to* SAMMY.)

SAMMY. Success?

MICHAEL. A good date, Sammy, nice and clean.

SAMMY. No fighting?

MICHAEL. Not much.

SAMMY. Good, good. No fighting means no fear in the meat.

MICHAEL. She went down easy. Two glasses.

SAMMY. Nice and calm.

MICHAEL. Some anxiety, maybe, but no fear. Not that I could taste, anyway.

SAMMY. I'll be the judge of that. Now, for just a taste.

> (SAMMY *opens the package, takes out a pinch of meat, and tastes it.*)

Mmmmm, yum. So good.

MICHAEL. Yes, the meat.

SAMMY. Didn't realize how hungry I was.

MICHAEL. A dry spell. Over for the moment.

SAMMY. Happy again.

MICHAEL. The meat.

SAMMY. The meat.

> (SAMMY *bites deep into the meat, snurfling it down like a starving stray dog. After a while:*)

SAMMY. You see *True Blood* last night?

MICHAEL. Tivo'd it.

SAMMY. Such lies.

MICHAEL. I know, you hate that show.

SAMMY. As if blood makes a meal, a full meal. Meat makes a meal! Specially tenderized, specially seasoned HUMAN MEAT!

MICHAEL. SSSHH!!

SAMMY. The meat. Such power.

MICHAEL. Yes, but still, we must be careful.

(SAMMY *gobbles down some more. Then:*)

SAMMY. You want some?

MICHAEL. No. Thanks.

SAMMY. You sure? You look like you could use a piece of meat.

MICHAEL. Not right now, Sammy. Thank you. Maybe later.

SAMMY. Not eat?

MICHAEL. What can I tell you? Sometimes we want to eat, sometimes we don't.

SAMMY. No, Michael, we always want to eat.

(*Beat.*)

MICHAEL. She came to me, Sammy. Last night. Around midnight.

SAMMY. She came to you?

MICHAEL. Last night. I was in bed, asleep, and she came to me. She spoke my name.

SAMMY. I don't understand, Michael. Who came to you?

MICHAEL. Maria.

SAMMY. Maria?

MICHAEL. My wife Maria, from the old country.

SAMMY. Your wife Maria.

MICHAEL. Last night, around midnight.

SAMMY. You were dreaming.

MICHAEL. I wasn't dreaming.

SAMMY. It was late, you were sleeping. You had a bad dream.

MICHAEL. I'm telling you Sammy, this wasn't a dream. I could feel her there, I could smell the soil between her toes.

SAMMY. She's dead.

MICHAEL. I know she's dead.

SAMMY. Over 500 years dead.

MICHAEL. I know.

SAMMY. So how could she come to you?

MICHAEL. I don't know. But she did.

(SAMMY *feels* MICHAEL's *forehead.*)

SAMMY. You remember Sigfried? His woman came to him in the night, I remember him talking about it. A few weeks later he was dead.

MICHAEL. Sigfried?

SAMMY. Von Blaumstein. I remember him saying "Sammy, I'm thinking of going off the meat for a while." A few weeks later his body was found dissolving into the floorboards, his flesh turned to goop.

MICHAEL. Where was this?

SAMMY. Outside Naples, after Napoleon, before Garibaldi. That's why we had to leave town. You don't remember any of this?

MICHAEL. Not entirely.

SAMMY. It was a long time ago. Anyway, the peasants wanted to burn us after that. It was a long cart ride up to Rome, I can tell you that much.

MICHAEL. His woman came to him?

SAMMY. So he said, in a vision, late at night. I said he was dreaming, he said he wasn't, just like you. Helga. Blonde. Buxom. Skin like cream, her hair in those rings they used to keep back then. In the end he just couldn't take it anymore.

(*Beat.*)

I need a cutter, Michael, a good cutter. If I'm going to bag for you I need to know you're going to be there.

MICHAEL. I'll be there, Sammy.

SAMMY. To cut them down.

MICHAEL. I'll be there.

(SAMMY *takes out a small black book to consult.*)

SAMMY. Okay, so… I have a woman, older but in *excellent* condition. Met her at pottery class, recently divorced. She might be something for next month.

MICHAEL. He was always a bit of a lost soul, though, wasn't he.

SAMMY. Who?

MICHAEL. Von Blaumstein. Couldn't quite reconcile Holy War with Christ's teaching, if I'm remembering him correctly.

SAMMY. Not much of a soldier, if you ask me.

MICHAEL. Ja. Well, we all have our doubts, I suppose. From time to time.

(*Beat.* SAMMY *returns to his book.*)

SAMMY. I have a man.

MICHAEL. No men.

SAMMY. We used to eat men.

MICHAEL. When we were soldiers. We're not soldiers anymore.

SAMMY. Men can be easy.

MICHAEL. NO MEN! They can smell it on me, the old ways. I'm uncomfortable, they're uncomfortable. They get anxious, I get anxious, and then all that fear goes into the meat.

SAMMY. It's not so easy, Michael, getting a woman.

MICHAEL. Was it ever easy?

SAMMY. Women are getting more with the kunstfertigkeit, the empowerment, the independence. I can't just give them the googly eyes anymore, not like I used to.

MICHAEL. How men are supposed to learn how to be men today, I don't know. All our natural instincts, our ancient privileges, reduced to a kind of crime. A kind of sickness.

SAMMY. In the West, maybe. Not in the East.

MICHAEL. Christendom is not what it used to be.

SAMMY. Nein.

MICHAEL. Nein.

> (*Beat.*)

SAMMY. Give me a week. I'll find someone suitable.

MICHAEL. A week will be hard. I'll move what I have into the freezer until then.

SAMMY. You have a Cuisinart?

MICHAEL. A Cuisinart?

SAMMY. You know, for blending things.

MICHAEL. I have a blender. Why?

SAMMY. Make yourself a treat. You don't even need to unfreeze the meat, really, just put it in little cubes.

MICHAEL. A treat?

SAMMY. A frozen treat, with lemon, orange juice, anything citrusy.

> (*He takes the lid off his "milkshake" and shows it to* MICHAEL.)

It's great in the summer.

> (MICHAEL *tries a slurp and smiles at his resourceful friend. They both laugh fairly mirthlessly for a while as the lights fade.*)

Scene 5

MICHAEL's dream. In the dark, we hear MICHAEL *and his wife laughing. The lights stay dark throughout this initial exchange.*

MICHAEL. (*O.S.*) Oh, Maria.

MARIA. (*O.S.*) Michael.

MICHAEL. (*O.S.*) Maria.

MARIA. (*O.S.*) Michael.

MICHAEL. (*O.S.*) I live for the sound of your laughter, Maria. Beautiful Maria. Beautiful, beautiful Maria.

MARIA. (*O.S.*) Must you go?

MICHAEL. (*O.S.*) I must, I'm afraid.

MARIA. (*O.S.*) What business have you there? Leave Constantinople to the Constantinopolitans.

MICHAEL. (*O.S.*) Leave it to the Turks, you mean.

MARIA. (*O.S.*) Leave it to the Devil, for all I care. Just stay home with me.

MICHAEL. (*O.S.*) If only I could, dear Maria. For you see, my business is to save Constantinople, not to leave it. Save it for you.

MARIA. (*O.S.*) Save your*self* for me, Michael. Not some city, some collection of streets and buildings. What I'm interested in is the streets and buildings of your soul, Michael. Only the streets and buildings of your soul.

MICHAEL. (*O.S.*) Oh, Maria.

MARIA. (*O.S.*) Michael.

MICHAEL. (*O.S.*) Maria.

OTTO. (*O.S.*) Michael.

> (*Beat.*)

MICHAEL. (*O.S.*) Maria?

OTTO. (*O.S.*) It's me, Michael, wake up. Turn on the light. I'm tired of sitting here in the dark.

> (*He does so. We see now we're in* MICHAEL's *bedroom.* OTTO *sits beside him in full medieval battle dress.* MICHAEL *looks at him for a moment, then scrambles away, panic-stricken.*)

MICHAEL. Jesus fucking Christ!

OTTO. Michael.

MICHAEL. Otto.

OTTO. The Lord's name, Michael, do not take it in vain.

MICHAEL. Stay back. Stay back, Otto, okay?! Just—stay away!

OTTO. Don't be afraid, Michael. I haven't come to hurt you. I've come to deliver you a message.

MICHAEL. Look, Otto, about eating your body—I was against it!

OTTO. This isn't about that, Michael.

MICHAEL. I fought it, Otto, I said "He went out there to get us a salad, and this is how we repay him?!"

OTTO. Michael—

MICHAEL. "The shins are gone already," I said, "eat those if you have to, but not—"

OTTO. Michael! Stop talking, this isn't about that. I come to you with a message from The Knights—aus Der Unterwelt!

MICHAEL. Der Unterwelt?

OTTO. Der Underworld.

MICHAEL. The Underworld?!

OTTO. DER UNTERWELT!! There is great danger afoot.

MICHAEL. Mein Gott.

OTTO. For centuries you have feasted on the meat of the innocent, Michael, kept company with the worst of our kind and avoided the destiny for which you were born. You may have felt invisible over the years, unseen, a mystery to all but your victims in their final squealings. But you were not invisible, Michael. Not to the Knights aus Der Unterwelt.

MICHAEL. The Knights of Der Unterwelt.

OTTO. The Knights *AUS* Der Unterwelt have watched you closely, Michael. We watched you stalk the streets of Rome and London, Hamburg and Cancún, feasting as you went. You may have thought yourself safe, dear Michael, but you were not, you never were. The time has come to make good on the promise you made those many years ago.

MICHAEL. It has?

OTTO. It has.

MICHAEL. What promise?

OTTO. Take back Constantinople! Take it back! Unsheathe your sword, sail for the East, raise an army, and march on it! In the name of all that is holy, take back the City of God and install yourself upon it as its emperor!

    (*Beat.*)

Or find someone else to be emperor, it's up to you.

MICHAEL. Take it back?

OTTO. That's right, Michael, return it to Christendom.

MICHAEL. That's your message?

OTTO. That is your holy duty. Look, Michael, this may seem out of the blue to you, but this has actually been in the works for some time.

MICHAEL. I had no idea I was under scrutiny.

MARIA. (*O.S.*) Michael?

(OTTO *stands with a start, alert. He draws his sword.*)

OTTO. Who goes there?!

MICHAEL. That's probably Maria. She visits me in my sleep, too.

OTTO. Oh, you're not sleeping, Michael.

(OTTO *sniffs the air, listening.*)

Could it be?

MARIA. (*O.S.*) Michael?

OTTO. So, she has come. Just as I expected.

MICHAEL. Otto—

OTTO. Sshh!!

MARIA. (*O.S.*) Turn on the light, Michael, I'm tired of sitting here in the dark.

OTTO. Ha! Der Teufelfrau can't even tell that the lights are already on. She has yet to complete her journey, I'm guessing—her journey *AUS* Der Unterwelt.

MARIA. (*O.S.*) Don't be afraid, Michael. I haven't come to hurt you. I've come to take you home.

OTTO. Hasn't come to hurt you?! Well, I'll hurt her, Hell-Maiden that she is! Hurt her plenty.

MICHAEL. Otto, wait.

OTTO. Don't trouble yourself about it, Michael. Just remember what I said. Remember... Remember...

(*His voice trails off as he exits. There's a knock at the door,* MICHAEL *crosses to answer it.*)

MICHAEL. Maria?

(*No response. He opens the door.* MRS. ROSEMARY, *an elderly woman, frail but fierce, stands in the hallway holding a handful of fliers.*)

Oh. Hi, Mrs. Rosemary.

(*She hands him a flier.*)

MRS. ROSEMARY. The memorial service for my Reuben is gonna be this Sunday, down in the lobby.

MICHAEL. Yes, thank you. I was very sorry to hear of his passing. He was a kind man.

MRS. ROSEMARY. He was a trusting man. Too trusting for his line of work.

MICHAEL. I—can give you your rent check, now. If you're prepared to receive it.

MRS. ROSEMARY. I better be prepared. Reuben never liked me collecting money or fooling around with the boiler or any of that, but now it's just me. I guess I'm the new sheriff in town.

MICHAEL. One moment.

(MRS. ROSEMARY *lingers in the doorway as* MICHAEL *retrieves his checkbook and writes out a check.*)

MRS. ROSEMARY. I heard voices, I figured it was all right to knock.

MICHAEL. Just…um…listening to a record.

MRS. ROSEMARY. A record?

MICHAEL. Oh, yes. I love records.

MRS. ROSEMARY. People don't listen to records anymore.

MICHAEL. It's making a comeback. They call it vinyl now.

MRS. ROSEMARY. Sounded like voices.

MICHAEL. Spoken word. A comedy album.

MRS. ROSEMARY. You don't seem like much of a comedy person to me.

(MICHAEL *returns with the check.*)

MICHAEL. It's the accent. People hear me speak and they think I must be one of those humorless, teutonic types, preoccupied with death and dying and the disposition of the soul after a lifetime of defying God and so forth.

MRS. ROSEMARY. That must be it.

MICHAEL. Yes. Well… Good night, Mrs. Rosemary.

MRS. ROSEMARY. Good night, Mr. Siebenburg.

(*She doesn't move. Lights fade and battle sounds grow as* MICHAEL *closes the door. The battle sounds rise to a roar.*)

Scene 6

Purgatory. Lights come up softly, so we can just make out the outlines of a medieval beauty making her way onstage.

MARIA. Michael? Schalten sie das licht, Michael, Ich bin müde von hier sitzt im dunkelm.

(*A voice sounds in the darkness.*)

OTTO. (*O.S.*) Maria?

MARIA. Michael?

OTTO. (*O.S.*) Nein, Maria. Es ist Otto.

MARIA. Otto?! Was machst du denn hier?!

OTTO. (*O.S.*) Ich?! Was machst DU denn hier?!

MARIA. Ich komme um Michael zu retten!

(MARIA *flees.* OTTO *rushes on, sword drawn.*)

OTTO. Dumme frau! Sie kämpfen die Knights Aus der Unterwelt!

MARIA. (*O.S.*) Und SIE kämpfen die Maidens Aus der OBERwelt! Ja, Helga?

(*From off, we hear an unfamiliar voice.*)

HELGA. (*O.S.*) Ja, Maria.

OTTO. "Helga"?

MARIA. (*O.S.*) Und Anna?

(*We hear another unfamiliar voice.*)

ANNA. (*O.S.*) Ja, Maria.

OTTO. "Anna"?!

MARIA. (*O.S.*) Auf wiedersehen, Otto. Für den moment.

(*The women laugh creepily in the dark.* Romantic music plays. OTTO *flees as the dim light fades.*)

Scene 7

Romantic music, another date, this time with APRIL. *It's not going so well.*

APRIL. You don't really believe that—*bullshit*, do you?! All those war stories glorifying murder and mayhem and all the rest of it?!

MICHAEL. War is a part of history, it's a part of us!

APRIL. It's not a part of me, thank you very much.

MICHAEL. How can you know what is or isn't a part of you?! You're American, you don't feel your present let alone your past!

APRIL. Oh, I feel my past, all right. History is another matter.

MICHAEL. History lives with us! It lives beside us, within us! Sniff the air you can smell its stink-breath!

APRIL. "The murdering, coffee-drinking Turks"?! I mean, maybe they did some bad things in the past, the slaughters, or whatever, but that was then! This is now!

MICHAEL. The fall of Constantinople wasn't that long ago!

APRIL. I've been to Turkey! They're wonderful people!

MICHAEL. "Wonderful"?!

APRIL. They were wonderful to me! And with all the *actual* shit that's going on these days, why the fuck would anyone worry about the Turks and what they did to Constantinople?!

(*The two fume. Finally:*)

MICHAEL. Forgive me. I didn't mean to bring up politics.

APRIL. It's hard to avoid these days, I suppose.

MICHAEL. Listen, how about we start again?

APRIL. I didn't mean to snap. I'm just not a big fan of war stories, that's all.

MICHAEL. Of course you're not. War has come to your people as it came to mine—suddenly, mysteriously, without end and without pleasure for those who tend the home fires. To talk of war is to invite the poison into your soul.

APRIL. That's one way to put it.

MICHAEL. But I am weak. In the presence of beauty I retreat to my war stories, hoping to match its power. Your power. I make of myself the buffoon.

APRIL. I don't know that I'd call you a buffoon.

MICHAEL. You are kind. And so your beauty flows not just from your face and, mm, body, but from the deepest part of you.

(*Beat.*)

More—wine?

(*He pours.*)

APRIL. You really are a baron, aren't you.

MICHAEL. Ah. Sammy told you about that, did he?

APRIL. Must be nice.

MICHAEL. It's all right. I feel out of place sometimes, but it's who I am.

APRIL. Don't be afraid, Michael. I haven't come to hurt you, I've come to take you home.

MICHAEL. Pardon?!

APRIL. Well, I was just wondering, what is it that makes you a baron, exactly, other than your title? Do you have—lands, or something?

MICHAEL. I do have lands. About—125,000 acres that overlook the Danube.

APRIL. One hundred and twenty five thousand?

MICHAEL. They're not in my control right now, of course, but I do still consider them my lands.

APRIL. That's a lot of lands.

MICHAEL. Beautiful country, farming country, at least it used to be when I lived there. My manor sat on a very high hill south of Clausenburg, clear views of the Carpathians to the east. Saxon country, but being Austrian I was more than welcome.

APRIL. Sounds—unbelievable.

MICHAEL. It was.

APRIL. Did you live there—alone?

MICHAEL. Was I married, do you mean?

APRIL. Yes, I suppose that is what I mean.

MICHAEL. I was.

APRIL. Divorced?

MICHAEL. Widowed. She was slaughtered by Turkish horsemen.

APRIL. Here we go with the Turks again.

MICHAEL. I was sailing at the time to join Giustiniani at Chios, and then on to Constantinople. Mehmed the Conqueror sent his raiding parties far and wide, retribution, you understand. I didn't know till much later, of course, but as I sailed, my wife, our servants, everyone, all put to the sword.

(APRIL *stands, unsteadily.*)

APRIL. I think I'd like to go now.

MICHAEL. Go?

APRIL. I have a terrible headache all of a sudden and—I think I'd just like to get the fuck away from you right now.

MICHAEL. But—there's dessert.

(APRIL *staggers back, now clearly struggling with the effects of the wine.*)

APRIL. Mehmed the Conqueror?! 125,000 acres?! What kind of game are you playing, here?!

MICHAEL. No game. Just a relaxing dinner.

APRIL. I haven't come to hurt you, I've come to take you home!

MICHAEL. What did you say?

APRIL. I said the relaxing dinner is over, Michael! So, please, just stay away from me! Stay back!

(MICHAEL *approaches again, now with the bottle and a glass.*)

MICHAEL. I've alarmed you. But please, before you go, let us finish the bottle. It's so rare, this bottle. So, mm, flavorful.

(APRIL *pulls a can of mace from her purse and sprays* MICHAEL *full in the face.*)

AAHHHH! My face! My *eyes!*

(APRIL *tries to make it to the door, but finds she can hardly walk.*)

APRIL. All night with the wine! What did you do, drug me?!

MICHAEL. Dear Gott, the stinging of it!

(APRIL *staggers toward the door. Blinded,* MICHAEL *pursues.*)

APRIL. I should have known! You and that creepy friend of yours! Both of you going on and on and on about the Bloody Turk and the rape of Constantinople! What have you got against the Turk?! They're in NATO, for Christ's sake!

(MICHAEL *reaches* APRIL, *she sprays him again.*)

MICHAEL. Yyaaaiiiii!

APRIL. I mean, they're a secular people! They're modernizing!

(*He grabs her and pulls her toward the bathroom.*)

MICHAEL. I'll show you what I've got against the Turk!

APRIL. Michael, please! Turn on the light!

MICHAEL. You have eaten! Now I must eat!

(*They disappear into the bathroom.*)

APRIL. (*O.S.*) It's me, Michael! Wake up!

MICHAEL. (*O.S.*) I am awake!

APRIL. (*O.S.*) I'm tired of sitting here in the dark!

MICHAEL. (*O.S.*) You're tired?! I'm tired!

APRIL. (*O.S.*) I haven't come to hurt you! I've come to take you—

(*From offstage, we hear the sickening thud of a Turkish war hammer being put to bloody use.*)

(*O.S.*) AAIIIEEE!!! MY SHINS! DEAR GOD IN HEAVEN, WHAT ARE YOU DOING TO MY—!

(*Blackout.*)

Scene 8

We hear the following in the blackout.

OTTO. (*O.S.*) Steam it, Michael! Use some of the paprika we found on Abdul! Or some ground cumin, that's also nice!

MICHAEL. (*O.S.*) I will, Otto.

OTTO. (*O.S.*) And Michael?

MICHAEL. (*O.S.*) Yes, Otto?

OTTO. (*O.S.*) Don't let them eat my body.

MICHAEL. (*O.S.*) What?

OTTO. (*O.S.*) Don't let them eat my body, Michael! Promise me!

MICHAEL. (*O.S.*) I promise you, Otto.

OTTO. (*O.S.*) On your word as a Christian!

MICHAEL. (*O.S.*) On my word as a Christian.

OTTO. (*O.S.*) Farewell, my friend. I'll be watching you from Himmel. And remember… remember… remember…

(MICHAEL *wakes with a start, turning on the light beside his bed. He's panting, sweaty, and doesn't notice that* MARIA, *an ethereal beauty from the Middle Ages, is sitting beside him.*)

MARIA. Michael.

(MICHAEL *scrambles in a panic to the farthest corner of the room.*)

MICHAEL. Jesus fucking Christ.

MARIA. The Lord's name, Michael, please.

MICHAEL. Maria?

MARIA. Don't be afraid. I haven't come to hurt you.

MICHAEL. Maria? Mein Gott, you scared me.

MARIA. You're in great danger, Michael, you should be scared. I mean, I said don't be afraid, but you actually should be afraid, just not of me.

MICHAEL. Mein Gott. Mein *GOTT*, is it you? Is it really you?

MARIA. Yes, Michael. It really is me.

(*Overcome,* MICHAEL *rushes forward to embrace her. She steps away.*)

NO! Don't touch me.

MICHAEL. Don't touch you?

MARIA. I'm sorry, Michael, but you mustn't touch me. Not yet.

MICHAEL. Why not?

MARIA. The meat of the innocent is still in your belly and you ask "Why not?"

MICHAEL. Maria.

MARIA. Michael.

MICHAEL. How I've missed you.

MARIA. And I you.

MICHAEL. I can't believe I'm seeing you.

MARIA. Believe it. Believe it with all your heart.

(MICHAEL *slaps and pinches himself.*)

You see?

MICHAEL. I want to kiss you.

MARIA. No kissing, Michael. Kissing is touching, no touching.

MICHAEL. But—

MARIA. Michael Karl Josef von Siebenburg, I have come from Der Oberwelt to take you home.

MICHAEL. Der Oberwelt?

MARIA. Der Overworld.

MICHAEL. The Overworld?!

MARIA. MICHAEL! You have to prepare for your journey.

MICHAEL. I'm dead?

MARIA. Well, no, not exactly. But you're very, very close.

MICHAEL. I feel okay.

MARIA. It's not about how you feel, Michael, it's about what must be.

MICHAEL. Have you spoken to the Knights of Der Unterwelt?

MARIA. The Knights *aus* Der Unterwelt?!

MICHAEL. Aus Der Underworld, that's right. Do you know them?

MARIA. Oh, yes, Michael, I know them. But you must listen to me, now, there is great danger afoot.

MICHAEL. Yes, that's what Otto said.

MARIA. Otto?

MICHAEL. You remember Otto, we fought together in Constantinople.

MARIA. Oh, yes, I remember Otto. But you must listen to me and no one else! A great conflagration is in the making! The forces of life and light are gathering to cast out the darkness! And for that we need the Souls of the Innocents that even now occupy your body and animate your flesh!

MICHAEL. The "Souls of the Innocents"?

MARIA. The Souls of the Innocents borne into your body by the meats of the innocents! They must be released, Michael, and only you can release them! The time has come—

(*Someone knocks on the door. The two are quiet for a moment.*)

You're expecting someone?

MICHAEL. No. Not now, at least.

MARIA. You have your women, yes, I know.

MICHAEL. It's not what you think.

MARIA. I know exactly what to think! I know of your crimes, Michael, against Gott! Against yourself! But if you only—

(*More knocking, now increasingly urgent.*)

MICHAEL. Just a minute!

MARIA. I must go.

MICHAEL. NO! It's probably my landlady, I'll get rid of her!

(MARIA *begins backing offstage.*)

MARIA. The conflagration is coming, Michael! You may yet redeem yourself, but to do that we need those souls!

MICHAEL. I'm listening, Maria. I'm listening, tell me!

MARIA. For if we don't have them—mein Gott!—what is coming will make die Göotterdämmerung look like Oktoberfest!

(*More knocking!* MICHAEL *moves to the door.*)

MICHAEL. Okay, all right! I'm coming!

(MARIA *disappears.* MICHAEL *swings open the door to reveal the bloody ghost of* JANE *from the first date. She stands in the doorway, unmoving, lost, as if in a trance.*)

Gott im Himmel.

(MICHAEL *slams the door shut and staggers back, aghast. To* MARIA.)

Did you see that? Maria?

(*But* MARIA *is gone. Tentatively,* MICHAEL *returns to the door and opens—it's* MRS. ROSEMARY.)

Mrs. Rosemary.

MRS. ROSEMARY. I heard some banging around.

MICHAEL. Banging around?

MRS. ROSEMARY. Earlier tonight. And then I heard some talking.

MICHAEL. I hope you haven't been lurking outside my door again.

MRS. ROSEMARY. What happened to your face?

MICHAEL. My face? Oh, my face. I prepared some shellfish for my, um, my date, earlier tonight. I'm allergic, but every now and then I eat some to see if I'm still allergic. I guess I'm still allergic.

(MRS. ROSEMARY *pushes past* MICHAEL.)

MRS. ROSEMARY. Where is she?

MICHAEL. Where is who?

MRS. ROSEMARY. "Who?" Your date, that's who. I met her in the lobby.

MICHAEL. Ah, yes. She's—in the bathroom at the moment.

(MRS. ROSEMARY *moves to the bathroom door.*)

MRS. ROSEMARY. Uh-huh. Taking a bath, I suppose? At this hour?

MICHAEL. She is bathing. So to speak.

(MRS. ROSEMARY *knocks on the closed door.*)

MRS. ROSEMARY. Everything all right in there?!

MICHAEL. Mrs. Rosemary, I'm afraid you have interrupted us at a most intimate and, if I may, inopportune moment.

MRS. ROSEMARY. I won't have hanky-panky in my building, Mr. Siebenburg, with the voices and the women and the banging around! I'll call the police, don't think I won't!

MICHAEL. I might have expected such intrusions in the old country. But here? In America? At this time in your history?

MRS. ROSEMARY. Meaning what?

MICHAEL. Meaning tenants have rights. I know my rights—as did Mr. Rosemary. And so, perhaps, I should be calling the police.

(*Long beat. Then, to the bathroom door.*)

MRS. ROSEMARY. I'm leaving, okay?! But if you need anything—for the shellfish, or whatever—you can knock on my door! The one by the lobby!

(MICHAEL *escorts* MRS. ROSEMARY *to the exit.*)

MICHAEL. I am a man, Mrs. Rosemary, with all the appetites of a man. I hope to help you understand as your husband understood.

MRS. ROSEMARY. My Reuben was a lonely, gentle soul who tried to understand everybody. I'm not a gentle soul. And I'm watching you.

MICHAEL. Goodnight, Mrs. Rosemary.

MRS. ROSEMARY. Gutenacht, Herr Siebenburg. Baron Michael von Siebenburg.

(*She exits, and as she does, we hear her calling from further and further down the hall.*)

(*O.S.*) Baron Michael Karl Josef von Siebenburg. Von! VON!!

(*Lights fade as* MICHAEL *closes the door.*)

Scene 9

SAMMY *and* ANGELA *sit on the edge of the loading dock,* ANGELA *eats a bag lunch.*

SAMMY. London?

ANGELA. No.

SAMMY. Paris?

ANGELA. No.

(*He thinks.*)

SAMMY. Vienna?

ANGELA. I haven't really traveled that much.

SAMMY. But we have met. I know we have met.

(*She thinks.*)

ANGELA. Well, there's this idea that we live and then we live again.

SAMMY. Live again?

ANGELA. Our bodies are vessels for the soul, that sort of thing. I see people all the time I'm sure I've met, can't remember from where. Maybe because we knew each other in a past life. And maybe because I'm a rootless temp, flitting about from job to job. Everyone seems to blur together after a while.

SAMMY. You are new, then.

ANGELA. I'm always new. That's sort of the deal when you're a temp.

SAMMY. And so no one knows you are here.

ANGELA. It's a pretty anonymous existence. I come, I type a few letters, alphabetize some folders, and then I'm gone. Whoosh. Like the wind.

SAMMY. Mail room.

ANGELA. I figured, from your, um, badge.

SAMMY. It is required. So people know who I am.

ANGELA. (*Reading his shirt.*) Sammy.

SAMMY. (*Offering his hand.*) Angela.

ANGELA. (*Taking it.*) Right. How'd you know that?

SAMMY. I make it my business to know when a beautiful, mm, soul enters my domain.

> (*But instead of shaking her hand, he kisses it.*)

ANGELA. Oh.

SAMMY. I do not mean to offend.

ANGELA. No, it's nice.

SAMMY. I believe in the old ways, the old notions.

ANGELA. I'm that way, too.

SAMMY. Ja?

ANGELA. Not that I believe in, like, slavery, or whatever. I'm just drawn to old things for some reason.

SAMMY. Ah.

ANGELA. "Old Soul." That's what my mom used to call me.

SAMMY. Old Soul.

ANGELA. I was always doing stuff that made her think I was living in the wrong place, the wrong time.

SAMMY. I know this feeling.

ANGELA. She found me once in the backyard, burying all my Barbies. She said, "Angie, what happened to your Barbies?" And I said, "Plague."

SAMMY. Plague is very serious. The bodies must be buried quickly.

ANGELA. Or burned.

SAMMY. Also acceptable.

ANGELA. And then I made her pray with me.

SAMMY. For their souls. Their Barbie souls.

ANGELA. Children believe everything has a soul. A tree. A shoe.

SAMMY. Adults used to believe such things, too. Once upon a time.

ANGELA. But not anymore.

(SAMMY *pulls closer, meaning to transfix* ANGELA.)

SAMMY. We live in a time of science, ja? The body—the body is nothing more than a petri dish, cells and fluids and a bit of electricity all mixed together for a time in a bag of skin until the spark of life fades and we return to the mud from whence we came. This is what science teaches us. But once—once men *believed*, as you say, that the body was not just mud but a sacred vessel which carried the soul. Once men believed in the soul, it's true. And once women believed in the men who believed those beliefs.

(*Beat.* ANGELA *is not transfixed.*)

ANGELA. I should be getting back.

SAMMY. Yes, of course.

ANGELA. It was nice talking.

SAMMY. Come to me again. I'm almost always here around this time.

ANGELA. I will, assuming my agency doesn't send me someplace new.

SAMMY. The rootlessness you mentioned.

ANGELA. That's me.

SAMMY. And tell no one that we talked. I'm—supposed to be sorting mail, now.

ANGELA. Mum's the word.

(ANGELA *exits.* MICHAEL *stumbles on, his condition is worsening.*)

SAMMY. Jesus. What happened to you?

MICHAEL. Rough night.

SAMMY. Looks like it.

MICHAEL. I got maced.

SAMMY. Hammered?

MICHAEL. Sprayed. It's a chemical. They spray it in the face.

SAMMY. Looks like an allergic reaction or something.

MICHAEL. It's nothing, I'm fine. I had an incident, but I'm fine.

(MICHAEL *tosses the package onto the loading dock.* SAMMY *starts to open it with great care.*)

SAMMY. The new *Twilight* opened last night.

MICHAEL. I know, I got your text.

SAMMY. Infuriating. I mean, who climbs trees like that? Do you know even *one* of us who climbs trees? Or has special powers, other than the googly eyes, and even that doesn't always work so well. I mean, if you had special powers, would you be getting "maced," or eating shrimp, or whatever it is that happened to you?

MICHAEL. Mrs. Rosemary's getting suspicious.

SAMMY. Your landlady?

MICHAEL. Might be time to move on.

SAMMY. Pity. This city's been good to us.

MICHAEL. But like you say, things are getting harder.

SAMMY. Now for just a taste.

(SAMMY *takes a bite, then spits it out.*)

There's fear in this meat, Michael.

MICHAEL. There is?

SAMMY. Yeah. Like, a lot of fear.

MICHAEL. Too much?

SAMMY. Of course too much! What did you do, tenderize her while she was awake?!

MICHAEL. Sorry, Sammy.

SAMMY. We can't eat any of this! What am I supposed to do now, I'm totally out of frozen!

MICHAEL. Maybe we could find someone for tonight.

SAMMY. What are you talking about?! It's 1:30 in the afternoon! I have to go back to work! And then I have pottery class!

MICHAEL. In a club, or something. After hours.

SAMMY. Jesus, Michael, it was supposed to be an easy kill.

MICHAEL. I know, Sammy, I slipped up.

SAMMY. Slipped up?

MICHAEL. I started hearing voices then the whole thing fell apart.

SAMMY. Butchering a conscious woman is not slipping up, Michael, it's suicide!

MICHAEL. She wasn't that conscious.

SAMMY. Not *that* conscious?!

MICHAEL. She was almost out.

SAMMY. This isn't like the old days, Michael, when we could eat whatever we liked! We're older people now! Our systems are fragile! My system is für Scheiße, you know that!

MICHAEL. You don't need to shout at me, Sammy.

(SAMMY *tosses* MICHAEL *the package.*)

SAMMY. Taste that. Taste it, Michael, and tell me she wasn't completely and totally conscious.

MICHAEL. I tasted it already.

SAMMY. Oh, you did, did you?

MICHAEL. Yes, Sammy, I did.

SAMMY. So, what did you think?! That I wouldn't notice?!

MICHAEL. I was hoping the meat might be better than I thought, that the problem might be with me and not with the meat.

SAMMY. Oh, the problem's with you, all right.

(SAMMY *feels* MICHAEL's *forehead.*)

You've got some veins starting to show.

MICHAEL. Where?

SAMMY. On your nose, around the nostrils.

(*Beat.*)

Sit down, Michael, let's take a moment.

(*They sit.* MICHAEL *breaks down, sobbing.* SAMMY *comforts him.*)

Okay.

MICHAEL. She fought hard, Sammy.

SAMMY. I know.

MICHAEL. She wouldn't stop screaming.

SAMMY. Shhhh, I know.

MICHAEL. We started talking politics, Sammy! Politics! You'd think I would have learned by now.

SAMMY. It's this damn country is what it is, it's rotting from the insides. Maybe we should start thinking about Canada.

MICHAEL. I keep getting these visions, these visits in the middle of the night, from Maria, from Otto.

SAMMY. Otto?

MICHAEL. You know, Otto. Von Klargsfeld. From the bluff.

SAMMY. Von Klargsfeld.

MICHAEL. Big guy, kind of scary, snuck out to get some moss.

SAMMY. Oh, right, Otto. Hard line guy.

MICHAEL. It's so—schrecklich, to see him, standing there. How he can stand, after what we did to his shins, I don't know.

SAMMY. Otto didn't make it, Michael. We ate him.

MICHAEL. He says we should return to the fight, that we've betrayed The Cause by lingering so long. And Maria—I think she wants me to die.

(SAMMY *sighs, then takes out his black book.*)

SAMMY. Okay. So. I've got a lead for, well, as soon as possible.

MICHAEL. Maybe Otto is right.

SAMMY. Otto is dead.

MICHAEL. Maybe we should get back into the fight, give our lives some direction, some purpose.

SAMMY. We have a purpose.

MICHAEL. We do?

SAMMY. Survival. That's our purpose.

MICHAEL. Survival is not a purpose.

SAMMY. Survival is the only purpose! Life! Living! Pottery! Everything else is kompletter Unsinn!

MICHAEL. Redemption was our purpose!

SAMMY. "Redemption"?

MICHAEL. Yes, redemption! Imagine it, Sammy, to be relieved of all guilt, all fear! Forever!

SAMMY. Gott im Himmel.

MICHAEL. That's what brought us to Constantinople in the first place, remember?! Fight the infidel and reclaim your soul! That's what the Popes said! That was their promise!

SAMMY. There is no redemption.

MICHAEL. Our crimes were many, even before Constantinople! But now?! After all we've done?! How can we find redemption after all we've done?!

SAMMY. THERE IS NO REDEMPTION!! NOT FOR US!!

(MICHAEL *is silent.*)

I have to get back to work, Michael. My lunch hour is up.

MICHAEL. Okay.

SAMMY. I have this lead, but I'm not going to set you up with her if you're going to fuck it up again.

MICHAEL. I won't fuck it up.

SAMMY. I don't have to start thinking about joining von Goldenhauser's operation in Cincinnati, now do I?

MICHAEL. Von Goldenhauser's operation?

SAMMY. I'm a good bagger, Michael, I'm in demand. And I need to eat. No matter what.

(*Beat.*)

MICHAEL. You can trust me, Sammy. Really. I'm just—having an off day. That's all.

SAMMY. She's an easy mark. Take it slow. Give her her space. And make her drink that wine.

MICHAEL. I will. I promise.

(SAMMY *hands* MICHAEL *the sandwich.*)

SAMMY. Here, take this for later.

MICHAEL. What is it?

SAMMY. Take it! Save it for just before the date, I don't want you having pangs.

MICHAEL. A sandwich?

SAMMY. Ja, a sandwich, it's all I have.

MICHAEL. I'm perfectly capable of buying a sandwich, Sammy.

SAMMY. Not this kind of sandwich.

MICHAEL. Ham?

SAMMY. Oh, that's not ham, Michael. It's meat, but it's not ham. It's Pam.

MICHAEL. Pam?

SAMMY. Oh, yes, Michael. Pam! It's a Pam sandwich! Get me?! Pam!

(*They laugh joylessly at* SAMMY's *terrible joke. Lights fade.*)

Scene 10

(MICHAEL's *apartment. In the kitchen we hear the bustle of a cook at his stove. The buzzer buzzes.* MICHAEL *emerges from the kitchen, an apron over his clothes, and crosses toward the intercom by the front door.*)

MICHAEL. Hello?

(*No response.*)

Angela?

(*Still no response.*)

Three flights up, Angela, I'll leave the door open.

(*He unlocks the door and opens it a crack. On his way back he drops a needle on a record, romantic music begins to play. Tentatively, the front door opens and* OTTO *makes his way into the apartment. Sensing someone's arrived,* MICHAEL *calls to his guest from the kitchen. Offstage:*)

Garlic! I hope you like it! I love it, can't get enough! Some people, they can't stand it, too strong! Use it to ward off demons, not hunger, this I have heard, many times!

(OTTO *takes a moment to check out* MICHAEL's *record collection, marveling at the technology.*)

But here's the thing: People thought garlic could protect you from black magic because garlic can actually protect you from disease! I went to war with a man who ate a clove of garlic every morning, and while others succumbed to the plague, bad humors, he stayed strong!

(MICHAEL *re-enters, still holding his sauce pan.*)

All those old wives' tales, they all have some basis in fact, so if someone tells you to wear garlic as protection—

(MICHAEL, *seeing* OTTO, *stops in his tracks.*)

Gott im Himmel.

OTTO. Michael.

MICHAEL. Otto.

OTTO. There is great danger afoot.

MICHAEL. Yes, I know.

OTTO. Has the Hell-Maiden Maria returned? I have searched for her, but she remains as yet invisible to me.

MICHAEL. Pardon?

OTTO. She means to destroy you, Michael. She means to smother the newborn babe of our fondest hopes and wishes beneath the sagging folds of her womanhood. This is why I call her Hell-Maiden.

MICHAEL. You can't be here now, Otto, someone's coming over.

OTTO. Yes, the meat, Christ forgive us. You'll need it to be strong for your journey.

MICHAEL. I'm not dead yet.

OTTO. Not to Der Unterwelt—to Constantinople. We're all counting on you.

MICHAEL. Right, you mentioned that.

OTTO. When will you leave?

MICHAEL. When? Well, the first thing for me is to cook this meal. Then I can think about Constantinople.

OTTO. Michael, look here. I have pamphlets. Good rates to Turkey. By ship, or *air,* believe it or not, with "frequent flyer miles." What it is, these "miles," I don't know.

MICHAEL. I'll be happy to look at them.

OTTO. Yes, look at them. Then go, the sooner the better. As an American passage will be easy for you. Go as a pilgrim, mm, "tourist," then raise an army from within to crush the Ottomans at their heart! Seize Topkapi, palace of the sultans, and legions of the faithful will rise to conquer Nicaea, Anatolia, Antioch—then on to Jerusalem!

MICHAEL. Topkapi is a museum now.

OTTO. I know it's a museum, but it still has symbolic value. $499 round trip, good discounts on four-star hotels in the heart of the city. That's a good rate, Michael, you won't do better than that.

MICHAEL. I don't have $499.

OTTO. I do.

(OTTO *tosses a purse filled with medieval coins onto the table.*)

2,000 ducats, Michael. There's a good exchange rate now, get your dollars, go to Turkey.

MICHAEL. There is no exchange rate for ducats.

OTTO. Take it to the Jews of the Diamond District, they'll get you your dollars.

MICHAEL. Otto! You can't be here now!

(OTTO, *furious, moves to the front door.*)

OTTO. SO BE IT! But I must warn you, Michael, make haste! For behold! The demons of Hell—are upon us!

(OTTO *throws open the front door to display the bloody ghost of* JANE *standing there once again.*)

MICHAEL. Yes, I saw this one once before.

OTTO. You did?

MICHAEL. A few nights ago. I almost had a heart attack.

(OTTO *moves to another door.*)

OTTO. Okay. But did you see—her!

(OTTO *throws open another door to display the bloody, entranced ghost of* APRIL.)

MICHAEL. No. She's new.

OTTO. The presence of these specters makes it clear that it is not only your soul, but the very order of the natural und supernatural worlds that hang in the balance! A conflagration is coming, Michael, a battle that will make die Götterdämmerung look like Oktoberfest.

(*Both doors slam shut on their own.*)

MICHAEL. Yes. I know.

(*The intercom buzzes.*)

She's here.

OTTO. Maria?!

MICHAEL. My date.

OTTO. Ach, ja, of course. You've got wine?

MICHAEL. I've got wine.

OTTO. You look puffy. You should be wearing powder. You want some?

(OTTO *produces some powder and rouge.*)

It's good powder. You want rouge? It's from the Sultan's camp, it's good, very healthy looking.

(*The intercom buzzes again.*)

I'll leave it in your chambers, if you want it.

MICHAEL. Don't leave anything, just go!

OTTO. For The Cause, Michael! The banner of Christendom shall fly once more above the City of God! Place it there, Michael! Place it!

(*The door buzzes again,* MICHAEL *crosses to the intercom to answer it.*)

MICHAEL. Hello?

ANGELA. (*O.S.*) Michael?

MICHAEL. Angela?

ANGELA. (*O.S.*) Sorry I'm late, Michael. There was a thing on the subway again.

MICHAEL. Three flights up, Angela. I'll leave the door open.

(*He buzzes her in, then turns.*)

Okay, Otto, now listen, about those specters—

(*But* OTTO'*s not there.*)

Otto?

(MICHAEL *checks the kitchen, the bathroom, the bedroom—no* OTTO. ANGELA *enters and makes her way into the apartment.* MICHAEL *returns, still holding his saucepan.*)

ANGELA. Hi, Michael.

(MICHAEL *freezes, dumbstruck.*)

MICHAEL. Maria?

ANGELA. I'm Angela. Actually. Sorry I'm late, there was a thing on the subway. It gets so crazy, you know? Being stuck down there, no way to call up above and everyone's just crammed together, staring at the advertisements. And I'm a little claustrophobic, so I have to really breathe and concentrate otherwise I lose it because I start to feel like I've been buried alive. I'm sort of preoccupied with death. Sammy probably told you.

(MICHAEL *drops his saucepan.*)

MICHAEL. Gott im Himmel. It's you.

(MICHAEL *faints. Blackout.*)

Scene 11

In the dark we hear SAMMY.

SAMMY. Michael.

> (*Beat.*)

Michael.

> (*Beat.*)

Michael, wake up.

> (*Lights up on* MICHAEL, *still splayed out on the floor where he collapsed.* SAMMY *is shaking him.*)

MICHAEL. What?! What is it!

SAMMY. The girl. Where is she?

MICHAEL. The girl?

SAMMY. From last night. Das faulein, ja? Das fleish der macht!

MICHAEL. What time is it?

SAMMY. It's after five, Michael. You were supposed to meet me at the loading dock at one.

> (SAMMY *crosses to the door to check that the hallway is clear, then he crosses throughout, speaking as he searches.*)

Where is she? In the tub? I'm telling you, Michael, I've got the hunger in me. Last night around midnight I was thinking the knife's probably going into her now, all right. One bucket for the blood, one for the guts, the rest skinned and boned and ready for the hammer.

MICHAEL. I don't know where she is, Sammy. I think—she probably just left.

> (SAMMY *stops.*)

SAMMY. She probably just left?

MICHAEL. That's my guess. She walked in the door. I saw her. I dropped my sauce pot. That was it.

SAMMY. I'm having trouble following you, Michael.

MICHAEL. I think she probably just walked out the door. It was open, right?

SAMMY. Right.

MICHAEL. So she probably just let herself out.

SAMMY. You know, Michael, I want to follow you, I'm trying to follow you, but for the life of me I just can't seem to follow you.

MICHAEL. She looked like Maria, Sammy. That's the thing. I thought she was Maria.

SAMMY. You thought she was Maria.

MICHAEL. It was like she was just standing there, right in front of me. I saw her and this rush of heat just flooded my body. The funny thing is I had this talk with Otto just before she arrived. He had these brochures and he was telling me—

SAMMY. Gott im Himmel.

MICHAEL. He wants me to return to Turkey, to reclaim it for Christ.

SAMMY. She was an easy mark, a fucking easy mark.

MICHAEL. And there's something going on with some Hell-Maidens. What it is, I don't know. Otto was a little vague.

SAMMY. God damn you! You said you were all right! You stood there and told me you were up to the job!

MICHAEL. I thought I was up to the job.

SAMMY. Ach, mein GOTT! I had von Goldenhauser on the phone the other day, you know that?! I was talking to him! Me! With von Goldenhauser!

MICHAEL. I don't know what happened, Sammy.

SAMMY. Oh, I know what happened!

MICHAEL. I saw her and I just fainted.

SAMMY. Your mind turned to goop, that's what happened! A little part of your brain melted because it was so hungry, and then you started seeing things!

MICHAEL. It was her.

SAMMY. It was goop! Mush! In there, in your skull! Did you at least eat Pam?!!

MICHAEL. Pam?

SAMMY. The sandwich!

MICHAEL. No, not yet.

(SAMMY *charges* MICHAEL *and throws him against a wall, holding him there.*)

SAMMY. You arschloch! You *schwein*hund!

MICHAEL. It's in the fridge if you want it.

SAMMY. If *I* want it?!

MICHAEL. The sandwich.

SAMMY. Look at my face, Michael, at the pallor of my face. Healthy? Rosy? No, my friend, a bit greenish if you ask me. A bit ashen. So, yes, I would like to eat the sandwich, I DID want to eat the sandwich, but I gave it to you! Why?! Because you had a job to do! But you didn't do that job, now did you?!

(MRS. ROSEMARY *appears in the doorway, brandishing a saucepan for defense.*)

MICHAEL. I thought she was Maria, Sammy. Then I fainted.

SAMMY. You thought she was Maria?! Of course you thought she was Maria, you motherfucker, you *ficken*-kopf! In a couple of days you'll think I'M Maria!

MRS. ROSEMARY. Who's Maria?

(*The men break apart, taken by surprise.*)

SAMMY. Your landlady?

MICHAEL. Ja. Reuben's widow.

MRS. ROSEMARY. And who's this? One of the undead like yourself?

MICHAEL. We're not undead, Mrs. Rosemary. Not exactly.

MRS. ROSEMARY. I'm calling the police.

(MICHAEL *crosses to stop her.*)

MICHAEL. I wouldn't do that if I were you.

MRS. ROSEMARY. Why?! So you can do to me whatever it is you do to those poor girls?!

MICHAEL. Bathe them, do you mean?

MRS. ROSEMARY. You don't fool me! And you don't scare me! I don't know what you had over my Reuben, but whatever it was you don't have it over me!

MICHAEL. Reuben and I did have an "understanding," it's true.

MRS. ROSEMARY. What "understanding"?

MICHAEL. I had something that I wanted to give your husband, Mrs. Rosemary. Something precious. But in the end he was too fearful to receive my gift.

MRS. ROSEMARY. What gift?

MICHAEL. You wouldn't believe me if I told you.

SAMMY. Michael.

MICHAEL. We have to tell her.

SAMMY. It's too dangerous.

MRS. ROSEMARY. What gift?!

MICHAEL. Immortality.

(*Beat.* MRS. ROSEMARY *moves toward the door,* MICHAEL *blocks her.*)

You know what I say is true. I've been here a long time, as long as you. But I am young—youngish—and you are old. Wouldn't you like to be youngish again, too?

MRS. ROSEMARY. You're insane.

MICHAEL. I wanted to give this gift to Reuben. Eternal life for a safe place to live at below-market rent.

MRS. ROSEMARY. Your rent is WAY below market!

MICHAEL. And still he was too fearful to let me keep my end of the bargain. He feared for his soul and now he's dead. But you are not afraid, Mrs. Rosemary. Join us.

SAMMY. You're telling her too much, Michael.

MICHAEL. I'm telling her what she already knows.

MRS. ROSEMARY. I'm calling the cops.

MICHAEL. Yes, call the cops. But without our gift you will die, like Reuben, like everyone. You will turn to dust and all you know or ever knew will disappear into the soil—except people aren't put in the ground anymore, are they? They're incinerated and disposed of like so much medical waste.

MRS. ROSEMARY. What are you?

MICHAEL. I'm practical.

MRS. ROSEMARY. You're sick.

MICHAEL. Well, yes, I am a little under the weather at the moment.

MRS. ROSEMARY. I want to go.

MICHAEL. I'm going to let you go. But before I do, consider this: There is no Heaven. No Hell. Just the vast eternity of The Void. Some think it peace. Others know that the agony of our final moments echo to the end of time. Call the police and that is your due. Let me help you, and you can escape what your Reuben was too afraid to escape.

(MICHAEL *steps aside.* MRS. ROSEMARY, *horrified, scrambles past* MICHAEL *and disappears down the hallway.* MICHAEL *closes the door behind her.*)

SAMMY. That was a mistake.

MICHAEL. She won't call the police.

SAMMY. She might.

MICHAEL. Not for a few days, at least.

SAMMY. Time for us to go.

MICHAEL. Set it up again.

SAMMY. Set what up again?

MICHAEL. Angela.

SAMMY. Forget Angela! Forget Maria! It's *over!*

MICHAEL. I want to see her again.

SAMMY. So see her! Go to sleep, have a dream, you'll see her!

MICHAEL. It's not the same.

SAMMY. You remember Schmidt?

MICHAEL. Schmidt?

SAMMY. Let himself get caught down in Juárez. Lingered in some hacienda too long, fedarales came and hauled him away. He turned to goop in some Gott-forsaken prisión south of the border. Los federales were so erschrocken they swore each other to silencio, covered the whole thing up. And that was—what?—over a hundred years ago.

MICHAEL. I'm not seeing things, Sammy. I mean, I am seeing things— like a lot of things—but not her. I believe in her.

SAMMY. You just told the old woman you don't believe in anything but The Void!

MICHAEL. I don't know what to believe. But I want to believe. Don't you? I mean, most people wouldn't believe we're possible, would they? And yet we are. So maybe there's more to the world than what we know.

SAMMY. I'm going to Cincinnati, Michael, next couple of days. If he'll have me. I've done what I can for you, now you have to help yourself. Recognize you have a problem, choose to do something about it, and save yourself.

(SAMMY *gets up to leave,* MICHAEL *follows.*)

MICHAEL. If she's an easy mark she's still an easy mark.

SAMMY. Take a walk down to the nearest prisión if you like. It'll expedite the process and leave me out of it.

MICHAEL. Give me her number, I'll set it up myself. What do you care, I'm dead to you, anyway.

SAMMY. You're not dead to me, Michael. You're my friend. I'm just hungry, that's all.

(SAMMY *opens the door to leave,* MICHAEL *slams it shut. As the two argue, the ghosts of* JANE *and* APRIL *appear once again, seen by* MICHAEL, *unseen by* SAMMY.)

MICHAEL. And what if I'm right?!

SAMMY. About what?!

MICHAEL. About her!

SAMMY. You're not right!

MICHAEL. But what if I am?! What if what I told the old woman is wrong and what I suspect about the young woman is right?! What if she is Maria, in some way?! What if her spirit—?!

SAMMY. 500 years, Michael! 500 years we've had to witness some kind of miracle, some kind of sign that there's more to life than what we see! And you know what?! NO SIGN! You say that a miracle is happening to you now?! You're not dying, no, not hallucinating! An angel has descended from on high to say "Michael Karl Josef von Siebenburg, you have been murdering blameless, beautiful human beings for centuries—CENTURIES!—but you, even *you* can be saved if—" WHAT?! What does she want from you?!

(The ghosts beckon to MICHAEL, *as if calling him to them.)*

MICHAEL. I don't know!

SAMMY. You don't know because she doesn't exist!

MICHAEL. But what if she does?!

SAMMY. Hilf mir, Jesus.

MICHAEL. What if it really is her, not in my dreams, my fever dreams, but here, alive, in this city, on this Earth?! What if she really is?!

SAMMY. Then we live again!

MICHAEL. Wouldn't that be wonderful?

SAMMY. Yes, Michael. Yes it would.

MICHAEL. You see?

SAMMY. But we don't live again.

MICHAEL. You don't know that. Not for sure.

SAMMY. No. I don't.

(The ghosts disappear.)

MICHAEL. Give me her number.

(Beat.)

SAMMY. I'll call her.

MICHAEL. Thank you, Sammy.

SAMMY. I'm the one with the secure line, I'll do the calling.

MICHAEL. Yes, absolutely.

SAMMY. Any resistance, any suspicion, and it's off.

MICHAEL. I just need to see her again, Sammy. Just once.

SAMMY. And then I'm going. I'm leaving. With or without you. Verstehen, sie?

MICHAEL. Ja. Verstehe.

*(*SAMMY *starts toward the door, then stops.)*

SAMMY. And if you're wrong? If you know you're wrong?

MICHAEL. About her?

SAMMY. That's right, Michael, about her.

(Beat, MICHAEL *thinks it through.)*

MICHAEL. Then I'll kill her.

(Blackout.)

Scene 12

Battle sounds roar and fade to be replaced by romantic music which also fades away. Lights up on MICHAEL *and* ANGELA, *the end of another meal.* MICHAEL *holds a bottle of wine in his lap.*

ANGELA. Well, that was a wonderful meal.

MICHAEL. Thank you.

ANGELA. Sammy was right. You really can cook.

MICHAEL. I know one or two dishes.

(*Beat.*)

ANGELA. I'm sorry I ran out on you.

MICHAEL. Don't be.

ANGELA. I should have called an ambulance or something.

MICHAEL. You did what anyone would do. I mean, after all, you don't know me.

ANGELA. I guess I just don't like to think of myself as the sort of person who would leave another person just lying there in the middle of his apartment, his head busted open.

MICHAEL. My head wasn't busted open.

ANGELA. Oh. Sammy told me—

MICHAEL. I fainted, that's all. I'm fine. Anyway, I have a feeling you're not that sort of person.

ANGELA. I did the sort of thing that that sort of person would do.

MICHAEL. Perhaps we're more than what we do. Or what we've done.

ANGELA. More?

MICHAEL. A baby hasn't done anything, but still, he is a person, is he not? He has a personality, an identity.

ANGELA. A soul?

MICHAEL. If you believe in the soul, then certainly, a baby must have one.

ANGELA. I used to believe in the soul. When I was a kid.

MICHAEL. But not anymore.

ANGELA. Maybe not. I'm still trying to decide.

MICHAEL. Me, too.

(*Beat.*)

ANGELA. I think I'm ready for that wine, now.

MICHAEL. The wine?

ANGELA. If it's not too late.

MICHAEL. Yes, of course. The wine.

(MICHAEL *sets about opening the wine.*)

ANGELA. I love the bottle.

MICHAEL. It's very old, this wine. Very ancient. Very—flavorful.

ANGELA. I'm drawn to old things. Sammy probably told you.

MICHAEL. He did. He told me about the Barbies, too.

ANGELA. The Barbies? Oh, right, the Barbies. I went through this whole medieval phase when I was a kid. The Black Death, chastity belts, that sort of thing. Not bathing.

MICHAEL. Bathing was considered unhealthy, back then. Bad humors.

ANGELA. I got into a lot of fights with my mom about not bathing.

MICHAEL. You would have had to wear perfume to cover the smell.

ANGELA. I did. God, I used to wear so much perfume.

(*Beat.*)

MICHAEL. Can I ask you a question?

ANGELA. Yes.

MICHAEL. You don't have to answer if you don't want to.

ANGELA. I bathe, now. Regularly. If that's what you're wondering.

MICHAEL. You don't know me.

ANGELA. No.

MICHAEL. But do I look—familiar to you?

ANGELA. Familiar?

MICHAEL. Even in the slightest way.

(*Beat.*)

ANGELA. No.

MICHAEL. Oh. Okay.

(MICHAEL *pops the cork.*)

ANGELA. It's more like you feel familiar to me. If that makes any sense.

MICHAEL. It might.

ANGELA. I feel like I've met you before.

MICHAEL. You do?

ANGELA. Sammy, too. He was sort of looking at me the way you're looking at me. The same sort of scrunched up thing going on with his eyes, like he thought he met me somewhere. Which made me think I had met him.

MICHAEL. The power of suggestion.

ANGELA. Maybe. Or maybe just wishful thinking.

MICHAEL. Wishful thinking?

ANGELA. I *wish* I had met you before. I mean, that would be great, wouldn't it? To have lived some past life that you don't even know about, but you do, kind of, when you get that, I don't know, that déjà vu kind of feeling when you meet someone you're sure you've met before. Sorry. I'm babbling.

MICHAEL. No you're not.

ANGELA. I mean, we want so much to—to *believe*, don't we? In the soul. Past lives. Anything. We want the world to be more than what we see because what we see can be pretty awful.

MICHAEL. Medieval times were full of such beliefs.

ANGELA. We could learn a lot from those people! I mean, don't get me wrong, I know, most people back then lived short, brutal lives full of squalor, filth, poverty and ignorance.

MICHAEL. Not bathing.

ANGELA. But they gave death its due. Nowadays, we do everything we can to push death away. We end our lives in hospitals, connected to tubes. But in medieval times—they were in the thick of it, you know?

MICHAEL. I do.

ANGELA. Anyway. When I meet a person that I think—I *feel* I've met before, it gives me hope. Like there's more to the world than what we know.

(*She holds out her glass to be filled. Beat.*)

MICHAEL. It's off, I'm afraid.

ANGELA. The wine?

MICHAEL. Turned to vinegar.

ANGELA. That's a shame.

MICHAEL. And it's late.

ANGELA. The wine?

MICHAEL. The evening.

ANGELA. Oh. Okay.

MICHAEL. You must forgive me, but I have big day tomorrow.

ANGELA. I put you off, didn't I. The thing about me not bathing.

MICHAEL. You were charming. And captivating and really very clean. I simply fear that if you don't leave now I will do something that you and I will both regret.

ANGELA. And you have a big day tomorrow.

MICHAEL. That, too. I'll get your coat.

(MICHAEL *retrieves* ANGELA's *coat and returns.*)

ANGELA. Listen, I know we got off to a rocky start. But I'd love to see you again.

MICHAEL. I'm about to make a journey—a very long journey. If, by some miracle, I return, I shall come for you. I will find you. And I will tell you things about the olden days. Things that no one knows but me.

(*With full medieval flourish,* MICHAEL *takes* ANGELA's *hand and kisses it.*)

ANGELA. You really are a baron, aren't you.

MICHAEL. I was. I don't know what I am, now.

(ANGELA *kisses* MICHAEL.)

ANGELA. Sammy has my number.

(*She exits.* MICHAEL, *happy, closes the door.* OTTO *appears from the shadows.*)

OTTO. Michael.

(MICHAEL *jumps, taken by surprise.*)

MICHAEL. Otto, Jesus. You scared me.

OTTO. So. You are going.

MICHAEL. Yes.

OTTO. On your journey.

MICHAEL. Yes. Ja. Jawhol.

(OTTO *embraces his comrade.*)

I saw the specters again.

OTTO. Hell is splurting up its souls in anticipation of our downfall. But we won't fall down, Michael, now will we.

MICHAEL. I must pack.

(OTTO *follows as* MICHAEL *retrieves a suitcase and begins packing, sloppily, trying not to falter.*)

OTTO. And the girl?

MICHAEL. The girl?

OTTO. Das fraulein. Das fleisch der macht. You don't need her?

MICHAEL. Not anymore.

OTTO. But the meat, Michael. Surely you must eat.

MICHAEL. We don't need to eat them, Otto. We just need to love them.

OTTO. "To love them"?

MICHAEL. Gott, I feel fantastic.

OTTO. You look awful.

MICHAEL. I feel like a kid again, like how we were when we first set out to save Christendom from The Turk.

OTTO. That's good. But that may just be your body shutting down, the last gasp of your corporeal form before it collapses.

MICHAEL. I will hail a cab. I will ride to the Diamond District, to exchange your ducats. It's late, I know, but I trust at least one hungry soul will remain to receive my offering.

OTTO. The path you are about to take will be difficult, Michael.

MICHAEL. I will ride to the airport, purchase my ticket, and fly across the ocean just as Jesus walked across the sea.

OTTO. I need to know you've the strength to do what must be done.

MICHAEL. In ten hours' time I will arrive and stand once again on the soil of Constantine, in the city he built by the Bosporus!

OTTO. Yes, that's what we've been hoping for—for centuries!

MICHAEL. I will take another cab, this time to the Hagia Sophia, Protector of Relics, Cathedral of Old, and I will ascend the steps once covered with the blood of the innocent!

OTTO. If Gott is with us, let it be so!

MICHAEL. I will stride, through the Imperial gate, across the Ottoman carpets, and under the heavenly dome—to the Altar! Or what remains of the Altar! I will kneel!

OTTO. Gott *IS* with us!

MICHAEL. And I will pray! To Jesus! To Mohammed! To Buddha, if he'll hear me! I will ask their forgiveness, for the crimes we have committed! Against Man! Against GOTT!

OTTO. Gott has answered—!! Wait a minute, what?

MICHAEL. The time has come to put down the sword, Otto, forever. The time has come to see the sacred in each and every soul, whether Christian or Muslim, gentile or Jew. We are all Gott's creatures, you see. And from this day forth, we shall treat each and every soul as we would our Maria—with grace and gratitude, tenderness and joy.

OTTO. "Maria"?

(MICHAEL *snaps shut his suitcase and heads for the door.*)

MICHAEL. And so I go, to spread this new Gospel! In Constantinople! In Jerusalem! In Mecca, if they'll allow it! I may not be a prophet—or, who knows, maybe I am—but I will be Gott's messenger on Earth, for as long as my body permits.

(MICHAEL *throws open the door, but* OTTO, *with his ghostly powers, commands the door to shut.*)

OTTO. HALT!!

MICHAEL. You said go to Constantinople. I'm going to Constantinople.

(OTTO *advances, enraged.* MICHAEL *retreats.*)

OTTO. I have spent time with you, Michael. I have spoken with you and I have offered you my ducats.

MICHAEL. I know, and I appreciate it, Otto, I do.

OTTO. And now you tell me the Hell-Maiden Maria has infected your heart so deeply that you would travel to the City of Gott, not to conquer it, but to surrender?! TO THE INFIDEL?!!

MICHAEL. You can't think of it as surrendering, Otto, you have to think of it as embracing the true Word of Gott. And stop calling Maria a Hell-Maiden!

(OTTO *grabs* MICHAEL *by the throat and, with godlike strength, lifts him up with one hand.*)

OTTO. Look at you, Michael. Already your muscle is turning to mush, your bones soft as pudding. Already your faith has turned to goop, long before your body.

(OTTO *throws* MICHAEL *to the floor.*)

The Knights *AUS* Der Unterwelt warned me about you, Michael. "He is weak at heart" they said, "Best to pick another pony." But I didn't want to believe them. I wanted to believe in you, and now you have betrayed me. You have betrayed yourself.

MICHAEL. I just want to tell people to love each other! You know, love thy neighbor as thyself!

(OTTO *unsheathes his medieval sword.*)

OTTO. I will give you your turn at the sword, then, Goop Man. I will push the goop from your heart and fill it with steel! So ends this blaspheme! So ends all blasphemers!

(*The front door opens to reveal* MARIA *standing in the hallway, holding a sword of her own.*)

MARIA. It is you who blasphemes, Otto. It was always you.

OTTO & MICHAEL. Maria!

MARIA. Step away from my Mann and give him his peace on this, his final day.

MICHAEL. Final day?!

MARIA. Final one or two days. Step away or you will taste the tang of my blade.

OTTO. Well well well, the original Whore of Europe, the flower that distracted the pride of Christendom with its scent.

MARIA. I distracted no one, Otto. I was a wife to my Mann, my beloved Michael.

OTTO. You were married to a soldier, wife, a soldier who betrayed his destiny. He must die!

MARIA. He will die!

MICHAEL. I'm going to die?!

MARIA. Not right away, but yes, Michael, you need to die.

OTTO. So he shall, and like a soldier that my soldier-tool might be filled with martial fury!

MARIA. He will die like a saint and so join me in Himmel!

MICHAEL. But—what about my journey?!

OTTO. I will send you on your way—to join the specters who call you home! So stand aside, woman! See how a true Mann does his manly duty!

MARIA. I will not stand aside! So show me, Herr von Kargsfeld! Show me how a Mann fights a woman!

(OTTO *rushes* MARIA, *they fight viciously,* MICHAEL *crawls out of their way.*)

OTTO. Can't you do better than that, woman?! Or is your only power in the whore-scent of your flower?!

MARIA. The souls are within him, Otto, Souls of the Innocents! And as fear can live in meat so too can it live in souls—unless released amidst a shroud of love!

MICHAEL. That's what I'm going to do on my journey! Be loving!

MARIA. Yes, meine Leibe, but it must be a death-shroud of love.

OTTO. Surrender the souls to her and she will build a "Frau-Reich" in Himmel as it is being built on Earth! And to this I say nein! NEIN! So I seize said souls! My sword will drink in his blood and glow with the power aus Der Gott-Leben! If the living will not fight, then so must the dead!

(*They fight,* MICHAEL *flees to his room.* OTTO *drives* MARIA *back.*)

MARIA. Do you like how this dead woman fights?!

OTTO. I like it well, far better than the non-fighting of your schwanzlutscher husband!

(OTTO *knocks the sword from* MARIA's *hand. Helpless, she retreats as* OTTO *advances.*)

MARIA. Get used to it, then, for there are many flowers yet left in the garden now willing to fight!

OTTO. When the time comes I'll cut them, too!

(HELGA *appears in the distance. She can see us, but cannot join in the fray.*)

MARIA. Von Blaumstein's Helga, to name one. Blonde, buxom, her hair in those rings they used to keep back then.

OTTO. I remember her!

(ANNA *also appears in the distance.*)

MARIA. Or Schmidt's Anna! Or even your beloved Gretel!

(OTTO *stops.* MICHAEL *returns, now holding a crossbow.*)

OTTO. Gretel?

MARIA. That's right, Otto, Gretel. Your Gretel.

OTTO. Gretel? *My* Gretel?!

MARIA. I know her well, Otto! We have lunch together!

OTTO. Gretel?! You have lunch with my Gretel?!

MARIA. With Gretel—in Himmel! She waits for you!

OTTO. In Himmel?! Gretel?! When can I see her?!

MICHAEL. Immediately, if you like!

(OTTO *turns to face* MICHAEL.)

OTTO. Immediately?! Gretel?!!

(MICHAEL *shoots: Sssssssswpank!*)

Ah, yes. Yes of course.

(OTTO *sinks down, collapsing to the floor.*)

To die again, the death of a dead man. How is it possible? I'm going, Michael. Farewell. I'll be watching you from Himmel. Forever. Remember, Michael! Remember… Michael… remember… White…light!

(OTTO *dies.*)

MICHAEL. He gets to go to Himmel?

MARIA. Oh, he's not going to Himmel.

(MICHAEL *stumbles a step toward* MARIA.)

MICHAEL. Sweet Maria.

MARIA. No touching, Michael. Remember.

(MICHAEL *collapses onto the couch.*)

MICHAEL. And what of me? Do I go to Himmel, now? Or to that other place?

MARIA. Rest, then, husband. We'll be together before too long.

(*As* MICHAEL *speaks,* HELGA *and* ANNA *join* MARIA *to drag* OTTO *away with her.*)

MICHAEL. Because—I guess I feel like I'm just starting to figure a few things out, you know? And if I just had a little more time, just a little, there's so much I could do.

(MRS. ROSEMARY *enters from the hallway, holding a knife.*)

MICHAEL. You know? Maria?

MRS. ROSEMARY. No, Mr. Siebenburg. It's me.

(MRS. ROSEMARY *checks the apartment out thoroughly as they talk.*)

MICHAEL. Oh, hi, Mrs. Rosemary. I thought you were someone else.

MRS. ROSEMARY. I heard fighting.

MICHAEL. It's over now.

MRS. ROSEMARY. I've been thinking about your offer.

MICHAEL. Yes?

MRS. ROSEMARY. I think I'd rather join Reuben, wherever he is.

MICHAEL. That's a very romantic notion.

MRS. ROSEMARY. I'm—what's the expression? I'm "old-school," that way.

MICHAEL. Me, too.

MRS. ROSEMARY. What's wrong with you, are you sick?

MICHAEL. I feel great. My body won't work anymore, that's all.

MRS. ROSEMARY. My Reuben used to say things like that.

MICHAEL. It's so cold all of a sudden. Are you cold?

MRS. ROSEMARY. No, Mr. Siebenburg, I'm not cold.

(*Beat.*)

You want a blanket?

MICHAEL. Yes. Please.

MRS. ROSEMARY. I'll bring you a blanket. Then I'm calling the police, not that they'll believe me.

MICHAEL. God, I'm freezing.

(*Lights fade as* MRS. ROSEMARY *exits.*)

Scene 13

MICHAEL *lies asleep on his couch, a blanket covers him.* SAMMY *enters, trailing his suitcase. He crosses toward* MICHAEL *and stands above him for a moment or two, considering his old friend.*

SAMMY. Michael.

(*Beat.*)

Michael.

(MICHAEL *awakes, he is in very bad shape, quite close to death.*)

MICHAEL. Maria?

SAMMY. It's me, Michael. Sammy.

MICHAEL. It's gotten…it's gotten to my shins, Sammy. It's gotten all the way up to my shins.

(SAMMY, *quite carefully, lifts the blanket to look at* MICHAEL's *feet and shins. He winces at what he sees, then, after a moment, he replaces the blanket.*)

SAMMY. Are you comfortable?

MICHAEL. I'm terribly cold. But I'm not uncomfortable, if that's what you mean.

(SAMMY *produces a small, clay container.*)

SAMMY. I brought you some meat. It's old, old frozen, but it's all right.

MICHAEL. I don't want it.

(SAMMY *places the container by* MICHAEL.)

SAMMY. I'll leave it. For later, maybe.

MICHAEL. (*Noticing the container.*) I do love the, um—What do you call this?

SAMMY. A pot. I don't know, I made it in class. Something for you to remember me by.

MICHAEL. So. You're leaving.

SAMMY. I got the call from von Goldenhauser. He says I can start right away.

MICHAEL. I have a message for him. For you, too.

SAMMY. Yeah?

MICHAEL. We don't have to eat them, Sammy, we just have to love them. This is my message to the world.

(*Beat.*)

SAMMY. That's a great message.

(MICHAEL *convulses,* SAMMY *steadies him.*)

SAMMY. Oh, Gott, Michael. I'm so sorry this is happening to you.

MICHAEL. You warned me.

SAMMY. Yes, Michael, I did. I did.

MICHAEL. They're not even there any more, are they, Sammy? The shins.

SAMMY. They're not looking particularly appetizing right now, no.

(ANGELA *appears at the door, unseen.*)

ANGELA. Hi, Sammy.

MICHAEL. Maria? Is that you?

ANGELA. It's me, Michael. I was going to call, but I don't have your number. I hope it's okay that I just came by.

MICHAEL. It's fine, Angela. I'm glad you're here.

SAMMY. Mmm…meat. *Meat.*

ANGELA. I can leave if you like.

MICHAEL. No, Sammy's the one who's leaving. Right, Sammy?

SAMMY. Yes. But perhaps, before I go, some—wine?

MICHAEL. Sammy!

(SAMMY *trundles his suitcase to the door, then turns to face his old friend.*)

SAMMY. We're going to make it, Michael. We really will take back Constantinople. And when we do, there will be a hundred thousand knights to lift their glasses to you, Baron Michael Karl Josef von Siebenburg, the greatest among us.

(*Beat.*)

Tschüss.

(SAMMY *exits*, ANGELA *crosses to sit beside* MICHAEL.)

ANGELA. My God, you look awful.

MICHAEL. I feel wonderful.

ANGELA. You want me to call somebody?

MICHAEL. No! No doctors. Please. Just sit with me.

(*She does so. Beat.*)

ANGELA. Mrs. Rosemary told me not to come.

MICHAEL. Mrs. Rosemary?

ANGELA. She's downstairs talking to some cops.

(*Beat.*)

MICHAEL. There's a purse on the table. Bring it to me, please.

(ANGELA *crosses to the table.*)

ANGELA. A purse?

MICHAEL. Filled with coins.

ANGELA. I feel like I should be calling an ambulance or something.

MICHAEL. NO! No doctors, no ambulance.

(*She returns with the purse, he digs through it.*)

ANGELA. You don't look good, Michael.

MICHAEL. (*Taking two coins.*) Two for me, the rest for you. Now, listen. Take the purse. Sell the coins. Go to Constantinople. Tell the people to love thy neighbor as they would thyself. Themself. Themselves. You must do this. Promise me.

ANGELA. You want me to go to Istanbul?

MICHAEL. It doesn't have to be right away. In a month. A year. Whenever your schedule permits. The coins are worth thousands—tens of thousands of dollars.

ANGELA. Michael, I'm not going to take your—What are these?

MICHAEL. Ducats, from the olden days. Take them. Then go.

ANGELA. We'll go together. When you're feeling better.

MICHAEL. I have my own journey to make, a different sort of journey.

>   (ANGELA *feels his forehead.*)

ANGELA. There's a paramedic with the cops, I'm going to get him.

MICHAEL. Okay. But give me a few minutes. I need time to prepare.

ANGELA. Prepare?

MICHAEL. You know, for the Ferryman and all that.

>   (ANGELA *kisses* MICHAEL *gently on the forehead.*)

ANGELA. I'll be right back.

>   (*She rushes out.* MICHAEL, *barely alive, takes the two ducats and gently places one over each eye. Then, barely audible.*)

MICHAEL. It's...it's...just...fantastic.

>   (*Lights fade.*)

End of Play

THE VERI**ON PLAY
by Lisa Kron
with music by Jeanine Tesori

Copyright © 2012 by Lisa Kron. All rights reserved. CAUTION: Professionals and amateurs are hereby warned that *The Veri**on Play* is subject to a royalty. It is fully protected under the copyright laws of the United States of America and of all countries covered by the International Copyright Union (including the Dominion of Canada and the rest of the British Commonwealth), the Berne Convention, the Pan-American Copyright Convention and the Universal Copyright Convention, as well as all countries with which the United States has reciprocal copyright relations. All rights, including professional, amateur stage rights, motion picture, recitation, lecturing, public reading, radio broadcasting, television, video or sound recording, all other forms of mechanical or electronic reproduction, such as CD-ROM, CD-I, information storage and retrieval systems and photocopying, and the rights of translation into foreign languages, are strictly reserved. Particular emphasis is laid upon the matter of readings, permission for which must be secured from the Author's agent in writing.

Required royalties must be paid every time this play is performed before any audience, whether or not it is presented for profit and whether or not admission is charged.

All inquiries concerning rights, including amateur rights, should be addressed to: Patrick Herold, International Creative Management, Inc., 730 Fifth Avenue, New York, NY 10019. 212-556-5782.

ABOUT *THE VERI**ON PLAY*

This article first ran in the January/February 2012 issue of Inside Actors, *Actors Theatre of Louisville's subscriber newsletter, and is based on conversations with the playwright before rehearsals for the Humana Festival production began.*

"Working on this play has revealed to me that, with the possible exception of birth and death, there is no experience as universal as a customer service nightmare," says playwright and performer Lisa Kron. An encounter with the phone company inspired Kron's wickedly funny revenge fantasy, *The Veri**on Play,* about a woman whose attempt to fix a seemingly innocuous billing error sucks her into a gas-lit vortex of horror. "It was one of those Kafkaesque experiences one has that goes on for many months," she recalls. "I was in a state of apoplectic rage, and found myself screaming at this poor customer service person: '*I'm going to write a play about this!*' There was a brief pause which I interpreted to mean, 'Okay, good luck with that. Knock yourself out.' I needed to write a play that was a primal scream. But that would be unbearable to watch, so I attempted to counterbalance it with my love of theatrical craft, my devotion to cheap laughs, and my interest in the alchemy that occurs between stage and audience and lifts us into that delicious 'we're all in this together' feeling."

Kron's primal scream at corporate malfeasance takes the form of a delightful mash-up of screwball comedy and noir thriller parody. *The Veri**on Play* abounds with pointed silliness as our heroine Jenni Jensen (played by Kron herself in the Humana Festival production) tries to get her billing problem resolved, with increasingly ridiculous results, and journeys down a widening rabbit hole of absurdity. Along the way, she makes a series of discoveries revealing that the problem goes much deeper than she'd ever imagined. A mysterious woman invites her to a support group called PHBICS—an acronym for "People Hurt Badly by Inadequate Customer Service." Jenni hesitantly visits this odd assortment of cranks and nerds, finding that they are indeed the "whining weirdos" she fears becoming herself. But she also learns that amid their wounded obsessions with evil fine print and bad mortgages, credit scams and whose turn it is to bring snacks...well, they may just be on to something about what's happening in America. And they might be the only ones who can help her.

Out of this premise spins a goofy adventure, powered by a theatrical engine that Kron describes as "giddy, fast-paced theatre fun and surprise stagecraft." Citing as influences the scrappy, inventive stage magic of Charles Ludlam's Ridiculous Theatrical Company, as well as her own roots in parody as a young writer-performer at New York's WOW Café, Kron revels in a madcap comic sensibility with *The Veri**on Play*. There are crazy cross-continental chases and dangerous late-night confrontations, an ensemble of actors who deftly morph into different roles, and *two* pairs of twins—which adds the fun of watching one actress play sisters in the same scene. "Theatre is nothing if not transformation," says Kron. "Everything turns into something else: characters, locations. That's one of the things that so deeply engage us. So this is the kind of theatre that really embraces the down-and-dirty bedazzlement of how cheaply—as in *stupidly*—we can do these things. Through the force of your will and drive, you can turn one thing into something else onstage. You just *make* something."

Kron also plays with the conventions of a noir thriller. "Genre spoofs are really fun," observes the playwright. "The audience recognizes the structure, so it allows you to have this kind of wildness of content." But in addition to generating laughs, the suspense and anxiety associated with the thriller matches Jenni's growing apprehension that her customer service nightmare may be one from which she'll never wake—inflicted by a power that's beyond her control. "It taps into our impotence against a nonsensical corporate monolith that claims to be caring about you while it's grinding you to a pulp," Kron explains. Jenni learns that she's dealing with a completely amoral entity, and hers is just one of many sad stories in the support group. "They are getting so screwed over, and there's nothing to do. That's the world we're living in," says Kron.

The Veri**on Play, then, also captures the energy of the moment we're experiencing right now, cracking jokes that speak to the same fed-up frustration reflected in the Occupy Wall Street protests. "We're all getting kind of beaten up," Kron says, "but we're starting to realize: This isn't just happening to me. This is actually widespread and pernicious. Corporations don't have responsibilities like people, they don't suffer the same consequences for their actions, and yet we have handed over to them a huge amount of control over our daily lives. I think we're in a moment of dawning consciousness about the extent and effects of this shift." Tapping into this deep disquiet, Kron's sharp eloquence about the strange time we're living in has found an outlet through raucous humor. "I *had* to write a funny play," she insists, "because otherwise I'd go down the path of crazy-lady ranting." In doing so, Kron has given us an uproariously cathartic comedy for our troubled times—a silly, silly light to laugh by in the dark.

—Amy Wegener

BIOGRAPHY

Lisa Kron has been writing and performing theater since moving to New York from Michigan in 1984. Her work has been widely produced in New York, regionally, and internationally. In addition to *The Veri**on Play*, her plays include *In the Wake* (Lortel and GLAAD best play nominations, Susan Smith Blackburn Prize finalist, included in the annual *Best Plays of 2010-2011*); *Well* (included in *Best Plays of 2003-2004* and produced on Broadway in 2006 in a production that earned two Tony Award nominations); *2.5 Minute Ride* (Obie, L.A. Drama-Logue and GLAAD Media Awards); *101 Humiliating Stories* (Drama Desk nomination); and *Fun Home,* a musical adaptation of Alison Bechdel's graphic novel written with composer Jeanine Tesori. Honors include playwriting fellowships from the Lortel and Guggenheim Foundations, Sundance Theater Lab, the Lark Play Development Center, and the MacDowell Colony, the Cal Arts/Alpert Award, a Helen Merrill Award, and grants from the Creative Capital Foundation and New York Foundation for the Arts. Lisa is a founding member of the Obie and Bessie-Award-winning collaborative theater company The Five Lesbian Brothers. She is a resident playwright at the American Voices New Play Institute at Arena Stage. She is on the playwriting faculty of the Yale School of Drama, and serves on the Council of the Dramatists Guild of America.

ACKNOWLEDGMENTS

The Veri**on Play premiered at the Humana Festival of New American Plays in February 2012. It had original music by Jeanine Tesori and was directed by Nicholas Martin with the following cast:

JENNI ....Lisa Kron
ANISSA...Carolyn Baeumler
JERRY NYBERG, et al...Joel Van Liew
WANDA, et al.............................. Kimberly Hébert-Gregory
CAROL K. ANDERSON, et al. ....Ching Valdes-Aran
STEVE, et al.. Clayton Dean Smith
BRYCE/LARS .... Calvin Smith
INGRID/CYDNEY.. Hannah Bos
ENSEMBLE ....Sabrina Conti, Chris Reid

and the following production staff:

Scenic Designer...Tom Tutino
Costume Designer .... Kristopher Castle
Lighting Designer..Kirk Bookman
Sound Designer... Benjamin Marcum
Properties Designer.. Joe Cunningham
Wig Designer.. Heather Fleming
Music Supervisor..Scott Anthony
Movement Director ....Delilah Smyth
Stage Manager .... Stephen Horton
Dramaturg..Amy Wegener

Directing Assistant ....Caitlin Ryan O'Connell
Assistant Costume Designer.................... Lindsay Chamberlin
Production Assistant ....Jessica Potter
Fight Supervisor...Nick Vannoy
Assistant Dramaturg..Molly Clasen

The Veri**on Play was originally commissioned and produced by The Theatre Arts Department of Drew University, Madison, New Jersey. It was developed at the Lark Play Development Center, New York City.

CHARACTERS

JENNI—Smart, hip, young aspiring professional working in the not-for-profit earnest and helping professions.

ANISSA—Also a smart, hip, young aspiring professional who says she works in the not-for-profit helping professions but is actually the head of training and management at Ferizon customer service.

Jenni and Anissa live together and are twin sisters.

INGRID—Appears at first glance to be another smart, hip, young aspiring professional but is actually the mysterious head of the underground resistance against bad customer service. She speaks in a compellingly unidentifiable foreign accent and can often be seen gazing off into the middle-distance with an ironic half-smile as if looking through a private window onto the absurd pain of the world. If this were the movie made 20 years ago, she would be played by Isabella Rossellini. Estranged sister of Cydney.

BRYCE—Friend of Anissa and Jenni. Hipster dude who happens to have a job as an investment banker. Super laid-back.

CUSTOMER SERVICE LADY #1—Pleasant customer service lady. Sincerely trying to do her job.

CUSTOMER SERVICE GUY (STEVE)—Pleasantly empathetic customer service guy. Sincerely trying to do his job.

CYDNEY—Pleasant customer service lady, sincerely trying to do her job. Not quite aware that she's working for a company that would like to snuff out her small but bright spark of humanity. Long-lost sister of Ingrid.

BILLING LADY (MS. TAYLOR)—Doing an assembly line job. Her disaffected affect is laid on top of a thin sheen of suppressed rage.

BILLING GUY (MR. JOHNSON)—Similarly soul-dead.

CAROL K. ANDERSON—Old-school cranky New York lady.

LARS—Young, well-meaning gay guy. Bit of a caretaker.

JERRY NYBERG—Single, probably works in a video duplication place. Hyper-enunciator. Has figured out how to decipher his Con Ed bill.

WANDA—Older professional woman. Warm but not inclined to suffer fools.

APATHETIC GREYHOUND CLERK—As described.

THUGGISH BILLING GUYS—As described.

ASSORTED AUTOMATED VOICES—As described.

SPECIAL THANKS

Special thanks to Anne Kauffman and Madeleine George.

Lisa Kron
in *The Veri**on Play*

36th Humana Festival of New American Plays
Actors Theatre of Louisville, 2012
Photo by Alan Simons

THE VERI**ON PLAY

Scene 1

A small pool of light comes up on JENNI.

JENNI. Life changes on a dime, doesn't it?

(She drifts off into a reverie, then—)

I'm sorry… I lost my train of thought. Uh…

(Remembers the dime she's holding in her hand.)

Oh. Dime.

They say in the old days you could make a phone call with a dime. Can that really be true? Was it really that simple? Were there really little booths on corners where you could just slip a dime into the jingling slot and…

(Sliding into an imaginary conversation.)

Hi. I'm good, how are you? Oh, I don't know, what do *you* want to do tonight? Oh, that sounds fun. That sounds like so much… Funny, the things we take for granted until one day a little billing problem with Ferizon rips your life to shreds and everything you thought you knew about yourself and your world and everything just…just…

(She takes her cell phone out of her pocket and looks at it.)

How can something so little cause so much pain? It's not supposed to be that way. It comes with a PLAN! I thought it was a plan to make my life easier and better—but I was wrong. Oh my god, I was so wrong.

(Collapsing.)

Oh why??? Why can't it all go back to the way it was???

(Ten months earlier. The sounds of a party in full swing—music, chatter, laughter. The lights come up on the shared Williamsburg apartment of JENNI *and her sister* ANISSA. *Way too cool people are lounging, chatting, looking bored with how cool they are, holding cans of PBR, smoking, texting, watching videos on their iPhones, and grooving to the music in a hip and ironic way. A group of party goers gathered around* JENNI *and* ANISSA *in the wind-down section of a big laugh.)*

ANISSA. Oh, that's a good one.

PARTY GOER #2. That is funny.

JENNI. Oh, that is so funny. I've told you what's happening with me and Ferizon, right?

PARTY GOER #1. Oh no.

JENNI. Oh yes.

PARTY GOER #1. What?

JENNI. Okay. So—a couple of months ago, I got this Ferizon bill that said I had an unpaid balance of $153.64.

PARTY GOER #1. Those fuckers.

JENNI. Right? And I was like—I know I paid that bill. So I looked though my records and discovered that I had paid the bill but I'd paid it to Ferizon *Wireless* because—okay, so boring—I used to pay Ferizon and Ferizon Wireless separately but then they changed it and put it together into one // bill and—

PARTY GOER #1. This is so like what happened to me—

JENNI. Okay, but just let me finish. It turns out that when I'd paid in March I'd clicked on the old Ferizon Wireless line instead of the Ferizon line in my automatic bill paying.

PARTY GOER #2. Uh-oh.

JENNI. I know. So I call Ferizon customer service and they're like—Yeah, we see you did that. No problem, we'll credit that amount to the correct account.

PARTY GOER #2. Yeah, see? This is how they do it—

JENNI. Right? So I was like, Great. How long until that money is credited? And they were like: Five or six weeks.

PARTY GOER #2. Mother. Fucker.

JENNI. And I was like: because you're sending a small pouch of ducats from one part of your company to another via mule team?

ANISSA. Did you really say that?

JENNI. I did. I was like—Do the divisions of your company communicate with each other via, like, notes on parchment paper that are transported by mule team?

> (JENNI *is now back in the conversation with the* CUSTOMER SERVICE LADY.)

CUSTOMER SERVICE LADY #1. I'm sorry?

JENNI. No, no, I'm sorry. I know it's not your fault. I'm just not sure why it takes so long for a credit to be processed. I mean, you are a telecommunications company so I thought you had computers but, I'm sorry. I know it's not you. Apparently it just takes that long. So… So… If that's how long it takes I guess there's nothing I can do about it. So… Thanks for your help.

CUSTOMER SERVICE LADY #1. You're welcome. Is there anything else I can do for you today?

JENNI. No. Just get the money transferred to the right place. That'd be great.

CUSTOMER SERVICE LADY #1. (*Cheerful.*) Okay then, thank you for choosing Ferizon.

(JENNI *back in party.*)

PARTY GOER #1. That is totally fucked up.

JENNI. I know.

PARTY GOER #2. So the thing that happened to me was—

JENNI. But hold on, that's not the end. So, like, two months pass and the charge is still there!

PARTY GOER #1. Unbelievable.

(JENNI'*s back in the phone call.*)

CUSTOMER SERVICE GUY (STEVE). (*Super nice, super helpful.*) Oh yes, I can see here that two requests have been made. I see them right here. I'm going to put another one in here for you and we'll hope this one goes through.

(*Beat.*)

JENNI. So… Should I like, light a candle? Or buy an amulet or something like that?

CUSTOMER SERVICE GUY (STEVE). (*Genuine.*) I'm sorry?

JENNI. Well, if I'm interpreting you correctly it seems that our method here is just to hope. I'd thought maybe Ferizon had some kind of computerized systems that might enable one part of the company to communicate with other parts of the company but apparently it's more of a mystical system so I was wondering if you thought, like, praying or something might be helpful?

CUSTOMER SERVICE GUY (STEVE). Uh, I'm sorry… I don't…

JENNI. Never mind. I'm sorry. I know it's not you. I don't mean to take out my frustration on you personally.

CUSTOMER SERVICE GUY (STEVE). No, it's fine. I understand. If I were you I'd be way more frustrated than you are.

JENNI. Oh. No—

CUSTOMER SERVICE GUY (STEVE). Yeah. Oh yeah. Oh yeah, I can see this must have been really frustrating.

JENNI. It really has.

CUSTOMER SERVICE GUY (STEVE). Wow. Yeah. I can see that. Yeah. Jenni, I'm going to personally make sure this gets taken care of for you.

JENNI. Well, that would be great.

CUSTOMER SERVICE GUY (STEVE). Of course.

JENNI. What's your name, by the way?

CUSTOMER SERVICE GUY (STEVE). (*Micro pause—which* JENNI *doesn't notice.*) Steve.

JENNI. Steve. Thank you so much, Steve.

CUSTOMER SERVICE GUY (STEVE). No problem. Is there anything else I can do for you today, Jenni?

JENNI. No. But thanks. If you can get that money moved to where it's supposed to be and get that outstanding balance off my bill I will be totally happy.

CUSTOMER SERVICE GUY (STEVE). I'm going to take care of it right now.

JENNI. Fantastic.

CUSTOMER SERVICE GUY (STEVE). Thanks for choosing Ferizon, Jenni.

JENNI. Thank you, Steve.

CUSTOMER SERVICE GUY (STEVE). You have a great day, Jenni, okay?

JENNI. I will, thanks, Steve. You too.

CUSTOMER SERVICE GUY (STEVE). Alright then. Bye-bye, Jenni.

JENNI. Bye.

> (*She looks affectionately at the phone for a second before coming back to the party.*)

So, that's what happened.

PARTY GOER #1. Steve fixed your bill?

JENNI. Uh, yeah. That call was just last week—but yeah, I'm sure he did. But isn't that crazy?

PARTY GOER #2. It's *crazy.* So listen, this is what happened to me—

JENNI. Oh, right, you had a story...

> (*She and* ANISSA *exchange a subtle look.*)

PARTY GOER #2. Okay so, my identity has been stolen 17 times—

> (*The next song on the playlist comes up—Daniel Powter's "Bad Day."*)

JENNI. Oh my god no! Who put this song on? No.

PARTY GOER #2. (*Shrugging.*) I don't know. So anyway—

JENNI. Anissa, is this you?

ANISSA. (*Affectionate.*) J.J., if I wanted to irritate you I could think of better ways than that to do it.

JENNI. Bryce!

BRYCE. Ladies!

JENNI. *You* put this on!

BRYCE. Most excellent par-tay. No I did not. But I wish I had. I am diggin' it!

(INGRID, *standing in a corner and moving to the song in a peculiar 1970's foreign film way, begins to sing along in a strange and tuneless way.*)

JENNI. Who is *that?*

BRYCE. That's Ingrid. You know Ingrid.

(*They shake their heads, no.*)

Dudes! Yo, Ingrid. Come meet my peeps.

INGRID. Good party.

JENNI. Did you put this song on?

ANISSA. J.J., be nice.

(*To* INGRID.)

I don't think we've met. I'm Anissa and this is my sister, Jenni.

INGRID. Jenni or J.J.?

JENNI. It's Jenni, my sister is the only one who calls me J.J.

INGRID. Jenni. Jenni. Jenni. Hello.

JENNI. Hi.

INGRID. Anissa.

ANISSA. You look familiar to me. Have we met before?

INGRID. I don't know. Where do you shop?

JENNI. Bryce, I thought we knew all your friends. Where did you two meet?

INGRID. Oh, kind of, the swirl of the Billyburg scene.

BRYCE. Yeah, like, just—on the street?

INGRID. Yeah.

BRYCE. Yeah, and she was like, "I'm looking for a party, do you know any?" And I was like, "Dude! I'm going to one right now," and she was like, "Can I come wees you?" And I was like "Totally!" And she was like, "Whar ees eet?" And I was like, "Uh, right here." And then…we just, like, came in. And here we are.

ANISSA. Wait—You *just* met? Just now?

BRYCE. I know, dude, it's awesome!

INGRID. Time is so elastic.

BRYCE. I'm *loving* this *chick!*

INGRID. And how do *you* all know each other?

BRYCE. Well those two met, like, in the womb.

INGRID. No. No. *Twins?*

JENNI. Well, not identical.

ANISSA. We're the mirror image kind of twins.

BRYCE. Cool, right. Cool. They're like a sister team. Like opposite day but in sisters. Like: good sister-bad sister. But which is the good one and which is the bad one? You can't tell because they're both so cool and nice. *It's breaking my mind, man!* Wait, what was your question again?

JENNI. She asked how we all know each other.

BRYCE. Oh yeah! I don't remember.

JENNI. You came to Kimberly's House.

INGRID. Who is Kimberly?

JENNI. No. No… "Kimberly's House."

BRYCE. (*Astonished.*) You haven't heard of Kimberly's House? It's the most awesome place!

JENNI. (*Modest.*) Oh, Bryce.

BRYCE. It is! I get, like, choked up just thinking about it.

JENNI. (*To* INGRID.) Kimberly's House is a free clinic for poor children in the Financial District.

INGRID. Are there a lot of poor children in the Financial District?

JENNI. There are poor children *everywhere.*

INGRID. Of course.

JENNI. The brokerage firm where Bryce works is one of our sponsors. Yay, Bryce!

      (BRYCE *makes prayer hands and bows.*)

And Anissa's company, VSOP is // our—

ANISSA. VCI

JENNI. VCI, I always get that wrong, is our *largest* corporate sponsor.

      (*Side-hugging her.*)

Yay, Anissa!

ANISSA. (*Shrugging it off, modest.*) We try to contribute where we can. And helping poor people has been Jenni's dream since she was a little girl.

JENNI. (*Glowing, blushing.*) Stop.

ANISSA. (*Poking* JENNI, *affectionately.*) Why? I'm proud of you.

JENNI. (*Poking her back.*) Well, I'm proud of *you.*

ANISSA. (*Playful, sweet.*) No you're not. You think I'm a sellout.

JENNI. Are you kidding? Your company's support is what keeps our doors open for those kids!

ANISSA. (*Laughing.*) Not to mention it pays your rent here in this apartment.

JENNI. (*Laughing, mock incredulity.*) Anissa! *I* pay my share of the rent.

ANISSA. Well, most of the time.

JENNI. I can't believe she said that!

ANISSA. I'm kidding.

     (*Starting a slap fight. Laughing.*)

JENNI. You're terrible!

ANISSA. I'm so much worse then you even know!

JENNI. I can't believe you!

     (*Slap fight climaxes and ends in a hug.*)

ANISSA. Love you, sis!

JENNI. Love you!

BRYCE. Twins, man. I get *off* on that twin *vibe!*

JENNI. So what do you do, Ingrid?

     (INGRID's *Blackberry vibrates.*)

INGRID. Sorry. (*Takes it out and*—) Damn! My Blackberry just crashed!

JENNI. Oh no.

ANISSA. Oh god, I feel sick to my stomach. That is my worst fear!

JENNI. I know.

INGRID. I need to text my boss or she's going to freak.

JENNI. Okay…

INGRID. I noticed your MacBook? Do you think it'd be alright if I…

JENNI. Oh, sure. Come on.

INGRID. Thanks, I really appreciate it.

     (INGRID *and* JENNI *go into another room.*)

JENNI. Let me log you on.

INGRID. Yeah, thanks, this is really going to—

     (*As they both bend over the computer.*)

It's not over with Ferizon.

JENNI. What?

INGRID. Believe me. I've been there. It's never over that quickly.

JENNI. Well, it's been three months and two phone calls. So. And the last guy I talked to, Steve, is going to take care of it. He told me. He's going to take care of it personally.

INGRID. (*Short bitter laugh.*) Steve?

JENNI. Yeah?

INGRID. Is that what he told you his name was?

JENNI. Why wouldn't he tell me his correct name?

INGRID. You are so naive… It almost hurts…

     (INGRID *starts furiously typing into* JENNI's *computer.*)

JENNI. What are you doing?

INGRID. (*Typing into her computer.*) I'm putting some information in your address book.

It's a group of people who've been hurt…like you're already being hurt. Do you understand me? No. Of course not. You don't believe me. I can see. But, Jenni, do me this favor…okay? Or…do this for yourself. Don't erase this number.

   (JENNI *looks skeptical.*)

Don't.

   (JENNI *still looking…*)

Don't.

   (INGRID *takes a Gauloise out of her purse, preparing to smoke in a Bergmanesque way.*)

JENNI. Please don't smoke in here.

   (INGRID *flicks the cigarette away, rips a nicotine patch off her own arm, holds it to her nose and inhales deeply, then flicks that away as well.*)

INGRID. I give it three months…maybe just two, until they break you.

JENNI. What are you talking about?

INGRID. Listen to me. Someday you will need us. And we'll be there for you. We're the only ones who can help you.

   (*They stare at each other for a moment.* INGRID *mysterious,* JENNI *confused and skeptical. Then:*)

Could I send that e-mail? My Blackberry really did crash.

JENNI. Sure.

Scene 2

Jenni and Anissa the morning after the party.

   JENNI *sits in the kitchen, looking so day-after.* ANISSA *comes in, dressed for work, scrolling through her Blackberry.*

ANISSA. Morning.

JENNI. Morning. Want some coffee?

ANISSA. No, I'll stop at Starbucks on the way in. How'd you sleep?

JENNI. Terrible! I couldn't get that "Bad Day" fucking bullshit nightmare of a song out of my head.

   (*Shaking her fist.*)

Ooh, if I could get my hands on the demon who put that on…

ANISSA. Then what? You'd thank me?

JENNI. I *knew* it was you!

ANISSA. You're welcome.

JENNI. I can't believe you did that.

ANISSA. What? Saved the party?

JENNI. In what way???

ANISSA. That song came on just as people were revving up to tell their own customer service stories. I had to do something or we'd *still* be listening to how *this* one got strung along by the cable guy and *that* one got screwed over by Best Buy...

JENNI. Wow. I think you might be right. You are good! Where do you learn this stuff?

ANISSA. (*Goes back to scrolling through her Blackberry.*) It could be that you don't know everything about me.

JENNI. Doubtful, but I guess it's possible. Oh my god, I can't believe I forgot to tell you this! Remember that weird girl last night?

ANISSA. Weird girl...?

JENNI. Yeah, Bryce's friend. You know. You know, the one whose Blackberry // crashed.

ANISSA. Oh my god, don't even say it. That is my worst nightmare!

JENNI. Yes, yes I know. But last night, after her // Bla—

ANISSA. Don't!

JENNI. Alright—after her...hmm-hmm, she asked if she could use my computer. Remember?

ANISSA. Yeah.

JENNI. And I was logging her on and suddenly she went all Julian Assange on me and started going on about some big conspiracy.

ANISSA. What kind of conspiracy?

JENNI. Something about Ferizon breaking people and making them criminally insane or something. I don't know, it was *nuts!*

ANISSA. Wow.

JENNI. And she wrote down a secret phone number for some, like, support group. And she kept looking at me in this super-intense way and saying "It's not over with Ferizon."

ANISSA. Wow. That is crazy.

JENNI. Right?

(*An uneventful beat.*)

ANISSA. (*Nonchalant.*) Are you going to go?

JENNI. Where?

ANISSA. Oh, to the support group.

JENNI. Oh. No. Why?

ANISSA. I don't know. Might be kind of fun.

JENNI. In what way?

ANISSA. I don't know. Don't you want to kind of see what it's like? See what kinds of things people are talking about?

JENNI. Well, we know what they're talking about—it's just like you just said. When people start talking about their customer service problems they *must speak aloud* every detail of their own bad experiences. It's like women who lactate when they hear a baby cry. It's like a biological imperative. Must. Tell. Own. Story.

ANISSA. (*Laughing.*) Oh god, it's true, isn't it?

JENNI. Totally.

ANISSA. (*Back to her Blackberry for a beat—then an innocent idea.*) You know what, though—You could tell about it at Ass-Slappers.

JENNI. At where?

ANISSA. Ass-Slappers. J.J. Where have you been? Ass-Slappers.

(JENNI *has no idea what she's talking about.*)

It's, like, a downtown theater thing. It's in the Lower East Side. People get on stage and tell their funny stories.

JENNI. Oh. Okay. Well, I don't need to go to some support group just to come up with a funny story.

ANISSA. (*A bit stung.*) Okay. Never mind.

JENNI. What?

ANISSA. Nothing.

JENNI. What just happened?

ANISSA. Nothing. I was...trying to help. It seems like you've been having a kind of a hard time with Ferizon and I thought—never mind. Stupid.

JENNI. No. I'm sorry. Stupid *me!* Anissa, you're the best sister! I think you're probably right. That Ferizon thing really was getting to me. Luckily that Steve guy took care of it.

(JENNI *gets up.* ANISSA *goes back to scrolling. A funny thought occurs to* JENNI.)

Oh my god! But what if my bill came next month and that charge was still there??

ANISSA. (*Pulling her focus from her Blackberry.*) I'm sorry, what?

JENNI. (*Laughing.*) Never mind. I'm just yammering on about something that's *not* going to happen.

Scene 3
Ferizon customer service encounter number three.

One month later. JENNI *goes through the mail.*

JENNI. Doctors Without Borders, Save the Children, Smile Train, Vermont Country Store, Vermont Country Store, Vermont Country Store... Oh, my Ferizon bill. Wow, has it been a whole month already?

(*She opens it and reads it.*)

I can't *believe* it.

(*She dials a number from the bill, listens for a beat, then:*)

One.
347 992 5568
Jennifer Jensen
Jenn I Fer Jen Sen

(*Over-enunciating.*)

I'm Having A Billing Problem.

(*Continuing to over-enunciate.*)

I'm Having A Billing Problem, Fuckers
I said: fuckers. *Fuh—kers. Fuh—kers.* You're all a bunch of fuh—

CYDNEY. (*Warm, friendly and easygoing throughout this conversation.*) Thank you for calling Ferizon. // How can I help you today?

JENNI. Oh, hi, yeah, thanks, hi. Uh... I've been having a problem with my billing, uh, it's been going on for, uh, for a while now.

CYDNEY. Oh yes. I see that here.

JENNI. Oh, you do. Great. Yeah. It's been about five months now.

CYDNEY. Oh, gosh yeah, I see that.

JENNI. So—

CYDNEY. Let me get Ferizon Wireless on the phone here and let's see if we can get this taken care of for you today.

JENNI. That'd be great.

CYDNEY. Okay, I'm going to put you on hold for 2 to 5 minutes.

(JENNI *waits.*)

Is that okay with you? If I put you on hold?

JENNI. Yeah. Sure.

CYDNEY. Okay, great. I'm going to put you on hold for 2 to 5 minutes and, just in case we get cut off, // can—

JENNI. Why would we get cut off?

CYDNEY. I'm sorry?

JENNI. I just—It just seems like you're the—Never mind.

CYDNEY. Okay…

JENNI. I'm sorry. In case we get cut off…?

CYDNEY. Yes in case we get cut off can I get the number you're calling from.

JENNI. I'm calling from my cell phone.

CYDNEY. And that number is…?

JENNI. I gave it at the top of the call, I—doesn't matter, it's 347

CYDNEY. 347

JENNI. 992 // 5—

CYDNEY. 992

JENNI. 5568

CYDNEY. 5568. So right now I'm going to put you on hold for approximately 2 to 5 minutes.

JENNI. Okay. Thanks.

(*A full minute of bad hold music.*)

CYDNEY. Okay, Mrs. Jensen // Thank you for—

JENNI. I'm not married, // it's not—

CYDNEY. I'm sorry, what?

JENNI. Never mind. Go on.

CYDNEY. Thank you for your patience and letting me put you on hold.

JENNI. No problem.

CYDNEY. I spoke with the people over at Ferizon Wireless and that matter's been taken care of for you today.

JENNI. It has?

CYDNEY. Yep.

JENNI. Are you sure?

CYDNEY. Yep.

JENNI. The outstanding balance has been taken off my account?

CYDNEY. Definitely. It's all been taken care of.

JENNI. Okay.

CYDNEY. Anything else I can help you with today?

JENNI. Yeah. Just in case, could I have your name? I'm sure if you say it's resolved I'm sure it's resolved but it's, it's just been five months of, you know. So, just in case, if I could have your name.

CYDNEY. No problem. I'm Cydney.

JENNI. Cydney?

CYDNEY. Yep.

JENNI. And what's your extension, Cydney?

CYDNEY. We don't have extensions.

JENNI. You have no extensions?

CYDNEY. No.

JENNI. Are you on, like, a rotary phone?

(*Small beat.*)

CYDNEY. Yes.

JENNI. Well, how do people get in touch with you?

CYDNEY. Just call the number you called today and any of us will be more than happy to help you with any further assistance you may need.

JENNI. But I mean, you don't even have extensions for if your mother wants to reach you?

(*Small beat.*)

CYDNEY. Nope.

JENNI. So, if your mother had an emergency situation she would just have to keep calling and talking to random people and hope that eventually she'd get lucky?

(*Beat.*)

CYDNEY. Yes.

(*Beat. Just the tiniest bit shaken.*)

Anything else I can help you with today?

JENNI. Uh-uh.

CYDNEY. Thank you for calling Ferizon.

(JENNI *hangs up.*)

Scene 4
Jenni and Anissa talk.

JENNI *and* ANISSA *at their kitchen table in robes and pajamas.* JENNI *has her MacBook open,* ANISSA *scrolls through her Blackberry. Morning coffee.*

JENNI. I mean, no extensions?! It's the phone company!!!

ANISSA. Seriously!

JENNI. I mean, I'm picturing like *Green Acres*, you know, where Oliver had to climb to the top of the telephone pole to make a call.

ANISSA. Oh my god, totally.

JENNI. I wish I would have thought of that while I was talking to her! I would have been like—is it like *Green Acres* over there?

ANISSA. That would have been funny.

JENNI. I know. What do you think the deal is with those Ferizon customer service people?

ANISSA. What do you mean?

JENNI. I don't know. What kind of people do you think work there?

ANISSA. Well… I don't know. What kind of people do *you* think work there?

JENNI. That's just it, I don't know. Something doesn't add up. They're so convincing when they talk to you, so sincere. They seem to genuinely believe they're helping you.

ANISSA. But they're not?

JENNI. Well, no, because they tell you the problem is resolved but then it goes on and on and on. It's like they're playing us. *Or…* Are *they* being played?

ANISSA. By who?

JENNI. I don't know. By the evil customer service cabal.

ANISSA. Oh right, a whole cabal!

JENNI. The one I talked to yesterday was really nice. If it turns out *she* didn't solve my problem I'll… I don't know what. Maybe I'll go to that support group. Remember that?

(*A beat.* ANISSA *is writing a text.*)

Anissa?

ANISSA. What?

(*Done, she looks up.*)

What? Sorry.

JENNI. No, I was just—

ANISSA. Oh, it's later than I thought. Sorry.

JENNI. No, it's okay.

ANISSA. I gotta get moving or I won't have time for Starbucks.

JENNI. Go.

(JENNI's *phone vibrates. She looks at the phone.*)

Who is this?

(*She pushes the talk button.*)

Hello.

(*No response.*)

Hello.

AUTOMATED VOICE. ...ding your Ferizon account. Please call 1 800 668 6668 regarding your Ferizon account.

JENNI. What? Fuck.

>(*She dials the number. Split screen of* JENNI *in her house and* BILLING LADY *at Ferizon.*)

MS. TAYLOR. (*Mumbled, sullen, barely intelligible.*) Accounts payable, Ms. Taylor speaking.

JENNI. I'm sorry... Is this Ferizon?

>(*Beat.*)

MS. TAYLOR. Yes?

>(*We see* ANISSA, *somehow miraculously fully dressed and in her coat, pass behind* JENNI. *On her way out she slips a note onto the table.* JENNI, *absorbed in her call, doesn't notice any of this.*)

JENNI. Uh... I just received a message saying I should call this number regarding my Ferizon account?

MS. TAYLOR. What's your number?

JENNI. I'm sorry.

MS. TAYLOR. Your cell number, please.

JENNI. 347-992-5568.

MS. TAYLOR. Hold on.

JENNI. Hello?

>(*Hold music comes on. She waits on hold for five minutes.*)

MS. TAYLOR. Ma'am?

JENNI. Yes?

MS. TAYLOR. You have an overdue balance of $153.64.

JENNI. Okay. Okay. Oh my god. I don't even know where to start here. I don't have an outstanding balance. Okay? I've been dealing with this issue now for five months and I have been told repeatedly that it was resolved. Just yesterday I spoke with a woman named Cydney in customer service who assured me this matter had been taken care of so if you could please correct your records as well I would very much appreciate it.

MS. TAYLOR. Okay, Ma'am, I don't know anything about any of that. You do have an outstanding balance of $153.64. Would you like to make that payment now?

JENNI. I paid that money five months ago, on time, when I owed it, like I do every month, which you can see in my account history.

MS. TAYLOR. I have no access to your account history, Ma'am.

JENNI. You can't see my account history?

MS. TAYLOR. No, Ma'am.

JENNI. So every single person I've talked to previously about this for the past five months has been able to see my account history but you can't.

MS. TAYLOR. Ma'am, the only thing I have in front of me is your outstanding balance. Would you like to make a payment now?

JENNI. I don't have an outstanding balance!

MS. TAYLOR. Ma'am, you have an outstanding balance of $153.64.

JENNI. I don't know what to do. I'm going to cry.

MS. TAYLOR. Ma'am do you want to make that payment now?

JENNI. I DON'T HAVE A BALANCE. I'm going to have a heart attack. I'm shaking. I am literally shaking right now.

> (*Long beat.*)

MS. TAYLOR. Is there anything else I can help you with today.

JENNI. Wha? I… I ca… I…

MS. TAYLOR. Thank you for choosing Ferizon.

> (MS. TAYLOR *hangs up.* JENNI *hangs up, shaken.*)

JENNI. I'm going to lose my fucking mind. Anissa? Where'd you go?

> (JENNI *exits. At the Ferizon center, behind* MS. TAYLOR, *lights up on* ANISSA, *still in her coat.*)

ANISSA. That was good work, Ms. Taylor.

> (MS. TAYLOR *jumps. She didn't know* ANISSA *was behind her.*)

MS. TAYLOR. Oh! You startled me. We received your text just a few minutes ago—I didn't realize you were in the building.

ANISSA. I'm always in the building. I was listening in for quality assurance purposes. As you know we do. How did that go for you?

MS. TAYLOR. I think it went fairly well. I followed the protocol. She sounded fairly rattled by the end.

ANISSA. Job well done, then.

MS. TAYLOR. (*Glowing.*) Thank you, Ma'am.

> (JENNI *returns, now dressed.*)

JENNI. Anissa?

> (*She sees the note.*)

Oh. When did you leave this?

> (*Reading.*)

"Sorry those people are such assholes." No shit.
When did you leave? I didn't even see you go.

Scene 5
A few weeks later.

JENNI *runs into* BRYCE—*literally. She's looking at her cell phone and he's watching something on his iPhone.*

JENNI. Hey, wa—   **BRYCE.** Whoa, there—
Bryce!   Dude!

BRYCE. What's shakin'?

JENNI. Not much. It's nice to run into you—literally! Sorry about that. I'm getting a call—I don't know who this is—never mind, it can go into voicemail. So what's going on? What are you up to?

BRYCE. Just watching this freakin' hi-larious episode of *Good Times* on Hulu. Jimmy J.J. Walker, man. Where *is* that guy?

JENNI. Don't know.

BRYCE. I gotta Google him. So, Jenni. How's life hangin' witchu?

JENNI. Oh, it's alright I guess…

BRYCE. This is not a happy vibe I see before me.

JENNI. Oh, I'm okay… It's just, if you can believe it, I'm still dealing with that Ferizon thing!

BRYCE. (*Searching—doesn't know what she's talking about.*) Ferizon thing…

JENNI. Yeah, you know the… Remember the story I told…? At that party we threw… Last fall.

BRYCE. Oh right, right. Still not resolved? Bummer.

JENNI. It's making me nuts!

BRYCE. Yeah, yeah. Well? Yeah. This is why I never look at the bills, I just pay whatever.

JENNI. But how do you know you're not being overcharged?

BRYCE. *Exactly.*

JENNI. But… How can you stand it that you might be paying money you don't owe?

BRYCE. Ah. See? That's the flaw in your logic. The real question is, how can you stand to *know* you're paying money you don't owe.

JENNI. Uh…

BRYCE. One way or the other you'll end up paying. You can just pay the bill. Or you can wage a full-time, personality-warping battle you will never win. Either way, you end up paying, my friend.

JENNI. Well, I just cannot bend over like that, Bryce.

BRYCE. I hear you, my friend. But Be-Ware. Because people lose their freakin' minds over this shit. On YouTube you can see like, videos of, like, support groups for these people who are, like, damaged, man. It's hi-larious.

JENNI. Your friend Ingrid invited me to one of those support groups.

BRYCE. She did? Man! I love that chick. She is hooked *up*. Dude, you should totally go.

JENNI. Really?

BRYCE. To-tally.

JENNI. It's just going to be a bunch of whining weirdos.

BRYCE. Exactly, and you in there, checkin' it out—like an urban adventurer. Hey, you could go tell about it at Ass-Slappers!

JENNI. What is with this Ass-Slappers?

BRYCE. Oh, it's so great. It's this downtown theater thing. It's like, I don't know, people and their stories…? Sometimes it's really funny, sometimes it's really moving… You should come with me. I go all the time. It's cool. It's down on the Lower East Side.

(*Gets a text, gets absorbed in his iPhone, chuckles.*)

Oh, shit, oh shit, my friend keeps sending me these links to '80's hair band videos but, like, remade with babies. Hi-*larious*.

(*He wanders off without saying goodbye, totally absorbed.*)

JENNI. See you later Bryce.

(*She looks at her phone.*)

Okay, who called me.

(*Dials the voicemail and listens.*)

VOICE OF CYDNEY. Hello, this is a message for Jenni Jensen. This is Cydney at Ferizon.

JENNI. No shit.

CYDNEY. We spoke a while back. I just wanted to let you know that I was doing some follow up and I noticed your case was still open so I'm just calling to say I'm gonna do a little more checking and make absolutely sure that gets resolved for you today. Okay? You have a good day now. And thanks for choosing Ferizon.

JENNI. Wow. That's so nice! And a good thing too because one more round with them would have been the straw that broke the camel's back.

(*The phone rings again.*)

Who's this?

(*She pushes the talk button.*)

AUTOMATED VOICE. ...ding your Ferizon account. To avoid a disruption in your service, please call 1 800 668 6668 immediately regarding your Ferizon account.

(*She snaps it shut.*)

JENNI. Fuck!

Fuck, fuck, fuck, fuck, FUCK

(*A beat, thinks.*)

Am I really going to do this? I guess I am.

(*She scrolls through her contacts, finds the number she's looking for, and dials.* INGRID *answers.*)

INGRID. Hello?

JENNI. Hi. Is this Ingrid?

INGRID. Yes?

JENNI. This is Jenni.

(*Small beat.*)

I'm Bryce's friend?

(*Beat.*)

It was a while back that we met. You came to a party my sister Anissa and I threw, last fall?

INGRID. I remember. How are you, Jenni?

JENNI. Good. I'm good. Um... When you were at the party that night, you mentioned something about a support group?

INGRID. PHBICS. (*"Fibbicks."*)

JENNI. I'm sorry?

INGRID. It's called PHBICS.

(*A beat.* JENNI *doesn't know what to say.*)

It's an acronym for "People Hurt Badly by Inadequate Customer Service."

JENNI. Huh.

INGRID. Would you like to come to a meeting?

JENNI. Oh. I don't know. I wondered if I could just ask you a couple of questions about it.

INGRID. Sure, yeah. I think you'd like it. It's super chill. Super low key. Great group of people.

JENNI. Oh. You know, the thing is I don't really know if I need a whole support group.

INGRID. Oh sure. So you'll come this Tuesday.

JENNI. You know, at this stage I'm really just information gathering so—

INGRID. See you there.

> (INGRID *hangs up.*)

JENNI. Oh. My.

Scene 6
Jenni's first PHBICS meeting.

We see JENNI *walking down a somehow un-gentrified East Village block, holding an address in her hand.* INGRID *appears.*

JENNI. Oh, hey! I'm glad I ran into you. I was having a little trouble finding the place.

INGRID. Yes, the numbers fell off.

JENNI. Oh. I wondered why I…

INGRID. Come.

> (INGRID *pushes the door open on a shabby building. They walk up the dark, narrow tenement stairs. At the door:*)

This is it. Knock-knock.

> (WANDA *opens the door to the shabby rent-stabilized Manhattan apartment of* CAROL K. ANDERSON *where the PHBICS members are gathered.*)

WANDA. You must be Jenni.

JENNI. Hi.

WANDA. I'm Wanda. How are you Ingrid?

INGRID. Oh you know, can't complain.

WANDA. Then you're in the wrong place!

> (WANDA *laughs.*)

INGRID. Oh, Wanda, how you make me laugh.

> (WANDA *and* INGRID *step inside,* JENNI *follows, and finds an argument already going full swing.*)

JERRY. What is the problem, Carol?

LARS. Okay, everybody, let's calm // down—

CAROL. Oh, you know what the problem // is, Jerry.

JERRY. All I did was request basic information preemptively, should there be a medical emergency.

CAROL. Jerry, you are a grown man.

LARS. (*Seeing* JENNI. *To the group:*) You guys?

JERRY. (*Pulling his medic alert necklace from inside his shirt.*) Yes. And hypoglycemic!

LARS. Guys?

CAROL. Yes, we all know // you're hypoglycemic, Jerry.

JERRY. It's a medical issue, Carol. If I was in a wheelchair you wouldn't crucify me for asking if you had a ramp.

(JERRY *and* CAROL *finally see* JENNI. *They stare.*)

LARS. You guys? This is Jenni. Remember Ingrid told us she was bringing someone new today?

JERRY. (*Eyeing her suspiciously.*) I remember.

CAROL. This isn't exactly what I expected—

INGRID. Shall we start?

CAROL. Might as well. I've given up hope we're ever going to start on time.

JENNI. I'm sorry. Did I hold you up?

LARS. Oh no. It's only five minutes to seven.

CAROL. If you say so.

LARS. (*Bewildered at implication that the time is a matter of opinion.*) If I say so?

INGRID. Jenni, welcome to our group. This is Jerry and this is Wanda, and Carol, and Lars.

JENNI. Hi. Thanks for letting me come and sit in.

CAROL. What's your issue?

JENNI. I'm sorry?

CAROL. What's your issue? How're you getting screwed?

JENNI. Oh. Um. I'm having a little billing issue with Ferizon.

(*Audible rage reaction from the group.*)

I know right, Ferizon—*arrrgghh!* But in the scheme of things it's probably not that big of a deal.

LARS. How long has it been going on, Jenni?

JENNI. Oh, I don't know, about nine months, // or…

CAROL. Is that what you call a long time? Try *seven years*. You just wait till you've been fighting with the phone company for *seven years!*

JENNI. Oh yeah, no. That's a, that's a long time // to—

CAROL. They say I'm dead.

(*She pauses for effect.*)

Do I look dead to you?

JENNI. No, uh-uh.

CAROL. My father died, seven years ago. I sent the phone company a copy of his death certificate to close his account. Would you like to see the letter they sent me in return?

(*Pulls out a crumpled form letter and reads:*)

"Dear Ms. Anderson. Our sincerest condolences on the recent death of

Carol K. Anderson."

> (JENNI *still doesn't get it.* CAROL *looks to the group.*)

She doesn't get it.

JENNI. I'm sorry, I—

JERRY. (*To* JENNI.) *She's* Carol K. Anderson!

CAROL. They cut off my phone service *seven years ago* and still they won't turn it back on because according to them *I'm dead!*

> (*Her rage turning into grief.*)

I go there in person, I stand by the payment windows, I scream: *I'm alive!! Look at me! I'm alive!!!*

> (*Crying now.*)

Nothing makes a difference. Nothing helps. Seven years! Seven goddamned years!!!

> (*She collapses, sobbing, and the group comforts her.*)

Let me tell you something, Janey. These people, these *brave* people are the only thing that gives me hope.

> (*Gratefully taking the Kleenex that* JERRY *is offering her.*)

Thank you, Jerry.

JERRY. Sure.

> (*He turns to* JENNI.)

I don't suppose you're interested in my story.

JENNI. (*Tentative.*) Of course I am.

JERRY. Let me describe my situation to you this way: In the eyes of the great and glorious company known as Consolidated Edison, I, Jerry Nyberg, am *persona non grata, numero uno.*

INGRID. Jerry has created a series of formulas which allow him to actually understand his gas and electric bill.

JERRY. Correct. And that, my friend, is not a recipe for popularity with the potentates of Con Edison. Making full use of the Freedom of Information Act, along with my pre-existing math skills, I have calculated that every person in this room is being overcharged *an average of 62 cents every single month.*

JENNI. (*Trying to look like she thinks that matters.*) Wow. *Wow.*

JERRY. Oh, I take it that sounds like pocket change to you. Well, try doing the math, sister! Sixty-two cents times twelve months a year times umpteen years since the public service commission in this region has had any real teeth times three million plus customers in New York City alone! *I invite you to do the math!*

LARS. (*Calming him.*) Okay, big guy, okay.

JERRY. I have asked you not to touch me.

INGRID. Lars, would you tell Jenni your story?

LARS. Oh god. Okay. Uh… I get so flustered!

WANDA. You just take your time.

LARS. Okay, so… I'm Lars…

>   (JERRY, *for some reason even he's not aware of, claps lightly.*)

Okay…

>   (*Takes a breath to center himself.*)

The incident that brought me here was with a credit card company.

>   (*Taking strength from them, he holds CAROL's hand as he continues with his story.*)

Wow, I can't believe this is always so hard.

WANDA. Stay strong, honey.

LARS. My um…my *boyfriend*

>   (*Deep sigh.*)

is not very good with money, to say the least. He had some debt, and an offer came in the mail. A credit card that was offering a cash advance at 4% interest.

JENNI. That's a good rate.

LARS. That's what Alex said. He said, "Honey, you're always telling me I'm paying too much interest." And it's true. I was. I was always telling him that.

JENNI. Sounds like you really love him.

LARS. I said, "Alex, I just don't trust these mail offers," and he said, "Why are you always undermining me?" And I guess, I don't know, I guess I was afraid he was right, because I said "Okay, Alex, I'll check it out." And I called the company and I was on the phone with a representative for at least 45 minutes going over every line of fine print and it seemed like Alex was right, it was a good deal, and as the call was ending, just to confirm, I said, "Just to confirm, we are talking about a 4% interest rate." And the man said, he said, "Yes sir, you're all set at 32%." And he hung up the phone.

JENNI. That can't be legal.

JERRY. Well, according to the Supreme Court's 1978 decision, Marquette vs. First Omaha Services, it is.

LARS. I called him right back and said cancel, cancel, cancel, cancel. And he said, "Don't worry. The loan can't go through until you sign the papers so don't sign them and you'll be fine."

JENNI. What a relief!

CAROL. Is she mentally retarded in some way?

JENNI. What happened?

LARS. There were no papers. They just deposited the money into our account.

JENNI. But you didn't agree to the terms!

LARS. I called them and said that.

JENNI. And what did they say?

LARS. They said we did.

JENNI. But it wasn't true.

WANDA. Honey, do you know anyone who hasn't been told an outright lie by a customer service representative?

JENNI. Well, Lars, I'm so sorry. But thank god you could pay it back before they hit you with that crazy interest.

> (LARS *tries to respond but a mangled sob comes out instead.*)

What happened?

WANDA. (*Softly to* JENNI.) His man spent the money.

> (JERRY *makes a sound of wounded rage.*)

LARS. (*Quiet, ashamed.*) Not only is my credit rating destroyed. But every day I have to come home to that...*Bowflex machine.*

JENNI. I'm so sorry.

JERRY. Bastards! Lying right to our faces! Except there are no faces! Right? We never see them! We don't know who they are! Lying, hiding bastards! Carol, is there *nothing* in the way of snacks?

WANDA. (*Under her breath.*) Okay, here we go.

> (*Unflustered, to* JERRY, *while fetching her purse.*)

Hold on now, Jerry.

> (LARS *hugs his knees, tucks his head and rocks, emitting a soft, high-pitched, keening wail as* WANDA *mumbles to herself and* JERRY *and* CAROL *fight. Somewhere in the midst of all this,* INGRID *slips out.*)

CAROL.	**WANDA.**
I do enough waiting on people already, // don't you think, Jerry?	(*Looking through her purse.*)
JERRY. Yes, I know, we all know, what you do, Carol—	Now I know...
All I did was make a completely neutral request for information. Did I not? People? Did anyone hear me criticize Carol // in any way shape or form?	...there's something in here...
	What did I do with those Pecan Sandies? ...
	I know there's gotta be a Life Saver...

CAROL. I have told you time and time and time again that you are welcome to bring // whatever kind of snack you desire—

JERRY. I didn't say there *should* be food. I asked if there was any food in the apartment.

CAROL. You can bring a five-course gourmet meal // or an intravenous feeding tube—

JERRY. I did not request a "meal." Did anyone here hear me request a "meal"?

CAROL. —but I cannot be responsible for the dietary needs // of every person in this group!

WANDA.

something in here...

What is this...

Look at that?

I looked for this receipt for two weeks!

...finally took a store credit.

That just makes me mad.

There must be trash in this bag...

been here since Ben Chavis was still running the NAACP.

JERRY. *For godssake, Carol, I have a //* medical condition!

CAROL. *Carry cookies like anyone else with a sugar problem, Jerry!*

(INGRID *rushes back in the front door with a bag of Combos which she thrusts at* JERRY.)

INGRID. Here.

LARS. (*Exhausted.*) Oh thank god.

(JERRY *opens the bag with trembling hands and begins to eat.*)

INGRID. Jenni, would you like to talk a little more about your issue?

JENNI. Um... No thank you.

INGRID. But... It's been now, what, about nine months?

JENNI. Yeah... I don't know why it's taking so long and, I guess I am a little irritated, but, you know, these systems all have their little glitches, right? Eventually they work out.

(*A beat as the group suppresses their reactions to this.*)

INGRID. Wanda, I think maybe Jenni should hear *your* story.

LARS. (*Flinching in pre-emptive pain.*) Oh!

(*Seeing* JENNI *look at him in alarm.*)

I'm sorry, it's just... It's... Go ahead, Wanda.

WANDA. You've heard about the "mortgage crisis."

JENNI. Sure.

(*The group prepares themselves for the harrowing story to come.* WANDA *starts quiet and steady.*)

WANDA. I bought my house fifteen years ago. Got a 30-year fixed-rate mortgage from a reputable bank. Beautiful house. I love my house.

JENNI. That's wonderful.

WANDA. Yes it is. Yes it is. Now, few years back, I get a letter saying my bank had sold my mortgage to another company. Form letter. You know. But companies are bought and sold all the time, right? So I don't think anything of it.

JENNI. No, right, sure.

WANDA. Until I started getting letters from collection agencies.

JENNI. Why?

WANDA. Well, that is a very good question. I do not know. Of course I immediately sent off copies of every one of my cancelled mortgage checks. Not one of them a day late.

JENNI. No, of course not.

WANDA. And they stopped calling.

JENNI. Whew!

WANDA. And now my house is in foreclosure.

JENNI. *Why???*

WANDA. That's what I would like to know. But I will tell you what I think: We are living in an *insane world.*

Let me tell you a little story.

Every day I used to listen to Kai Ryssdal on *Marketplace.* And every day, as you know, he signs off saying "Don't make any big decisions without consulting a financial expert." And every day I would think, that is some good advice, Kai Ryssdal. I like you. I like the way you think. *Now* I think—Hold up, Kai. Who are you talking about? Who are these "experts" you want us to consult? Do you mean the "experts" running the mortgage consolidators taking my house for no explicable reason? Do you mean the "experts" who trashed our entire economy shoveling our money into their own pockets and who now have the nerve to tell us the only way to fix it is to keep shoveling our money their way?

My grandmother used to say me, when I was a little girl, she used to say to me, "Do not trust a bank, baby. Never trust a bank. You keep your money in your shoe. You get a shoe with a false bottom and you keep all your money there because you cannot trust no man in no bank." You know what my grandmother had to show for this way of thinking at the end of her life? I'll tell you what. Nothing. Except what would fit in the bottom of her trick shoe. So what are we supposed to do? They got us coming and going. I used to imagine introducing my grandmother to Kai Ryssdal. I did. I used to imagine that he could talk some sense into her so she could have a better life.

I still have that dream but now it's so I could watch my grandmother slap Kai Ryssdal right across his face. That is an ugly thought. I need my Rescue Remedy.

> (LARS *hands* WANDA *her Rescue Remedy and she squeezes a few drops under her tongue as everyone else looks to* JENNI *for some sort of response.*)

JENNI. Thanks everybody…for letting me come…and for the, uh, support…

Scene 7
Five minutes later.

> INGRID *and* JENNI *stand outside* CAROL's *apartment and smoke.*

INGRID. So what do you think?

JENNI. They, um, they seem really nice.

INGRID. Don't be put off by first impressions, Jenni.

JENNI. Well, since you bring it up, they seem a little unhinged.

INGRID. (*With an ironic laugh, to herself.*) Unhinged…that's an ugly word.

JENNI. (*Confused.*) It is?

INGRID. Would you have come, Jenni, if I'd told you what they're like?

JENNI. I don't know… I…

INGRID. I'm not going to lie to you, Jenni, these are damaged people. You don't get through these kinds of prolonged customer service nightmares like what these people have suffered unscathed. A toll is taken on the human psyche.

JENNI. Uh huh.

> (*Both finish their cigarettes, flicking them to the ground and stepping on them to put them out.*)

INGRID. I don't need to convince you, Jenni. You'll see for yourself soon enough. I just hope you're not hurt too badly in the process.

> (*They part, walking in opposite directions.*)

JENNI. Wait.

> (INGRID *turns around.*)

I didn't hear your story.

INGRID. Oh.

Next time.

JENNI. I'm not really sure there'll be a—

> (INGRID *is gone.*)

Scene 8
The apartment, the next day.

In the kitchen, morning coffee. ANISSA *scrolls through her Blackberry while* JENNI *talks.*

ANISSA. So what was it like?

JENNI. It was a crazy rant-a-thon. Those people are completely invested in their insane paranoia.

ANISSA. Like…what sorts of things were they saying?

JENNI. Oh you know… "The big bad companies *deliberately trying* to hurt us."

ANISSA. Did they have, like, ideas about how they think companies are doing that?

JENNI. I don't know. They're nuts! They kept wanting me to talk about my "terrible problem" and they got pissed off when I said my problem wasn't so bad so I didn't dare tell them there's a person at Ferizon who's trying to help me.

ANISSA. Wait, there is?

JENNI. Yeah, I told you that. Didn't I?

ANISSA. No, uh-uh.

JENNI. Oh, yeah. This woman from Ferizon left me a message saying she was doing, I guess, some follow up and she wanted to let me know she was personally looking into my case.

ANISSA. Huh.

JENNI. Yeah. Cydney. Is her name. She's really sweet. I mean my issue's still not resolved but at least I know someone there is working on it.

ANISSA. (*Absently, while writing a text.*) That's amazing.

JENNI. I know, right?

ANISSA. (*Sending the text.*) Um-hm.

Gosh look at the time. I gotta go.

(*Heading for the bedroom.*)

Damn, I'm not going to have time for Starbucks.

JENNI. Where are you going?

ANISSA. (*From the bedroom.*) I've got a training session.

JENNI. A training session? This early? That's kind of strange, isn't it?

ANISSA. (*Emerging from the bedroom, fully dressed.*) Just came up.

(ANISSA's *already out and crossing into a corporate classroom where a group of customer service representatives are gathered for their training session.*)

Who can sum up for me, in one sentence, the number one reason for Ferizon's existence…let's see…Mr. Robertson?

MR. ROBERTSON. To provide phone service?

ANISSA. Yes, but no.

> (*She scans for more hands.*)

Mrs. Davis?

MRS. DAVIS. So people can have DSL lines?

ANISSA. Uh-huh. Good answer. No. Anyone else? Mr. Allenby?

MR. ALLENBY. FIOS?

ANISSA. Someday, yes. But right now? Anyone?

> (*A beat, then writing, then underlining on her SmartBoard.*)

Customer Service. Okay? All the services provided by Ferizon are just a framework for our main purpose which is the world's best customer service. As you well know, J.D. Power and Associates has rated Ferizon the number one provider of customer service for the past seventeen years.

> (MR. ROBERTSON *raises his hand.*)

ANISSA. Yes?

MR. ROBERTSON. Doesn't J.D. Power and Associates review cars?

ANISSA. Yes, exactly. Thank you Mr. Robertson. Okay, any questions?

> (CYDNEY *raises her hand.* ANISSA *looks at her notes to get the name.*)

Yes…

CYDNEY. Cydney.

ANISSA. *Cydney.* Hanson. Yes. Ms. Hanson.

CYDNEY. It's fine if you just call me Cydney.

> (*A tense beat.*)

ANISSA. Okay.

CYDNEY. Well, I had a question about follow-up.

ANISSA. Shoot.

CYDNEY. It's just that, I know there's no official mechanism for follow-up but I sure wish I could follow up with my customers sometimes. You know, some of them, their issues have been persisting for a while and a lot of times I just wish I could check on 'em, you know, to just make sure everything is resolved.

ANISSA. That's a great impulse, Cydney. Is it okay if call you Cydney?

CYDNEY. Sure.

ANISSA. Cydney, I need to correct you here, just a little bit, okay?

CYDNEY. Sure, okay.

ANISSA. We most certainly do have an official mechanism for follow up here at Ferizon. But it's invisible.

CYDNEY. Oh.

ANISSA. You don't see it because customer service at Ferizon is organized into a highly structured tier system that was developed for us at M.I.T. which is why you never talk to the same customer twice. It's this *circuit breaker* element of the system that makes our customer service so good. It protects you from getting emotionally involved. Which is crucial. Crucial. You are professionals—like doctors. The studies show—good customer service people keep a professional distance. So your impulse to check back—it makes you a good human being, but not a good customer service person. Clear?

CYDNEY. Kind of.

ANISSA. Well, Cydney, this is not a line of work everyone is cut out for.

CYDNEY. Right, well, sure.

ANISSA. And those people might need to be cut out.

(*A super tense silence.*)

Just kidding! Now everyone? Back to work. Get out of here. Have a great day.

(JENNI, *still at the apartment, reading the paper online, sees she's got a text.*)

JENNI. I have a text? When did this come in?

(*She reads the text. A dead calm rage comes over her.*)

Mother. *Fucker.*

(JENNI *dials.*)

MR. JOHNSON. Ferizon Billing. Mr. Johnson speaking.

JENNI. Yes. Hello. I just got a text saying that my service is going to be turned off at 5:00 today.

MR. JOHNSON. Account number, please?

JENNI. 346 992 5568

MR. JOHNSON. Hold.

(*She waits on hold.*)

Okay, Ma'am.

(*She doesn't respond.*)

You still there?

JENNI. I'm here.

MR. JOHNSON. Yes Ma'am. You have an overdue balance of $153.64.

JENNI. (*Barely contained RAGE.*) I just got a message just last week from this woman, Cydney, in customer service, telling me this matter was being resolved.

(*Beat.*)

MR. JOHNSON. Would you like to make that payment now?

JENNI. I don't owe you any money!

MR. JOHNSON. Is there anything else I can help you with today.

> (*Beat.*)

JENNI. I have half a mind to go tell the story of how I'm being treated by you people on stage at Ass-Slappers!

> (*Beat.*)

MR. JOHNSON. Is there anything else?

JENNI. No. Nothing else.

MR. JOHNSON. Alright then, Ma'am, thank you for…

JENNI. Don't say it.

MR. JOHNSON. I have to say it Ma'am. Thank you for ch…

JENNI. Don't say it. Don't say thank you for choosing Ferizon! Don't say it.

MR. JOHNSON. I'm required to say it Ma'am. Thank you for—

JENNI. No! No! I didn't choose you. This is not my choice. I chose none of this. Do you hear me? This is a toxic relationship and I'm just not that into you!

MR. JOHNSON. Thank you for—

> (JENNI *hangs up on him. She's shaking like a crack baby. She dials another number, listens, then—*)

JENNI. What? What? Marque dos? No. One. One, please. English. I spoke in English. To Cydney. And it made sense. And she listened to me. Can I speak with Cydney, please? Please? Please?

AUTOMATED VOICE. To send this message press one. To record a new message—

> (*She lets the phone drop from her ear and stares out blankly into space, shattered.*)

Scene 9

Carol's apartment.

> JENNI *sits straight upright on the couch, smoking like a madwoman, eyes darting back and forth.* CAROL, WANDA *and* LARS *sit on either side of her, petting her and trying to talk her down.* JERRY *is across the room, pressed up against the wall, stiff, watching in silent, anguished horror.*

WANDA. Jenni, now you stay with us, honey. Don't drift. Don't drift. Hey! You gotta stay with us here.

LARS. Come on, Jenni. You did the right thing calling us and we're going to get you through this, okay?

(INGRID *rushes in.*)

INGRID. I got here as soon as I could. How is she?

JERRY. (*Suddenly breaking down.*) How is she? They've broken her! Jesus Christ, what have they done??

(*Covering his face and falling to the ground.*)

Oh God, oh God, oh God...

LARS. Jerry...

JERRY. (*Still wailing.*) She was so beautiful and now—look at her...

INGRID. Jerry, when was the last time you ate something?

JERRY. (*Through his tears.*) I don't know, I don't know, I don't know...

WANDA. (*Taking a donut from her bag, hands it to* LARS.) Get him to eat this.

LARS. Jerry, come here.

(*Still sobbing,* JERRY *eats the donut which* LARS *feeds to him and it seems to quickly end his crying jag. The others turn their attention back to* JENNI.)

WANDA. How you doing, girl?

(*Smoothing the hair from* JENNI'*s forehead.*)

Those people really got to you this time, didn't they?

JENNI. No, Wanda, it's fine. They told me they'd fix it and, so they'll fix it. Right? It's all fine. It's all fine.

(WANDA *looks to* INGRID.)

INGRID. (*Gently but firmly doling out the stark, horrible truth.*)

Jenni, it's very painful

When you realize

That they really just don't care.

JENNI. (*Standing up, shaking them off, crazy eyes.*) That's crazy talk! They DO care about us. And you know why I know that? Because we're their customers and they have to care about us because *that,* my friend, is what the free market is all about. That's why I'm just going to get Ferizon on the horn, and tell them that I'm getting another cell phone provider. Oh, you'll see. That'll get 'em hoppin'.

INGRID. Who will you go to, Jenni? Sprint? AT&T? You really think things are different there?

JENNI. (*A new, better idea which makes her maniacally chipper.*) Wait. Wait. Wait. I know what I'm going to do. Duh! I can't believe I didn't think of this before! *I'll just pay the bill.*

(*The group draws a collective breath. She's hitting bottom.*)

INGRID. But you did pay the bill, Jenni. You paid it nine months ago.

JENNI. (*Crazy eyes.*) Yeah, yeah, yeah, yeah, yeah, but see, this is the thing I just realized. I can pay it *again.* And then it will all be over. Then things will go back to the way they used to be. And I'll be happy again. Ingrid, let me use your Blackberry, okay? Okay? Just for a minute. Okay?

(*The others all exchange a look and a slight nod.*)

INGRID. (*Holding out her Blackberry.*) Here you go, Jenni.

(INGRID *holds out the Blackberry,* JENNI *reaches for it.* INGRID *tosses it over her head to* WANDA *who catches it and holds it out for* JENNI *who has spun around to get it. As she reaches for it,* WANDA *tosses it over her shoulder to* JERRY *who is behind her.* JENNI *extends her arms, reaching for it, and* LARS *and* CAROL *each grab an arm and pull it behind her back, leaving her face to face with* WANDA, *who takes her chin in her hand to make* JENNI *meet her gaze.*)

WANDA. You listen to me. The only reason you're going to call Ferizon is to demand that your service is reinstated!

JENNI. (*Sobbing.*) I can't, I can't. I give up! I can't do it anymore!

(WANDA *slaps her.*)

WANDA. Now you listen to me, little girl. You are not giving up, you hear me?

(JENNI *is unresponsive.* WANDA *slaps her again.*)

Do you hear me? My people worked too long and too hard to gain admission to the promised land of decent customer service only to find that you all are giving up on it! Oh no. Oh no. And you don't even know what it is you're giving up. You all been livin' in a paradise so perfect you didn't even know you were livin' in it. You *assumed* that's the way the world is. Everything you touch is on time, well made, reasonably priced, non-toxic and if it's not, you *know* somebody's gonna fix it for you. Well let me tell you something little miss Abercrombie and Fitch, that kind of world is something you gotta *fight* for. You understand me?

JENNI. No.

WANDA. (*Another slap.*) That's right. You don't. Whole country filled with people talking about how bad they've been treated, shocked, like each one of these stories was some bizarre, isolated glitch. Ain't no glitch! It's what happens when you give up and I won't have it! Now, what are you going to do?

JENNI. I'm going to pay the bill.

WANDA. (*Slaps her several times.*) Now, you hear me and hear me good. My parents and my grandparents and my great-grandma Sally and my aunts and my uncles and my cousin James would be ashamed of you. Now what are you going to do? Hm? What are you going to do?

JENNI. I don't care anymore! I'm going to pay the bill!

(WANDA *slaps her a couple of more times.* INGRID *punches her in the stomach. Still nothing.*)

WANDA. Alright then. Maybe you need to see what a world truly without customer service looks like.

(*She looks at the others.*)

Plan B.

(*The group freezes.*)

CAROL. Is that...really necessary?

WANDA. I don't see any other way, do you?

(*They shake their heads no.* WANDA *hands* LARS *her purse.*)

Honey, heat up my chamomile neck wrap.

(*To* JENNI.)

Get yourself up, girl. We're going to the bus station.

Scene 10
At the Greyhound Bus Station.

JENNI. (*Wide-eyed horror.*) What is this place?

WANDA. (*A chamomile neck wrap around her neck.*) This, little girl...is a Greyhound Bus Station. You say you're willing to do without customer service, it's too much trouble, it's not worth it. Well, before you do that, you look around here. You ready, Jerry?

(JERRY *nods, grim-faced.*)

Alright, baby, we're right here and we got your back. If it gets too bad over there, you pull out. You hear me?

(JERRY *nods, steels himself, and heads toward the information window.*)

WANDA. (*To* JENNI.) You watch!

(JERRY *approaches the* CLERK *who is sitting behind bulletproof glass in his booth, engrossed in a personal phone call.*)

JERRY.	APATHETIC GREYHOUND CLERK. (*Talking on the phone.*)
	Yeah, I read about it online. It's a 200
Excuse me.	pound rat and it's got a human elbow
Excuse me? Sir?	growin' out of its ear.
(JERRY *knocks on the glass.*)	(*To* JERRY.)
	Hey!
	(*Returning to his phone call.*)
	And it growled like a dog. Kind of like
Sir?! Excuse me!	grrr, grrrr.

APATHETIC GREYHOUND CLERK. (*Into the phone.*) Hold on.

> (*With deep irritation and a bit of malevolence the clerk resentfully slides the window open.*)

What?

JERRY. Hi. Thanks. Is the bus in from Cincinnati yet?

APATHETIC GREYHOUND CLERK. (*Chillingly even.*) Is it up on the board?

JERRY. What board? I don't see a board.

APATHETIC GREYHOUND CLERK. If it's on the board it's in, if not it's not.

> (*He slides the window closed.*)

JERRY.	**APATHETIC GREYHOUND**
(*Knocking on the window again.*)	**CLERK.** (*Into the phone.*)
	Wait, go back, so you were at Fuddruckers
I'm really sorry // Sir but—	and—

APATHETIC GREYHOUND CLERK. (*Opens the window, irritated, contemptuous.*) Can you see I'm on the phone?

JERRY. Yes, but my 98-year-old mother's supposed to be on that bus and I'm worried she missed her connection in Chicago.

APATHETIC GREYHOUND CLERK. Do I look like I'm in charge of Chicago?

> (*Into the phone, with a derisive chuckle.*)

Who the hell knows. Somebody with some problem he thinks I can fix.

> (*Laughs.*)

Yeah.

> (*Amused, looking* JERRY *up and down.*)

Yeah.

Oh yeah, you got that right.

> (*Sliding the window shut.*)

Now wait, *what* kind of sandwich was it?

JERRY. (*Knocking on the glass, urgency rising.*) Excuse me, I would like to speak to your supervisor.

APATHETIC GREYHOUND CLERK. (*Sliding the window open.*) I'm the supervisor.

JERRY. Can I have your name?

APATHETIC GREYHOUND CLERK. Sure. My name is—

> (*He raises his middle finger, then shuts the window and returns to his phone call.* JERRY *knocks on the window and tries to hold it together but is starting to unravel.*)

JERRY.	APATHETIC GREYHOUND
But I…	CLERK.
But sir…	Have you talked to Chad? Yeah. 17. 17
Pardon me…	hot dogs. I kid you not.

LARS. Oh Jesus, Wanda, it's bad!

WANDA. I know, I know.

LARS. Let me pull him out! I gotta pull him out!

WANDA. Go, baby, go!

> (LARS *runs and grabs* JERRY *and drags him away.*)

JERRY. No, I can get his name! // Please! I can do it!

LARS. It's okay big guy. It's okay!

JERRY. I can go one more round. // I can. I can.

LARS. It's enough, Jerry, It's enough.

JERRY. Wanda, I tried! I tried my best. But he wouldn't…even…look… at…me…

WANDA. We know, baby. We know. You're a good man. You're a good man Jerry Nyberg.

CAROL. *Oh, the humanity!*

WANDA. Honey, take him over to Sbarro. Get him a calzone.

> (LARS *and* JERRY *go.*)

WANDA. (*To* JENNI.) That was your wake-up call, little girl. That's what you say you're willing to accept. Can you live with that?

JENNI. (*Starting to cry.*) I can't! It's terrible. It's terrible!

> (*She sobs and collapses onto* CAROL's *couch which has miraculously appeared behind her. Then, rousing herself:*)

How can we just sit by and let this go on? Well, we can't. We have to do something. We have to take action. But what, what? Let's see… Carol, you flood the Congressional switchboard with irate calls. Jerry, you fire off some pithily-worded letters to the editor. Wanda, we need you to pen an incendiary broadsheet. Lars, you…stuff some envelopes. What'll I do? What'll I do? Who do I have to fuck to get some customer service around here? Just kidding. But I feel drunk with possibility!

INGRID. Your passion is truly inspiring, Jenni. However, in our experience, political activism is not an effective tool.

JENNI. What are you talking about? Of course it is.

WANDA. It used to be, but not anymore, Jenni. People today are just more interested in personalities than issues.

JENNI. Well, I can tell you that *this* person is extremely interested in the issues.

JERRY. (*Scoffing.*) Oh, is that right?

JENNI. Oh, indeed it is!

> (*The group looks to* INGRID—*all of them now thinking the same thing.*)

INGRID. In that case, perhaps you'd like a small tutorial from Jerry.

JENNI. I would like that very much.

JERRY. (*Taking out a tall stack of dog-eared reports tabbed with many Post-It notes.*) Alright then.

> (*Selecting a report.*)

You're going to want to start with the Telecommunications Act of 1996.

JENNI. Excellent.

> (*As* JENNI *reaches for the report,* CAROL *nonchalantly drops a copy of* US Weekly *on the coffee table.* JENNI *is drawn to it like a moth to a flame.*)

Wait a minute, Beyoncé had her baby?

JERRY. (*Snapping his fingers at her.*) Jenni!

JENNI. (*Pulling her focus back to the task at hand.*) Sorry, sorry! I'm with you.

JERRY. (*Handing her another report.*) This is an analysis of the myriad extra fees we pay monthly, we are *told*, for the construction of a nationwide high-speed infrastructure which, thus far, exists only in myth.

> (JENNI *has been drawn back into the irresistible magazine.*)

JENNI. Did you guys know The Situation is a person?

JERRY. (*Tossing a pile of folders on the table.*) Articles on exploitation of the Universal Service Fund // in which you will find multiple…

JENNI. (*Still bewitched by the magazine.*) I love Sandra Bullock but this kid does not look happy.

JERRY. (*Offering another folder.*) Donations to Congress by telecommunications companies // increasing exponentially…

JENNI. (*Lost in the magazine.*) What? No! Jennifer Hudson definitely wore this better.

CAROL.	**INGRID.**
(*Prying the magazine out of her hands.*)	(*Snapping her fingers.*)
Give me that!	Jenni! Jenni!

JENNI. What? What? Oh my god! *Oh no!*

INGRID. Now do you see?

JENNI. (*Horror dawning.*) My god! You're right. It's hopeless!

INGRID. It's not hopeless, Jenni.

JENNI. But…without political action what is there? There's nothing left.

CAROL. What are we supposed to do with her? She's not even as sharp as a bag of hair.

JENNI. What are our options??? I mean, what are we supposed to do? Start an underground resistance movement?

(*A beat. She looks at the group, a realization dawning.*)

Wait a minute…

INGRID. Yes, Jenni. PHBICS is actually an acronym for Committee to Wipe Out Blatant and Inhuman Consumer Slavery.

JENNI. Isn't that…CWIBICS?

INGRID. We had to disguise the acronym until we knew we could trust you.

JENNI. Yes, that makes sense.

INGRID. The way we see it, the only way to take this system down is to find a way to get inside.

JENNI. You need a *mole.*

INGRID. Yes!

JENNI. Yes!

INGRID. But the trick is finding that person. All of us are working on a different front. For instance, Wanda has set herself up as a diversity trainer—

JENNI. (*With dawning awe.*) And you got yourself hired at Ferizon.

WANDA. I'm trying. So far the closest I've gotten is Working Assets.

INGRID. Lars goes to every single networking event held by the G-FAG.

LARS. It's the Gay Ferizon Associates Group.

INGRID. (*With steely-eyed respect.*) It's a lot of happy hours.

(LARS *nods, grimly.*)

Jerry. Every night Jerry sifts through hundreds of bags of Ferizon garbage.

JERRY. Do you happen to know what a diamond-cut shredder is?

JENNI. Oh, Jerry.

JERRY. I can handle it. I'm just saying.

INGRID. And Carol—

ALL. (*Murmuring appreciatively.*) Oh, Carol!

CAROL. All right everybody calm down.

INGRID. Carol got herself hired at the Starbucks next to the Ferizon building where the executives get their morning coffee. She had to file an age discrimination claim to make it happen but she did it. She's just started working double shifts.

CAROL. I get free coffee, it's not so terrible.

JENNI. You're all just… I had no idea.

INGRID. Nobody does! You understand that right? This work must be kept completely secret.

JENNI. Of course. Obviously. I would never tell anyone. And I want to help you in any way I can but—I can't imagine what I could do for you.

INGRID. We're thinking it might be possible that someone, a higher up at Ferizon, might be a person in your orbit.

JENNI. Me? Know someone who works at Ferizon? I don't think so. I mean, if I knew someone who worked at Ferizon and they hadn't helped me after all I've been through, well…that'd be a pretty rotten person, wouldn't you say? No, I definitely do not know anyone who works at Ferizon.

INGRID. Well, mull it over and perhaps something will occur to you.

JENNI. Wait…

INGRID. Yes?

JENNI. There is…

INGRID. Yes?

JENNI. You know what? Let me think this through. I don't want to say anything…before I think this through.

INGRID. Alright.

JENNI. This person is…well, she's—She's been really good to me and…*if* this person *is* the right person to be your mole…I want to be really careful about how I proceed.

INGRID. Yes, fantastic. Jenni. We understand. We will be patient. And you remember—top secret. Ssshhh.

JENNI. Gotcha. Top secret!

Scene 11
The next morning.

ANISSA *at the table with her Blackberry.* JENNI *enters from her room.*

JENNI. Morning.

ANISSA. You were out late last night. Where were you?

JENNI. Oh… I was at the, uh, the support group.

ANISSA. Really? I thought you weren't going back there.

JENNI. Yeah. No. Yeah. I, yeah, I decided to go back. Give it another try. Yeah.

ANISSA. But I thought you said they weren't helpful.

JENNI. They, um, it turns out they're more helpful that I had thought. So…

ANISSA. Helpful in what way?

JENNI. Oh, uh… They, um… They, um… You know what the thing about them is? Um… They… Uh…

(ANISSA *lets her hang for a moment.*)

ANISSA. Jenni, are you feeling okay?

JENNI. Yeah, yeah, yeah. Yeah. How are you?

ANISSA. I'm good.

It seems like there's something you want to tell me.

JENNI. Oh my god, there is. I swore I wasn't going to tell anyone but, oh right, like I'm not going to tell you.

ANISSA. What? Tell me.

JENNI. PHBICS is not a support group. *It's an underground resistance movement!*

ANISSA. I know!

JENNI. What?

ANISSA. I mean, that's *wild.*

JENNI. I know!

ANISSA. Do they have, like…guns and stuff?

JENNI. Oh no! Their plan is to find a mole, someone who works inside the company who can help us take them down from the inside and they recruited me because they think there's someone in my orbit who works for Ferizon and at first I was like, that's not even possible, but then I was like… Wait a minute. I think I *do* know someone who works for Ferizon.

ANISSA. And who is that?

JENNI. Cydney.

ANISSA. Oh, right. Cydney.

(*She begins to text furiously.*)

JENNI. So I'm going to try to get in touch with her and—

ANISSA. (*Her Blackberry freezes.*) What's going on? Oh my god, my Blackberry froze! Fuck! It's my nightmare. I need to be in touch—I need to make sure that everything—Give me your cell—

JENNI. I wish I could but Ferizon turned off my service.

ANISSA. Oh right. Damn.

JENNI. I borrowed this phone from Bryce but I need it to try and get in touch with Cydney.

ANISSA. Oh right. Cydney.

JENNI. They don't give them any extensions, remember? So I guess I'm just going to have to keep calling until she picks up. I have no idea how long that's going to take.

ANISSA. (*Briskly gathering her stuff to leave.*) Alright, alright, alright, whatever.

JENNI. Anissa, calm down. You'll be fine without your Blackberry between now and the time you get to—

(ANISSA*'s out the door.*)

Have a good day.

Okay. Might as well get started.

(*She dials a number on her cell phone.*)

One.

347 992 5568

Jennifer Jensen—oh, you know what?

Representative.

Rep Re Sentative.

Rep—

CHARLENE. Ferizon Customer Service how can I help you?

JENNI. Oh hi. Who am I speaking with, please?

CHARLENE. This is Charlene speaking.

JENNI. Never mind. Thank you.

(*She hangs up and hits re-dial.*)

Representative.

Rep—

MOLLY. Ferizon Customer // Service—

JENNI. Who am I speaking with, please?

MOLLY. This is Molly.

JENNI. Okay, thank you, bye.

(*Hangs up and hits re-dial.*)

Representative—

KYLE. Good morning—

JENNI. Who is this?

KYLE. Uh, this is—

JENNI. Oh you're a guy, never mind.

(*Hangs up. Hits re-dial.*)

Representative.

Representative.

Repre—

CYDNEY. (*Hushed, terrified.*) Hello?

JENNI. Hello. Hi. Who is this please?

CYDNEY. This is Ferizon, can I help you?

JENNI. Yeah. Who am I speaking with?

CYDNEY. This is Cydney?

JENNI. Cydney? Cydney! Oh my god you can't believe how many times I had to call to get through to // you

CYDNEY. Who is this?

JENNI. This is Jenni. Jensen. Cydney, I was—

CYDNEY. Please stop calling me!

JENNI. What? Are you okay? You sound kind of funny.

CYDNEY. I'm fine. I'm fine… I just need you to stop calling me.

JENNI. Okay but could we meet somewhere? I'd love to have a conversation with you.

CYDNEY. It's not a good idea.

JENNI. Please, Cydney, please? It's kind of important.

CYDNEY. Okay. Do you know the switching building?

JENNI. The what?

CYDNEY. Meet me there tonight at 4 a.m.

JENNI. *In the morning?*

CYDNEY. (*Hearing someone coming.*) *Oh my god I've gotta go.*

      (*Trying to cover, trying to sound normal and bright.*)

Is there anything else I can do for you today?

JENNI. Yeah, where am I supposed to meet you?

CYDNEY. (*Trying to sound normal.*) Alright then, you have a great day. Thank you for calling Fer—

      (*The line goes dead.*)

JENNI. Cydney? Cydney? Dammit!

      (*She re-dials.*)

Come on… Come on… Cydney…

      (*Responding impatiently to the prompts.*)

Yes. One.

Yes.

Representative, representative, representative, represen//tative—

ANISSA. (*Her voice disguised.*) Thank you for calling Ferizon, what can I help you with today?

JENNI. Oh! Yes. Hi. I'm trying to reach Cydney.

ANISSA. I'm sorry, Ma'am, but there's no one who works here by that name.

JENNI. I was just speaking with her!

ANISSA. And the name again was Cynthia?

JENNI. No. Cydney! Not Cynthia. Cydney!

ANISSA. I'm so sorry Ma'am. No one by that name works here.

JENNI. Oh my god. I was talking with her one second ago! She was helping me with a billing problem that no one else seems able to resolve—

ANISSA. Oh, well I can fix your billing problem.

JENNI. (*Taken aback, wary.*) Really?

ANISSA. Absolutely I can. Would you like me to take care of that for you? It'll only take a quick minute. I promise.

JENNI. (*Still wary but willing to try.*) Okay, yeah.

ANISSA. Hold on for just one moment.

(*She holds the phone down to the CD player and turns on Daniel Powter's "Bad Day."*)

JENNI. Aaahh! You're kidding me! Oh my god! It burns!!

(*As* JENNI *writhes on hold we see that on* ANISSA's *end this call is being observed by a group of trainees. This is a "higher tier" than the class we saw earlier. They're a bunch of thugs, all smoking and drinking and sprawled out around the classroom. They've been listening to this call with thuggish satisfaction.* ANISSA *crosses the room to sit on the desk with her legs crossed.*)

ANISSA. Are you paying attention, boys?

THUGGISH BILLING GUY. Magnificent!

THUGGISH BILLING GUY 2. Question.

ANISSA. Shoot.

THUGGISH BILLING GUY 2. What if she threatens to call the FCC?

ANISSA. On what? We cut off her phone service.

(*Raucous, thuggish laughter.*)

THUGGISH BILLING GUY. Jesus, I love this job!

ANISSA. Okay, let's finish it up. Watch and learn, people.

(ANISSA *crosses back to the phone and turns off the CD.*)

Okay Ma'am. Are you still there?

JENNI. Yes, I'm here.

ANISSA. I checked into your account and I don't see any record of a problem.

JENNI. You don't see a problem????

ANISSA. It's not showing up here on my system.

JENNI. Oh my god, what's wrong with me? Of course it's not! Because this company is one big fucked-up gaslight machine. There's no problem with my account—except you turned off my service! There's no Cydney—except I just talked to her one minute ago! Just, please, I beg you, I beg you, human being to human being, please just say to me that I'm not crazy and that you know that none of this makes any sense.

ANISSA. I'm so sorry, Ma'am, I can't do that.

(JENNI *collapses in existential despair.*)

Is there anything else I can help you with today?

JENNI. (*Broken.*) No. Thank you.

ANISSA. Alright then. Thank you for choosing Ferizon, J.J.

(*A beat. Then, suddenly—*)

JENNI. *J.J.?*

ANISSA. *Damn!*

Scene 12
Emergency PHBICS meeting.

CAROL, LARS, JERRY *and* WANDA *sit knee-to-knee with a hysterical* JENNI. INGRID *stands in the back, smoking a Gauloise and looking out into the middle distance.*

JENNI. Okay, okay. So I was trying to reach…my contact, you know? That I thought I had. And I was trying and trying to reach her, you know, but they don't have any extensions, like, one time I made a joke that it must be like *Green Acres—*

WANDA. Okay honey, fast forward through the jokes.

JENNI. Okay, right. So finally I reached her and like, now I realize she sounded kind of funny, kind of stressed, but at the time I didn't notice and—

CAROL. Get to the part about your sister.

JENNI. My sister… My sister… Oh my god! My sister works for Ferizon!

ALL. We know.

JENNI. You WHAT???

JERRY. For the record I questioned the ethics of this whole operation.

JENNI. I don't understand! She's my sister! She's my twin sister!

INGRID. (*Still gazing out, rueful.*) Sisters… Yes… Your best friend can turn out to be your worst enemy.

LARS. Jenni, tell us about Cydney. What did Cydney say?

INGRID. Cydney. How ironic. I knew a Cydney once. A long time ago…

LARS. Cydney.

JENNI. Right, right. Cydney. The last thing she said before the line went dead was, "Meet me in the switching building."
What is that?

JERRY. It's Ferizon's main telecommunications switching center. Five sub-basement levels that house 3.6 million data circuits.

JENNI. She said I should meet her there tonight at 4 a.m.

WANDA. In the *morning?*

JENNI. I know. I'm going to have to set two alarms.

INGRID. You can't go, Jenni.

JENNI. But I have to.

INGRID. No. Anissa knows now that you know and believe me, there's nothing more ruthless than a sister whose betrayal has been uncovered by her sister.

JENNI. Really?

INGRID. Yes. And so it will be me who will go and I will try to get this Cydney out in one piece and then I will try to get out myself and if I do not... I trust you will carry on the work I have started.

WANDA. Ingrid, don't even talk like that!

INGRID. I am saying only what is true. And now, I must assign one of you to take my place in charge if I don't return.

(*She surveys the group, weighing the pros and cons of each.*)

Lars. Your empathy is a beautiful tool which we need and use. But to be in charge...? No, you would be pulled too much by your heart. Jerry. We would be lost without your skills of analysis. But they are an impediment to quick decision making. Wanda. Few people know how your calm and canny facade teeters on the precipice of a bottomless chasm of bitterness, rage and despair.

WANDA. I wouldn't say it's that bad.

INGRID. That's because your finely calibrated regimen of yogic breathing and the Bach Flower Remedies keeps you balanced. But the pressures of leadership might be too much. It would not be fair. And so... Carol. This leaves you.

CAROL. Oh, for godsakes, you're not serious.

INGRID. Yes, my no-nonsense friend.

CAROL. I feel exhausted just thinking about it.

INGRID. You see? She is a leader.

My friends, tomorrow I will rise at four a.m. to face whatever awaits me. If things go badly we shall not meet again. If fate smiles upon our mission I will see you all...tomorrow afternoon. And now I must prepare...for the switching building.

(*She leaves. Everyone looks at CAROL.*)

CAROL. Oh, for godsake. Alright. I guess I'm in charge. Alright. Everybody, listen up.

(*They all come to attention.*)

When we head out, take your trash with you. I'm sick of cleaning up after you people.

Scene 13
One hour later.

(The apartment. ANISSA *is at the table, scrolling through her Blackberry.* JENNI *walks in. They are both startled.)*

JENNI. Oh hi.

ANISSA. Hi.

JENNI. You're home early.

ANISSA. Am I? It's 5:30. It's not so early. It's normal after work time.

JENNI. I've never known you to be home before 7.

ANISSA. Sure I have. Lots of times.

JENNI. Oh well, my mistake, then.

    (Long beat.)

ANISSA. So what are you up to tonight?

JENNI. Me, nothing?

ANISSA. No, no plans?

JENNI. No, why, do you have plans?

ANISSA. Me, no.

JENNI. Actually, I was thinking I'd turn in early.

ANISSA. Yeah, me too.

JENNI. Oh yeah? Early day tomorrow?

ANISSA. Not more than usual. You?

JENNI. Me, no. Everything's the same as usual for me. Yep just like normal, nothing new, nothing different.

ANISSA. You look a little different.

JENNI. In what way?

ANISSA. I don't know, just different somehow.

JENNI. That's funny 'cause I was going to say that about you.

ANISSA. Is that right?

JENNI. Yeah. Something's…different.

ANISSA. Huh.

JENNI. Yeah. Can't exactly say what it is.

    (Beat.)

ANISSA. Okay, well, I'm going to head off to bed now.

JENNI. Yep, me too.

ANISSA. Okay then, have a good night.

JENNI. You too, sleep well.

ANISSA. I expect to.

JENNI. Me too. I'll be out like a light by—

(*Looks at her watch.*)

5:45.

ANISSA. 'Kay. Night.

JENNI. Night.

Scene 14
At the switching building.

Down in the sub-basement of the switching building, dim light illuminates the spaces between the rows of stacked computer switching equipment. The whole building is suffused with a loud humming drone.

From between two stacks INGRID *appears, smoking a Gauloise. She hears a sound and ducks behind another set of stacks.*

From behind another set of stacks, CYDNEY *appears. She carries a cardboard box. She looks like she's been through something. She looks like she's on the lam.*

CYDNEY. (*Whispering, tentative.*) Jenni?

Jenni?

Yoo-hoo?

You're not standing me up, are you?

(*She walks away, looking for* JENNI. *From behind the stacks where she was hiding,* INGRID *re-emerges.*)

INGRID. It can't be! I can't believe it. But *of course!* How many Cydneys are there?? Oh Ingrid! What is your *damage.*

(*She hears footsteps.*)

I can't let her see me. Not yet.

(*She ducks behind the stacks.* CYDNEY *reappears.*)

CYDNEY. Oh, Jenni, why aren't you here!

(*Re: her box.*)

I should have taken this home, I guess.

(*She puts it down on the ground.*)

Oh, I don't know which way is up, anymore. Jenni?

(*She walks away again.* INGRID *re-emerges. She sees the box, she looks to see what's inside.*)

INGRID. What is this…?

(*She lifts out a magnetic paperclip holder shaped like a porcupine.*)

Oh the contents of her desk. They fired her!

(Flipping through a folder.)
COBRA forms.
(She closes the folder.)
It hurts just to look at them. I never would have thought in a million years that the Cydney I was hearing about who was working at Ferizon could possibly be the same Cydney who is my estranged twin but why should I be surprised. She must have taken this job for the benefits. She would have had to—after—Oh! The old remorse comes back, sharp, like a brand new slash of the knife.

(She puts the folder back in the box, then, slowly, lifts out a framed photograph.)
Cydney, you carry this photo with you. Look at us, you and me, Cydney, in Mom's Taurus. I don't remember where we were going. But we look happy.

(She reaches into a pocket and takes out another photo.)
I carry a photo with me as well. You and me at the grand opening of your company, your dream, "Composting for Peace." To this day you still don't know that it was because of me you lost your beautiful company and had to leave Madison and take a job you must have hated with Ferizon, all so you could pay off your medical bills. Oh, you vaguely knew I worked in the insurance industry—but it never occurred to you that I worked for the enemy: Blue Cross/Blue Shield. It never occurred to you that it was me, personally, who said that your broken leg was a pre-existing condition and refused to pay. I felt proud when I was destroying you. I felt that you were too romantic, that you didn't understand about the real world. But after you went away I realized—*I* was the one who didn't understand—and then *I* went away. And since then I have made it my mission to try to put something back, to make up, in whatever small way, for what I took away from you.

(She hears footsteps.)
Oh shit, I gotta go.

(She dives behind a stack, not realizing she's dropped her picture into CYDNEY's *box.* CYDNEY *re-emerges.)*
CYDNEY. I guess she's not going to come.

(Picking up her box, she sees the snapshot INGRID *dropped.)*
What's this?

(Confused.)
Ingrid?

(And then, the penny drops.)
Ingrid!

(She looks around, then runs into the stacks, looking for her long-lost sister.)
CYDNEY. *(Offstage.)* Ingrid?

(INGRID *comes running out looking for her.*)

INGRID. Cydney?

(ANISSA *enters. Using a special feature on her new iPhone she freezes* INGRID.)

ANISSA. Hello there Cydney.

INGRID. Hello.

(ANISSA *uses the phone to make* INGRID *dance like a puppet, then releases her.* INGRID *falls to the floor.*)

ANISSA. This is a terrific app.

(*She sees that* CYDNEY—*really* INGRID—*has escaped into the stacks.*)

Oh for Chrissakes.

(*She tries to make her come back with the app but it doesn't work. She looks to see why.*)

Upgrade $2.99? I'm not paying for that.

(*She pulls a rope and a hood out of her pocket.*)

We'll just have to do this the old-fashioned way.

(*She reaches into the stacks.*)

Ah! There you are!

(*Though we can only see* ANISSA, *we see she's tying* CYDNEY *[really* INGRID*] up.*)

I knew those Catch your own Prey exercises we did at the Corporate Retreat would come in handy one day.

(*Pulling her partway out, leaving her head behind the stacks.*)

You didn't really think I was going to just hand you a full severance package and then let you waltz over here and betray me, did you?

(CYDNEY *emerges from the stacks and sees* ANISSA *and* INGRID.)

CYDNEY. You leave my sister *alone!*

(ANISSA *looks at* CYDNEY, *startled. She pulls a hooded* INGRID *the rest of the way out.*)

ANISSA. (*Looking from one to the other.*) Wait a minute... You're...
But you're...

(*Putting it together.*)

Damn! Twins!

(*The group peeks out from behind one set of stacks.* JENNI *steps out from behind another.*)

JENNI. That's right, Anissa. And you'd better let them both go.

ANISSA. Or what?

JENNI. Or I'm going to call Mom and Dad and tell them what you're really like!

ANISSA. You think I care?

JENNI. Anissa, you don't have to do this. It's not too late.

ANISSA. Oh really? What time *is* it?

(*She takes out her iPhone, and checks the time.*)

Oh right!

(*She snaps open a switchblade attachment and holds it to* INGRID'*s throat.*)

It's hostage time!

(*Everyone freezes, panicked.*)

JENNI. Stay cool, everybody, stay cool…

(CYDNEY *takes a cautious step toward* INGRID.)

CYDNEY. Ingrid, I'm right here. I can see you. Everyone can see you. And me. At the same time.

(*Muffled noises in response from under the hood.*)

You're right. This whole thing feels like a cheap joke. But don't worry. We'll get you out of this.

ANISSA. Enough funny business!

(*She starts backing out with* INGRID.)

Now your friend and I are gonna take a little walk, and—

(*Suddenly, re:* WANDA *who has taken a step toward her.*)

Put down the Rescue Remedy!

(WANDA *drops it to the floor.*)

You don't wanna see me any calmer than I am right now. Got me? Adios suckers.

(ANISSA *exits with her hostage. A beat.*)

CYDNEY. What just happened??? For seven years I have no idea where my sister is and then suddenly she's right here. And then, *poof*, my boss takes her hostage!

JENNI. Cydney, calm down.

CYDNEY. *You* calm down!

LARS. Cydney, Cydney, it's under control. Listen. Last week Carol dropped a tracking device into Anissa's latte. We know her every move.

JERRY. (*Looking at the Lo-jack receiver for the tracking device.*) They're exiting the building right now and onto Pearl Street heading…south.

WANDA. We're gonna get your sister back, honey.

LARS. (*Eyes on his watch.*) We're giving them a five-minute head start so Anissa lets down her guard.

CAROL. Then we're going to be on 'em like deodorant on a black sweater.

LARS. 3, 2, 1… Go!

    (*They race out of the switching building. Out on the street,* JERRY *studies the Lo-jack.*)

JERRY. It looks like they're headed to Boston.

LARS. Amtrak right? Come on. Penn Station.

CAROL. It's rush hour. Penn Station will be a madhouse. I'm going to order the tickets on the phone.

JERRY. We should just go.

CAROL. (*Dialing her phone.*) Just hold your horses.

VOICE OF JULIE. Hi. I'm Julie—

CAROL. Hello?

VOICE OF JULIE. —Amtrak's automated reservation agent. I'll be helping you with your reservation today.

CAROL. Fantastic.

VOICE OF JULIE. Let's get started.

CAROL. Yes. Let's.

VOICE OF JULIE. I'm sorry. But I didn't understand what you said.

CAROL. I didn't say anything.

VOICE OF JULIE. Tell me the name of the city you want to depart from.

CAROL. New York Penn Station.

VOICE OF JULIE. I think you said Chattanooga Tennessee. Is that correct?

CAROL. I said Penn Station! Chattanooga Tennessee?

VOICE OF JULIE. I'm sorry. Let's try again.

CAROL. I'm leaving from Penn // Station.

VOICE OF JULIE. Hold on. I'm working on it.

CAROL. Alright.

VOICE OF JULIE. I think you said Bismarck, North Dakota. Is that correct?

CAROL. Oh for crying out loud.

VOICE OF JULIE. Got it.

CAROL. Got *what?*

    (LARS, *a few steps away, snaps his phone shut.*)

LARS. I got 'em. Come on.

    (*They race down the subway stairs and all swipe successfully through the turnstile except* CYDNEY *who swipes. Then swipes again. And again. And again.*)

WANDA. What's happening?

CYDNEY. It keeps saying swipe again.

WANDA. Well swipe it again, honey.

> (*She swipes, and swipes, and swipes.*)

CAROL. Somebody swipe her through!

JENNI. You guys, the train is coming!

LARS. I can't I have a monthly card!

CAROL. Me too.

> (*Sound of an approaching train.*)

WANDA. We all have monthly cards. Honey buy yourself another card.

> (*The train pulls in.*)

JENNI. Here's the train!

CYDNEY. Go without me.

LARS. We can't.

CAROL. Yes we can. Everybody on.

> (*They get on. The doors close.*)

ALL. (*Waving to* CYDNEY.) Bye!

> (*Terminal C. Boston Logan Airport.* CAROL, JENNI, LARS *and* JERRY *study the Lo-jack.*)

JERRY. Looks like they're on their way to the gate.

JENNI. Hey you guys, where's Wanda?

> (WANDA *stands at the airport Duane Reade self-scanner checkout. She swipes an item.*)

SCANNER. *Dentyne. Ice.* Two dollars Ninety-*nine* cents.

> (WANDA *puts the gum in the bag.*)

Move your *Dentyne. Ice.* to the bag.

WANDA. I did it already!

> (*She swipes an item.*)

SCANNER. *Cheeze. Itz.* Three dollars Eighty-*two* cents.

Move your *Cheeze // Itz* to the—

WANDA. Alright, keep up.

> (*She swipes.*)

SCANNER. *Jumbo. Tampons.* Nine dollars Ninety-*eight* // cents

WANDA. Oh good lord!

SCANNER. Move your *Jumbo. Tampons.* // to the bag

WANDA. (*Angry whisper.*) Shush! You shush!

SCANNER. The weight is not correct for your *Jumbo. Tampons.*

WANDA. Oh, forget it!

(She flees the Duane Reade and rejoins the group.)

Come on, let's go.

JENNI. Where were you?

WANDA. Never mind. Here are your boarding passes.

LARS. They're on a flight that leaves in ten minutes to Paris.

JENNI. Ours leaves in half an hour. We'll be right behind them. Come on.

(They enter the security line and all struggle to comply with the instructions.)

TSA AGENT. *(In an "I've repeated this ad nauseum" tone.)* All cell phones must be removed from your pockets and placed on the belt. Keep your boarding passes in your hand. Sweaters, jackets and coats must be removed and placed on the belt. Keep your boarding passes in your hand at all times. All shoes must be removed and placed on the belt. Boarding passes in your hands, people. Alright, move it along. What's the hold up?

(They run to the plane carrying their shoes and coats in their hands.

They get off the plane in Paris. JERRY studies the Lo-jack.)

WANDA. Which way, Jerry?

JERRY. They're at the Eiffel Tower, heading toward the Seine.

JENNI. We'd better take the Metro. It looks like tickets are over here.

(They all gather around a machine for tickets to the Paris Metro.)

VOICE OF THE PARIS METRO. Bienvenue au Métro de Paris.

WANDA. Oh, that's nice. Classy.

CAROL. Here, use my credit card.

(JERRY pushes the card into the machine.)

VOICE OF THE PARIS METRO. Non. Cette carte de est déplaisante. Bleh.

(It spits out the card.)

CAROL. What's wrong with my card? Try again.

(She pushes it back in to the machine.)

VOICE OF THE PARIS METRO. Bleh.

(It spits the card out.)

CAROL. Why??

VOICE OF THE PARIS METRO. Votre carte n'a pas la microchip electronique plus sophistiquee de la carte européenne.

WANDA. *(Paging through a phrasebook.)* Wait, I'm checking my phrasebook— It says it wants a card with some kind of a microchip.

CAROL. This is ridiculous.

(She pushes the card back in.)

VOICE OF THE PARIS METRO. (*Spitting it back out.*) Bleh. Ptui. Votre carte est inferieure.

CAROL. (*To the machine.*) I don't like your tone.

VOICE OF THE PARIS METRO. I don't like your outfit.

CAROL. Why I...!

> (LARS *runs up from another machine with tickets in his hand.*)

LARS. I got 'em. Come on you guys. Let's go!

> (*They emerge from the Metro and gasp at the sight of the Eiffel Tower.*)

JERRY. It looks just like the Eiffel Tower!

CAROL. It *is* the Eiffel Tower, Jerry.

JENNI. Damn! It looks like we just missed them!

LARS. (*Looking at the Lo-jack.*) It looks like they're heading for Germany.

CAROL. I knew I should have worn my other shoes.

WANDA. (*Doing a bit of mime.*) Look everybody. I'm Marcel Marceau.

LARS. Jerry, are you okay? You look a little shaky.

JERRY. I'm fine! I'm fine!

JENNI. The train to Berlin is this way. Come on!

> (*They hop on a train and arrive in Berlin.*)

JERRY. (*Fading fast.*) Uh, not to...alarm anyone, but...I...food...or eating... might be.

LARS. I've got to find something for him.

> (*Realizes.*)

Wait—does anyone have any Euros?

CAROL. We were in New York ten minutes ago.

LARS. Oh, right.

JENNI. Is that an ATM?

LARS. Let's go.

> (*They go into the* ATM.)

VOICE OF THE GERMAN ATM. Wilkommen im Deutsche Sparkasse Geldautomat. Bitte Sie seine Geldkarte hineinstecken.

LARS. Uh... okay. Looks like the card goes here...

> (*He puts his card into the machine.*)

VOICE OF THE GERMAN ATM. *Nein!* Falsche Antwort. Bitte Sie Geldkarte hineinstecken.

WANDA. (*Handing him another card.*) Here. Try this card.

> (*He inserts the card.*)

VOICE OF THE GERMAN ATM. *Nein!* Geldkarte hineinstecken, bitte.

LARS. I don't know what it wants.

CAROL. Try this.

LARS. That's a library card.

CAROL. Just try it. It's frightening me!

    (*He puts it in.*)

VOICE OF THE GERMAN ATM. Geldkarte hineinstecken!

WANDA. Give it money!

LARS. But we're trying to get money.

WANDA. I think it wants money!

VOICE OF THE GERMAN ATM. *Geldkarte!*
GELDKARTE!

    (JENNI *looks at the Lo-jack.*)

JENNI. Uh-oh. Come on you guys. They just landed in Irkutsk.

    (*They fly on a scary, tiny Russian plane, bumpy, lights flashing, and deboard in Irkutsk.*)

JERRY. (*Deboarding the plane, hysterical.*) Who lands a plane like that? Tray tables... *willy-nilly!* Seat backs in non-upright positions!!!!

LARS. Guys, we've got to get some food in him! This way Jerry.

JERRY. What have I told you about touching me.

CAROL. Are those vending machines?

LARS. I guess. But what's in them?

    (*They approach the vending machine.*)

VOICE OF THE RUSSIAN VENDING MACHINE. Privyet! Ya Vesyoli-Vendink-Avtomat—

CAROL. What's it saying?

LARS. (*Slowly, clearly, to the machine.*) We need food.

VOICE OF THE RUSSIAN VENDING MACHINE. Dlya sosisechki, pozhaluista nazhmitye sosisechkuyu knopku.

WANDA. "For a cute little sausage, please press the sausage button."

LARS. Which do you think is the sausage button? Oh.

    (*He pushes a button. A sausage is dispensed. He starts to hand it to* JERRY *but a* BABUSHKA *appears out of nowhere.*)

BABUSHKA. (*Snatching the sausage.*) Vy shto, zachem zdyes tak kushetye? Kak zvyer? Eto shto, svinarnik? Nyelzya zdyes tak kushat. Bezobrazoye kakoye. Kak vam nye stydno? Otvratityelno. Obidna! Uzhas takoi!

    (*"What are you doing eating here like that? Like an animal? What is this, a pigsty? It's not permitted to eat here. What appalling behavior. How is it you are not ashamed? Disgusting. Insulting! Appalling!"*)

JENNI. (*Looking at the Lo-jack.*) Guys! They're back in New York... Somewhere in the Financial District. Looks like... Oh my god! They're at Kimberly's House! Come on!

LARS. Wait, who's Kimberly?

JENNI. No... It's Kimberly's House! It's a free clinic for poor children in the Financial District. Come on!

WANDA. But wait— There are poor children in the Financial District?

JENNI. Wanda, please! There are poor children // everywhere!

CAROL. Come on. We're going back to New York.

> (*Whirlwind montage of trip back to New York, depositing them outside the door of "Kimberly's House—A Free Clinic for Poor Children, yes, in the Financial District."*)

JENNI. What does the Lo-jack say, Jerry?

JERRY. She's in there. She's in there right now.

JENNI. Oh god, okay, okay, okay, how are we going to handle // this?

JERRY. Swat Team. We go in Swat Team style // and—

CAROL. The ducts! I want you to crawl into // the ducts!

JENNI. This seems // extreme.

WANDA. I have a fuchsia belt in Tae Bo, // I don't like to use it but—

JENNI. No, you // guys, no.

JERRY. Swat. Swat. // Swat. Swat.

LARS. Something. We have to do something to get Ingrid out of there.

WANDA. Let's just blast in. We'll just blast right in. And we'll figure it out when we're in there.

JERRY. Boo-ya!   **CAROL.** Let's go.   **LARS.** Let's do it!

JENNI. No, no, no, no! People, people, listen to me! Listen. Listen. Whatever else Anissa is involved in, she cares about Kimberly's House and she cares about those kids and she's just not going to put them in the middle of some big, ugly "Rescue at Entebbe" situation. Alright? So we're just going to go in there nice and calm and she's going to give us Ingrid. Okay?

> (*They nod.*)

Okay. Calm.

> (*They enter.*)

WANDA. Seems awfully quiet in here.

> (ANISSA *enters with a teddy bear in one hand and* INGRID, *bound and gagged, in the other.*)

Um-um. This does not look good.

ANISSA. Oh, hi, everybody. Looking for the kids?

JENNI. Where are they?

ANISSA. Hopefully looking for jobs.

JENNI. Oh my god!

ANISSA. Apparently they weren't aware chemo costs money.

WANDA. You monster!

LARS. (*Low, even.*) Stay focused, people.

JERRY. Yes. Madam? I request that you release our friend and then we will bid you a good day.

ANISSA. Oh, that makes sense. This woman was plotting the overthrow of my company so what will I do about it? Oh, I know. I'm just going to let her go.

JERRY. I see your point but I'm going to have to insist.

LARS. And I back him up.

> (*Two burly* THUGS *appear.*)

ANISSA. Oh yeah? What are you two tough men gonna do?

> (*The burly men face off with* LARS *and* JERRY *for a beat. Then,* LARS *and* JERRY *leap…and are easily subdued.*)

LARS.	**JERRY.**
Bullies! You're so mean!	I'm stronger than I—OW!
—Ow! Ow!	(*Grabbing his groin area.*)
	Jesus! I just had that repaired!!

LARS. (*To the* THUG *holding* JERRY.) You're hurting him.

JERRY. (*To the other* THUG.) If you mark his beautiful skin, I'll—

> (*Their eyes meet.*)

LARS. Jerry?

JERRY. I was never going to say anything. You're with Alex.

LARS. I'm not.

JERRY. You're not?

LARS. Well, on paper maybe, in a way, he hasn't technically moved out but…no. I didn't even know you were—

JERRY. I didn't either. Since I first met you I felt like I don't know anything anymore.

LARS. Is that…a good thing?

JERRY. You tell me?

ANISSA. Oh for Chrissakes! Where's that pepper spray?

> (*As the* THUGS *grab* LARS *and* JERRY, WANDA *and* CAROL *suddenly leap on the* THUGS, *wailing like characters from* Xena, Warrior Princess, *The* THUGS *easily detain and corral all four.*)

JENNI. Anissa, why are you doing this?

ANISSA. Why do you think?

JENNI. It's because Grandma loved me best, isn't it?

ANISSA. Oh, please, I was Grandma's favorite and you know it.

JENNI. What I know is that this is bigger than you and me and Grandma, *and* Mittens, *and* my Barbie Dream Camper which you stole and don't deny it. This is about every consumer everywhere at the mercy of mega-corporations like yours. Why do you treat people this way? Can't you see that all we want is decent phone service?

ANISSA. Can't you see that we don't care about phones!

JENNI. What do you mean you don't care about phones? You're the phone company!

ANISSA. Hello. Twenty-first Century calling for Jenni Jensen. We're not a phone company. We're a *telecommunications giant*.

JENNI. Either way you still owe us good service! You're still our public utility!

ANISSA. Public utility! Don't make me laugh. That's like saying Cable TV is a public utility.

JENNI. Cable TV *is* a public utility! Oh my god! How did you manage to hoodwink us all into thinking our collective public resources were your own privately owned money factory?

ANISSA. Because we're smarter than you?

JENNI. You're not smarter. You're just evil.

ANISSA. Oh Jenni, I'm not evil.

JENNI. Well you're not good.

ANISSA. Right. I'm not good *or* evil—I'm *corporate*. Which means I'm morally neutral.

JENNI. But you're not. You're not morally neutral. You present yourself as a caring entity! But then you hurt people.

ANISSA. Yes! Jenni! Do I really have to spell everything out for you? That's what a corporation *does*—we project all the warmth of a human being without any of the pesky human responsibilities.

JENNI. Like a psychopath?

ANISSA. If that's liberal psychobabble for profitable, then yes, good analogy. And it's time you woke up and smelled the coffee picked by under-compensated workers. Your little protest is for naught. The die is cast and the deal is done. We run the world.

JENNI. But Anissa, I know you. This isn't you.

ANISSA. Oh, but it is me. I'm your mirror image. And if you're surprised it's probably because you weren't all that interested in looking very closely as long as my "evil" life made your "good" one possible. Huh. What do you know? Turns out, sister, dear, I'm no faker than you are.

JENNI. (*To herself, her worldview collapsing around her.*) Oh my god. Can it be true? While I was claiming the higher moral ground was I so enamored of great Groupon offers and Words with Friends that I didn't notice the world of justice and light was slipping away? Can it really be too late? Is there really no place left on God's green earth that your corporate tentacles don't reach?

ANISSA. Nope.

(INGRID *runs in.*)

INGRID. Oh yes there is!

(*A sign descends that says "Ass-Slappers."*)

ANISSA. What the…?

INGRID. Welcome to Ass-Slappers!

EVERYONE. (*Exclaiming things like:*)
Yay!
What?
Amazing!
I've *heard* about this place!

INGRID. For anyone who'd like to be in the show the non-hierarchical sign-up sheet is right here. Anyone here to watch, pay what you like, admission is on a sliding scale.

JENNI. Put my name on that non-hierarchical sign-up sheet. I've got a story to tell.

ANISSA. (*Scoffing.*) Oh yeah? What story is that?

JENNI. The story of the theft of our public utilities!

ANISSA. Nobody wants to hear it.

JENNI. Oh I think they do. I think people are aching to see a staged representation of the daily experience of being pummeled by a million tiny fists which is the condition of daily life under your regime.

ANISSA. And you think this is going to help, do you? Theater? No one goes to the theater. The last effective piece of political theater was what? *Lysistrata?* You think you're Jenni Odets or something? "Strike! Strike! Strike!" You think everyone is going to march out of here and raise hell with Ferizon? I don't think so.

JENNI. I think they just might.

(*To the audience, raising her hand.*)

How many people here have ever had a problem with your cell phone carrier?

(*To* ANISSA.)

See?

ANISSA. What the hell do you think you're doing?

JENNI. It's called direct audience address.

ANISSA. Alright, I'll see your direct audience address and I'll raise you.

(*Also to the audience, raising her hand.*)

How many of you are going to do something about it?
Put your hand down! Put it down!

JENNI. Just because we've been lulled into submission doesn't mean we're going to stay that way.

ANISSA. (*To the* THUGS.) Shut this down! Now!

THUG #1. (*Not hearing* ANISSA *because he's talking to* THUG #2.) Seriously? You never heard of Ass-Slappers! It's so great. Sometimes it's really funny, sometimes it's really moving. Come on, let's get a good seat.

ANISSA. (*To the audience.*) Listen people, nothing is happening here. My company is very powerful. In fact, we control reality. So none of this is actually happening.

JENNI. Oh I think it is. I think you're the one who needs to wake up and smell the coffee.

(*Sniffs.*)

Mmmm. Smell that?

(*Everyone sniffs.*)

Fair trade.

(*Music in. That's right. Here comes the big number.*)

JENNI. *Your free-wheeling free market*
had its day in the sun
You thought deregulation
was a whole lot of fun
You didn't care if we lost
but you made damn sure that you won
that you won, that you won, that you won
Well guess what my friend
that bullshit is done

ANISSA. (*To the audience.*) Politics of envy.

WANDA. *We've finally wised up*

LARS AND CAROL. *We wised up*

WANDA. *And we're making a link*
Your net worth keeps rising
while ours continues to shrink

Were you just blind
or did you really never bother to think

LARS AND CAROL. *Think*

WANDA. *Never think*

LARS AND CAROL. *Think*

WANDA. *Never think*

LARS AND CAROL. *Think*

WANDA. *Yah never, never think*
Folks lose their shit when they are pushed to the brink—

ALL. *Can you hear us now?*

JERRY. *No more! No more! No more! No more!*

ALL. *Can you hear us now?*

JERRY. *No more! No more! No more! No more! No more!*

ALL. *Can you hear us?*
Can you hear us now?
Can you hear us?
Can you hear us now?
Can you hear us?
Can you hear us now, now, now

INGRID. *There was a time that like you*
I was skeptical of my twin sister
She seemed so naive in her world view
that I mocked and dismissed her
Now I am filled with remorse for the years that I tried to resist her, resist her, my long-lost
twin sister
I can't seem to shake the sense that she was right here and I just missed her...

ALL. *Can you hear us now?*

INGRID. *I swear that Cydney was just right here!*

ALL. *Can you hear us now?*

INGRID. *Come on, come on, come on, come on, come on, come on, Cydney!*

ALL. *Can you hear us?*
Can you hear us now?
Can you hear us?
Can you hear us now?
Can you hear us?
Can you hear us now, now, now.

ANISSA. *(To THUG #1.)* You! Shut this down! Now!

THUG #1. *Listen, I'm no lefty freak*
I'm just a plain old working slob

I don't get into politics
I show up. I clock in. Do my job

ALL. (*Soft.*) *Can you hear us now?*

THUG. *But listen to that sound…*

ALL. (*Soft.*) *Can you hear us now?*

THUG. *That's freedom's plaintive, aching, distant throb*
Hell, I quit Ferizon! Let me join your rag-tag mob!

ALL. *Can you hear us now?*

THUG. *Look at me!*

ALL. *Can you hear us now?*

THUG. *Free, Free, Free!*

ALL. *Can you hear us*
Can you hear us now?
Can you hear us?
Can you hear us now?
Now, now, now, now—

> (*Sound of a cell phone ringing.*)

JENNI. Oh my god, you guys, my service is back on!

> (*Everyone cheers.*)

Sorry. Just one minute—

> (*She answers.*)

Hello?

AUTOMATED VOICE. …—ding your Ferizon account. Please call 1 800 668 6668 regarding your Ferizon account.

JENNI. NOOOOOOOOOOO!

ALL. *There is only so long you can go on like you do*
You think you've got all the power
and we used to think that too
But the day is dawning when we stop taking your crap
Are you with us? Come on people!
You know what to do

> (*They clap and the audience claps along.*)

Can you hear us?
Can you hear us now?
Can you hear us?
Can you hear us now?
Can you hear us?
Can you hear us now?
Can you hear us now, now, now, now, now?

Can you hear us?

ANISSA. *NO!*

ALL. *Can you hear us now?*
Can you hear us?

ANISSA. *NO!*

ALL. *Can you hear us now?*
Can you hear us?

ANISSA. *NO!*

ALL. *Can you hear us now, now, now, now, now?*

ANISSA. No, no, no, no, no, no, no!

ALL. *Can you hear us?*
Can you hear us now?
Can you hear us?
Can you hear us now?

End of Play

THE HOUR OF FEELING
by Mona Mansour

Copyright © 2012 by Mona Mansour. All rights reserved. CAUTION: Professionals and amateurs are hereby warned that *The Hour of Feeling* is subject to a royalty. It is fully protected under the copyright laws of the United States of America and of all countries covered by the International Copyright Union (including the Dominion of Canada and the rest of the British Commonwealth), the Berne Convention, the Pan-American Copyright Convention and the Universal Copyright Convention, as well as all countries with which the United States has reciprocal copyright relations. All rights, including professional, amateur stage rights, motion picture, recitation, lecturing, public reading, radio broadcasting, television, video or sound recording, all other forms of mechanical or electronic reproduction, such as CD-ROM, CD-I, information storage and retrieval systems and photocopying, and the rights of translation into foreign languages, are strictly reserved. Particular emphasis is laid upon the matter of readings, permission for which must be secured from the Author's agent in writing.

Required royalties must be paid every time this play is performed before any audience, whether or not it is presented for profit and whether or not admission is charged.

All inquiries concerning rights, including amateur rights, should be addressed to: The Gersh Agency, 41 Madison Ave., 33rd floor, New York, NY 10010, ATTN: Jessica Amato. 212-997-1818.

ABOUT *THE HOUR OF FEELING*

This article first ran in the January/February 2012 issue of Inside Actors, *Actors Theatre of Louisville's subscriber newsletter, and is based on conversations with the playwright before rehearsals for the Humana Festival production began.*

It's the summer of 1967 and the map of the Middle East is about to change drastically. But Adham doesn't know that. Young, determined, and eager to greet his future, the Palestinian scholar has been invited to deliver a lecture on William Wordsworth's poem "Tintern Abbey" at University College, London. Thousands of miles from Beit Hanina—the village outside East Jerusalem where Adham lives with his mother, Beder—London represents more than a bustling center of ideas and culture. For Adham, it represents the beginning of the rest of his life, his lecture the first rung on the tall academic ladder he plans to scale. "You become well-known in Cairo, you teach in Cairo," he explains, referring dismissively to the city where he trained as an undergraduate. "You become well-known in London, you can go anywhere."

As he prepares for his journey, Adham falls in love with Abir: a beautiful young woman whose fierce intelligence and independent mind belie her provincial background. To his mother, who has made enormous sacrifices to protect her son and promote his education, Abir is a distraction. Beder would prefer that he progress in his career before turning his attention to women. Nevertheless, Adham and Abir quickly wed and travel to London. As the young lovers navigate the city and embark on their first tentative explorations of married intimacy, Adham suffers a crisis of confidence, suddenly doubting his ability to fulfill his great ambitions. Meanwhile, political tensions back home begin to escalate. Though they don't know it, Adham's lecture has taken them from the West Bank on the eve of what Arabs call *an-Naksah*, or "the Setback"—known to most Westerners as the Six-Day War.

Playwright Mona Mansour's dramatic affinity for the Middle East is almost instinctual. Though she was raised in Southern California, Mansour's father is Lebanese. "Arab culture is so pervasive," she says, reflecting on a childhood in which the cadences of the Arabic language rang through the house along with English. Her family frequently hosted relatives from Lebanon, and Mansour recalls feeling self-conscious as a child about what she perceived as her family's "difference." "My cousins would come over and everyone would put on a Fairuz record," she remembers, speaking of the famous Lebanese singer whose music appears in *The Hour of Feeling*. "And I would think 'God! Why are we so weird? Why can't we listen to normal music like a normal American family?'" But with time youthful embarrassment transformed into a profound appreciation of her heritage. "Now I listen to Fairuz all the time," says Mansour. "I'm so deeply moved by her music."

Beyond instilling pride in the richness of Arab culture, Mansour's childhood also fostered an early awareness of the political divisions rocking her father's homeland. His village in southern Lebanon became a "hot spot" when civil war broke out in 1975. The war had a profound effect on Mansour's family, even though, she says, "no one ever said explicitly why all our male cousins were coming to live with us. But one by one they came." That period in her life promoted a heightened level of global consciousness. Perhaps more significantly, it forced Mansour to confront and internalize the personal impact of conflict on the human psyche. "One of my cousins in Lebanon started to sleep with a gun," she recalls. "I had always been vaguely aware of the political situation in the Middle East. But at that point it stopped being an abstract thing." Years later, that ignited consciousness would fuel Mansour's dramatic imagination.

In *The Hour of Feeling*, Adham struggles to reconcile his dreams with the pull of family and home. Suddenly confronted with the possibility of extending his stay in London beyond the expected few days, he must wrestle with huge decisions about the shape of his future life. "I'm fascinated by the crisis implied by choice," says Mansour. "By those moments in our lives which we only recognize in retrospect as turning points: crucial junctures when a decision we make will define the course of our destiny." Questions about the significance of *place* also ring through the play. Are selfhood and geography inextricably linked? To what extent are our souls shaped by the land of our birth? What if the boundaries of that land are unstable? Is identity something we inherit—or something we define? The poetry of William Wordsworth appears throughout the play in both English and Arabic translation, adding to an already rich linguistic landscape. Beyond providing the impetus for Adham's departure from home, Wordsworth's verse supplies a cartographic key as Mansour maps the young scholar's journey, and as Adham attempts to locate himself in a disorienting world. But what if he is destined to be an outsider no matter where he goes?

Is *The Hour of Feeling* a political play? "It depends on how you define 'political,'" counters Mansour. "If you're asking me where I think borders should be, well, if I had some kind of practical solution in mind, I'd probably be trying to make that happen instead of writing plays. But as a writer I'm interested in how displacement affects people, how it impacts them psychically, how it wears on their souls. And to me, that is political. It is the political reality of Adham's life."

—Sarah Lunnie

BIOGRAPHY

The Hour of Feeling was part of the High Tide Festival in the United Kingdom as part of the Rifle Hall Plays. *Urge for Going* (directed by Hal Brooks) received a LAB production in the 2011 season at The Public Theater, and before that was read in New Work Now! at the Public, and developed at the Ojai Playwrights Conference. Mansour was a member of The Public Theater's Emerging Writers Group and a Playwright Fellow at the Lark Play Development Center and is currently a Core Writer at The Playwrights Center in Minneapolis. Other plays include *Across the Water, Girl Scouts of America* and *Broadcast Yourself* (part of Headlong Theater's *Decade*, which premiered in London) and *The Way West*. Her work has been developed at the Cape Cod Theatre Project, Williamstown Theatre Festival, New York Stage and Film, and Lincoln Center Directors' Lab. Television credits include *Dead Like Me* and *Queens Supreme*. Newest works include a piece on journalist Anna Politkovskaya for Continuum Theater and *The Letter*, a play co-written with Tala Manassah that premiered in November 2012 at Golden Thread's ReOrient Festival. She received an honorable mention for the 2010 Middle East America Playwright Award. Mansour received a 2012 Whiting Writers' Award for playwriting.

ACKNOWLEDGMENTS

The Hour of Feeling premiered at the Humana Festival of New American Plays in March 2012. It was directed by Mark Wing-Davey with the following cast:

ADHAM	Hadi Tabbal
ABIR	Rasha Zamamiri
BEDER	Judith Delgado
GEORGE	David Barlow
THEO	William Connell
DIANA	Marianna McClellan

and the following production staff:

Scenic Designer	Michael B. Raiford
Costume Designer	Lorraine Venberg
Lighting Designer	Brian J. Lilienthal
Sound Designer	Matt Callahan
Properties Designer	Mark Walston
Media Designer	Philip Allgeier
Wig Designer	Heather Fleming
Stage Manager	Kathy Preher
Dramaturgs	Ismail Khalidi, Sarah Lunnie
Casting	Judy Bowman

CHARACTERS

ADHAM, handsome, intense. Early 20s. Palestinian. A scholar. Equal parts cocky and unsure.

ABIR, Palestinian, 19. Smart, beautiful, un-self-conscious.

BEDER, Adham's mother, 50s. As intense as her son. World-weary but fierce. Funny, too. Not a great cook.

GEORGE, English scholar, late 20s/early 30s, but could be older. Very polished, more confident than Adham. A bit argumentative; loves the sound of his own voice. The ladies like him.

THEO, English scholar, mid-20s. Affable. Energetic, sweet, willing to look foolish at times.

DIANA, English ex-scholar/current bohemian, early 20s. Very friendly, very curious about the world. Sexy in a *joie de vivre* kind of way.

SETTING

The play takes place in the summer of 1967 in two places: London, and Beit Hanina, a village considered a "suburb" of East Jerusalem. In 1948, Beit Hanina was captured by Jordanian forces, so it became part of the Hashemite Kingdom of Jordan. But residents there considered themselves Palestinian first and foremost. This is still the case when the play begins.

PLAYWRIGHT'S NOTES

ABOUT LANGUAGE

I've indicated supertitles for Arabic translation. There are other ways of getting this out, and I would welcome exploring those. Dialect-wise, it seems to fit the rules of the play that in scenes with just Arab characters, no dialect is present. But in scenes with the British, ADHAM has a Palestinian accent, as does ABIR.

On page 389 a scene begins that is entirely in Arabic. While I would strongly suggest this scene play as such, should no supertitles/alternate form of translation be available, there is a slightly modified version of the scene, all in English. See Addendum on page 415.

PRONUNCIATION GUIDE

The Arabic in the script has been transliterated to English. Below is a guide showing how a sound appears in the script, its Arabic counterpart, and the pronunciation.

aa – (ا) extended *a*, as in "happy"

A – (ع) when capped, this stands for the *ayn* sound in Arabic; a consonant, it has no real equivalent in English; a guttural sound

' – (ء) glottal stop (hamza) as in the stop in *uh-oh*, between syllables

H – (ح) no real English equivalent; an overaspirated *H*

th – (ث) unvoiced *th* sound, as in English "theater"

dh – (ذ) voiced *th* sound, as in "the"

kh – (خ) guttural, as in Hebrew "challah"

gh – (غ) like the French *r*

SPECIAL THANKS

The playwright gratefully acknowledges Liz Frankel and Mandy Hackett at The Public Theater; Mark Wing-Davey; Johanna Pfaelzer and New York Stage and Film; Hayley Finn and The Playwrights' Center; Professor Nina Schwarz; Noor Theatre; Ismail Khalidi; Sarah Lunnie at Actors Theatre of Louisville; and The Public Theater Emerging Writers of 2009.

Hadi Tabbal and Rasha Zamamiri
in *The Hour of Feeling*

36th Humana Festival of New American Plays
Actors Theatre of Louisville, 2012
Photo by Alan Simons

THE HOUR OF FEELING

"We do not weep for the mill of the village but for the bookshop and the library."
—Mourid Barghouti, *I Saw Ramallah*

PART ONE

Prologue – The Party

Lights up, very close in on:
ADHAM, *25, intense, lean, dark unruly hair, who stands, reads out loud from Wordsworth's poem "To My Sister," first in Arabic:*

ADHAM.

Hunaaka baraka feelhawaa'	[There is a blessing in the air,
tabdoo idraakan lil'ibtihaaj, yoohab	Which seems a sense of joy to yield
lil'ashjaar aljardaa' wa ljibaal alAaariya	To the bare trees, and mountains bare,
wa lilAushb al akhdar fee lHuqool.	And grass in the green field.]

(Then in English:)
My sister! Tis a wish of mine
Put on your woodland dress;
And bring no book: for this one day
We'll give to idleness.

BEDER. Idleness? Hm.

(ADHAM shushes her.)

ADHAM. Love, now a universal birth,
From heart to heart is stealing,
From earth to man, from man to earth:
– It is the hour of feeling.

(Lights widen a little to reveal: late afternoon. A small, stifling apartment, in which his mother, BEDER, 50s, cooks—energetically but not necessarily skillfully.)

BEDER. Keep going.

ADHAM. I can't. It smells terrible in here.

BEDER. You don't have to eat it.

ADHAM. Someone does. All these years and she's never learned to cook.

BEDER. So what. No one starved.

ADHAM. Can I open the window? Please.

BEDER. No. I just killed a mosquito. I don't want to have to run around chasing them off all night.

ADHAM. It's stifling in here. It's only going to get worse when the guests arrive. (*Sarcastic and playful, more the former.*) Whatever guests there are, actually. Who's coming?

BEDER. Half the village. They better show up.

ADHAM. Is that what you said when you invited them? I'm opening a window. I can't breathe in here.

BEDER. You're antsy? Have a smoke.

ADHAM. I will if I feel like it. Not because you told me to.

BEDER. So spoiled.

      (ADHAM *laughs.*)

Like a child. It's hard to believe you're a college graduate, the way you act.

ADHAM. Believe it.

BEDER. Intellectually, yes. Emotionally?

ADHAM. What are you doing?

BEDER. Putting down a bowl. Is that so shocking?

ADHAM. For what?

BEDER. Nothing you need to worry about!

ADHAM. Food?

BEDER. Maybe.

ADHAM. I see. So what's with the coins you threw in? Are they edible?

BEDER. Leave it alone.

ADHAM. My god, she has no class! All these festivities to "celebrate my accomplishments"?

BEDER. (*Rhetorically.*) Do you need money for your trip?

ADHAM. No! It's funded by a scholarship, all of it!

BEDER. Leave it alone.

ADHAM. So we're begging people for money now?

BEDER. We're not going to London with you in that suit.

ADHAM. We? We? Ha.

BEDER. (*Correcting herself.*) You. You.

ADHAM. She thinks she's coming along? Good god.

BEDER. Does the scholarship pay for new shoes and a suit?

ADHAM. I'm leaving.

BEDER. The bowl is for gifts! This is common practice!

ADHAM. Then why force it upon people?

BEDER. These cheap villagers? You have to make it explicit!

ADHAM. Why don't you put that on the bowl: "Dear cheap villagers, please pay up or leave!"

BEDER. They put on such airs when we got here. Acting superior, because we were the refugees!

ADHAM. Not this again.

BEDER. And you don't know this, but people aren't naturally generous. Left to their own devices, they're petty. Selfish. They don't think about things like how much it will cost to get you a new suit, or to bribe someone to get your passport.

ADHAM. Well, I don't want to think about such things.

BEDER. You're above all such worldly considerations? I've created a monster.

ADHAM. Yes, you have.

BEDER. Where are you going?

ADHAM. Out for a walk.

BEDER. Where?

ADHAM. I need to give you a report?

BEDER. I'm asking.

ADHAM. The hill, above the village. Where I used to walk all the time.

BEDER. Hm.

ADHAM. You don't approve?

BEDER. It's dangerous.

ADHAM. What, I'll twist my ankle?

BEDER. There are things going on.

ADHAM. I am reminding you I lived in Cairo. An actual city.

BEDER. Bad things happen to Palestinian men walking around these days. Here, not Cairo. You forget how close we are to the border.

ADHAM. (*Under.*) No I don't.

BEDER. You think you can just amble along like one of your poets. They think you're involved in some bit of business against the Israelis, and that's it.

ADHAM. Thank you, Mother. I'll make sure I don't shout political slogans and accidentally amble into No Man's Land.

BEDER. You think it's funny? Be careful! (*As he goes.*) You can't leave! It's your party!

ADHAM. No it's not.

(ADHAM exits. As he opens the door, lights widen to reveal ADHAM's world: 1967 West Bank. He pulls across the stage a giant panel, on which is a series of pictures that represent—)

The City – a village outside Jerusalem (April 1967)

We hear the sounds that surround ADHAM:
First, music. Fairuz, the great Lebanese singer: "Old Jerusalem."
More sounds: argument and speeches in Arabic, English and Hebrew.
Carrying a book, he makes his way up a hill. As he does so, men run in with posters and "paste" them all over the city: cartoons of 1960s Arab/Israeli figures—Dayan, Eshkol, Nasser—framed by Arabic or Hebrew.
A beautiful young woman, ABIR, 19, runs in and flips a panel, revealing a photo of Sixties British singer Lulu, and the words: LULU SHOUT. Into the sound mix we hear a few lines of "To Sir With Love." ABIR bops to the music for a split-second, then looks around like she might get into trouble—and leaves. Fairuz music fades up once more as other sounds fade out.
ADHAM walks over to a small panel and turns it, revealing: "SOMEWHERE IN THE MIDDLE EAST."
Then another panel: "IN WHAT USED TO BE CALLED PALESTINE."
And one more panel: "AND NOW IS JORDAN. KIND OF... IT'S COMPLICATED."
Finally, he finds the spot he loves, top of the hill. Settles in, making notes in his book. Laser focus. Beat.
ABIR enters, seems startled to see him. He's not flustered. Nothing flusters him.

ADHAM. Meeting someone?

ABIR. Oh. Hello. No. I'm just taking a walk.

ADHAM. It's a long way up from the village.

ABIR. Clears my head. So. *(She reaches into a small cloth bag, pulls out a pack of cigarettes, takes one out and lights up.)*

ADHAM. Wow!

ABIR. Want one?

ADHAM. Are you allowed to do that?

ABIR. No. But I don't ask anyone for permission.

ADHAM. All right then. *(She holds up a cig for him. He reaches to take it.)* Your hand is shaking.

ABIR. No.

ADHAM. Okay.

ABIR. It's cold up here.

ADHAM. Sure.

ABIR. It is!

ADHAM. Yes.

ABIR. And windy.

(They light up; smoke in silence for a beat.)

ADHAM. If you're going to transgress, at least enjoy yourself. I don't know why it's considered shameful anyway. The prophet never saw a cigarette. If he had, who knows? Maybe he'd have liked Gauloises.

ABIR. You shouldn't be talking that way about the Prophet.

ADHAM. Says the girl who's sneaking a smoke. *(Studies her.)* You're...? I'm sorry, I know we've met before. But I've been away for school.

ABIR. I'm Abir.

ADHAM. Abir. *(Playing with her name.)* Abir... So why are you not at my party?

ABIR. Well.

ADHAM. Everyone in the village was invited. I can't believe you're not attending.

ABIR. Why are you not there?

ADHAM. I don't like smiling and pretending to be gracious.

ABIR. But it's your party!

ADHAM. Let me ask you something.

ABIR. Okay.

ADHAM. You like my shoes? My clothes? You think they're acceptable?

(He "models" for her for two seconds.)

ABIR. The shoes are worn out. And you could use a new pair of pants.

ADHAM. *(Amused.)* I see. And they say the village girls have no taste!

ABIR. Who says that?

(He laughs. Which makes her mad.)

I know what looks good! I read magazines. I see movies. I speak French fluently and some English.

ADHAM. And Arabic, of course, with a little bit of a peasant accent.

(She starts to leave.)

I mean that in a good way!

ABIR. *(Incensed.)* We had a farm. But I'm probably more educated than most city girls.

ADHAM. *(Overlap.)* All right—

ABIR. I learned how to draw and design irrigation tunnels from my father. How many people can say that?

ADHAM. (*Overlap.*) Of course.

ABIR. I was second in my class, overall.

ADHAM. I believe you! So let's hear some English then.

ABIR. What?

ADHAM. You said you spoke English.

ABIR. I mean, just some phrases. Here and there.

ADHAM. Such as?

ABIR. (*Caught.*) *Tosir Widloh.*

ADHAM. What?

ABIR. (*Hedging.*) *Toh. Sir. Widloh.* The song? To. Sir. That one. You know that one.

      (*He lets her squirm.*)

ADHAM. I really don't.

ABIR. The one, To. Sir. Lulu.

ADHAM. "To Sir With Love"?

ABIR. Yes!

ADHAM. So that's your English.

ABIR. And a few lines from a movie. The Julie Christie one. I see all her movies. Do you go to the movies?

ADHAM. No.

ABIR. Are you really going to Oxford to speak?

ADHAM. Oxford? No. Who said that?

ABIR. Someone. I thought I heard that.

ADHAM. No. University College. London. A conference on Romantic Literature. I'm one of the keynote speakers.

ABIR. Oh.

ADHAM. So I'll deliver a paper. I was chosen out of, uh…300 or so entries? Every year they highlight one speaker from abroad, and this year it was me.

ABIR. Praise to God.

ADHAM. I'll keep the praise for myself.

ABIR. You don't believe God had a hand in this?

ADHAM. I don't believe he has a hand, a face, an arm, a tooth; I don't think he exists.

ABIR. (*Challenging, a little.*) At least you pray.

      (*Beat.*)

ADHAM. Not for a long time.

(*Beat.*)

ABIR. So...what happens after you go to London?

ADHAM. Who knows? You become well known in Cairo, you teach in Cairo. You become well known in London, you can go anywhere.

ABIR. So that's what you want, to teach?

ADHAM. Well, I've finished my masters, so that's done. Then when you complete the Ph.D., teaching is the next step. But then, anyone can do that, you know? It's another thing to be—sought after. To have other scholars, people you respect, say, "Yes, I've heard of you. I've read your work." It's an imprimatur, you see. You keep building your reputation, and eventually you chair a department, and then... You think I'm too much?

ABIR. I think that, to get anywhere, one must have a lot of confidence.

ADHAM. What do you want?

ABIR. Well, I studied civic engineering in secondary school.

ADHAM. And now?

ABIR. Now I'm supposed to wait at home for a husband.

ADHAM. How's that going?

ABIR. I don't like any of them. It feels forced.

ADHAM. Oh no. It should feel natural.

(*Beat. They both smoke and look out.*)

Why did you come up here?

ABIR. So you don't believe in any god? Not ours, no one's?

ADHAM. I believe in Fate. If anything.

ABIR. Yes?

ADHAM. When I was a child, my mother took up with a stupid man.

ABIR. I don't...understand. Your father...died?

ADHAM. May as well have. When we had to—leave the Galilee, we ended up at a refugee camp in Southern Lebanon.

ABIR. I'm sorry.

ADHAM. I was three, barely remember it. Anyway, my mother says she would've killed herself if she stayed. So she got us out of there somehow. Left my father, and we came here.

ABIR. And the stupid man? Where does he come in?

ADHAM. Oh! Well, he was from the next village. He was nice enough, good at fixing things. But not a good fit with my mother. It wasn't his fault! He had a low I.Q. Couldn't understand her books or make proper conversation. So he gave up, and she gave up. She stopped speaking to him, except to say, Go get flour. Get me a magazine. Shut up. He finally got the hint and stopped coming around.

ABIR. That's terrible! And you?

ADHAM. I don't want to talk about this.

ABIR. Tell me.

ADHAM. Just. She put all her energies on me. I read to her in the mornings, translated Latin… If I didn't get it right?…

> (*He laughs at the memory.*)

She demanded I be her equal.

ABIR. Where is the fate in that?

ADHAM. If my mother had found a smarter man, I wouldn't have achieved a thing.

> (*Beat.*)

You think I'm strange.

ABIR. I think you say strange things.

ADHAM. (*Mock horror.*) Oh I say terrible things sometimes.

ABIR. Do you still read to her every day?

ADHAM. No!

ABIR. She must be proud of you.

ADHAM. She should be.

> (*Beat.*)

Why did you come up here?

ABIR. You saw. To smoke.

ADHAM. Why else?

ABIR. I don't know.

ADHAM. Really?

ABIR. I don't know.

ADHAM. You don't? (*He keeps getting closer to her.*) Why don't you tell me?

ABIR. It's wrong.

ADHAM. (*Reaches out to her, barely brushes her arm.*) What's wrong? Tell me.

ABIR. I saw you walk up the hill. And I thought, if I don't talk to him now, I'll never get to talk to him.

> (*And now he runs his hand up her arm.*)

ADHAM. And how does it feel? Talking to me?

ABIR. I'm not sure. Not altogether good.

ADHAM. Oh?

ABIR. And not altogether bad.

ADHAM. And how does it feel now?

    (*He lifts his hand to her face.*)

ABIR. Stop making fun of me.

    (*He takes her hand.*)

ADHAM. I'm not making fun of you.

ABIR. Do you think I'm beautiful?

ADHAM. You know you are. Don't you? You look like your actress, like Julie Christie.

ABIR. No.

ADHAM. More beautiful.

ABIR. I'm not supposed to think that.

ADHAM. Too late.

    (*She looks at him. She tries to pass, and he doesn't let her. They stand there, a couple feet apart. He leans in, takes her hand, and kisses her on the lips, very lightly, very slowly.*

    "To Sir With Love" starts playing: "If you wanted the sky I would write across the sky with letters, that would soar a thousand feet high.")

At Home (May)

    BEDER's *apartment.*

    She turns a panel, revealing: a giant picture of ADHAM, *14, looking very serious, holding a certificate. She then sits down next to* ABIR, *who has come in with a plate of food on her lap.* ADHAM *stands, leaning against the door frame.*

BEDER. That's him getting the Jowett.

ABIR. Oh.

BEDER. (*Overlap.*) The youngest recipient in the history of the award.

ABIR. So impressive.

BEDER. (*Barely lets her get it out.*) And then the Partington. That got him into University. That one was from the Catholics, they made him do some of these (*She waves her hands carelessly in the air, doing something resembling the Sign of the Cross.*) and write a letter to the Pope, but I didn't care. They want to pay for his education, we'll do anything they want.

ADHAM. It's this. (*He makes the Sign of the Cross, doing it the right way.*) Left to right. Father, Son, Holy Spirit. (*Teasing her.*) Get it right, Mother.

BEDER. And this is his graduation picture. (BEDER *hands* ABIR *a small Polaroid photograph.*) Careful.

(ABIR *looks at the picture, anxiously, balancing her plate.* ADHAM *reaches his hand out to take the picture.*)

ADHAM. I'll take that.

BEDER. More food?

ABIR. Oh. Yes. It's delicious.

BEDER. It's passable.

ABIR. I don't agree.

BEDER. Keep eating.

(*Mini-beat.*)

Did my son tell you what I did for him as a child?

ABIR. You made him read to you. And uh, you tested him…? Right?

BEDER. That's what he said?

ABIR. Well. I mean—

BEDER. That's one-tenth of what I did. After an-Nakba…

ADHAM. Oh no…

BEDER. You want to tell the story?

ADHAM. Of 1948? I'll pass. She knows, anyway. The Israelis took her family's farm. Her father died.

BEDER. They killed him?

ABIR. No, not from that. It was all the smoking. His lungs. He smoked a couple packs a day.

BEDER. (*Her mind is made up.*) They killed him. What about the rest of your family?

ABIR. I live with my sister and her husband. And my mother lives with my brother. In Detroit, Michigan. America.

BEDER. What does he do there?

ABIR. He makes cars.

BEDER. (*Not impressed.*) Oh.

ABIR. He likes it… Adham told me you were from the Galilee.

BEDER. Before they cleaned out every village, yes.

ABIR. And then…Lebanon?

BEDER. It wasn't a pleasure trip.

ABIR. I know that.

BEDER. We get there, and we sit in, excuse me, a shithole refugee camp. I realize: This isn't temporary. This place is Death. I grabbed my youngest son, and came back here. With nothing but my education, that's it. Did he tell you I had started a degree in philosophy? Before I was married.

(*Loud explosions are heard in the distance. Everyone jumps.* BEDER *gets up.*)

God help us.

> (*Another explosion, and now light bursts through the window.*)

The war is on? It's happening?

ADHAM. It can't be.

> (*Jumpy, everyone goes outside.*
> *A few beats while the explosions continue.*
> ADHAM *and* ABIR *come back in.*)

I knew it was just fireworks.

ABIR. So loud.

> (*He takes the opportunity to get close to her.*)

ADHAM. She likes you.

ABIR. I don't know about that. She thinks I'm common.

ADHAM. Doesn't matter. I like you. (*He takes her plate away.*) And I like this. (*He kisses her hands.*) And this…

> (*He kisses her neck.*)

ABIR. We can't.

ADHAM. She's not religious.

> (*He starts to caress her arms when* BEDER *comes back in.*)

Disappointed, Mother? Did you expect to see Egyptian jets, here to liberate us all?

ABIR. That's not funny.

BEDER. (*Fuming.*) Independence Day fireworks. How can the Israelis call it Independence Day and not choke on the words? They celebrate forcibly removing people from their homes? Killing men, women, children? This is cause for a party?

ADHAM. Let's not get political.

BEDER. Who's getting political? Anyway, we leave Lebanon. We come here, we know no one. I take a job. Menial labor, a clerk. Our own people talk to me like I'm nothing, as dumb as a dog running in the streets: "Take this number and write it three times in three books." Same number, over and over. I said, What is this? I explain to them: this is inefficient! They don't care. They're not interested. No wonder the Arab world hasn't advanced in the last two hundred years!

ADHAM. Thank god we cleared that up.

ABIR. (*Changing the subject.*) You did so much for him. I know you did everything to help him be successful.

BEDER. When the Quakers opened the new school, I begged them to let him in. We couldn't afford more than him being a day student. He was so frightened the first time I took him there.

ABIR. (*Touched.*) Oh?

BEDER. You remember?

ADHAM. No.

ABIR. Why do you think he was afraid?

ADHAM. Who cares.

BEDER. Who knows? He'd been at the little village school before that. This one was farther away, toward Ramallah. We had to take a bus. There's the entrance, where the gate is. Then you have to go down these stone steps, and you're on a path between a grove of fig trees, the building in the distance. Well. I get him there and he starts crying. And I am thinking, who is this child? What is wrong with him? So fearful! Did I make him this way?

ADHAM. (*Under.*) Yes.

BEDER. Then he tells me: He thinks bandits are going to come from behind the trees and slit his throat. You remember?

ADHAM. No. And I don't remember you, actually. What was your name again?

BEDER. And I'm thinking, What to do? I can't send him away like this, his face covered in tears. So I make it a game. This wasn't my nature, this kind of whimsical approach.

ADHAM. Really.

BEDER. I say, Do you see this sign, my son? This entrance to the school? This is a magical entrance. Once you go through these gates, you are safe. Just be careful as you walk these first few steps. (He was always running, everywhere.) They used very old stones when they built the school. They say these were from the front steps of the great hall that housed Alexander the Great.

ADHAM. I didn't believe that. Even then.

BEDER. Of course you did.

ABIR. Did he stop crying?

BEDER. No he didn't.

ADHAM. Because he didn't recognize this strange new mother, full of kindness!

BEDER. That's not the story.

(*Beat. He looks at his mother.*)

We walk through the gate, and I take your hand, and the wind comes up. I say, Do you feel yourself drifting, as you take this walk? (Because none of us was ever allowed to drift, really.) Let yourself drift, my son, as the ancient grove makes way for you. The trees will bow to you. See? Each one nods! Each one says, This is a scholar! Each tree had a name, do you remember this?

ADHAM. *Khalas*, mama.

BEDER. And you look at me, and you look at the trees, and you say: "Tell me then. Tell me each tree's name." This is when I realize, this boy has exceptional intelligence. Such imagination.

ADHAM. Or he was crazy. Did you consider that?

BEDER. And I think, quickly: What is the name of each tree? And I say: Al-Mutanabbi, the great poet. Al-Yajizi. Al-Barudi. Aristotle. Shakespeare. You see? And then you took a breath, and you walked, and you let go of my hand, and it was like I was barely there.

(*Long beat.* ADHAM *waits it out, displaying a rare show of sensitivity.*)

ADHAM. So. I don't want to have to ask your blessing. We're not traditional that way.

BEDER. So don't ask.

ADHAM. I've already talked to her brother-in-law, and we spoke to the sheikh.

BEDER. Oh.

ADHAM. But I'm giving you the chance.

(BEDER *looks right at* ABIR.)

BEDER. You're a beautiful girl.

ABIR. Thank you.

BEDER. But my son is too young to make his way with a woman.

ADHAM. What?

BEDER. In ten years or so, when he's established, that's when he starts looking for a wife. And then, he'll be at a higher level, if you understand.

ABIR. I should...go.

BEDER. Finish your food.

ADHAM. I can't believe you!

BEDER. We've discussed this. I said the same thing about your Egyptian girlfriends.

ADHAM. You're unbelievably insulting, on every level.

ABIR. I'm leaving.

BEDER. I'm insulting? I waited with you for your passport for hours, begging them to issue it to you. They're suspicious of every Palestinian these days, and I'm standing there, pulling out my birth certificate from the British Mandate! Telling them lies, that your father died! Performing the sad widow act! Bribing them!

ABIR. I don't want to cause a problem...

(*She starts to leave.* ADHAM *grabs her arm.*)

ADHAM. Wait.

ABIR. She doesn't want me.

BEDER. I didn't say that. I like you.

ABIR. (*To* ADHAM.) Why would you bring me here, if you knew this would happen?

ADHAM. I wanted her to see you.

ABIR. Well, she saw me, okay?

BEDER. You have your mind made up? Then why go through the motions? You're making a mistake if you go with her! I know what mistakes are! So even though you really don't want to hear my opinion, I'm giving it. This is my house!

ADHAM. You're right. I did just go through the motions. I like her. I liked her the moment I saw her. You've decided everything! This is the one thing that's mine.

> (*Blackout.*
>
> ADHAM *stands in front of his mother, in a suit, holding a suitcase. Beat.* BEDER *hands him a small envelope.*)

BEDER. Take this. Just in case.

ADHAM. I told you already, I don't need it.

BEDER. You have no idea how the world works.

> (*She holds the envelope to him. He takes it. A beat. There could be a hug goodbye—but there isn't.*)

ADHAM. Okay.

> (*Just as he starts to leave—*)

BEDER. There's one thing I never told you, part of that story. I wanted to walk you all the way down the steps, through the trees. To take you inside the building, and sit next to you, and sit there all day to make sure we were getting our money's worth! I wanted nothing more than to take you all the way in. It was the last thing in the world I wanted, to leave you to go down those steps alone.

ADHAM. (*Playfully.*) So why did you leave?

BEDER. I had to stand there and watch you go.

> (*She's fixed on him. He stands there, hovering, excited for the trip, but can't quite move to go yet.*)

You know what I did after I left you? I came home and I threw away every picture I had of your brother.

ADHAM. (*Genuinely shocked.*) What?

BEDER. I had very few to begin with. Baby pictures.

ADHAM. (*Still not quite believing—this can't be true.*) What do you mean—you just tossed them in the trash?

BEDER. Tore them to bits, each, and then, yes.

> (*Beat.*)

ADHAM. Why on earth would you do that?

BEDER. The way I felt with you on the steps. This—this—

> (*She puts her hand on her chest: a pang she doesn't have words for.*)

This was—the way I—felt—every time I looked at those pictures. I couldn't stand to look at them anymore.

ADHAM. (*Devastated.*) Why would you tell me this?

BEDER. (*Ignoring his question.*) What does that emotion serve? It's going to help me get your brother out of Lebanon, rescue him? I knew that if I got rid of him, his pictures, I could do anything. I knew that to get you where you needed to go, all such feelings would have to be gotten rid of.

ADHAM. You left them. He and my father. That was your choice.

BEDER. There was no choice to be had! What a ridiculous thought! Choice. What a myth. Choice is a luxury.

ADHAM. You left your son there.

> (ADHAM *takes his suitcase and leaves.*)

BEDER. To raise you in a better place! Don't forget that.

ADHAM. See you later.

> (*Sounds of a jet plane. Lights shift.*)

Strand Palace Hotel, London (June)

> *Summer, late afternoon. Panels have turned to reveal 1967 London, with parts of the original ancient city still showing.*
>
> ADHAM *and* ABIR *enter their hotel room—not huge, but well-appointed. A desk with a lamp. Two chairs and a table, on which has been placed a tea service, and a bottle of champagne. A bed.*
>
> *They close the door behind them and take in the room.*

ABIR. This is, uh.

ADHAM. Nice.

> (ADHAM *carries the suitcase into the room. Leaves it by the window. He peers through the sheer curtains.*)

ABIR. What's out there?

ADHAM. Theaters. Lots of things.

ABIR. Can anyone see in?

ADHAM. I don't think so. I don't think anyone cares.

> (ABIR *goes into the bathroom.* ADHAM *opens the window. Sounds of the street come in.* ABIR *comes back.*)

ABIR. So many towels.

ADHAM. Yeah? (*She giggles a little bit. He smiles.*) What's going on?

ABIR. Nothing. We just haven't been. Alone.

ADHAM. Sure we have. That first day. The day of my party.

> (*Beat.*)

ABIR. What was the man talking about, something "downstairs"?

ADHAM. Oh, bomb shelters. During the war. Down there.

ABIR. He talks so fast.

ADHAM. Why do you ask? You want to go look at them again?

ABIR. No. (*She opens a cabinet. Excited.*) A television set.

ADHAM. All the nice hotels have them now.

> (ABIR *turns it on. It's Tom Jones on the BBC, singing "Show Me." We see it projected on one of the panels behind them. It's Tom Jones, so it's kind of amazing/sexual, obviously.* ABIR *shuts off the TV. Closes the cabinet. Awkward beat.*)

You like that?

ABIR. I don't understand it.

ADHAM. (*Flirting.*) I think you do.

> (*She scans the room, sees something on the tea service.*)

ABIR. Tea?

ADHAM. Not now.

> (*She picks something up off the tea service.*)

It's an English cookie. Try it.

> (*She takes a bite.*)

Good?

> (*It's heinous.* ABIR *nods politely.* ADHAM *walks over to her, holds it up to his mouth, eats the rest.*)

That's terrible.

> (ABIR, *exhausted, fluttery, sits on the bed. Bounces back up. Grabs the champagne off the tea service.*)

ABIR. Let's have some of this.

ADHAM. You can't have alcohol!

ABIR. A little. With my husband.

ADHAM. A little, huh? You found that out. Read it somewhere?

ABIR. No. I know it. (*She impulsively starts to open the bottle.*)

ADHAM. You don't know what you're doing.

ABIR. No one did, the first time they did it. (*The cork goes flying. Hits a painting on the wall.*) Oh no.

      (ADHAM *walks over to look.*)

Do you think anyone could hear it?

      (*He checks the painting.*)

ADHAM. It's fine.

      (ABIR *pours some into a glass, drinks.*)

ABIR. Oh.

ADHAM. Good?

ABIR. It tastes like juice. Very strong juice. (*She pours some for him, holds it out.*) You have to have some.

ADHAM. Look at you.

ABIR. Go.

      (*He takes it, drinks it quickly.*)

ADHAM. It's good.

      (*She stands and looks at him. He goes over to her, puts his arms on her, runs his hands up her back. This is new for both of them. His grip gets tighter.*)

ABIR. Ouch.

ADHAM. (*Letting go.*) Shit.

ABIR. No. It's okay.

      (*She takes his hands, places them on her waist. The hands stay there, still firm, but not going anywhere. He stalls. Breaks off.*)

Did I do something wrong?

ADHAM. No, no. You. You're beautiful. (*He goes to the window. Looks out. Takes a big breath.*) Maybe I'm no one to come here and tell them what their poetry is.

ABIR. What? No. You're everyone.

      (*She walks up behind him, places a hand on his back. He turns. She kisses him quickly, almost surprising herself.*

      She takes his face in her hands, looks at him. He kisses her back. Wraps his arms all around her body.)

Everyone.

      (*Now she kisses his face, his chest, his hands. He kisses her hands back, lets go, puts his hands on her breasts. She inhales. Doesn't know where to put her hands.*)

I want another glass.

> (ADHAM *wordlessly goes over to the champagne, pours more. Holds it up to her...*
> *Lights fade on the room, as the two move onto the bed.*)

Wives, Too

Next morning. In bed, ADHAM, alone, asleep. He rustles, slightly. ABIR, wearing a robe, her hair up, makeup "done," stands watching him, smiling. She leans over him, studies him. Dares herself to touch his face. He reaches for her, touches her breasts, smiling. He half sleep-talks.

ADHAM. Yes. All right.

ABIR. (*Amused.*) Yes what?

> (*His eyes open suddenly. He pulls his hands away.*)

ADHAM. Where am I?

ABIR. The hotel, silly.

> (*He bolts up, panicked.*)

ADHAM. Oh god. What time is it?

> (*He finds his watch on the nightstand, checks the time.*)

This is terrible.

ABIR. Are you all right?

> (*He looks at her, taking her in for the first time.*)

ADHAM. Oh.

ABIR. (*Re: the robe.*) I didn't want to wear it at your mother's. (*She suddenly gets self-conscious, pulls the robe more tightly around her waist.*) Should I make you tea?

ADHAM. I'm late.

ABIR. Now?

ADHAM. I will be. Why didn't you wake me? Where are my books. Notes? I need to know where they are at all times!

ABIR. I put your things on that desk.

> (*In only his underwear, he goes to the desk, starts to rifle through two neat piles of books and folders.*)

Are you speaking today?

ADHAM. I'm meeting everyone. Why didn't you wake me?

ABIR. I tried. I didn't know you had to be somewhere.

ADHAM. You have to give me a shove. It's—you have to do that 'til I wake up.

ABIR. I'll remember.

ADHAM. It's not just about presenting the paper. It's about fellowship, camaraderie, you understand?

ABIR. I think so.

(*He finds the folder he was looking for, sets it on the bed, then grabs the pants he wore on the plane, folded over a chair. Puts them on. He goes to his suitcase, pulls out a button-down shirt and puts it on. The shirt is very, very wrinkly.*)

ADHAM. Oh no. Oh no.

ABIR. I saw an iron.

(ADHAM, *helpless, says nothing.*)

Let me get it for you.

(*She opens a closet and pulls out an ironing board and iron. Holds her hands out.*)

Give it to me. Here. I'll take care of it.

ADHAM. I can do it.

(ABIR *steps back as he walks his shirt over to the iron. He clearly has no idea what he's doing.*)

Shit!

ABIR. I said, let me…

ADHAM. We don't have time for that.

(*She takes it from him, and irons the damn shirt.*)

ABIR. It just takes a minute… I should've hung this up last night when we got here. I didn't know you were going somewhere important today.

ADHAM. We. You're coming too.

ABIR. We?

ADHAM. Yes. Wives. Wives, too.

ABIR. Oh. I have to get dressed.

ADHAM. You're not interested in going?

ABIR. Of course I am.

ADHAM. (*Snatching the shirt from her.*) Give me that.

ABIR. I only finished one side!

ADHAM. It'll be fine. I'll keep my jacket on. You keep your coat on at these things.

ABIR. It's warm outside. You'll be too hot—

ADHAM. The jacket stays on. It's fine.

(*He grabs a tie from the suitcase, puts it on, and then puts on the coat he wore on the plane, the only one he has.*)

It's fine.

(Rushed, he pulls out of his suitcase some kind of hair cream, gops it into his hair, tries to push it down.)

Now you get ready. Why are you laughing?

ABIR. Your hair.

(She rushes into the bathroom, comes out with a comb, sits him down on the bed.)

ADHAM. No one cares.

ABIR. I do. No one will listen to a word you say if this isn't fixed.

(ABIR tries to comb his hair. As she finishes, she puts her hands through it, slowly, trying not to give away how much she likes it. She steps away.)

There.

ADHAM. Okay. So go. Get ready.

(She goes back into the bathroom.
He lights a cigarette, then goes to the window and looks out at the city.)

All the fellows in the literary department will be there. They're probably expecting someone older.

(A few beats as he smokes and waits. Then, calling to her:)

Okay?

ABIR. *(From inside the bathroom.)* One minute.

ADHAM. We have to go!

ABIR. *(From inside the bathroom.)* I know! *(Moments later, ABIR comes out, wearing her "travel" dress.)* Do I look like the wife of an academic?

ADHAM. I don't know. What does one look like?

(Stung, she tries to zip the back of her dress.)

Let me do that.

(She turns her back, lets him.)

ABIR. Are you upset with me?

ADHAM. *(Clueless.)* No.

(And now she cries.)

ABIR. I thought maybe—

ADHAM. Oh no—what?

ABIR. Are you happy with me?

ADHAM. What? Yes!

(She cries for a beat. ADHAM's lost.)

I'm sorry.

(He takes her hands, holds them, softens. Re: her hands:)

This smell…

ABIR. You like it?

ADHAM. It smells like the countryside.

ABIR. That's not good!

ADHAM. Yes it is.

(*She throws her heels on.*)

Can you run in those shoes?

ABIR. I don't know.

(*He throws his cigarette in the ashtray, not bothering to put it out.*)

ADHAM. Hold on to me.

(*As they disappear into the panels, now London, we hear Petula Clark's "Don't Sleep in the Subway."*)

The Lunch

Lights up. Two English scholars, GEORGE *and* THEO, *open the panels to reveal a domed building above the words: "UNIVERSITY COLLEGE." They sit down at a table and hold up teacups to* ADHAM.

GEORGE. To the next wave of literary criticism.

THEO. You're embarrassing him.

GEORGE. But he is. You are.

ADHAM. Thank you.

GEORGE. Don't you feel it's so?

ADHAM. (*Cocky, pretending to be humble.*) I feel I'm finding an interesting angle in my approach.

GEORGE. Angle? You're far too humble. Look how humble he is.

ADHAM. No one's ever called me that before. Humble, I mean.

(*They laugh.*)

GEORGE. And funny.

THEO. I think we needed it, frankly. A fresh infusion.

GEORGE. What—you didn't think we got that from the German scholar last year? (*To* ADHAM.) Dreadfully boring he was.

THEO. It's refreshing. A different perspective on our dusty old poets. Will you tackle Tennyson as well?

ADHAM. I don't find his work particularly engaging, actually.

GEORGE. His love has limits. Not willing to take on old Alfred Lord?

ADHAM. Nothing has inspired me to do so yet.

GEORGE. But have you read Tennyson, actually?

THEO. George…

GEORGE. I'm just asking. Everyone loves to malign Tennyson but most haven't actually bothered to read him.

ADHAM. No, I have. I appreciate the imagery in his, uh, (*Confidently, but hitting the "T" hard, and following it with the Arabic "H" sound.*) Tet-HO-nus.

GEORGE. Which one?

ADHAM. One of his blank verse…?

> (*They don't seem to know what he's talking about.* ADHAM *covers his panic. Faking confidence, slowing the word down.*)

Tet. Honus…

GEORGE. "Tithonus"? Of course. Yes.

THEO. Adham, we've been looking forward to meeting you. We want to show you the town.

GEORGE. Where have you been so far?

ADHAM. Just here. And the hotel.

THEO. Oh, that's unacceptable! We must give you a tour.

ADHAM. Yes, absolutely.

GEORGE. Oh! Forgive my manners! I almost forgot. We have something for you.

> (GEORGE *reaches onto the seat next to him, and pulls out a paper bag. He pulls out a large towel-like thing with an old painting on it.*)

To our most esteemed guest of the international language exchange.

> (*He hands the thing to* ADHAM, *who holds it up appreciatively.*)

ADHAM. Oh this is, it's perfect.

THEO. It's hideous!

GEORGE. He hasn't a clue as to what the hell it is. Have you?

ADHAM. No.

GEORGE. It's a tea towel.

ADHAM. Oh. Of course.

THEO. 'Cause everyone needs a tea towel.

> (GEORGE *points to the figures on the towel.*)

GEORGE. Ah, but this is a University College tea towel. These are our founders, Jeremy Bentham et al., fighting our blood enemies from Kings College.

ADHAM. Who's winning?

GEORGE & THEO. We are, of course.

ADHAM. What's the fire?

GEORGE. The pits of hell. Into which our rivals will fall. Gorgeous, right? So you'll remember us when you take your tea.

THEO. Or wipe your bum! It's awful! Adham, I for one won't be insulted if you leave it in the hotel when you go.

ADHAM. I will treasure this. Thank you. I wish I had brought something.

GEORGE. Relax. You're our guest.

THEO. Now give him the real gift.

GEORGE. That old thing?

(GEORGE *pulls out a book. Hands it to* ADHAM.)

Your Wordsworth. Third edition. It was the oldest one we could find.

ADHAM. Thank you. I don't know how to thank you. (*He opens the book. Amazed. Reads.*) "Third printing, Macmillan Publishing…"

GEORGE. Didn't believe me, eh?

THEO. Smart fellow.

ADHAM. "Sixteen Colborn Street."

GEORGE. That's close by.

ADHAM. (*Breaks out of his reverie.*) Thank you.

(*He closes the book and sets it down carefully.*)

GEORGE. I must ask, how did you find your way to the English Romantics?

ADHAM. Find my way?

GEORGE. I can't imagine you woke up every day hearing Wordsworth.

ADHAM. My mother decided I should be a scholar. It was this or Cicero.

GEORGE. You chose right! Was she a teacher?

ADHAM. No. Just full of opinions.

GEORGE. You should've brought her along.

ADHAM. (*Laughs.*) No I shouldn't have.

GEORGE. And she grew up in, uh, Israel? Or…um, of course. Palestine.

ADHAM. Yes.

THEO. The landscape there is splendid. Mountains and the sea, yes?

ADHAM. I don't know. I never get out that way.

THEO. Really? The famous road down the coast, on the way to Jerusalem. I'm dying to try it one day. The Phoenicians, the Romans…

ADHAM. I've heard that. The road is cut off now, so.

GEORGE. What do you mean?

ADHAM. We can't go back there. It's off-limits. To—us.

THEO. Sorry.

ADHAM. No no. It's. You can't miss it if you don't know what you're missing.

(*Just then* ABIR *walks up, a tea in hand.*)

My wife—she's from the countryside. You can ask her.

GEORGE. *Vous etes de la campagne?*

ABIR. *Oui.*

GEORGE. She's delightful. Isn't she delightful. I'm saying you are delightful.

ABIR. Oh, yes. Yes.

GEORGE. Have you been to London before?

(ABIR *nods tentatively.*)

ADHAM. That was the extent of her English.

(ABIR *smiles, nervously, standing there, waiting. Beat.*)

Okay.

(ADHAM *nods, as if to say, you're done. She goes.*)

GEORGE. Ah. Darling girl. So she's never been to England?

ADHAM. No.

GEORGE. Brave girl.

ADHAM. Why brave.

GEORGE. To come all this way.

ADHAM. I thought you meant, to marry me.

(*They don't know* ADHAM *well enough to know he's joking.*)

GEORGE. Oh. Well.

(*Awkward beat.*)

ADHAM. In which case I'd agree.

(*They realize* ADHAM*'s joking. They all laugh.*)

THEO. Because you're a penniless academic like the rest of us?

ADHAM. Because I have no sense of the practical concerns of life. I'm useless in every way.

(GEORGE *smiles, leans in to* ADHAM, *confidentially, man to man.*)

GEORGE. In every way?

(ADHAM *takes a beat: Is he really going to go there? He is.*)

ADHAM. Well…no. Not in every way.

(*They laugh.* GEORGE *puts an arm around* ADHAM.)

GEORGE. Listen to this, Adam: We've a friend who runs a society called The Old Stagers. They take the month of August, go to a giant house in the Cotswolds and do nothing but play cricket all day and amateur theatricals at night. You must come back and join me there.

ADHAM. I would love that.

THEO. I can't imagine he'll come all this way to see our countryside before he's seen his own.

ADHAM. You never know.

    (ABIR *approaches. She speaks to* ADHAM *in Arabic.*)

ABIR. [What should I eat?] Shoo akul?

    (*All of the following is in Arabic.* ADHAM *is jarred; immensely embarrassed to be speaking in his native tongue.*)

ADHAM. [What?] Shoo?

ABIR. [The food. I can't tell what anything is.] Al akl, maa baArif shoo hel aklaat.

ADHAM. [Eat what the other wives are eating.] Kulee shoo biaklu azzawjaat ittanyeen.

    (*She makes a face.*)

[Just take your best guess, okay?] IHzeree, maashi?

THEO. Everything all right?

ADHAM. (*To* THEO, *in English.*) Yes. (*To* ABIR, *in Arabic.*) [Go. We're talking.] RooHee iHna bniHkee.

    (ABIR, *hurt, goes.*)

THEO. She doesn't like the food?

GEORGE. Can't blame her for that!

ADHAM. Oh. No. No no. She's fine.

THEO. But she did mention food? Bad food?

ADHAM. Yes.

THEO. (*To* GEORGE.) See? I'm not as hopeless as you think.

GEORGE. Hurray, hurray, you understood one sentence.

ADHAM. You speak Arabic?

THEO. I try.

GEORGE. Very hard, sadly. With little results.

THEO. Not true.

GEORGE. Actually, Theo here is a bit of a pan-Arabist.

THEO. An Arabist. Although this pan-Arabist phenomenon is fascinating. Nasser is rather inspiring.

GEORGE. (*To* ADHAM.) Do you think?

ADHAM. Do I think?

GEORGE. Nasser. I'm curious what the word on the street is about him.

    (ADHAM*'s a bit thrown.*)

ADHAM. "On the street"? Well. I guess, he, uh, yes, he's seen as a, savior... by most people.

THEO. And you?

ADHAM. He's very charismatic. Sweats a lot.

GEORGE. (*Enjoying* ADHAM's *assessment.*) Brilliant.

> (ABIR *is back.*)

ABIR. [Are you going to sit with me?] Inta Hati'Aud maAay?

ADHAM. [In a minute. Talk to someone.] BaAd da'ee'a, itkallamee maA hada.

ABIR. [WHO?] MEEN?

ADHAM. [Anyone. Make some conversation.] Ayy hada. iHkee maA annas.

ABIR. [About what? None of those women speak French. Why is that? You said they were educated.] Aala shoo? wala waHde min ha nniswaan biHkoo faransawi. leish? inta ultillee inhum muthaqqafaat.

THEO. You'd think if they were really educated, those women would speak French!

ADHAM. [We'll talk later.] niHkee baAdein.

> (*She stands there for a beat.*)

Go.

> (*She goes.*)

THEO. She seems a good sport.

ADHAM. Ah. Oh yes.

> (GEORGE *offers* ADHAM *a cigarette. He takes it. All three men light up, looking back toward where* ABIR *went.*)

GEORGE. You've been married a long time?

THEO. That's rather a personal question, isn't it.

ADHAM. Not at all. We're just. Married.

GEORGE. Just?

ADHAM. Three weeks ago.

GEORGE. By God.

> (*They look at* ADHAM.)

THEO. Oh. It's very new, then.

ADHAM. Yes. We barely know each other. So. (*For some reason he starts to laugh.*) Here we are.

GEORGE. Sometimes that's best.

> (ADHAM *looks at them. He feels bad about this talk. But does it anyway.*)

ADHAM. Why is that?

GEORGE. Well, sometimes you need to just jump in. Don't look at how high the cliff is, or that you might hit the rocks on the way down.

THEO. So cynical.

GEORGE. How so? I love women.

THEO. Adham, he has three girlfriends! Three. And he rotates them from week to week. I can't fathom why they put up with it.

GEORGE. I mislead none of them! They're happier than if they were my only ones. They're all beautiful, Adam. Just gorgeous… Really, my man, we could take you to some parties…

THEO. Tell him about your theory.

GEORGE. So you'll make fun of me?

THEO. Of course. Tell him anyway.

GEORGE. Well, as I said, I love women. Always have. I love every bit of them. Their minds. Bodies. Their clothing. I mean, when a girl asks me what she should wear to go out, I put some thought into it! My father was the same way.

THEO. The theory—?

GEORGE. My theory is, well, my father and I both were raised by women, you see? Just women. Both our fathers were off at wars. So we spent an inordinate amount of time with the fair sex. We've got a sixth sense about how they operate, what goes on in their heads. (*To* THEO, *re:* ADHAM.) He thinks I'm touched.

ADHAM. No no. It makes sense to me. I was, uh, raised by a woman, also.

GEORGE. So you see? You're the same way.

ADHAM. I'm…not so sure about that.

(ADHAM*'s not so sure about that.*

ABIR *returns, and this time sits down next to* ADHAM.)

ABIR. [I came all this way. You can't ignore me.] ana jeet kul hal masaafeh. laa yumkin tatjaahalnee.

GEORGE. (*To* ABIR.) Would you care for a cigarette? (*He holds up a cigarette to her.*)

ABIR. Thank you.

(*He lights it. She inhales, exhales. Smiles at* ADHAM.)

ADHAM. She's not supposed to, so this is a special treat for her.

GEORGE. I'm sorry. It hadn't even occurred to me. Is she not allowed…?

ADHAM. She can do whatever she wants, as far as I'm concerned.

GEORGE. Ah. But it's not in line with the religion?

ADHAM. It's not about the religion. People talk.

THEO. I can't imagine how difficult it must be right now, down there. In your homeland, I mean.

(*Re:* ABIR.)

I feel terrible leaving her out.

(In Arabic, to ABIR.)

[I feel terrible…leaving you out of the conversation.] bHiss inno da raheeb… lam nushrikuki fil hadith.

ABIR. [Thank you for saying that!] ashkuruka Aala qawlika haadha!

THEO. [My Arabic is terrible, isn't it?] al Aarabi bitaAi, taAban, mish kida?

ABIR. [Not at all.] la'.

GEORGE. Can she understand a word he's saying?

THEO. Of course she can. *(To* ABIR *again, in Arabic.)* [I get to use it so infrequently. It's really not bad?] mabastaAmilhash kiteer. bi ged mish battal?

ABIR. [No. You sound like you're from Egypt. That's the only strange thing.] la'. tiHkee ka annak min masr. haada shee ghareeb.

THEO. *(In English, to* ADHAM.) What's that?

ADHAM. Egypt. She said it sounds like you're from Egypt.

GEORGE. So he is a pan-Arabist. One of Nasser's cronies. A spy, very likely. A rather inept spy, but still.

THEO. *(To* GEORGE.) Would you please be quiet. *(To* ABIR:) [I had no idea. Imagine that. I suppose that's the standard?] ma kansh Aindee ayy fikra. kunt faakir inno huwa da al mustawa?

(ABIR *shrugs.*)

She's absolutely unimpressed with me. She's very beautiful if you don't mind me saying.

ABIR. *(She understands this.)* Thank you. *(She smiles.)*

ADHAM. You understood that… *(In Arabic.)* …maheik?

(He puts his arm around ABIR.)

You see? So we can speak in English.

ABIR. [At least your colleagues like me. The women were all old and mean.] Aal aqal zumalaa'ak Habbounee. amma anniswaan, kullhum Aajaayiz wa ghaseesaat.

THEO. I agree! The women over there are old and mean.

(He and ABIR laugh.)

Rest assured they're not our wives. I mean, we don't have them.

(ABIR nods politely, not getting it.)

I wish my Arabic were better! *(To* ADHAM.) They are the repressed trophies of our doddery old faculty.

(Awkward beat.)

Beer, anyone?

ADHAM. Oh. Yes, thank you.

THEO. Certainly. Would your wife…?

ADHAM. No no.

    (THEO *leaves.*)

GEORGE. Are you ready for your talk tomorrow?

ADHAM. Oh, yes. Yes.

GEORGE. Some of our colleagues have got pretty worked up about the poem on which you're speaking.

ADHAM. Oh.

GEORGE. They take issue with Wordsworth's way of seeing. He sees something, then he doesn't.

    (THEO *returns with three beers.*)

THEO. Oh no. Is this your hedgerows discussion again?

ADHAM. Let me hear it.

GEORGE. Early on in "Lines Composed a Few Miles Above Tintern Abbey, on Revisiting the Banks of the Wye During a Tour, July 13, 1798"—you'll forgive me if I don't abbreviate—Wordsworth mentions the hedgerows he sees. But then in the same line, backs off from the observation. He who is the master observer of nature backs away from what he sees.

ADHAM. (*Not sure where it's going.*) Um-hmm…

THEO. That's what I say! "Um-hmmm." It doesn't go anywhere, this line of thinking. Trust me, Adham.

    (ABIR *reaches for the beer glass, but* ADHAM *stops her.*)

GEORGE. It's been said—not by me—that these hedgerows are a sign of enclosure, and, and, rural impoverishment.

THEO. By one neo-Marxist historian! Not even a Romantic specialist. (*To* ADHAM.) Should I get her a beer? (*To* ABIR, *in Arabic:*) BEDIK tarabeiza?

    (ABIR *laughs and shakes her head.*)

Oh no. What did I say? What've I done?

GEORGE. What did he say?

ABIR. (*In Arabic.*) ult "tarabeiza."

ADHAM. (*In English.*) You asked her if she wanted a table.

THEO. Oh dear. Just when I think I've made progress.

ADHAM. She's fine.

GEORGE. (*Resuming his argument.*) Do you feel this is way off the mark?

ADHAM. I don't understand.

GEORGE. That Wordsworth backs off from an indictment of the landed class!

THEO. So now it's an "indictment"? That reading isn't supported!

GEORGE. Some critics are taking that path, my friend.

THEO. (*To* ADHAM.) Tiny pocket of scholars out of Cambridge. They're just interested in being trendy. Most of their colleagues have said as much!

GEORGE. It's a reasonable discussion. Wordsworth sees this sign of social stratification, of the subjugation of the peasant, and then dismisses it. It bears some investigation.

(ABIR *sneaks in another sip of* ADHAM's *beer.*)

ABIR. (*To* THEO.) [I like whatever this is. I don't care if it's a table.] Aajabitnee hay mahma kaanat. hatta law kaanat tarabeiza.

(*She laughs, as does* THEO.)

THEO. Should I get her something?

(*But* ADHAM *is caught up in the discussion.*)

ADHAM. I read it as simply—Wordsworth says, "Once again I see these hedgerows, hardly hedgerows, little lines of sportive wood run wild." He sees the structures, the outlines of them, but then he reflects on what he's seen, almost instantaneously, and amends it. "Hardly hedgerows." Not because he's disturbed by the implication. But for the simple reason that the hedgerows have become overgrown with grass. That's what he sees.

GEORGE. That's the traditional reading of the poem, of course.

THEO. And the one that most readers of English adhere to!

ADHAM. He's giving himself license to let things fade in tableaux as they fade in the mind.

THEO. Ah. I like that!

GEORGE. Hm. What about the vagrant then?

ADHAM. From "The Ruined Cottage"?

GEORGE. No, from the same poem we're discussing. "Tintern Abbey." What about him?

ADHAM. Forgive me, but what about him? I don't understand the question.

GEORGE. My dear man, you need to be ready for this kind of question.

THEO. You're making him feel unwelcome.

GEORGE. Not at all. We're having a discussion. Exchange of ideas. You don't feel I'm making you unwelcome do you?

(ADHAM *shakes his head.*)

So, yes, in this same poem. Wordsworth suggests this life, this vagrant is there, but he clearly finds it distasteful, moves on.

ADHAM. I don't think he finds the vagrant distasteful.

GEORGE. There are readings that contradict that. That imply that the vagrant is tucked away, something marring the poetic vision.

ADHAM. What more did Wordsworth need to say about the vagrant?

ABIR. [Don't yell.] laa tsarrekh.

ADHAM. [I'm fine.] ana mneeH.

THEO. (*To* GEORGE.) Right. Did you want an epic poem about the vagrant? If you want a bloody epic poem about the bloody vagrant perhaps you should write it yourself. Sorry, Madam.

(ABIR *smiles. She hasn't understood, but decides to respond anyway, in English.*)

ABIR. It's all right. Where's my table?

THEO. Good lord, Adham, I had no idea your wife was a comedienne. She's perfectly charming.

GEORGE. I'm saying that no discussion of Wordsworth should be considered complete without an acknowledgement of this unseemly underbelly. Our friend Adam is in a perfect position to understand.

ADHAM. I am?

THEO. Ha.

ADHAM. I don't know how.

GEORGE. As a Palestinian, a, a, refugee.

ADHAM. Sorry, I don't understand.

GEORGE. Your world. Where you live. I mean, what's going on now. The sublime mixed with the horrific. The Egyptian army building up in the Sinai...

THEO. Some of that is overblown.

GEORGE. Not at all. And the Israeli generals panicking, taking the reins from the Prime Minister. We have been hearing about how dire it is, all over the Middle East.

ADHAM. I've never known things not to be dire.

(*Beat.*)

THEO. There was an, uh, interesting article in the *Times*. Saying that basically Nasser is bluffing, with no intention of going to war. But Moshe Dayan, who says he won't go to war, is actually readying the rifle, so to speak.

ABIR. (*Alerted.*) [Dayan is a liar.] Dayan kdhaab.

(ADHAM *tries to quiet her.*)

ADHAM. All right, all right.

GEORGE. What'd she say?

THEO. She believes Dayan's a liar.

GEORGE. Well he may be, Madam, but he's saddled with the task of protecting his country. Israel is surrounded by those who wish them extinct. They must fight back if provoked. Clearly you grant them that?

ABIR. [What's he saying? He's defending the Israelis?] eish bee'ool? beedaafiA Aal israa'eeliyyeen?

ADHAM. *(To* ABIR.*)* La'! *(To the men.)* I'm sorry.

GEORGE. No need to apologize. I like the passion.

ABIR. [What did he say?] eish yaHkee?

ADHAM. [Don't worry about it.] wala yhimmik.

ABIR. [Dayan is just doing the dirty work, while Eshkol gets to sit back and pretend he knows nothing about it. It's all part of their plan to look innocently provoked.] Dayan bass byaAmal al Aamal al wisikh. fee nafs el waqt Eshkol biHibb yi'Aad wara wa byeAmil Haloo innu maa byiAraf shee. haada kullu mukhattat Aashaan ybeinoo abriyaa' mustafazzeen.

THEO. What's all that?

ADHAM. I guess this is an area she has strong feelings about.

ABIR. [People should know. You can listen to Dayan, but ninety-nine percent of what comes out of his mouth is lies.] annas lazim yaArafoo. mumkin yastamAoo li dayan, bas tisAa wa tisAeen fil meyya min elli bee'ooloo kidhb bi kidhb.

ADHAM. [We didn't come here to talk about this, all right?] ma jeenaa hon naHkee Aan haada?

ABIR. *(To* GEORGE.*)* [But you know, if you want to stay ignorant, stay ignorant. What can I do?] bas ibtiAraf eish, iza biddak itdal jaahel, khalleek jaahel. eish baddak aAmal?

ADHAM. [Shut up!] uskutee!

THEO. What's she saying?

ABIR. [Don't talk to me like that. Why would you talk to me like that?] lei Aam teHkee maAee heik. leish ibteHkee maAee heik?

ADHAM. I think Wordsworth sees the vagrant as much as he cares to. As much as he sees anything else in the poem. And that I for one don't feel any particular affinity for the vagrant dweller in that poem, or any other.

(ADHAM *takes the beer away from* ABIR *again, and downs the rest.*)

Rehearsal

ADHAM *enters, turns a panel, revealing: "ADHAM'S REHEARSAL."
A beat of panic upon seeing this title, then he takes his place behind a podium, leans into a microphone, and starts his lecture.*

ADHAM. Wordsworth's poem—

(ADHAM *backs away. There's a tremendous echo, almost surreal.*)

—begins with the mention of time passing: "Five years have passed." Is this the way it's supposed to sound?

(*The others are heard but not seen.*)

GEORGE. Sounds good to us.

ADHAM. It's very loud.

GEORGE. That's this hall. You have to fill it up or you get swallowed.

(ADHAM *looks supremely uncomfortable.*)

THEO. You okay up there?

GEORGE. It's just a rehearsal.

ADHAM. It's uh—yes. (*He laughs.*) It's so big in here. What's the word— (*In Arabic.*) [Cavernous.] *WasiA.* I don't know it in English. (*Laughs again, nervously.*) Oh well. *WasiA.* Leave it at that.

(*He wipes sweat from his face.*)

THEO. Take the coat off, you'll feel better.

ADHAM. Yes, thank you.

(*Starts to take his coat off, stops.*)

I'll be all right.

(*We hear the low sounds of Fairuz's song "Dabke Libnan." ADHAM adjusts his coat.*)

GEORGE. Just a few more words.

(ADHAM *begins again, trying to be louder than the music [and we] seems to hear. But the music rises as well, until it drowns out his words.*)

ADHAM. Five summers, with the length
Of five long winters...
Once again
Do I behold these steep and lofty cliffs
Which on a wild secluded scene impress
Thoughts of more deep seclusion...
I have owed to them
In hours of weariness, sensations sweet
Felt in the blood, and felt along the heart,
And passing even into my purer mind,
With tranquil restoration: – feelings too
Of unremembered pleasure: such, perhaps
As have no slight or trivial influence
On that best portion of a good man's life.

(*Lights out.*)

PART TWO

Adham confronts his mediocrity

> *Early evening.* ADHAM, *in some kind of torment, enters the hotel room. Rain has come through the open windows, drenching the curtains.* ADHAM *doesn't seem to notice. He takes off his jacket, throws it on the floor. Starts to unbutton his sweat-stained, wrinkly shirt. Lays on the bed.*
>
> *Suddenly, his mother,* BEDER, *appears in the window—all garbed-out, wearing a hijab—totally different from how she looked at home before.*

BEDER. Tell me again why you brought the girl.

ADHAM. (*Springing up.*) What the hell?

BEDER. Tell me.

> (*He goes to the window. She disappears. He slams it shut.*
> *Now we hear her voice, from the opposite side of the stage.*)

(*O.S.*) Answer my question.

> (*Now she comes out of the bathroom, dressed normally.*)

She brought a lot of makeup. What is she hiding?

> (*He looks at her, decides not to question her being there, lays back down.*)

ADHAM. She helps me.

BEDER. By ironing your shirt? Half ironing it? She didn't even have it on the right setting.

ADHAM. She's not my maid. She's my wife. She's beautiful. She makes me look good.

BEDER. A word to you: You didn't look so good at that event.

ADHAM. What event?

BEDER. The tea. Whatever that was. You looked sideswiped. Like someone who'd never spent a day in a library. You made us look bad!

ADHAM. Well thank goodness you're not here then, right? What a relief.

BEDER. I'd have helped you handle that.

ADHAM. Handle what?

BEDER. The argument he made, the Englishman. You needed a minute to think about it. You'd have found the answer.

ADHAM. There is no answer. It's a literary discussion.

BEDER. One-sided! He made his point and you retreated.

ADHAM. I'd never heard it before—

BEDER. (*Overlap.*) —Doesn't matter!

ADHAM. (*Overlap.*) —what he was saying.

BEDER. (*Overlap.*) —You're educated! An educated man comes up with answers!

ADHAM. —He had an entirely new approach.

BEDER. Based on Marxism. So what. Like you've never heard any of that? It's the same babble we hear every day coming out of Cairo. These English want to be Marxists, let them. They have all the time in the world up here to sit and philosophize. Like the bourgeoisie that they are!

ADHAM. I did answer him. I told him that line of thinking doesn't interest me.

BEDER. What "interests" you doesn't matter. No one cares about that. You didn't dismantle what he said as irrelevant.

ADHAM. You're right.

BEDER. I knew I should've sent you away when you were five. I had the chance. Just packed you up and sent you to the States. Instead, we both stayed. What a waste. All that work!
How was I to know those schools weren't halfway decent? What a fool I was, thinking I'd set you up with a proper education.

ADHAM. I've done well!

BEDER. For an Arab in Palestine. Up here, you're practically a Bedouin, as far as they're concerned.

> (*He sinks.*)

Money, connections. We had nothing. And those teachers put on such airs, as if it was the Sorbonne! It just isn't enough, in the end. You can't hold your own here. God, I should've seen that. I should've seen how limited your education was.

> (*His hands start to shake.*)

ADHAM. I'm not giving up on myself.

BEDER. This could be the end of you.

ADHAM. How's that possible? Washed up at 25, mother?

BEDER. Not that unusual in our part of the world.

> (*And she's gone.* ADHAM *lays back down on the bed. Long beat of him alone.* ABIR *enters. Switches on the light. Shocked to see one of the windows still open. The scene is in Arabic, with superscript titles on the panels.*)

ABIR. [You're laying here letting the rain in? Are you all right?] leish naayem wa mkhalli al matar yadkhul? haasis innak mneeH?

ADHAM. [Sure, sure.] mashi lHaal.

> (*She rushes to close the window.*)

ABIR. [I hope it didn't damage anything.] inshallah ma kharrabish ishi.

ADHAM. [It's a hotel room. They don't care.] haadi ghurfat funduq. maa byehtammoo.

(She looks at him.)

ABIR. [Why did you go ahead so fast? I looked for you downstairs. The old man—the clerk?—wanted to show me the pictures from when Omar Sharif stayed here. He thought I'd be interested.] leish ruHt heik bsorAa? dawwaret Aaleik taHet. il Aajooz—il muwadhaf?—kaan bidou iyfarjeeni suwar Omar E-Sharif lamma kaan hon. fakkarni mehtammeh.

ADHAM. *(Sarcastic.)* [And you were.] wa kunti.

(ABIR sees the jacket on the floor, walks to it, picks it up, shakes it out.)

ABIR. [*What is it?*] shoo fee?

ADHAM. [*Nothing.*] wala shee.

(She takes the cigarettes out of the pockets and sets them on the desk. Hangs the jacket in the closet, looks at ADHAM, who goes to look out the window.)

ABIR. [You're tired. I'll make you a cup of tea.] inta taAbaan. raH aAmillak shay.

ADHAM. [I don't want anything.] ma biddi ishi.

(He sulks. She studies him.)

ABIR. [Something's wrong.] fee ishi ghalat.

ADHAM. [Forget it. You're on vacation. You should have a good time!] wala ishi. inti bi vacances. laazim itrooHi titbassati fHalik.

(Beat.)

ABIR. [Okay.] Haader.

(She goes into the bathroom. Stunned, ADHAM watches her go. He walks to the desk, grabs a cigarette and lights up. Goes back to the window. ABIR comes back out, her hair down.)

[So what is it?] tayyib shoo al ussah?

ADHAM. *(Incredulous.)*[If you have to ask!] Aanjad, lazim tis'ali!

(Now she walks over to him. Just stands there, waiting.)

[I looked like a fool. Ridiculous! I failed.] kaan shaklee zay liHmar. Fshilt.

ABIR. [Failed? At what?] fshilt? bi eish?

ADHAM. [They looked at me, like, you saw them – "Who is this idiot?" "Why did we bring him here?" "Someone felt sorry for him." Or they assumed I was brought here to show them how smart they are. Either way.] ittalaAoo feyyee, zay, inti shufteehum. "meen hal ahbal?" "leish iHna jibnaa la hon?" Hada shafa' Aalei. aw fakkaroo inhum jabooni la hon Aashaan afarjeehum addeish hummin azkiya. ma btifri'.

ABIR. [No one thought that.] wala Hada fakkar heik.

ADHAM. [I was an embarrassment. Scrambling for an answer, coming up with mishmosh, nothing.] kunt bahdaleh. Aam bafattish Aala jawaab, Aam battaleA takhareef, wala ishi.

ABIR. [It didn't sound like that!] ma bayyanish heik.

ADHAM. [You don't speak the language, my dear.] ma btitkallami il lugha, ya habibti.

ABIR. [Some.] baHki shway.

ADHAM. Beer. Please. Thank you.

ABIR. [I saw them talk to you. They liked you. I wish you could see that.] shuft hum biyiHkoo maAak. Aajabt hum. ya reit law inta shuft haada.

ADHAM. [You should be disgusted with me. I stood in that hall, and looked out... My legs beneath me, they couldn't hold me. I can't do it. I can't.] lazim ti'rafee minnee. wa'afit fissaaleh, wa ittalaAit, sakaAoo rukabi, ma Himlouni. maa raH a'dar. mish aadar.

ABIR. [It was just practice.] kaanat ibrova.

ADHAM. [I could barely get the words out. You didn't see that?] yadob tiliA ilkalaam min tummee. Ma shufteesh?

ABIR. [No.] La'.

ADHAM. [Well, then let me explain something. Your husband was flailing. I can't believe you couldn't see that! They ask me to defend my point of view, and what do I give them? Theories that took fifteen years to trickle down to us. Old thoughts, old theories. I'm useless.] khalleeni afassirlek. jozek kaan Aam bi saareA. mish maA'ool innek ma shuftee! sa'alooni adafiA Aan ra'yi wa eish aAteit hum? nadhariyyaat Aumurha khamastaAshar saneh. afkaar qadeemeh, nadhariyyaat qadeemeh. faashil.

ABIR. [By God, that's not true.] walla mish saH.

ADHAM. [By god, it is! We're backwards! While we've been fighting over this and that scrap of desert, crying over the last assassination, they've been living with the great thoughts. We've wasted so much time.] walla saH. iHna mutakhallefeen. aaAdeen minHarib Aala nitfeh min hon wa sha'feh min ha saHrah il khara, Aammin walwil Aala aakher ightiyaal, wa hummin Aaysheen maA al afkaar al Aadheemeh. daaA al wa'et minna.

(*He looks like he might cry, but he holds it together. She goes to him, touches his back.*)

ABIR. [You have a great mind.] afkaararak Aadheemeh.

(ADHAM *laughs.*)

ADHAM. [Is that right.] aah.

ABIR. [He said that.] aah heik al.

ADHAM. [Who?] meen?

ABIR. [The, uh, Theodore. In Arabic. He said that.] haada Theodore. bil Aarabi. heik aal.

ADHAM. [When?] eimta?

ABIR. [When you were practicing.] lamma kunt bil brova.

ADHAM. [He said that to you? He just wanted to get close to a beautiful woman.] huwweh allik heik? kaan bas biddoo yit'arrab Aala waHdeh Helweh mitlek.

> (*Beat.*)

[Flirting. You didn't know he was doing that? Men will say anything to look into a woman's eyes.] aaAid biAaaksik. ma intabahti? al rjaal bi'ooloo ayy ishi la yittallaAoo biAanein waHdeh.

ABIR. [I don't know. I don't even think of it that way. It doesn't matter. He also said you have a unique scholarly voice.] ana ma baAraf. ma bafakker fee hattaree'a. bihimmish. wa kamaan aal innu wajhit nazarak raheebeh.

ADHAM. [Because it comes with an accent.] Aashaan baHki maA lahjeh.

ABIR. [I don't know why you've forgotten how smart you are. The man I met—] ana mish Aarfeh leish inseet addeish inta zaki. al rujjaal illi baArafu—

ADHAM. [The man you met!—] al rujjaal illi ibteArafee!—

ABIR. [—Was smart, and sure of himself, and didn't care about what anyone thought.] —kan zaki, wa mit'akkid min nafsu, wa ma ihtammish eish al naas bifakru fee.

ADHAM. [Well, maybe that wasn't really me.] yumkin haada al rujjaal mish ana.

> (*He looks at her.*)

[Maybe this is me.] yumkin haada ana.

> (*Beat.*)

ABIR. [Then I want them both.] ana biddi al itnein.

> (*She reaches for his head, touches it.*)

[I can handle both.] ana ba'dar Aala al itnein.

> (*She takes his hands.*)

[Your hands are (shaking).] ideik (biroojjou).

> (*He pulls his hands away. She places her hands on his head, runs her hands through his hair, trying to fix it.*)

[I don't know what happens with this hair.] mish Aaarfeh eish biseer bi ha shaArat.

> (*He relaxes, just a little. She takes his cigarette from him, smokes, studies him...*)

ADHAM. [Wondering what you got yourself into?] nadmaneh?

ABIR. [No.] La'.

ADHAM. [You lie.] kazzaabeh.

> (*She goes and grabs his Wordsworth book.*)

ABIR. [Tell me what it says.] oollee eish bi'ool.

ADHAM. [You'll be bored.] ha tizha'ee.

ABIR. [You're so insulting, you know that?] btiAraaf innak inta kteer aleel il adab.

ADHAM. [It's in a different language!] haadi gheir lugha.

ABIR. [So?] wa kamaan?

(She starts reading it, in English. It's barely recognizable.)

Thus by day…

(She stops, but keeps her eyes on the page, as if she's reading and comprehending it.)

ADHAM. [You don't understand a damn thing.] inti mish faahmeh ishi bilmarra.

ABIR. [I get some of it. I'm very smart, too.] ana faahmeh shwayye minnoo. ana kteer zakiyyeh kamaan.

ADHAM. [I know.] baAraf.

(She hands the book to him.)

ABIR. [Go. Read.] yallah. iqra'.

(He shrugs. She watches intently. He takes a beat, then reads, speaking in English.)

ADHAM. "Thus by day / Subjected to the discipline of love—"

ABIR. [Translate.] tarjim.

(ADHAM shakes his head at first. ABIR waits. He then translates it into Arabic, haltingly. This feels very unfamiliar to him.)

ADHAM. wa haakadha maA el waqt, wa huwa khadiAan li qaaAidati lHub.

ABIR. [More.] kamaan.

ADHAM. "His organs and recipient faculties/Are quickened, are more vigorous." *(He looks at her. Translates again, into Arabic.)* Aada'uhoo wa quduraatuhu lHissiyya tatasaaraA, tatazaayadoo nashaatan.

ABIR. [I like this poet. He's not boring.] Aaajibnee haada il shaAir. ma bizahhi'.

ADHAM. [It doesn't translate well.] ma bittarjam imneeH.

ABIR. [I disagree.] mbala.

ADHAM. [You're not supposed to disagree with your husband.] mish mafrood itkhaalfee jozek.

ABIR. [I thought you weren't traditional.] Halla' serna taqleediyyeen.

ADHAM. [Sometimes I am.] ah, aHyanan.

(ABIR gives him a look.)

ABIR. [More.] kamaan.

ADHAM. [Ordering me about!] wa Aam btit'ammaree fiyyeh!

ABIR. [Go.] yallah.

ADHAM. "His mind spreads, tenacious of the forms which it receives." (*And translates again.*) Aaqluhu yanshareH, yatashabbathu bil 'ashkaali yalqaaha.

> (*As he finishes translating this last part,* ABIR *moves closer to him. Both of them are on the bed now. She kneels, places her hands on his hipbones. Leans in, kisses him there.*
> *Lights shift: early morning light.*)

Right at Exeter Street

> ABIR *is gone. It's raining again. We hear a shower. As* ADHAM *says the following, he gets out of bed very slowly. He's naked.*

ADHAM. No flinch, no fear.

Face. Eyes. Swallow. Normal swallow.

Hands, still. Hand, still.

> (*He puts on his shirt.*)

Shirt? Pretend it's nice. Pretend it's dry. Breathe. Slow. Slow.

> (*He breathes in and out, fast. Almost cries. Stops himself.*)

Remember why you're here.

> (*He puts his pants on. His jacket.*)

A proper gentleman. A student.

> (*He leaves the room and goes outside, into and through the panels/London.*)

On his way to do his work:

Right at Exeter Street, left at Wellington Street, Bow Street, Long Acre, Endell Street, High Holborn, Shaftesbury Avenue, Gower Street.

The Darwin Lecture Theater, University College.

> (*Inside. A simple washroom. A single sink, and a mirror. He takes a towel hanging there, and dries his hands.*)

A clean towel. With letters. England's letters.

> (*He hangs the towel. Looks in the mirror.*)

Vain.

> (*He fixes his hair for a second. He likes what he sees.*)

Not bad.

> (*He walks away from the mirror, goes through the vast hallways of the building.*)

New shoes. Clean shoes. Tight. On marble.

Solid. History in this floor. Scholars buried here. This history. Scholars underneath, learned men. Here. Shoes click above the great scholars. The poets. The poetry. And me. And me walking past, and through, and history, and honor, and great thoughts, and those that abide by language. Its laws, and its mandates. Me above, moving through.

(*He arrives at the door that takes him backstage.*)

Last breath. Hands, still.

(*He finds a folder, his folder.*)

Folder.

Pants zipped.

(*Checks his zipper.*)

Papers.

Hands still. Pants zipped.

Goddamn, hands still!

(*He opens the door, and steps into darkness, into the backstage area.*)

Darkness.

Breath. Last big breath.

Dust. Old air. A small light on a table. How are you sir? Do you have everything you need, sir? Glass of water for you sir? Glass of water for the scholar, for the man, for me. No smile, no thanks, this is expected, this is how it goes. This is my birthright. I've earned this. I'm in a long line. Shoes, shirt, zipper. Yes.

(*And now he takes his place at a podium, stepping into a very bright light.*)

Stand still. Paper. Light. Light.

(*We hear very faint, muffled clapping. He looks out over the audience.*)

Glasses. Hair. No one I know. Glasses, hair. Small, easy breath. Easy. You know how to talk. No rolling R's. No attack. The British, the English, they don't attack the language.

You know this: In England, the words are like water. One false sound, and a man is exposed. We Arabs? Our words are like hammers, hitting nails.

A thousand breaths, waiting for me. For this man, this scholar, ready to do the Work of God.

(ADHAM *stands at the podium, the lights go as bright as they can, and then blackout. Music: Joni Mitchell, "Night in the City."*)

The party

Lights up at a party in an apartment. THEO *is there, as is* GEORGE, *as is a very beautiful English woman,* DIANA, *20s, who sits languidly on a couch next to* THEO. ADHAM *and* ABIR, *having just arrived, stand and look at the group, awkward.*

GEORGE. (*To* ADHAM.) Have you met Diana?

DIANA. I'm George's girlfriend. (*Re:* GEORGE.) How he hates that word. He flinches, don't you George?

GEORGE. Not in the least.

(*Staying on the couch,* DIANA *reaches her hand out to shake* ADHAM's.)

ADHAM. Pleasure to meet you.

DIANA. Actually, we spoke for a moment right after your talk.

ADHAM. I'm sorry—

DIANA. It's all right. There were loads of people. As well there should've been.

THEO. And this is Adham's wife. Abir.

DIANA. Oh! My goodness. Yes. They said you were married.

ADHAM. Sorry—yes.

DIANA. (*To* ABIR.) You sat in front of me. I admired your dress.

ABIR. Hello.

(*Beat.*)

ADHAM. She doesn't speak English.

DIANA. Sorry. (*Now waving to* ABIR, *as if to make it clear.*) Hello.

ABIR. Hi.

THEO. (*To* ABIR, *in Arabic.*) [I'll be your translator tonight. If you even want to hear any of the nonsense that comes out of our mouths.] ana Hakoon mutarjimik illeileh. da iza kunti Aayza tismaAee el Aabataat illi btitlaA min bu'ina.

ADHAM. (*To* THEO, *in Arabic.*) [It's all right.] wala yhimmak.

THEO. [I love speaking Arabic.] ana bHeb etkallem Aarabee.

ABIR. [You've gotten better already!] seret kteer aHsan. Aanjad.

ADHAM. [He has.] ah, sar. aHsan.

THEO. [Thank you.] shukran.

(*Beat. They realize they are leaving the others out.*)

DIANA. (*Re: hearing the language.*) Marvelous. Don't stop.

GEORGE. I think we all need more of, whatever we're drinking. Adham, can I get you started?

(ADHAM *nods.* GEORGE *goes.*)

DIANA. So, she couldn't understand any of what you said tonight?

ADHAM. No, not so much.

DIANA. Tragic.

ADHAM. Maybe it was a relief. She has to listen to me a lot.

DIANA. Ridiculous! (*To* ABIR.) Your husband did very well. (*To* THEO.) Tell her that. (*To* ABIR.) Could you see how well he did?

ADHAM. (*To* ABIR, *in Arabic.*) [She wants to know how it was to watch me tonight.] bid ha taAraf keef shufteeni illeileh.

ABIR. (*To* ADHAM.) [You were the most comfortable I've ever seen you.] kunt mbayyan martaaH kteer.

DIANA. What did she say?

THEO. She—

ADHAM. (*Cutting him off.*) She enjoyed it.

DIANA. And how does she find London?

ABIR. (*To* ADHAM.) [What?] shoo?

ADHAM. [She wants to know how you like London.] bid ha taAraf keef Habbeitee London.

ABIR. (*To* ADHAM, *re:* DIANA.) [Who is she?] meen hiyyeh?

ADHAM & THEO. [His girlfriend.] saHbitoo.

ABIR. [Whose?] saHbit meen?

ADHAM. [Don't worry about it.] Laa ti'la'ee.

THEO. George's.

DIANA. What did she say?

ABIR. [Did she say I was pretty?] hiyya aalat inni hilweh?

ADHAM. (*To* DIANA.) Oh. Uh… she likes London very much.

THEO. (*To* ABIR.) [Yes, she did.] naAam.

ABIR. (*To* THEO.) [She's beautiful. Not angry, here…] hiyya jameela. mush zaAlaana, hon… (*Points to her mouth, pouty.*) […like so many of your English women.] …mitl kteer min anniswaan al engleeziyyat.

DIANA. What did she say?

(THEO *starts to translate.*)

THEO. She says you're beautiful, not like—

ADHAM. (*Cutting him off.*) We both like London very much.

DIANA. Well. You should both stay. Finish your studies here. I think Adham would do well. Don't you, Teddy?

THEO. (*Feigning nonchalance.*) Eh.

DIANA. (*To* THEO.) Stop it. (*To* ADHAM.) They're so gruff, these academics. No wonder I had to drop out.

THEO. Diana was halfway through her literature course.

DIANA. I met George, and that was it. He seduced me, and I couldn't concentrate anymore. I wasn't cut out for it anyway, though. Focus your whole life on one poet, or one bloody poem? I need variety.

THEO. Really? According to whom? Your fortune teller?

DIANA. She's been right about a lot of things.

> (*She smiles at* ADHAM. GEORGE *returns with a fresh bottle of wine and two glasses. He fills everyone's glasses, and pours for* ADHAM *and* ABIR.)

GEORGE. To a great speech!

THEO. Hear, hear!

ADHAM. You're too kind.

DIANA. No kindness. We're impressed.

THEO. Don't start being humble now, my dear chap.

GEORGE. You were good.

ADHAM. I mentioned your vagrant.

GEORGE. I noticed.

THEO. Funny that. The vagrant made it in. Satisfied, Georgie?

GEORGE. Surprised.

ADHAM. The vagrant had his place. Just a smaller place than you'd have liked.

DIANA. I heard all that. But I didn't remember a vagrant in the poem. I'm sorry.

THEO. Aw, Georgie, that's got to be hard to hear.

DIANA. I mean, it was really just about Wordsworth, this man. The individual. Oh God. You're afraid I'll massacre your point.

ADHAM. I'm not worried.

THEO. You haven't read her work, Adham. / Maybe you should be.

GEORGE. Let's hear it.

DIANA. Well, really, it was all sort of ironic, wasn't it? The way you put it. Old William was sort of going on and on about Nature, but in the end, it's not the things he sees at all. Or even the place… It's the imprint it leaves. He could be anywhere.

THEO. See? People were listening.

ADHAM. (*To* DIANA.) Maybe you should go back into academics.

DIANA. Right.

THEO. (*To* GEORGE.) Maybe she had the wrong teacher.

DIANA. Maybe.

GEORGE. I admit. It's a very close reading of the text. Not accounting for the socioeconomic underpinnings...

THEO. Oh no...

GEORGE. But it worked. In your hands, the poem was vital. Alive.

DIANA. (*To* ADHAM.) Did I get it right, though?

ADHAM. Well, it's the paradox of...

> (*He stops himself.*)

I don't want to go on too much. She... (*Meaning* ABIR.) doesn't understand any of this.

> (*Everyone looks at* ABIR, *who's been listening, smiling, not getting any of it.*)

DIANA. Isn't she a dear? She must be bored out of her mind.

ABIR. (*In Arabic, to* ADHAM.) [What?] eish?

ADHAM. (*In Arabic.*) [Nothing. I don't want to leave you out for too long.] ma fee shee, ma biddi akhalleekee lawaHdik kteer.

ABIR. [No. I'm all right. This is your night.] la'. ana martaaHa. haadi leiltak. (*She takes his hand, moves close into him.*) Talk.

> (ADHAM *smiles. As he speaks, we see his passion for the work unleashed.*)

ADHAM. For Wordsworth, this, uh, this meaning of home, it comes to him only after leaving. His tie to this part of Nature, uh, paradoxically helps him transcend the specific place itself. Line 63:
"The picture of the mind revives again:
While here I stand, not only with the sense
Of present pleasure, but with pleasing thoughts
That in this moment there is life and food
For future years..."
Essentially it's—Should I go on?

DIANA. Yes!

ADHAM. It's—the paradox is: Wordsworth, great poet of Nature, comes to know himself as part of the grand scheme of Spirit only when he lets go of his attachment to the very landscape that inspired him to write in the first place.

DIANA. And then he forgets all about it?

ADHAM. No. It stays here. (*Points to his head.*) And here. (*Points to his heart.*)

> (*Beat.* ADHAM *catches himself in his own reverie.*)

Well, enough. Can I have another drink? (*He holds up his glass.*)

GEORGE. I can do even better. (*He goes.*)

THEO. George just might be a bit pissed off.

ADHAM. I'm sorry—?

DIANA. He's fine.

ADHAM. I don't mean to cause any problem.

DIANA. George deserves a little trouble. He's got another girlfriend, you know. I'm not the only one.

ADHAM. I see.

THEO. You're the most important.

DIANA. He said that?

THEO. It's clear.

DIANA. That's too bad. Poor Theo's being forced to lie! What do you think, Adham—should a man be confined to one woman?

ADHAM. Yes.

DIANA. Ha!

ADHAM. If it's the right woman, of course.

> (ABIR, *exhausted from the day, slowly falls asleep on* ADHAM's *shoulder. He takes her glass.*)

DIANA. Sweet. I wish I could fall asleep like that.

ADHAM. I think she's just tired.

THEO. Been a long day for both of you.

DIANA. So one woman if it's the right one. It's conditional to you.

ADHAM. Well. Yes.

DIANA. Are there no gentlemen to be found anywhere?

THEO. Don't lump us in with Georgie.

DIANA. Too late. You're lumped.

> (GEORGE *returns with a rolled-up joint.*)

GEORGE. I didn't think anyone would object if I— (*Sees* ABIR.) Oh look at that. We've bored her.

THEO. No different than some of your first-years.

GEORGE. I've taken a fair amount of beating tonight.

THEO. Aw. Did you bring something to ease the pain?

GEORGE. I did. Adham, will you join us? It's good stuff. From Morocco, I believe.

> (GEORGE *lights up, takes a hit. Passes it to* THEO. *He passes it to* DIANA, *who takes a long drag, then passes it to* ADHAM.)

DIANA. It's all right— for you to— ?

ADHAM. Oh. Uh, yes.

> (ADHAM *takes a hit, holds it as the others have, exhales.*)

GEORGE. We've established all that. Adham is not a man of faith.

ADHAM. Not really, anyway.

DIANA. I went out with a man from Morocco.

THEO. Oh ho!

DIANA. Claimed he was some kind of royalty.

GEORGE. I'm sure he was.

DIANA. Spoke six languages.

THEO. I bet he did.

DIANA. He was lovely. My flatmates adored him. I found out later he was selling hash to everyone.

THEO. And none to you?

DIANA. It's not really my thing! (*Realizes she's holding the joint. Laughs.*) God, present circumstances excluded. Adham, you must think we're all so decadent.

ADHAM. No.

DIANA. You know, the children of the faded empire/ and all that.

THEO. "Faded empire"?/ Good god.

GEORGE. Let me have that.

> (*He takes her hand, wrestles the joint from her. Leans in and kisses her.*)

THEO. Ah, love.

DIANA. Fine, shut me up.

GEORGE. Never.

DIANA. (*To* ADHAM.) When do you go back?

ADHAM. To the hotel?

DIANA. No! You're so funny. Home. To your, to your country. Oh god, I've messed it up. It's not really a country, is it?

THEO. Not for 20 years.

ADHAM. Day after tomorrow.

DIANA. You should stay longer.

ADHAM. For more parties?

DIANA. To see London. Didn't you just get here? Why are we sending him off so quickly?

THEO. That's how the university works these things out. They rush you in, pat you on the back, and rush you out.

DIANA. Well, it's silly. There's so much to see.

THEO. I agree.

GEORGE. Seriously, Adham. You can't want to go back home now?

ADHAM. After meeting all of you?

GEORGE. After hearing the news.

ADHAM. What news?

GEORGE. The war is on. You didn't hear? *Evening Standard* said the Israelis destroyed the entire Egyptian air force this morning.

DIANA. No.

THEO. But that's not confirmed./ Radio Cairo is saying Egypt took down Israeli jets.

ADHAM. What?

GEORGE. Where did you see that?

THEO. I heard it on the Home Service. They say there was dancing on the streets of Damascus.

DIANA. So who's lying?

GEORGE. And it commences. The muddle of wartime rubbish begins promptly on schedule.

THEO. I didn't realize we were getting our news from the *Standard*.

GEORGE. I don't./ Normally.

DIANA. It's half past midnight.

ADHAM. Do you have the paper here?/ Can I see it?

GEORGE. Downstairs.

THEO. Adham, you shouldn't put any credence in the *Standard*. It's biased.

GEORGE. Not always.

DIANA. Isn't tomorrow's *Guardian* out?

GEORGE. And they're not biased at all.

THEO. Yes! Let's nip down to Euston station for the first edition. Adham?

> (ADHAM *gets up and joins them. To* DIANA:)

Be right back.

> (*They leave. Beat.* ABIR *sleeps,* DIANA *watches. Lights up a cigarette, stretches…*)

DIANA. Hm.

> (ABIR, *feeling* ADHAM *gone from next to her, wakes up, slowly. Sees* DIANA.)

Oh. Sorry. They'll be right back.

ABIR. [Where's my husband?] wein zoji?

DIANA. Oh. Em.

ABIR. *Ou est mon mari?*

DIANA. Oh, dear. *No parlez vous pas.* I mean, beyond that. So sorry. I'm sorry.

> (ABIR *gets up, looks around.* DIANA *gets it.*)

Oh! Sorry. Yes. He left. Just for a moment. They left. Just to get the newspaper. They'll come right back.

(DIANA *smiles, trying to reassure.*)

I promise, it'll be all right.

ABIR. [Do you have a cigarette?] Aindik sigara? (ABIR *gestures: a smoke.*)

DIANA. Cigarette? Oh, yes. Of course.

(DIANA *gets a cigarette, lights one for* ABIR. *They smoke for a moment.*)

ABIR. [I like your hair.] shaArek heloo.

(DIANA *doesn't seem to understand.* ABIR *reaches over, touches* DIANA's *hair lightly.*)

DIANA. Oh! I like your hair. I mean, it's beautiful.

(ABIR *seems to get this. They smoke, and smile at each other appreciatively.*)

Yes? God. I'm afraid they left you with the most illiterate of the bunch... Studied ancient Greek of course. Ancient Greek? "Thalassa! Thalassa!" Which is of course wildly helpful out in the real world.

(*Beat.*)

You. Like. It Here?

ABIR. (*Shy.*) Tosir Wid Loh?

DIANA. What's that—*To Sir With Lov*e? You like that film?

(ABIR *nods.*)

It is rather good, isn't it.

(ABIR *smiles. Emboldened, throws out:*)

ABIR. Julie Christie.

DIANA. You like her? I love her. God, did you see her in *Darling*?

(ABIR *nods.*)

Wasn't she fabulous?

ABIR. Three times.

DIANA. Really? (DIANA *does a bit from the film—Julie Christie, of course, furious:*) "A pound's not enough! A pound's not enough!" (*And another moment:*) "We're not married! At least not to each other!"

ABIR. So good.

(*The men return, each holding newspapers.*)

THEO. It doesn't look good for the Arabs.

(ADHAM *scans the newspaper. It's hard to tell how it's affecting him.*)

ADHAM. It doesn't, does it?

GEORGE. Well, then. They overplayed their hands, didn't they? They had to have known Israel would take their threats seriously.

(THEO *shakes his head to shush* GEORGE. ABIR *has been intently studying* ADHAM.)

ABIR. [What's this?] eish haada?

ADHAM. [News.] akhbaar.

ABIR. [What does it say?] eish tiHkee?

ADHAM. [It's all bad. I'll tell you later.] kulla raheeba. aHkeelik baAdein.

ABIR. [Tell me now.] aHkeeli halla'.

ADHAM. [I can't.] mish aadir.

ABIR. [What's that about Egypt?] eish haada Aan masr?

ADHAM. [The air force. Apparently it's gone.] silaaH aljaww. yabdoo innoo raaH.

ABIR. [In a day? I thought the whole thing was a bluff.] fe yom? ana shakkeit kullu kaan khidAa.

ADHAM. [The bluff got called, apparently.] yabdoo al khidAa inkashfat.

ABIR. [Oh, God.] ya, ilaahi.

ADHAM. [Don't worry.] laa ti'la'ee.

ABIR. [Why shouldn't I? We should go. Find out what's happening.] leish ma'la'sh? laazim nrooH. inshoof eish saar.

ADHAM. [It's all gone to shit! What else do we need to know?] kullu raH lil khara. eish aktar badna naAraf.

> (ABIR, *upset, grabs the paper from* ADHAM, *scours it.*)

THEO. I'm so sorry. I thought you knew.

ADHAM. Not today. We've been preoccupied.

> (*Recovers.*)

The news is always bad. We learn to not jump at every rumor.

DIANA. That's understandable. One hears so many things.

ADHAM. The Israelis have been digging trenches for months, getting ready. But no one thought anything would really happen.

THEO. We can put the wireless on if you want. I'm sure they're still covering it.

ADHAM. No no, not now.

GEORGE. Egypt's jets were parked in the open air. No hangars or sandbags, even. Shocking.

ADHAM. (*Trying to keep panic down.*) Yes, it is.

THEO. I didn't think Israel would move first without getting the green light from Johnson.

GEORGE. That wasn't going to happen. America can't be seen as giving a green light—

THEO. Not explicitly!

DIANA. (*Cutting them off.*) God. It's all so confusing. How can one keep track of any of it?

ADHAM. No one does.

DIANA. That settles it. You have to stay. Couldn't we work something out, with Adham's visa?

GEORGE. I suppose so.

THEO. Would you even want to?

DIANA. Of course they would. Why wouldn't they?

ADHAM. Uh—

ABIR. [What is this a picture of?] soorat eish haadi?

THEO. With the war happening, we could try to get the department heads to push through a fellowship.

ABIR. [Where are these hostages?] fein maHjuzeen?

ADHAM. I wouldn't quite call it a war.

ABIR. [Egypt?] masr?

THEO. The reporters are. Most assuredly.

ADHAM. How long would a fellowship last?

THEO. Depends. Six or seven months?

GEORGE. One term.

ABIR. [Where in Egypt?] wein fee masr haada?

DIANA. At least wait for things to calm down before you go back.

    (ABIR *stands up.*)

ABIR. [Let's go.] yallah.

ADHAM. Well. There's a lot to think about. (*Repeats this to* ABIR, *in Arabic.*) fee kteer lazmoo tafkeer.

ABIR. [You can do that as we walk.] fakker wa iHna mashyeen.

    (ABIR *stands up, looks at* ADHAM: *Time's up.*)

[Let's go.] yallah.

Seven Dials

    Outside. Midnight. It's dark. Panels reveal a London intersection where a large monument stands. ADHAM's *a combination of cocky, drunk and stoned mixed with a rising panic he tries desperately to push down.*

ABIR. I don't recognize this.

ADHAM. We were here yesterday. You don't remember it, civic engineer?

ABIR. It's dark.

ADHAM. Just look.

    (*She looks around: lights, sounds of automobiles…*)

ABIR. We've seen a lot of places.

> (*He steps close to her, puts his hands on her shoulders.*)

ADHAM. Boo!

ABIR. (*Jumps.*) Stop it! That's not funny.

ADHAM. Sorry. (*He turns her slowly, 360 degrees around.*) This will help: One, two, three, four...

ABIR. Seven streets—

ADHAM. —connect here.

ABIR. Seven Dials.

ADHAM. You remember. (*Pointing places out.*) Thieves and prostitutes were over there, pubs were here.

ABIR. Right. He told us that.

ADHAM. So we have options. (*Again, he turns her slowly, showing her each intersection as he does so.*) We can take Monmouth Street, Mercer, Earlham... Monmouth, the other way, Mercer, the other way, Earlham, and—shit. What's the other one? Can you remember?

> (ABIR *shakes her head.* ADHAM *pulls her closer, touches her hair, face.*)

You looked so beautiful today. I saw the way people were looking at you. Did you see the way people were looking at you?

> (*Beat.*)

No. You've been taught not to notice things like that.

ABIR. I noticed.

> (*He laughs.*)

ADHAM. Ha! Shorts Gardens. That's the other street. I knew I'd think of it. Damn I'm good.

> (ADHAM *sits down on the steps in front of the monument, lights a cigarette.*)

Come here.

ABIR. Why?

ADHAM. It's a nice night. Sit for a minute.

ABIR. I don't want to.

ADHAM. Why not?

ABIR. I don't feel safe.

ADHAM. What?

ABIR. Theo said this was a bad area.

ADHAM. During Dickens' time. Not now.

> (ABIR *shrugs.*)

ABIR. Well.

(*Beat. She still doesn't sit down. Something occurs to* ADHAM, *and he laughs, shaking his head.*)

What's so funny?

ADHAM. Nothing.

ABIR. Tell me.

ADHAM. It's wrong. I shouldn't think it.

ABIR. Well now you have to tell me.

ADHAM. Just—Your family was living in the country, the middle of nowhere, and they got pulled out of their house, guns on them, and watched it burn down. But you feel scared here.

ABIR. Don't make light/ of what happened.

ADHAM. I'm not!

ABIR. Don't you dare/ make light of it.

ADHAM. I'm not!

ABIR. You think it's a game. You think everything is a game.

ADHAM. I don't, *habibti!* Not you and me.

(*He springs up, gets close to her, kisses her hard.*)

ABIR. How much alcohol did you drink?

ADHAM. (*Overlap.*) Oh no.

ABIR. (*Overlap.*) How much?

ADHAM. I'm in trouble now. The wife is upset!

ABIR. You're so mean/ tonight.

ADHAM. I'm not mean, my dear—

ABIR. "My dear"? As if I'm your child?

ADHAM. Of course not! I'm being silly. I'm happy. I spoke in front of people. I succeeded. Did you not see that? They listened to me, a foreigner, tell them about their Poet Laureate. What he meant, what he didn't mean, why he used a comma, a semicolon, a dash.

ABIR. I know!

ADHAM. No you don't. Not really. (*Challenging her.*) You barely understood it.

ABIR. I don't speak English! You want an Englishwoman, is that what you want?

(ADHAM's *stunned she even asked, speechless.*)

Do you?

ADHAM. No!—No… I want you. You can't tell? (*Softens, takes her in.*) Habibti.
  (*Beat.*)

They offered me a fellowship.

ABIR. What?

ADHAM. Well, they didn't offer. But they think it can be arranged. It can be pushed through, maybe, they said. There's a lot to work out, but. (*Almost pleading.*) Come sit down. Why are you in such a rush?

ABIR. I want to hear the news.

ADHAM. I told you all of it.

ABIR. On the radio.

ADHAM. Paper, radio, it's all bad. You want specifics? Egypt lost its air force.

ABIR. I want to know what's happening now.

ADHAM. And uh, I'm not sure about Jordan, but I think they fired a few rounds and are making, what do they say in military terms, a hasty retreat? The Arabs lost. We lost. The whole thing's a bust. / But the British are happy. The Americans are happy. No world war. So far.

ABIR. Oh god. What's going to happen now? I can't believe it. There was so much talk/ about the Egyptians being superior.

ADHAM. Yes, yes, talk. Talk talk talk, bullshit bullshit bullshit. It's all bullshit, my dear.

ABIR. You talk like an old man.

ADHAM. That's what I'll be if we go back!

> (*Beat.*)

Please. Listen to me. We have, we have here, I have, this window of opportunity. You see? We should leave, just leave, our so-called lives and stay where we're wanted.

ABIR. We know no one here!

ADHAM. Sometimes that's preferable!

ABIR. You're crazy!

ADHAM. Please, come sit. Just for a minute.

> (*She relents, goes and sits next to him. He puts his arms around her.*)

See? All the world connects here.

> (*He takes her in, caresses her hands…*)

ABIR. If the Israeli army goes into Jerusalem—

ADHAM. They won't. They can't. It's their "holy place." Everyone's "holy place." It's so "holy," they don't want to destroy it.

ABIR. But if they do?

ADHAM. Then the old bat can fend for herself.

ABIR. You talk about your mother this way? At a time like this?

> (ADHAM *shrugs, laughs. Beat as she just watches him.*)

Some of the things you say… You joke now, but one day—

ADHAM. What? God will punish me?

(*Beat.*)

ABIR. Everything she's done, she's done for you! To advance your career!

ADHAM. Everything she's done, she's done for herself! Be careful what you believe, my love.

ABIR. You would leave her there to die?

ADHAM. She's always had a flair for the dramatic.

ABIR. I know you don't mean that.

(*Beat. They look at each other.*)

At least, let's go get her, bring her here/ to live with us!

ADHAM. A man, his wife, and his mother!

ABIR. Everyone lives like that.

ADHAM. Not here! Not here! These are civilized people! Do you not understand that? She doesn't even like you—why plead her case?

(ABIR, *stung, tries to keep her cool.*)

ABIR. I'm thinking only of her safety. You wouldn't be here if not for her. We have to go home and wait for the situation to stabilize.

ADHAM. Stabilize! Stabilize? Where? Where? Where are you talking about? When have we ever known stability, you stupid peasant girl?

(ABIR *is shocked. It's as if he's slapped her.*)

ABIR. You...

ADHAM. Shit.

ABIR. You mean that.

ADHAM. Godamnit.

ABIR. When you look at me. That's what you—

ADHAM. I didn't mean it. I'm drunk, don't listen to me!

ABIR. That's what you think I am? I'm a village girl you rescued, some girl with the smell of shit on her boots—

ADHAM. Okay, okay...

ABIR. —and dirt on her hands, who you get to show the world, is that how you think of me?

ADHAM. No.

(*He tries to comfort her.*)

ABIR. Don't touch me! Don't you ever touch me again!

(*She bursts into tears. Goes. Stunned, he stands, watching her. Long, long beat. He doesn't know what to do with himself. Suddenly looks very lost. He sits. Hands start to shake. Spent, spent, he runs them through his hair...*
On the panels around him, we see a silent film, dated June 6, 1967.)

No sound, a handheld camera, almost a home movie, of bombs going off, civilians running through the streets, soldiers. This is Jerusalem. The War. ADHAM just sits there in these images for a couple minutes. BEDER appears again.)

ADHAM. *(Jumps.)* Oh god, can you go away?

BEDER. Please. I know things are bad, but let's not start invoking god. You look like a beggar.

ADHAM. I walked all over the city today.

BEDER. Boo hoo. In '48, I ran out of the village, you on my back, and we walked for three days.

ADHAM. And now you're a refugee again.

BEDER. *(Finds this funny.)* I never stopped being one. You never stop being one. I've been packed for 20 years.

(She comes toward him, then sits on the steps at the foot of the monument.)

ADHAM. Are you all right?

BEDER. I'm tired. Just tired. Even I get tired sometimes.

(ADHAM studies her face, seems to notice as if for the first time:)

ADHAM. You look old.

(Beat.)

BEDER. "Many rich / Sunk down as in a dream among the poor."

ADHAM. "The Ruined Cottage."

BEDER. He wrote that poem, you know, to show who he would have been if he'd been born under different circumstances. "And of the poor did many cease to be / And their place knew them not."

(Considers, says it again.)

And their place knew them not.

ADHAM. Shall we discuss poetry now, mother? Is that what you want? To talk to your son, the scholar, about Wordsworth?

BEDER. Actually, no. I just want to rest for a while.

ADHAM. Are you all right?

(BEDER just sits there.)

Are you?

(She doesn't look at him. Doesn't answer.)

Will you miss me if I don't come back? Will you?

(She shakes her head no. But she lies as she says:)

BEDER. I've forgotten you already.

THE RUINED COTTAGE

The hotel room. It's very very late. Lights are off. The television is on, volume down—we see the images of the ground war in Jerusalem reflected on ABIR's *face.* ADHAM *enters.*

ADHAM. I was almost hoping I would fail. I was! If I failed, you see, then. Then it's not complicated. I go home, fade into obscurity. No choice. See? Where we come from, we get one chance. You know that right? That's it. We uh, we're not uh, designed for success, we. Arabs. From Palestine. It's—we're good at packing up, and leaving places, and waiting.

ABIR. You let me walk alone.

ADHAM. What was I supposed to do, run after you, like in one of your movies?

ABIR. I can figure these things out on my own if I have to. I studied engineering. I should've stayed an engineer! I should've stayed home with all that was going on. I shouldn't have left my family with a war coming. I was foolish to come.

ADHAM. (*Gently.*) If we stayed every time a war seemed near none of us would ever leave the house.

ABIR. Maybe.

ADHAM. I know I behaved badly.

(*He turns a light on. Sees on the floor a packed suitcase.*)

What's this?

ABIR. I'm leaving.

ADHAM. No, no, no, you're not. It's been a big day, okay? I talk sometimes, I don't know what I'm saying.

ABIR. I think you do.

ADHAM. Why are you doing this?

ABIR. What's "this"?

ADHAM. Packing your bag. Ruining everything for me?

ABIR. I'm leaving you. Don't you understand?

ADHAM. And going where?

ABIR. Home! My home. I tried calling my sister—I couldn't get through. All the lines are down. I don't know where they are.

ADHAM. Chaos. Wherever they are.

ABIR. I have to go back. I want to be with her.

ADHAM. Why? So we can all be refugees together?

ABIR. You don't know that.

ADHAM. So I don't. Maybe everything will turn out fine.

ABIR. I want to be with my family! There's something WRONG with people who don't.

ADHAM. You can't even get near the country—

ABIR. I'll go to the airport, and I'll wait. I can't be with you for another minute.

ADHAM. You're being ridiculous—

ABIR. I am? You're leaving your mother to die, Adham.

ADHAM. She's not dying—

ABIR. What is that? Who does this? I don't understand a man who has no ties! Who are you?

ADHAM. She taught me to be that way! She did! Because there was nothing in her life that wasn't taken away at some point or another. So she taught me to love that way, easy come, easy go.

ABIR. That's love.

ADHAM. That's— .

ABIR. So if I leave you now, just leave, and we, we separate, and get a divorce—

ADHAM. —She's so modern now! Listen to her!—

ABIR. —you would have no feelings about it. Would you? Would your heart break?

ADHAM. ...I don't talk that way. Use phrases like that.

ABIR. I'm asking you. Would you have a broken heart? Because I would.

(*He can't answer. She tries not to cry.*)

Okay. Well. At least I know now. It's only been a month. I have to go back. I was such an idiot to come here.

ADHAM. Just slow down, okay?

ABIR. Too late.

ADHAM. You can't get home now anyway.

ABIR. I don't care. I'll sleep at the Consulate until I get a ticket—

ADHAM. "Sleep at the Consulate"? You're crazy! It's going to get better.

ABIR. What is?

ADHAM. Everything.

(*She looks at him incredulously.*)

ABIR. What, what is everything?

ADHAM. ...My career.

ABIR. (*Stinging him.*) Your "career"? You gave one lecture. That's it.

ADHAM. (*Stung.*) So she can be cruel, too.

ABIR. I never was before.

ADHAM. So I've done good work then. Brought out the best in you.

(ABIR *starts packing again, crying as she does so.*)

Please, stop. It's okay.

ABIR. No it's not.

(*He watches helplessly as she cries.*)

ADHAM. I have no idea what to do.

ABIR. I do.

(*She gets up to leave. He grabs her arm.*)

ADHAM. I didn't say you could walk away!

ABIR. (*Wresting free.*) You don't get to pick and choose your traditions!

(*She goes to the bathroom, comes back with a little makeup bag, puts it in her suitcase, zips it up.*)

ADHAM. Don't tell me I don't love my mother. I LOVE her. She made me everything I am. But I don't need to be with her, you see. It's here— (*Points to his head.*) It's all in here, you see? She made an imprint. I have her. She knows this. And I know this.

ABIR. If you don't come with me now, you may never get to go back. Do you know that, Adham?

(*Beat. From somewhere inside, him, the answer:*)

ADHAM. ...Yes. Yes.

ABIR. Okay.

(*She packs up the last of her things, grabs her suitcase. He gets in front of her.*)

ADHAM. Don't do this. Please.

(*She stands there facing him.*)

You'll regret it.

(*Beat.*)

I don't want you to go.

(*Beat.*)

Come on. Look what you'd be giving up.

(*Beat.*)

ABIR. This feels like Nowhere to me.

ADHAM. (*Half joking?*) Well then it suits me.

(*She shakes her head, grabs her suitcase. He watches her go. Door shuts. He suddenly is completely alone.*)

Okay. Okay...

(*Slowly, without much emotion, ADHAM opens a panel that stretches the length of the room: blankness. Nothing.*

He goes over to the window, looks out. Goes to his desk, straightens his papers.

Does it again. Picks up his book. Goes to the bed. Sits on it. Opens the book. Begins to read. As he does, we see:
ABIR *on one side of the stage, suitcase in hand;* BEDER *on the other, holding cloth sacks, and* ADHAM *in the middle, with nothing.)*

The Ruined Cottage:
"The house-clock struck eight:
I turned and saw her distant a few steps.
Her face was pale and thin, her figure too
Was changed. …
She told me she had lost her elder child.
Today
I have been traveling far, and many days
About the fields I wander, knowing this
Only, that what I seek I cannot find.
And so I waste my time: for I am changed."
For I am changed.

(*As film freezes, so do* ADHAM, ABIR *and* BEDER.)

End of Play

Addendum

Should supertitles be impossible, and no other way of doing live translation presents itself, below is a version of the hotel room scene, entirely in English. This would replace the scene beginning on the bottom of page 389.

> *And she's gone.* ADHAM *lays back down on the bed. Long beat of him alone.* ABIR *enters. Switches on the light. Shocked to see one of the windows still open.*

ABIR. You're laying here letting the rain in? Are you all right?

ADHAM. Sure, sure.

> (*She rushes to close the window.*)

ABIR. I hope it didn't damage anything.

ADHAM. It's a hotel room. They don't care.

> (*She looks at him.*)

ABIR. Why did you go ahead so fast? I looked for you downstairs. The old man—the clerk?—wanted to show me the pictures from when Omar Sharif stayed here. He thought I'd be interested.

ADHAM. (*Sarcastic.*) And you were.

> (ABIR *sees the jacket on the floor, walks to it, picks it up, shakes it out.*)

ABIR. What is it?

ADHAM. Nothing.

> (*She takes the cigarettes out of the pockets and sets them on the desk. Hangs the jacket in the closet, looks at* ADHAM, *who goes to look out the window.*)

ABIR. You're tired. I'll make you a cup of tea.

ADHAM. I don't want anything.

> (*He sulks. She studies him.*)

ABIR. Something's wrong.

ADHAM. Forget it. You're on vacation. You should have a good time!

> (*Beat.*)

ABIR. Okay.

> (*She goes into the bathroom. Stunned,* ADHAM *watches her go. He walks to the desk, grabs a cigarette and lights up. Goes back to the window.* ABIR *comes back out, her hair down.*)

So what is it?

ADHAM. (*Incredulous.*) If you have to ask!

> (*Now she walks over to him. Just stands there, waiting.*)

I looked like a fool. Ridiculous! I failed.

ABIR. Failed? At what?

ADHAM. They looked at me, like, you saw them—"Who is this idiot?" "Why did we bring him here?" "Someone felt sorry for him." Or they assumed I was brought here to show them how smart they are. Either way.

ABIR. No one thought that.

ADHAM. I was an embarrassment. Scrambling for an answer, coming up with mishmosh, nothing.

ABIR. It didn't sound like that!

ADHAM. You don't speak the language, my dear.

ABIR. Some.

ADHAM. Beer. Please. Thank you.

ABIR. I saw them talk to you. They liked you. I wish you could see that.

ADHAM. You should be disgusted with me. I stood in that hall, and looked out... My legs beneath me, they couldn't hold me.
I can't do it. I can't.

ABIR. It was just practice.

ADHAM. I could barely get the words out. You didn't see that?

ABIR. No.

ADHAM. No? (*She shakes her head.*) Well, then let me explain something. Your husband was flailing. I can't believe you couldn't see that! They ask me to defend my point of view, and what do I give them? Theories that took fifteen years to trickle down to us. Old thoughts, old theories. I'm useless.

ABIR. By God, that's not true.

ADHAM. By god, it is! We're backwards! While we've been fighting over this and that scrap of desert, crying over the last assassination, they've been living with the great thoughts. We've wasted so much time.

> (*He looks like he might cry, but he holds it together. She goes to him, touches his back.*)

ABIR. You have a great mind.

> (ADHAM *laughs.*)

ADHAM. Is that right.

ABIR. He said that.

ADHAM. Who?

ABIR. The, uh, Theodore. In Arabic. He said that.

ADHAM. When?

ABIR. When you were practicing.

ADHAM. He said that to you? He just wanted to get close to a beautiful woman.

> (*Beat.*)

416

Flirting. You didn't know he was doing that? Men will say anything to look into a woman's eyes.

ABIR. I don't know. I don't even think of it that way. It doesn't matter. He also said you have a unique scholarly voice.

ADHAM. Because it comes with an accent.

ABIR. I don't know why you've forgotten how smart you are. The man I met—

ADHAM. The man you met!—

ABIR. —Was smart, and sure of himself, and didn't care about what anyone thought.

ADHAM. Well, maybe that wasn't really me. (*He looks at her.*) Maybe this is me.

(*Beat.*)

ABIR. Then I want them both.

(*She reaches for his head, touches it.*)

I can handle both.

(*She takes his hands.*)

Your hands are [shaking].

(*He pulls his hands away. She places her hands on his head, runs her hands through his hair, trying to fix it.*)

I don't know what happens with this hair.

(*He relaxes, just a little. She takes his cigarette from him, smokes, studies him…*)

ADHAM. Wondering what you got yourself into?

ABIR. No.

ADHAM. You lie.

(*She goes and grabs his Wordsworth book.*)

ABIR. Tell me what it says.

ADHAM. You'll be bored.

ABIR. You're so insulting, you know that?

(*She starts reading it.*)

Thus by day…

ADHAM. You want to hear something from the *Preludes*?

ABIR. I don't care. I just want to hear it, coming from your mouth.

ADHAM. Which poem?

ABIR. I don't care.

(*He shrugs. She watches intently. He takes a beat, then reads.*)

ADHAM. "Thus by day / Subjected to the discipline of love—"

ABIR. I like it. More.

ADHAM. "His organs and recipient faculties/Are quickened, are more vigorous."

ABIR. I like this poet. He's not boring.

ADHAM. We don't use such criteria to measure a poet's work.

ABIR. I disagree.

ADHAM. You're not supposed to disagree with your husband.

ABIR. I thought you weren't traditional.

ADHAM. Sometimes I am.

    (ABIR *gives him a look.*)

ABIR. More.

ADHAM. Ordering me about!

ABIR. Go. Just read. Read to me.

ADHAM. "His mind spreads, tenacious of the forms which it receives."

    (*As he finishes reading this last part,* ABIR *moves closer to him.*
    Both of them are on the bed now. She kneels, places her hands on his hipbones.
    Leans in, kisses him there.
    Lights shift: early morning light.)

THE BALLAD OF 423 AND 424
by Nicholas C. Pappas

Copyright © 2012 by Nicholas C. Pappas. All rights reserved. CAUTION: Professionals and amateurs are hereby warned that *The Ballad of 423 and 424* is subject to a royalty. It is fully protected under the copyright laws of the United States of America and of all countries covered by the International Copyright Union (including the Dominion of Canada and the rest of the British Commonwealth), the Berne Convention, the Pan-American Copyright Convention and the Universal Copyright Convention, as well as all countries with which the United States has reciprocal copyright relations. All rights, including professional, amateur stage rights, motion picture, recitation, lecturing, public reading, radio broadcasting, television, video or sound recording, all other forms of mechanical or electronic reproduction, such as CD-ROM, CD-I, information storage and retrieval systems and photocopying, and the rights of translation into foreign languages, are strictly reserved. Particular emphasis is laid upon the matter of readings, permission for which must be secured from the Author's agent in writing.

Required royalties must be paid every time this play is performed before any audience, whether or not it is presented for profit and whether or not admission is charged.

All inquiries concerning rights, including amateur rights, should be addressed to: Nicholas C. Pappas, nick@nicholascpappas.com.

BIOGRAPHY

Nicholas C. Pappas' play, *The Ballad of 423 and 424,* was the recipient of the 2012 Heideman Award as well as a finalist for the National Partners—American Theatre (NAPAT) award in playwriting and the Kennedy Center American College Theater Festival (KCACTF) Ten-Minute Play Award. His plays have been performed in London, Edinburgh, Washington, D.C. (The Kennedy Center), Kentucky (The Humana Festival of New American Plays at Actors Theatre of Louisville), California (San Francisco, Humboldt, Los Angeles), Michigan, Boston, and Vermont. Plays that have received productions include *The Dreams in Which I'm Dying* (reading, dir. Jon Tracy), *The Greatest American Porno, Go Or Go Ahead, The Sonnet Plays,* and *Know Thy Enemy.* He holds B.A.'s in Theatre Arts (Performance) and English (Creative Writing) and an M.F.A. in playwriting, all from San Francisco State University. He is currently working on a graphic novel called *Phinnaeus' Wake.* More information and samples of all his work can be found at nicholascpappas.com.

ACKNOWLEDGMENTS

The Ballad of 423 and 424 premiered at the Humana Festival of New American Plays in March 2012. It was directed by Sarah Rasmussen with the following cast:

RODERICK .... David Barlow
ELLEN.. Kate Eastwood Norris

and the following production staff:

Scenic Designer... Tom Burch
Costume Designer .... Lindsay Chamberlin
Lighting Designer .... Nick Dent
Sound Designer.. Paul Doyle
Properties Designer..Mark Walston
Wig Designer ....Hannah Wold
Production Stage Manager .... Kathy Preher
Dramaturg.. Hannah Rae Montgomery
Casting .... Zan Sawyer-Dailey

Production Manager..Michael Whatley
Production Assistant .... Katie Shade

CHARACTERS

RODERICK, a novelist. His popularity is on the scale of Steven King but his reclusive nature is on the scale of J.D. Salinger. His disorders control all, though he wishes otherwise.

ELLEN, the kind of woman that can put an unknown crying baby to sleep within seconds of it hitting her arms. She is new and exhilarating.

PLAYWRIGHT'S NOTES

The Blackouts:

The blackouts function almost as a rimshot. The scenes often end before the audience expects them to and the blackouts add to the surprise and pace. Use them to your advantage. Now, that being said, the blackout is not a long one. Literally, it should work like this: ending moment of scene, blackout, half a beat, lights up. Keep the pacing up and they will serve you well; long blackouts will equal death. I've been asked if the blackouts can be removed to allow the scenes to morph from one to the other. My response: I'd prefer not.

The Doors:

The Doors are the third character in the play. They add a certain rhythm and pacing. The refrain of the slam can be exciting.

The Hallway:

The hallway can be shaped two different ways: 1) The hallway runs across the stage parallel to the proscenium, the doors facing the audience side by side. 2) The hallway runs perpendicular to the proscenium, the doors facing each other. There are advantages to both. The first way gives space and it becomes a bit easier to stage with more options, but you give up that claustrophobia, the forced closeness that comes with the doors facing each other. I prefer option 2, but I've seen option 1 and it can be done.

Inside the Rooms:

We toyed with freestanding doors, which allowed us to remove the walls and see inside the rooms, giving us a unique perspective into the way the characters live behind closed doors... It failed miserably. Under no circumstance— other than what can be seen spied inside from the open door—should we be able to see inside the rooms.

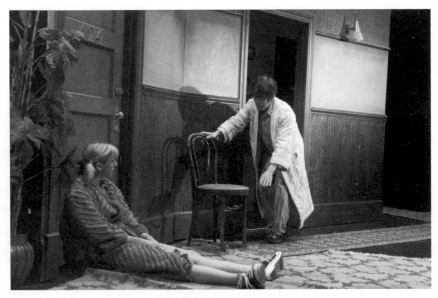

Kate Eastwood Norris and David Barlow
in *The Ballad of 423 and 424*

36th Humana Festival of New American Plays
Actors Theatre of Louisville, 2012
Photo by Alan Simons

THE BALLAD OF 423 AND 424

Based on William Shakespeare's 23rd Sonnet

Scene 1

It's the hallway of an apartment building. We can see two doors on opposite sides of the hall, before the hallway branches off into the bottom part of an L, disappearing into what is assumed to be the elevator doors or staircase. The numbers on the doors read 423 and 424. 423 is closed. 424 is wide open.

We are able to take the scene in for a moment when a woman enters carrying several huge boxes. After a struggle, she eventually gets them in her apartment. A moment passes. The door to 423 opens and a man dressed in pajamas exits, but doesn't quite get the door closed before the woman comes out of her apartment. They stare at each other for a brief moment. She puts her hand out.

ELLEN. Hey neighbor. I'm Ellen.

(A moment passes where she stands, hand out. He does not respond.)

As you can probably tell, I'm moving in.

(Again, nothing. Don't be afraid to let this silence stretch. Minutes, maybe days could pass.)

What's your name?

RODERICK. My name?

ELLEN. Yes.

(Another moment. He slowly reaches his hand towards her. She thinks he is trying to shake, so she reciprocates. He pets her arm. After one full stroke, she jerks her hand back.)

What are you doing?

(It frightens him. An excruciatingly long moment where neither talks; then, quite suddenly, the man darts back into his apartment and slams the door. She is shocked. Blackout.)

Scene 2

Time has passed. Between each scene time passes. Sometimes long stretches like weeks or months, sometimes days, very seldom should it be hours.

ELLEN *is walking down the hall with a few bags of groceries. As she gets to her door,* RODERICK *comes out of his apartment.*

RODERICK. Oh Jesus. You're not the Thai food guy.

ELLEN. Nope.

(*Beat. He stares at her. Halfway between creepy and endearing.*)

ELLEN. How's your day?

RODERICK. I'm hungry.

ELLEN. Explains the Thai food.

RODERICK. I guess.

(*Beat. He's still staring.*)

ELLEN. Oh, um… You didn't happen to see a tall guy, dark hair…beard, probably wearing tight pants…standing around here earlier, did you?

RODERICK. Is he the new delivery guy?

ELLEN. What? No. It's my boyfriend.

RODERICK. You mean he's. Unless you haven't seen his sexual organs, then "it" may be the correct word choice. But then again, you did imply that "it" was male when you said boyfriend, therefore "he's" would be the correct word choice.

(*Beat.*)

That settles it, if you want to be correct, you should have said "he's my boyfriend."

(*Beat.*)

ELLEN. Well. I'm going to go in.

RODERICK. If you see the Thai food guy…

ELLEN. I'll send him your way.

(*He nods yes. Takes one last look, and slams the door on her. She goes into her apartment. Blackout.*)

Scene 3

RODERICK *is standing at the end of the hallway, peering around the corner. He sees something and makes a mad dash to his apartment and closes the door. A moment later,* ELLEN *comes around the corner. As she tries to open the door to her apartment,* RODERICK *comes out from his.*

RODERICK. Hi Ellen.

(*He has said this a little loud. She is startled. She screams. He screams. They look at each other. He goes in and slams his door. Blackout.*)

Scene 4

ELLEN *is standing at her door looking at a bouquet of flowers on her doorstep. She picks them up and reads the card out loud.*

ELLEN. "Sorry for scaring the fucking shit out of you. Roderick."

(*Beat.*)

Who the fuck is Roderick?

(*From behind the closed door of apartment 423:*)

RODERICK. I am.

ELLEN. Oh. (*Beat.*) Thanks.

(*A moment passes without a response. She enters her apartment. Blackout.*)

Scene 5

ELLEN *comes out of her apartment and knocks on 423. A moment passes. She knocks again. From behind the closed door:*

RODERICK. Bark. Bark. Bark. Bark. Bark.

(*She knocks again. He barks again, but this time adds some scratching at his own door.*)

Oh man. You better come back another time. The dogs are going crazy. Bark, bark, bark, bark.

ELLEN. This building doesn't allow pets.

(*Beat.*)

RODERICK. That's what you think.

ELLEN. That's what I know.

RODERICK. Oh.

(*A long beat.*)

ELLEN. Roderick. Would you mind coming out?

(*Another long beat. After what seems like forever, the door opens.*)

RODERICK. I had to put the hounds away.

ELLEN. There aren't any dogs.

RODERICK. They're vicious.

(*Beat.*)

ELLEN. I've been asking about you.

RODERICK. That's silly.

ELLEN. You're interesting.

RODERICK. Sorry.

ELLEN. The super says you're a novelist.

RODERICK. In theory.

ELLEN. Well, do you write novels?

RODERICK. Stories.

ELLEN. You're Roderick Williams? The Roderick Williams.

(Beat.)

RODERICK. Bark, bark, bark, bark, bark, bark, bark. I better check on the dogs. If they got loose, they'd rip your throat out. Then we couldn't have these pleasant conversations in the hall.

(He goes in and slams the door.)

ELLEN. I thought so.

(She turns back to her place. Blackout.)

Scene 6

She is leaving for work. It's quite early in the morning. He opens the door and hands her a travel coffee mug.

RODERICK. Coffee.

ELLEN. You're odd.

RODERICK. Thanks.

(He slams his door. She leaves. Blackout.)

Scene 7

She is coming home from work. When she gets to her door, she drops her stuff on the floor in front of her door. She starts to rummage for her keys. Eventually she gets so frustrated she lays her jacket out, and dumps the entire contents of her purse on the jacket. Shit cascades everywhere. It's obviously been years since she cleaned that bad boy out, and has probably kept every receipt she has received in that amount of time. She starts to pick through it. A moment, then he comes out.

RODERICK. What are you doing?

ELLEN. Hello, Roderick.

RODERICK. You are going to clean all that up, right?

ELLEN. Yes, Roderick.

RODERICK. Good.

(Beat.)

Well?

ELLEN. Well what?

RODERICK. Where is it?

ELLEN. What?

RODERICK. The mug?

ELLEN. The what?

RODERICK. The coffee mug. That I gave you. How am I supposed to give you coffee tomorrow morning if you don't give the mug back?

ELLEN. I left it at work.

(Beat.)

RODERICK. I only have two.

ELLEN. I'm sorry.

(Beat.)

RODERICK. I'll give you my personal mug in the morning. I'll just have to go without coffee tomorrow.

ELLEN. You don't have to do that.

RODERICK. It's what a friend would do. Right?

ELLEN. I guess so.

RODERICK. Okay. It's settled then.

(A very long beat as she continues her search. She starts checking her pockets again.)

What are you doing?

ELLEN. Looking for my keys.

RODERICK. Why?

ELLEN. I can't find them.

RODERICK. Don't you always keep them in your front, right pants pocket?

ELLEN. No.

RODERICK. That's stupid.

ELLEN. Thank you.

RODERICK. No problem.

(Another beat. He reaches out and pats her on the head. She doesn't react negatively.)

Oh, sorry. I forgot.

ELLEN. Forgot what?

RODERICK. You don't like to be pet.

ELLEN. What?

RODERICK. You don't like to be pet.

ELLEN. Why do you think that?

RODERICK. You do like to be pet?

ELLEN. What?— That's not the point. —What makes you— Why do you think I don't like to be pet?

RODERICK. I tried to pet you.

ELLEN. When?

RODERICK. The day you moved in.

ELLEN. Why in the hell would you do that?

RODERICK. When I was little, I wanted to make friends with dogs, but they would always bite at me. My mom said that if I wanted to make friends with dogs I should hold my hand out to them, and let them get comfortable, let them smell me. Then I could pet them, and that would mean we would be friends.

>   (*Beat.*)

ELLEN. Roderick, I'm not a dog.

>   (*A long beat.*)

You can tell the difference, right?

>   (*An even longer beat.*)

The only person who is allowed to pet me is my boyfriend.

RODERICK. Does he like dogs?

ELLEN. I don't think so.

RODERICK. He's not a very nice person then.

>   (*He turns around and goes back into his apartment. Blackout.*)

Scene 8

>   *She is coming back from a run. As she approaches her door she notices a present on her doorstep. She opens it. It's an accordion-style file folder with a note. She reads it.*

ELLEN. To help keep your purse organized so you don't lose your keys and make the hallway a mess again.

>   (*She turns to the door.*)

Thanks.

>   (*From behind his door:*)

RODERICK. Thank you.

>   (*She reacts. Blackout.*)

Scene 9

She again is leaving for work. He opens the door and hands her the mug.

ELLEN. Thanks.

(*He goes inside. She leaves. Blackout.*)

Scene 10

She exits her apartment in a robe, closes her door and walks down the hall. A moment passes. She comes back and goes to her door, tries to open it. It's locked.

ELLEN. Crap.

(*A beat. She thinks a moment and then goes over to 423. She knocks on the door.*)

RODERICK. Bark. Bark. Bark. Bark. Bark. Bark.

ELLEN. Roderick. It's me.

RODERICK. Bark. Bark. Bark. Bark.

ELLEN. Ellen.

RODERICK. Bar— Oh. You should be more specific so as not to get the hounds' hackles all hackled.

ELLEN. Will you please come out?

RODERICK. Maybe.

ELLEN. I need your help.

(*A long moment, then the door opens, just a crack.*)

RODERICK. Yes.

ELLEN. I went out to get the mail, and I've locked myself out.

RODERICK. You don't have mail.

ELLEN. Yes. I forgot my keys inside. Now I can't get into my mailbox or my apartment.

(*He opens the door wider.*)

RODERICK. Want me to use my battering ram to break down your door?

ELLEN. No.

RODERICK. Oh.

ELLEN. I would like to use your phone to call the landlord or maybe a locksmith.

RODERICK. What about your boyfriend?

ELLEN. He won't be around anymore. I don't know. I thought moving out of our old place would give us a chance. You know, time apart. I don't know why, I couldn't really afford it. And it had clearly ended. I don't know, I was just being—

(*He closes the door on her.*)

stupid.

(*Beat. She shakes her head and sits next to her door. She cries. Nothing big. Just some tears.*
A moment, and then, RODERICK *opens his door. He is holding a chair.*)

RODERICK. I called a locksmith. He's on his way.

(*Beat.*)

Why are you sitting on the ground?

ELLEN. You left me.

RODERICK. I had to get you a chair. It might be a while.

ELLEN. Thanks.

(*She takes the chair and sits down. Long pause.*)

RODERICK. You can finish your story if you want. But if you don't mind I'm going to go inside and listen to you through the door.

(*He goes in and closes the door. Beat.*)

Are you still there?

ELLEN. Yes.

RODERICK. Okay. I'm ready.

(*She laughs. Blackout.*)

Scene 11

She is coming home from work. She opens her door and puts the coffee mug on his doorstep. She knocks a rhythmic knock on the door (think "shave and a haircut," but be more creative), and disappears into her apartment, door closed. A moment passes. He opens his door, picks up the mug, closes the door. A moment. And then… Blackout.

Scene 12

It is very late. He comes out of his apartment holding a book and stands in front of her door. He tries to knock, but can't bring himself to do it. He sits on her

doorstep and cries. He stands and tries to knock again. He can't. It's as if she
set up an invisible force field. He turns around and goes back into his apartment.
Blackout.

Scene 13

She is leaving for work. He opens the door and hands her the mug.

ELLEN. How about you come over for dinner sometime?

RODERICK. That's preposterous.

(*He closes the door. She leaves. Blackout.*)

Scene 14

She leaves her apartment holding a plate. She knocks on his door with the same
rhythm she did previously. After a moment, he opens his door.

RODERICK. What? I'm writing.

ELLEN. Sorry.

(*Beat.*)

RODERICK. Why are you looking at me?

ELLEN. It's Easter.

RODERICK. So?

ELLEN. I made Easter dinner.

RODERICK. I don't believe in Jesus. Or God for that matter.

ELLEN. I'm not very religious either. It's just that it's usually a day I spend
with—

RODERICK. Food?

ELLEN. Yes. Food.

(*Beat.*)

I know you don't want to come over for dinner, but I thought you might
want something to eat. It's my first Easter alone, but I made a whole dinner
anyway. I figured you might want.

(*She hands over the plate, he peels back the foil, looks, and hands the plate*
back.)

RODERICK. The mashed potatoes are touching the turkey and the gravy
is on the green bean casserole.

(*He goes back in, slamming the door in her face.*)

She takes a moment, and then knocks.)

RODERICK. What is it? I'm writing.

ELLEN. Why won't you eat my food?

RODERICK. I don't like it when my food touches other food.

ELLEN. What?

RODERICK. I won't eat food that touches other food. How is that not clear.

ELLEN. Is that why you always order Thai and Chinese? Because it comes in separate containers?

(He's embarrassed that she figured him out so fast.)

It all goes to the same place.

RODERICK. I'm not a pig eating scrap.

(Beat.)

ELLEN. You order fried rice.

RODERICK. Yes.

ELLEN. Isn't that rice mixed with egg and vegetables?

RODERICK. It's served like that.

ELLEN. So?

RODERICK. It's meant to be eaten that way.

ELLEN. Oh.

(Beat.)

Well, this is supposed to be served like this. With the gravy on the green bean casserole.

(Beat.)

RODERICK. You're lying.

ELLEN. No. I'm not. This is a family recipe that is supposed to be served like this.

RODERICK. You're being tricky you tricky trickster.

ELLEN. Would I do that?

RODERICK. Most likely.

(Beat.)

Okay. I'll try it.

(He grabs the plate from her hands and closes the door. She smiles. Blackout.)

Scene 15

It's late again. He exits his place holding a book. He practices the rhythmic knock on the air. Mastering it, he goes across and tries to knock. Can't. He leans against the door, face in the crack, and whispers:

RODERICK. Please come out and talk to me.

(*He waits a moment. Goes back to his place. A beat. She comes to the door. Opens it, looks around. Closes the door. Blackout.*)

Scene 16

She is leaving for work. His door doesn't open. She stands there for a few moments. Checks her watch.

ELLEN. Odd.

(*She goes. Blackout.*)

Scene 17

It's late. He opens his door and stands in front of hers. He has a book under his arm. After some time, he tries to knock. He stops. He takes in a very deep breath. He knocks the rhythmic knock. A long time passes before a very sleepy ELLEN *opens the door.*

ELLEN. Roderick? It's so late. What's wrong?

(*No response. It's a long time before anybody speaks.*)

I miss my coffee in the mornings. I've missed you.

(*He holds out a book for her. She takes it and looks it over.*)

It's your book.

(*He grabs it from her. Opens it to a certain page. Hands it back. She reads.*)

For my neighbor Ellen.

(*Beat.*)

You dedicated your book to me?

(*She looks at him.*)

RODERICK. Can I come over for that dinner now?

ELLEN. Come in.

(*He steps toward the door. Stops.*)

RODERICK. Only if we can keep the door open. In case I need to make a quick escape.

ELLEN. Sure.

> (He *steps into the apartment. She follows after. Both doors are open. Fade to* black.)

End of Play

THE DUNGEONS AND
THE DRAGONS
by Kyle John Schmidt

Copyright © 2012 by Kyle John Schmidt. All rights reserved. CAUTION: Professionals and amateurs are hereby warned that *The Dungeons and the Dragons* is subject to a royalty. It is fully protected under the copyright laws of the United States of America and of all countries covered by the International Copyright Union (including the Dominion of Canada and the rest of the British Commonwealth), the Berne Convention, the Pan-American Copyright Convention and the Universal Copyright Convention, as well as all countries with which the United States has reciprocal copyright relations. All rights, including professional, amateur stage rights, motion picture, recitation, lecturing, public reading, radio broadcasting, television, video or sound recording, all other forms of mechanical or electronic reproduction, such as CD-ROM, CD-I, information storage and retrieval systems and photocopying, and the rights of translation into foreign languages, are strictly reserved. Particular emphasis is laid upon the matter of readings, permission for which must be secured from the Author's agent in writing.

Required royalties must be paid every time this play is performed before any audience, whether or not it is presented for profit and whether or not admission is charged.

All inquiries concerning rights, including amateur rights, should be addressed to: Kyle John Schmidt, kylejohnschmidt@yahoo.com.

BIOGRAPHY

Kyle John Schmidt is a writer from Montezuma, Iowa. His plays have been produced by Actors Theatre of Louisville, Crashbox Theatre, the Kid Magicians, Theatre in a Bar, University of Texas New Theatre and the David Mark Cohen New Works Festival. Kyle was the co-winner of the 2010 Heideman Award, a recipient of the Theatre Masters Award, is published by Playscripts, Inc. and is featured in the anthology *The Best American Short Plays 2010-2011*. He received his M.F.A. from the Michener Center for Writers and is an alumnus of the National Theatre Institute and Grinnell College.

ACKNOWLEDGMENTS

The Dungeons and the Dragons premiered at the Humana Festival of New American Plays in March 2012. It was directed by K.J. Sanchez with the following cast:

BRETT	Jordan Brodess
JEAN VERLAINE	Sean Mellott
MARLIN BRICKS	Sarah Grodsky
FELICITY HYDRANGEA KARMIKAL	Trent Stork

and the following production staff:

Scenic Designer	Tom Burch
Costume Designer	Lindsay Chamberlin
Lighting Designer	Nick Dent
Sound Designer	Paul Doyle
Properties Designer	Mark Walston
Wig Designer	Hannah Wold
Production Stage Manager	Kathy Preher
Dramaturg	Hannah Rae Montgomery
Casting	Zan Sawyer-Dailey
Production Manager	Michael Whatley
Production Assistant	Katie Shade

CHARACTERS

BRETT, the Dungeon Master.

FELICITY HYDRANGEA KARMIKAL ONYX WIZARD, a gender ambiguous Destruction Wizard. Wears glittery robes and carries a magic staff. She is the character of a teenage boy who is absolutely fabulous.

JEAN VERLAINE, Elf. Wears a tunic and carries a bow and arrow. He is the character of a teenage boy who thinks he has a +5 literary sensibility and a +2 twink factor.

MARLIN BRICKS, Valkyrie Warrior. Has mithril chainmail and a sword. She is the character of a teenage girl who wants to be tough as nails.

STAGING AND COSTUMES

This play takes place in a magical fantasy world created as the characters play Dungeons and Dragons, the popular role-playing game. The audience does not necessarily see any "real world" business (rolling dice, eating Hot Pockets, etc.) and the actors shouldn't feel like they need to mime these things.

In actuality, the characters of this play live in rural America.

Jordan Brodess, Sarah Grodsky, Sean Mellott
and Trent Stork
in *The Dungeons and the Dragons*

36th Humana Festival of New American Plays
Actors Theatre of Louisville, 2012
Photo by Alan Simons

THE DUNGEONS AND
THE DRAGONS

A blank stage. BRETT *sits to one side. He is the Dungeon Master and controls what happens in the fantasy world.*

BRETT. You come to a village. It's a small place. Only one street. There's an apothecary. A tavern. A blacksmith. A few houses. It's morning but you can't see anyone in the streets. Except. At the end of the street there's a mangy goat tied to a hitching post in front of one of the houses.

(JEAN VERLAINE *enters. He is an Elf.*)

JEAN VERLAINE. Danger check.

BRETT. Roll your dice.

JEAN VERLAINE. Which one?

BRETT. D-20. The twenty-sided one.

JEAN VERLAINE. Eleven.

BRETT. What's your Perception Bonus?

JEAN VERLAINE. Four.

BRETT. You succeed. Jean Verlaine uses his heightened Elven sense and gets a creepy feeling from the direction of the goat.

(MARLIN BRICKS *enters. She is a Valkyrie Warrior.*)

MARLIN BRICKS. I slash off the goat's head with my Flutter Blade.

JEAN VERLAINE. The creepy feeling is near the goat. Not necessarily the goat.

MARLIN BRICKS. We hesitated with those kittens in the Murk Forest and they morphed into Steel Resistant Werepanthers and I got knocked unconscious.

JEAN VERLAINE. Jackie, jeez! That wasn't my fault!

BRETT. A flood of blood ravens swarm from the sky and peck out Jean Verlaine's left eye.

JEAN VERLAINE. Hey! What? Why?

BRETT. Her name is Marlin Bricks. She is a Valkyrie Warrior. You called Marlin Bricks by a non-game name, you lose an eye.

JEAN VERLAINE. I won't look cute with a missing eye.

BRETT. It's the rules.

JEAN VERLAINE. Jean Verlaine is supposed to be cute.

BRETT. Too bad. Jean Verlaine has one eye.

(JEAN VERLAINE *puts an eye-patch over an eye.*)

MARLIN BRICKS. The goat's going to be a monster. Remember the kittens. Brett's a bitchy Dungeon Master.

BRETT. Hey.

MARLIN BRICKS. My character has VD.

BRETT. You used a public toilet.

MARLIN BRICKS. That's not how it works.

BRETT. In this world it is.

MARLIN BRICKS. I slaughter the goat.

JEAN VERLAINE. Let's at least do a magic check.

MARLIN BRICKS. Fine. Where's Felicity?

JEAN VERLAINE. (*Yelling offstage.*) Felicity Hydrangea Karmikal! We need you in the living room.

FELICITY. (*Offstage.*) I'm making HOT POCKETS!

JEAN VERLAINE. You get to do magic.

FELICITY. (*Offstage.*) I'm coming! I'm coming!

(FELICITY HYDRANGEA KARMIKAL *enters grandly. She is a gender-ambiguous Destruction Wizard. With a flourish:*)

Spell Detection!

BRETT. Roll for it.

FELICITY. Sixteen! (*With a bigger flourish.*) Spell Detection!

BRETT. You succeed. Felicity Hydrangea Karmikal Onyx Wizard sends out a Spell Detection and feels magic wielded in the direction of the goat.

FELICITY. Yes! (*A microwave ding offstage.*) Hot Pockets!

(FELICITY *exits.*)

MARLIN BRICKS. I'm killing the goat.

JEAN VERLAINE. What if it's a transmogrified person?

MARLIN BRICKS. It's bait or it's guarding something. Metallurgical check. Fourteen.

BRETT. You succeed. You sense treasure near the goat.

MARLIN BRICKS. See, it's guarding treasure.

(FELICITY *enters.*)

FELICITY. Who's hungry?

JEAN VERLAINE. Oooo. Hot Pockets.

MARLIN BRICKS. I get cheeseburger.

BRETT. It's this one.

JEAN VERLAINE. Ouch hot. What is this, broccoli?

FELICITY. There's a truck that keeps driving by your house.

BRETT. Probably a dumb farmer looking at his field.

FELICITY. At night? You guys know Eric Caves tried to hit my car with his truck when I was leaving school today—

BRETT. Stop talking about it. We heard you already, like fifty times. He wasn't trying to hit your car. He must not have seen you coming out of the parking lot.

FELICITY. He tried to run my car over.

JEAN VERLAINE. Maybe if you didn't have such a flaming hood ornament.

FELICITY. It's not flaming.

MARLIN BRICKS. It's a disco ball.

FELICITY. That's not flaming.

BRETT. Your car might as well be on fire.

FELICITY. Eric Caves has been after me since the year began.

BRETT. You already told us. Fifty times.

JEAN VERLAINE. Stop wearing your Kelly Clarkson shirt to school.

FELICITY. I don't have a Kelly Clarkson shirt. I had a limited-edition Kelly Clarkson signed concert tee that I formerly liked to show off, until Eric Caves burned it with an acid compound in chemistry.

MARLIN BRICKS. Too bad he doesn't know you're actually an Onyx Wizard.

FELICITY. I know! (FELICITY *strikes a magic pose.*) ERIC CAVES! MAGIC MISSILE! METEOR STORM! COLOR SPRAY!

BRETT. Death by magic tranny.

FELICITY. Felicity Hydrangea Karmikal is not a tranny. Onyx Wizards don't have gender.

MARLIN BRICKS. Let's kill the goat and get the treasure.

JEAN VERLAINE. NO! It might be someone.

FELICITY. Looks like that truck stopped on the road.

BRETT. Stop being dramatic.

FELICITY. We should go check outside.

BRETT. If you don't focus on the game, I'll send a swarm of tranny-eating hornets into the village.

FELICITY. I'm not a tranny.

MARLIN BRICKS. Why are you being so safe about a mangy goat?

JEAN VERLAINE. It might be Rimbaud.

MARLIN BRICKS. Who's Rimbaud?

JEAN VERLAINE. Did you not listen to my back story? I'm on this adventure to find my one true love, the youthful Lord Oscar Rimbaud, who was kidnapped after we shared our first tender kiss by the evil Necromancer, Mastigious.

MARLIN BRICKS. We can have lovers? Why don't I get a girlfriend?

JEAN VERLAINE. Because you're the only lesbian in school.

BRETT. A blue metapede burrows out of the ground and gobbles Jean Verlaine's left hand—

JEAN VERLAINE. I meant that in character. Marlin Bricks said she was the only girl at Warrior School.

BRETT. Fine, the metapede was a phantom and you get your hand back.

MARLIN BRICKS. I forgot to tell you, I had a girlfriend and I'm trying to find her.

FELICITY. I think there's people outside.

JEAN VERLAINE. What!?! You're on this adventure 'cause your family was killed by owlbears.

MARLIN BRICKS. I lied. My family's alive and don't know I'm a Warrior. My girlfriend was at Warrior School and, like me, she dressed as a boy to escape detection. But the other Warrior students found out she was a girl because the evil Necromancer, Mastigious, revealed her identity. Now they're all hunting her and I must save her so we can go on hot adventures together.

FELICITY. Brett, I think there's guys outside your house with that truck.

BRETT. It's stupid farmers picking up varmints. They'll go away.

JEAN VERLAINE. You can't steal my back story.

MARLIN BRICKS. No one told me we could have love interests! I won't be the only single hero.

FELICITY. I'm staying single. There's no one in the world awesome enough for Felicity Hydrangea Karmikal Onyx Wizard.

(FELICITY *looks offstage.*)

Can you guys hear that?

BRETT. Suddenly, the party realizes that the sun has set.

JEAN VERLAINE. This conversation has not taken an entire day.

MARLIN BRICKS. The town could be enchanted. How much time do we feel has gone by?

BRETT. A few minutes. The goat starts bleating loudly.

MARLIN BRICKS. I'm approaching the goat, with my Flutter Blade out.

JEAN VERLAINE. I'm following.

BRETT. Felicity, are you following them?

FELICITY. Hold my character, I hear something outside.

(FELICITY *exits.*)

BRETT. You die, it's your own fault, tranny. As the party approaches, you see a shadowy alley near the goat. The goat tries to break its tether to come to you. The bleating gets more desperate.

JEAN VERLAINE. I put my hand on the goat.

MARLIN BRICKS. I don't like this.

BRETT. It licks your hand and nuzzles against your thigh.

MARLIN BRICKS. I'm going to use a Listen check.

BRETT. Roll for it.

JEAN VERLAINE. I'm talking to the goat: Rimbaud?

BRETT. It nibbles at your fingers.

MARLIN BRICKS. Crap. Nine.

BRETT. You succeed. Barely. You hear a scratching.

MARLIN BRICKS. From where?

BRETT. Near Felicity. The shadowy alley.

MARLIN BRICKS. Felicity moves away from the shadows.

BRETT. She can't until she tells me she does.

JEAN VERLAINE. I'm going to kiss the goat.

MARLIN BRICKS. Don't. Felicity!

JEAN VERLAINE. The goat might be under a spell.

BRETT. The scratching sounds like a ripping.

MARLIN BRICKS. Felicity! You need to move! Come back!

JEAN VERLAINE. I kiss the goat.

BRETT. Nothing happens.

JEAN VERLAINE. Dammit.

BRETT. The ripping becomes a rumbling.

MARLIN BRICKS. I stab into the shadows with my Flutter Blade.

BRETT. Roll for it.

MARLIN BRICKS. Dammit. Three.

BRETT. Major fail. You move to fight, but trip over the goat and fall. But it's too late! Out of the shadows, acid goblins leap upon Felicity, they spit in her face, eat off her shimmering gown, and tear her head clear off her shoulders. The acid goblins scurry back into the shadows from whence they arrived.

JEAN VERLAINE. I douse her in Revive Potion.

BRETT. Too late. Felicity Hydrangea Karmikal Onyx Wizard is dead by acid goblins.

> (FELICITY *enters wearing his normal clothes and holding a broken disco ball hood ornament.*)

JEAN VERLAINE. Felicity. You're dead.

MARLIN BRICKS. I'm running after the goblins.

JEAN VERLAINE. I'm following her with the goat.

FELICITY. Stop playing.

BRETT. The goat won't move.

JEAN VERLAINE. Can I pick it up?

MARLIN BRICKS. Just leave it.

BRETT. Roll for strength.

FELICITY. STOP PLAYING!

(*Pause.*)

JEAN VERLAINE. What happened to your disco ball?

FELICITY. I told you there were guys outside.

BRETT. Stupid farmers.

FELICITY. It wasn't stupid farmers. Farmers wouldn't smash up my car. Now I'm dead.

BRETT. You can roll a new character.

FELICITY. Not the game, asshole. The front of my car's all kicked-in and my dad's going to kill me. Don't worry, they didn't do anything to your cars. Just mine. They drove all the way out here for me.

MARLIN BRICKS. They can't do this. Let's go after 'em.

FELICITY. Are you going to bring your Flutter Blade?

JEAN VERLAINE. Don't be an ass.

FELICITY. Maybe you should've done something instead of hiding here playing pretend.

BRETT. You wanna make a new character? Felicity Part Two?

FELICITY. No. I quit.

JEAN VERLAINE. Don't you wanna see how it turns out?

FELICITY. Shitty and ruined. That's how everything turns out. Shitty and ruined.

BRETT. Suddenly, morning breaks over the town. But it feels like no time's gone by. A spell has been broken.

FELICITY. See you at school.

(FELICITY *exits.*)

BRETT. Someone steps out of the alley. Someone who looks exactly like Felicity Hydrangea Karmikal.

JEAN VERLAINE & MARLIN BRICKS. What?

FELICITY. (*Re-entering wearing her robes:*) What?!!?

BRETT. The dead body you thought was Felicity is actually Felicity's evil twin…the Necromancer Mastigious! He has been impersonating Felicity this whole time!

FELICITY. That doesn't even make sense.

BRETT. I thought you went home. Jean Verlaine turns to see that the goat has been transformed into—

JEAN VERLAINE. The youthful Lord Oscar Rimbaud?

BRETT. Yes.

JEAN VERLAINE. Are you serious? Rimbaud!

FELICITY. It's not real.

MARLIN BRICKS. What about me?

BRETT. Marlin Bricks realizes she never hit the ground when she tripped into the shadows. She was caught by two familiar arms. She peers up and finds—

MARLIN BRICKS. Her lost warrior princess.

BRETT. Alive and strong.

MARLIN BRICKS. And totally hot.

FELICITY. Like that would really happen.

BRETT. And all of our heroes live on for greater adventures. The end.

JEAN VERLAINE. Awesome adventure.

MARLIN BRICKS. Yeah, that was fantastic.

FELICITY. Brett! You can't end it. You never said what happens to me.

BRETT. You said you quit.

FELICITY. I did, stupid. But obviously, I came back.

BRETT. Well, too bad, it's over.

FELICITY. No! Sit down! I want an ending. Let me have a good ending!

BRETT. I yield the story to Felicity Hydrangea Karmikal Onyx Wizard.

FELICITY. I'm about to fly to my palace made of feathers. But then something catches my eye. On that Mastigious guy's body is a silver pouch encrusted with jewels. And it's filled with a super-powerful powder that grants wishes.

(FELICITY *looks at the broken disco ball. A trickle of glitter pours out.*)

I wish for a wonderful world of gowns and gems, where everything's grand and everyone's nice, where Felicity Hydrangea Karmikal can cast fantastic spells with other wizards of might and magic. And where everyone—everyone—is as awesome as she is.

(FELICITY *empties the glitter from the disco ball onto the floor. Then, a drizzle of glitter falls from the sky. And, for a moment, the world truly is beautiful.*)

End of Play

OH, GASTRONOMY!
by Michael Golamco, Carson Kreitzer,
Steve Moulds, Tanya Saracho and Matt Schatz

Copyright © 2012 by Michael Golamco, Carson Kreitzer, Steve Moulds, Tanya Saracho and Matt Schatz. All rights reserved. CAUTION: Professionals and amateurs are hereby warned that *Oh, Gastronomy!* is subject to a royalty. It is fully protected under the copyright laws of the United States of America and of all countries covered by the International Copyright Union (including the Dominion of Canada and the rest of the British Commonwealth), the Berne Convention, the Pan-American Copyright Convention and the Universal Copyright Convention, as well as all countries with which the United States has reciprocal copyright relations. All rights, including professional, amateur stage rights, motion picture, recitation, lecturing, public reading, radio broadcasting, television, video or sound recording, all other forms of mechanical or electronic reproduction, such as CD-ROM, CD-I, information storage and retrieval systems and photocopying, and the rights of translation into foreign languages, are strictly reserved. Particular emphasis is laid upon the matter of readings, permission for which must be secured from the Author's agent in writing.

Required royalties must be paid every time this play is performed before any audience, whether or not it is presented for profit and whether or not admission is charged.

All inquiries concerning rights to produce *Oh, Gastronomy!* in its entirety, including amateur rights, should be addressed to: Bret Adams Ltd., 448 West 44th St, New York, NY 10036, ATTN: Mark Orsini. 212-765-5630.

Inquiries concerning rights for individual scenes or monologues, including amateur rights, should be addressed to:

For Michael Golamco: Creative Artists Agency, 162 5th Ave., 6th Floor, New York, NY 10010, ATTN: Corinne Hayoun. 212-277-9000.

For Carson Kreitzer: Bret Adams, Ltd., 448 West 44th St, New York, NY 10036, ATTN: Mark Orsini and Bruce Ostler. 212-765-5630.

For Steve Moulds: stevemoulds@yahoo.com

For Tanya Saracho: Bret Adams, Ltd., 448 West 44th St, New York, NY 10036, ATTN: Mark Orsini. 212-765-5630.

For Matt Schatz: Paradigm Talent Agency, 360 Park Avenue South, 16th Floor, New York, NY 10010, ATTN: Jonathan Mills. 212-897-6400.

ABOUT *OH, GASTRONOMY!*

This article first ran in the January/February 2012 issue of Inside Actors, *Actors Theatre of Louisville's subscriber newsletter, before rehearsals for the Humana Festival production began.*

"I can reason down or deny everything, except this perpetual Belly: feed he must and will, and I cannot make him respectable."
—*Ralph Waldo Emerson*

"There is no sincerer love than the love of food."
—*George Bernard Shaw*

"Give me liberty or… OOOooo… A jelly donut!"
—*Homer Simpson*

Whoever you are and however you live, food is a great unifier; everybody eats. Speaking historically, food offers one of the most important lenses through which to understand world civilizations. Within families and communities, food is identity: it figures into many significant ritual expressions of culture and tradition. The table is a gathering place, around which people congregate to tell stories and endure awkward silences, settle business and make peace—not to mention to just plain relish the pleasures of really delicious fare.

The subject of food, in all its glorious complexity, forms the jumping-off point for *Oh, Gastronomy!* Every year, Actors Theatre of Louisville commissions a group of playwrights—this year they were Michael Golamco, Carson Kreitzer, Steve Moulds, Tanya Saracho and Matt Schatz—to collaborate on a new piece for our Acting Apprentice Company to perform in the Humana Festival of New American Plays. Now in its 40th year, the Acting Apprentice Company consists of 22 talented young actors who spend a season training at the theatre. In addition to honing their craft in master classes with local and visiting artists, these industrious performers appear in plays in the theatre's mainstage season, as well as their own series of projects. They also spend most weekday afternoons assisting in departments throughout the theatre and, significantly, comprise the run crew for all season and Humana Festival productions. For the Apprentices, *Oh, Gastronomy!* represents an opportunity to celebrate months of hard work and artistic growth, and to showcase their talent for the local community and our industry guests.

The playwrights came on board in the summer of 2011, and began sharing their culinary experiences with one another by email. These early conversations ranged from a discussion of food-related phobias to points of good-natured epicurean snobbery, and from vivid childhood memories to cherished gastronomical fantasies. In September, appetites whetted, they journeyed to Louisville to meet the Apprentices and director Amy Attaway. Over the course of an action-packed three-day workshop, the writers and actors traded stories and compared recipes before venturing out into the community to perform "field research"—speaking with growers, preparers and enjoyers of food all over Louisville. (Warning: Many calories have been consumed in the preparation of this play.) Scattering to explore their inspirations and begin writing, the authors returned for a second workshop in December, drafts in tow, to share and further develop their contributions to the cause.

Even the briefest reflection on the topic tends to remind one how scant are the areas of life in which food exerts no influence. Eating is necessary for survival, sure—but for people all over the world, it's also a favorite recreational activity. Food figures heavily into most people's dating repertoires (and their weathering-the-break-up routines), adds zest to the celebration of important milestones, and offers one of the most reliably comforting manifestations of our love for one other. Of course, its very primacy in our lives gives rise to certain unavoidable contradictions: plenty here can imply scarcity there. So to talk about food is to speak of both nourishment and deprivation, indulgence and self-denial (or punishment), abundance and the lack of it.

Oh, Gastronomy! combines these ingredients in a robust dramatic stew, exploring food's complexities while celebrating its most enduring pleasures. From a sweet behind-the-counter food truck romance to a fierce showdown at the farmers' market, and from a lost school lunch to a family feast of epic proportions, Golamco, Kreitzer, Moulds, Saracho and Schatz have chronicled the many various relationships we humans have to the stuff we eat with gusto (and, in composer and lyricist Matt Schatz's case, with song). Light yet filling and best enjoyed at odd hours, this play is delicious, nutritious, and was not processed in a facility containing nuts. Leave room in your theatrical tummy and get ready to dig in!

—Sarah Lunnie

BIOGRAPHIES

Michael Golamco is a Los Angeles-based playwright and screenwriter. His play *Year Zero* received acclaimed runs at Second Stage in New York City and Victory Gardens Theater in Chicago; his latest play, *Build,* is set for a world premiere at the Geffen Playhouse in Los Angeles. His play *Cowboy Versus Samurai* has had several productions since its premiere in New York, including in Canada and Hong Kong. Golamco is the recipient of the 2009 Helen Merrill Award and is a member of New Dramatists. He is currently working on new play commissions for South Coast Repertory and Second Stage.

Carson Kreitzer's plays include *Behind the Eye*, *1:23* and *The Love Song of J. Robert Oppenheimer,* all of which premiered at the Cincinnati Playhouse in the Park, directed by Mark Wing-Davey. Other work includes *The Slow Drag* (The American Place Theater, The Whitehall Theater, West End) and *SELF DEFENSE or death of some salesmen* (New Georges). Grants: National Endowment for the Arts New Play Development Program, New York Foundation for the Arts, New York State Council on the Arts, Theatre Communications Group, Jerome and McKnight Foundations, Loewe Award in Music-Theatre and the first Playwrights Of New York (PONY) Fellowship through the Lark Play Development Center. Kreitzer is a resident playwright at New Dramatists and a member of The Workhaus Collective and The Playwrights' Center. She is currently writing a play for Marin Theatre and a musical with Matt Gould for Yale Repertory Theatre. More information at www.carsonkreitzer.com.

Steve Moulds is a writer living in Los Angeles. Productions of his plays include an adaptation of Pirandello's *Six Characters in Search of an Author* for The Hypocrites (Chicago), which received a Jeff nomination for Best New Adaptation; *Emergency Prom* (University of Texas at Austin), published by Playscripts; *Oh, Gastronomy!,* a group-written anthology play (Humana Festival of New American Plays); *Compound/Complex* (the Brouhaha Comedy Festival); *Von Rollo* (Illusion Theater, Minneapolis); *Principles of Dramatic Writing* (Source Festival, named "Best of the Ten-Minute Fest"); and three plays in the Minnesota Fringe Festival—*Killer Smile, Buyer's Remorse,* and *See You Next Tuesday.* Steve has also seen three of his ten-minute plays produced at Actors Theatre of Louisville, including *Commodity* (published by Samuel French). Moulds has worked for Actors Theatre of Louisville, The Playwrights' Center in Minneapolis, and History Theatre in Saint Paul, and spent a year in Denver as the National New Play Network Playwright in Residence at Curious Theatre Company. Moulds holds an M.F.A. in playwriting from the Michener Center for Writers at the University of Texas at Austin.

Tanya Saracho is a native of Sinaloa, Mexico. Named "Best New Playwright" by *Chicago* magazine, she is a new Ensemble Member at Victory Gardens Theater, a resident playwright emerita at Chicago Dramatists, a Goodman Theatre Fellow at the Ellen Stone Belic Institute for the Study of Women and Gender in the Arts and Media at Columbia College Chicago, founder and co-director of ALTA and co-founder and former Artistic Director of Teatro Luna. Her plays have been seen at the Goodman Theatre, Mo'olelo Theater, Steppenwolf Theatre Company, Teatro Vista, Teatro Luna, the Fountain Theatre, Clubbed Thumb, Next Theatre Company, 16th Street Theater, and Oregon Shakepseare Festival. Her plays include *Enfrascada, El Nogalar, The House On Mango Street* (adaptation), *Our Lady Of The Underpass, Surface Day, Kita Y Fernanda, Quita Mitos, Song for the Disappeared,* and *The Tenth Muse.* Saracho is a winner of the Ofner Prize, a recipient of an NEA Distinguished New Play Development Project Grant and a 3Arts Artists Award. Saracho is a member of SAG/AFTRA and the Writers' Guild of America. Currently, she writes for the Lifetime series *Devious Maids.*

Matt Schatz won the 2012 Kleban Prize for Most Promising Musical Theatre Librettist for *Love Trapezoid* (workshop production with the Astoria Performing Arts Center, 2012). Also a playwright, lyricist, composer and screenwriter, Schatz's other works include the musical *Georama* with West Hyler and Jack Herrick (workshop with the Great River Shakespeare Festival, 2012), and the play *The Tallest Building in the World* (Luna Stage, 2011). Short musicals include *Richie Farmer Will Have His Revenge on Durham* with Diana Grisanti ("Best of Fest" at Austin's FronteraFest, 2011), and *Roanoke* with Michael Lew (Humana Festival 2009, Heideman Award Finalist). Schatz has received three commissions from the Ensemble Studio Theatre/Sloan Project, has been a finalist and twice a semi-finalist for the P73 Playwriting Fellowship, and was a finalist for the 2009 Fred Ebb Award for excellence in musical theatre songwriting (with composer Dina Pruzhansky). Member: ASCAP, the BMI Advanced Musical Theatre Workshop, the Dramatists Guild and EST. Alumnus: Youngblood and Interstate 73 writers groups (2009, 2012). M.F.A., Carnegie Mellon University. Schatz is currently working on a number of musical and non-musical projects for the stage and screen, including an original hip hop musical about a 1988 slam dunk contest. Mattschatz.com

ACKNOWLEDGMENTS

Oh, Gastronomy! premiered at the Humana Festival of New American Plays in March 2012. It was directed by Amy Attaway, and conceived and developed with Sarah Lunnie, with the following cast:

On Your Mark, Get Set, Eat! by Matt Schatz
COMPETITOR 1.. Daniel Kopystanski
HOST..Nick Vannoy
HOSTESS ....Erika Diehl
OTHER COMPETITORS...............................J. Alexander Coe,
Jonathan Finnegan, Alexander Kirby,
Liz Malarkey, Katie Medford,
Maggie Raymond, Trent Stork

Ingredients, The Mix and *First Taste* by Steve Moulds
MASTER BAKER... Calvin Smith
APPRENTICE ....Zoë Sophia Garcia

Fear and Loathing at the Food Truck by Carson Kreitzer
ADRIAN .... Marianna McClellan
JEANNINE.. Maggie Raymond
LANA...Rivka Borek
JIMMY .... Sean Mellott
DAVE..Jonathan Finnegan
FARMER ....Nick Vannoy

The Family Feast by Steve Moulds
SALLY ....Lisa Dring
MARY.. Sabrina Conti

Artisanal Foods Anonymous by Steve Moulds
CHARLES.. Doug Harris
DOROTHY..Kanomé Jones
JACK...Keaton Schmidt
RANDOM ATTENDEE............................ Amir Wachterman
ATTENDEES .... Erika Diehl, Zoë Sophia Garcia,
Marianna McClellan, Nick Vannoy

Code Fries by Tanya Saracho
GRRL..Trent Stork
ROOMMATE .... Sabrina Conti

The Game by Carson Kreitzer
ONE.. Alex Coe
TWO ....Keaton Schmidt
THREE.. Liz Malarkey
FOUR...Alex Kirby
FIVE.. Amir Wachterman

ORDERING: Memories, Eat What You Kill and *Free Lunch*
by Michael Golamco
RICK..Chris Reid
ZELDA ....Lisa Dring
POE/ZACK .... Sean Mellott
HERB .... Daniel Kopystanski
CHLOE..Rivka Borek
MACK...Chris Reid
DENNIS ....Keaton Schmidt
WAITER .... Amir Wachterman

Tastes Like Home by Matt Schatz
WOMAN... Katie Medford
MAN ....Alexander Kirby
THE BAND .... J. Alexander Coe,
                    Jonathan Finnegan, Liz Malarkey

In The Line by Tanya Saracho
IAN ....Chris Reid
ANNIE...Zoë Sophia Garcia

My Mom Won't Let Me Eat That by Michael Golamco
BILLY .... Daniel Kopystanski
MRS. SHRIVER... Katie Medford

Banana Girl by Tanya Saracho
BANANA GIRL ....Lisa Dring
JAY ....J. Alexander Coe
CO-WORKER..Kanomé Jones
CO-WORKER 2.. Sabrina Conti
MALE CO-WORKER...Nick Vannoy

A Numbers Game by Tanya Saracho
ONE... Liz Malarkey
TWO .... Katie Medford
THREE ....Nick Vannoy

How Do You Know? by Matt Schatz
GIRL...Erika Diehl

Tomatoes by Carson Kreitzer
FARMER..Nick Vannoy
WOMAN.. Maggie Raymond
GIRL..Kanomé Jones

C.S.A. Battle by Matt Schatz
FEMALE FARMER... Liz Malarkey
MALE FARMER...Trent Stork
PATRON 1...Lisa Dring
PATRON 2.. Katie Medford
PATRONS.......J. Alexander Coe, Sabrina Conti, Erika Diehl,
 Jonathan Finnegan, Zoë Sophia Garcia, Doug Harris,
 Alexander Kirby, Daniel Kopystanski, Calvin Smith

Last Supper by Michael Golamco
SAMANTHA..Erika Diehl
GIL... Doug Harris
CHRIS ....Alexander Kirby

and the following production staff:
Scenic Designer..Tom Burch
Costume Designer .... Lindsay Chamberlin
Lighting Designer..Brian J. Lilienthal
Sound Designer.. Paul Doyle
Wig Designer ....Hannah Wold
Music Director...Scott Anthony
Properties Designer...Mark Walston
Stage Manager .... Travis Harty
Dramaturg...Sarah Lunnie

Assistant Directors .... Lillian Meredith,
 Caitlin Ryan O'Connell
Assistant Lighting Designer...................Rachel Fae Szymanski
Assistant Dramaturgs..... Molly Clasen, Dominic Finocchiaro
Production Manager..Michael Whatley

Oh, Gastronomy! was commissioned and developed by Actors Theatre of
Louisville.

Calvin Smith and Zoë Sophia Garcia
in *Oh, Gastronomy!*

36th Humana Festival of New American Plays
Actors Theatre of Louisville, 2012
Photo by Alan Simons

OH, GASTRONOMY!

ON YOUR MARK, GET SET, EAT!
by Matt Schatz

The stage is empty.
Music begins to play. A riff on a guitar or a piano.
COMPETITOR 1 enters and sings "I Am Good At Eating A Lot."

COMPETITOR 1. MY MOTHER IS A GOOD LITTLE COOK
MY BROTHER IS A GOOD LITTLE CROOK
MY SISTER'S GOT A GOOD OUTSIDE SHOT
WELL, I AM GOOD AT EATING A LOT

(A HOST enters with a microphone. Or it could just be a voice coming from a speaker.)

HOST. Ladies and gentleman welcome to the Derby Pie Derby. Louisville's very own derby pie-eating competition.

(The music builds. Either in the arrangement, or with additional instruments joining in.
The COMPETITORS enter.)

COMPETITOR 2. IN PHILLY I ATE EIGHTEEN CHEESESTEAKS

COMPETITOR 3. IN BROOKLYN I ATE THREE WHOLE CHEESECAKES

COMPETITOR 4. AT THE CHILI EAT-OFF I CLEANED EVERY POT

ALL COMPETITORS. I AM GOOD AT EATING A LOT

(The music continues to build. Maybe something percussive is beginning to happen. More COMPETITORS could enter here.)

HOST. These talented competitors have traveled from all over the world to be with us today each of them will be vying for a $10,000 grand prize.

(All of the COMPETITORS have lined up to eat.)

HALF OF THE COMPETITORS. OHHHH
YOU CAN GET CLOSE TO YOUR DREAMS

THE OTHER HALF. IT ISN'T AS GROSS AS IT SEEMS

THE FIRST HALF. YOU CAN GET CLOSE TO YOUR DREAMS

ALL COMPETITORS. YOUR DREAMS

HOST. When the whistle blows, each competitor will have fifteen minutes to eat as many slices of derby pie as they can.

(*Here the arrangement is stripped down. Just the guitar or piano. Whatever started us off. Held chords.*)

COMPETITOR 1. MY DAD SAID WE ALL HAVE A GIFT
BUT I ALWAYS THOUGHT I WAS GIVEN SHORT SHRIFT

(*The full musical arrangement kicks in.*)

UNTIL OKTOBERFEST
WHERE I ATE EVERY BRAT

THE FIRST HALF. I AM GOOD AT EATING A LOT
I AM GOOD AT EATING A LOT
I AM GOOD AT EATING A LOT
I AM GOOD AT EATING A LOT

THE OTHER HALF. (*Over the above in harmony and in unison.*)
OHHHHH
YOU CAN GET CLOSE TO YOUR DREAMS
IT ISN'T AS GROSS AS IT SEEMS
YOU CAN GET CLOSE TO YOUR DREAMS
YOUR DREAMS

(*And* EVERYBODY *is just singing and playing and harmonizing and scatting and rapping and beatboxing and dancing and it has built to whatever it's going to be built to. And maybe the pies have been set out in front of all the competitors or maybe not.*)

ALL COMPETITORS. I AM GOOD AT EATING A LOT

HOST. On your mark, get set, eat!

(*The whistle blows. The music stops. Blackout.*)

INGREDIENTS
by Steve Moulds

A table. No chairs. The MASTER BAKER *waits.*

An eager APPRENTICE *enters carrying a bag of groceries. Whatever's in there, she didn't buy from a chain grocery store.*

The APPRENTICE *sets her bag down, and immediately starts to remove items.*

MASTER BAKER. Eh-eh-eh, not yet. Just 'cause it's our last class, you can't just start baking. We need to review our principles.

(The APPRENTICE *stops. She's used to this routine by now.)*

One: It don't matter how nice a dish looks. Catchy name, fancy presentation…

(He makes a dismissive noise. She makes it with him.)

A little powdered sugar never put a cookie over the top. Two: The fundamental measurement of any dessert is the journey it takes from taste bud to tummy.

Now number two leads us directly to number three: You never start with taste. You start with its components. Which means you gotta analyze. Break it down, flavor by flavor, each individual sensation. When done right, cuisine is a molecular pursuit.

(The APPRENTICE *has been following along. From time to time, she mimics his gestures precisely.)*

I get the sense you're not really listening.

(To prove that she is, the APPRENTICE *produces a small pad, where she has written all his principles. She shows it to him.)*

You didn't need to write 'em down. They're simple because they're true.

(He hands her back the pad.)

What might be nice is hearing you offer some wisdom for a change. You know, say a few words. Any words.

(She remains silent. Resigned, he continues.)

Why start now? Okay. You wanted our last lesson to be brownies, let's see your ingredients.

(The APPRENTICE *pulls out a box of instant brownie mix.)*

Yes yes, very clever. You've been waiting to make that joke, haven't you?

(The APPRENTICE *smiles, sets the box aside. One by one, she pulls the real ingredients out of the bag. As she does so, the* MASTER BAKER *comments.)*

Good. You went low-protein flour. That's good.

That's a…serviceable sugar. Not my favorite, but okay.

Vanilla, good, cocoa, good…

English butter, huh? So you weren't entirely undiscriminating. I like that.

You got some surprises left in you. That's good in a student.

(*The* MASTER BAKER *stops for a minute.*)

You decided to go with the Ghirardelli Bittersweet, huh? You realize that the chocolate basically forms the backbone of the brownie experience. You feel confident about this selection?

(*The* APPRENTICE *isn't sure how to respond.*)

I'm just messing with you. Ghirardelli's fine. People swear by their Callebaut, but most palates can't tell the difference. Plus you saved money.

Remember: You're not always looking for the best. You do what works now with what's available today. Anyone who says there's one right answer never spent no time in a kitchen.

(*The* APPRENTICE *nods. She's heard that before too.*
Finally, one last ingredient.)

Now <u>this</u> is interesting. You want to justify this?

(*The* MASTER BAKER *pulls out a bottle of Maker's Mark.*)

You said you wanted to make brownies. You didn't say anything about putting bourbon in them.

(*He leans in.*)

You got something you wanna tell me?

(*No.*)

I knew it. You got some surprises left.

FEAR AND LOATHING AT THE FOOD TRUCK
by Carson Kreitzer

Part One: Now

Two girls inside a gourmet ice cream truck, parked at a farmers market. There is barely room for both of them in there. Bumping, elbowing, near head-bashing… it would be much more comfortable with one.
ADRIAN *is training* JEANNINE. ADRIAN *is over it.* JEANNINE *is super-excited to be learning the ropes.*
Next to the truck is a farm stand/table, where LANA *sells microgreens. With a hand-lettered sign, with "micro" written really tiny: micro*GREENS.

ADRIAN. (*Rattling off instructions.*) …and make sure you tell them all our ingredients are locally sourced—

JEANNINE. (*Excited.*) all our ingredients are locally sourced?

ADRIAN. —to the extent they can be. With the exception of the vanilla, from Madagascar, the tropical nuts in the Tropical Nut Brittle, the cocoa and cocoa nibs, which are all fair trade certified, and the hazelnut in the Gianduja—

JEANNINE. (*Trying to follow, a little daunted.*) Tropical nuts?

ADRIAN. Which is of course imported from Italy. Cos what, are we gonna use Kentucky Hazelnuts in the signature confection of the Piedmontese, when we could get the actual nuts from Turin? (*She finds this funny.*) Coconut and Brazil nut.

JEANNINE. What?

ADRIAN. In the Tropical Nut Brittle. Have you tried it yet?

JEANNINE. No, I've only sampled a few of the—

> (ADRIAN *has already opened the aluminum freezer hatch, and reached in with a sample-spoon, which she shoves at* JEANNINE.)

ADRIAN. Here—

> (*Slams hatch shut.*)

JEANNINE. Oh, I, thanks—

> (JEANNINE *tastes the ice cream.*)

ADRIAN. You've got to become conversant with all our flavors, be able to describe them in detail when asked, not only about the sourcing but of course the specific flavor profiles of all the ingredients—

> (JEANNINE *is having a flavor epiphany. Her face records about five different reactions.*)

JEANNINE. Oh… wow…

ADRIAN. Yeah, not like that.

JEANNINE. It's…amazing. It's like—

ADRIAN. (*For a minute, remembering that this is actually an awesome job.*) Yeah, isn't it?

JEANNINE. Like I'm on a Tropical Island, caressed by lazy salt-air breezes—

ADRIAN. The Brazil nuts are toasted with a hint of sea salt, which gives it a more complex—

JEANNINE. And Vanilla—

ADRIAN. Madagascar. Really makes a difference.

JEANNINE. Vanilla…angels are singing…with rainbows emanating from their fingertips—

(ADRIAN *stares at her.*)

and little crunchy, buttery Tropical Nut Cherubs frolicking at their feet…

(JEANNINE *becomes self-conscious.*)

LANA. (*Sales-pitch singsong.*) MICROgreens. Teeny, tiny, little ARUGULA!

ADRIAN. Maybe we can get you a list of

JEANNINE. yes

ADRIAN. official descriptions of the flavors, cos

JEANNINE. sorry

ADRIAN. that is really not going to help anyone.

LANA. Tiny tarragon.
Baby romaine
Itsy bitsy oak leaf
Shiso

(*Observing the greens closely.*)

The cutest little shiso you've ever seen!

ADRIAN. And obviously you know how to run a cash drawer—

JEANNINE. Yes, yes I—

ADRIAN. Cos they wouldn't have *sent* me someone who didn't know how to run a *cash drawer.*

JEANNINE. (*Trying too hard.*) I have extensive retail experience!

ADRIAN. (*Looks at her, appraising.*) Fine. Show me.

JEANNINE. What do you want me to—?

ADRIAN. (*Nods to an approaching customer.*) Him.

(JIMMY *approaches. A little shifty.*)

JIMMY. Do you sell *snow cones?*

JEANNINE. All our flavors are listed on the chalkboard. Our ingredients are locally sourced, to the best of our abilities, with the exception of the tropical nuts, the nibs, the cocoa…

JIMMY. Um, can I get some *nibs?*

> (*He is looking at her intently.*)

JEANNINE. (*Confused.*) They're in the Midnight Chocolate Melange…

JIMMY. (*Trying again.*) Do you have any *green* ice cream?

JEANNINE. We use no artificial colors of any kind, so our Mint Chocolate Chip is a pure white—

> (ADRIAN *sighs heavily.*)

ADRIAN. Beat it, kid.

JEANNINE. (*Turns to her.*) *Why are you—scaring off a customer?*

ADRIAN. THERE ARE NO DRUGS HERE.

JIMMY. Come on, man, I'm cool—

ADRIAN. There is no special thing to order. You're not magically gonna get let into the club.

JIMMY. (*Trying a new tactic.*) I'd like to get enough to share with all the lovely ladies—

ADRIAN. No drugs.

How unoriginal would that be? An ice cream truck with "special orders"… Seriously, do you know how often we get searched by the cops?

JEANNINE. (*Shocked.*) How often?

ADRIAN. (*Gritting her teeth.*) *It doesn't matter how often, because there are never any drugs in here.*

> (JIMMY *moves off, but continues to lurk and listen, convinced there is something they're not telling him.*)

Christ almighty it never ends.

THE FAMILY FEAST
by Steve Moulds

Part One

Note: In the Humana Festival production, as a matter of logistics, we didn't set up the tables and the meal and so on, as described below, until the beginning of Part Two of "The Family Feast." It can all come together whenever it seems best, so long as it feels like a community-wide event.

> SALLY *appears, wearing an oversized winter coat, large pack strapped tight to her back, suitcase at her side.*

SALLY. A few years ago, my mother began her own ritual. Just up and declared it one day, like she was the Master of the Revels. "We're starting a new tradition," she told the four of us. "I'm calling it The Whitley Family Feast. And it's going to kick Thanksgiving's ass."

> (*A small group emerges and begins setting up tables.*)

Janet's always been a competitive person—not so much to keep up with the Joneses of the world but as a way to silence the gears grinding constantly in her head. So it's not like the idea itself was unusual. But something about the way she announced it felt a little tense, even for her. When I saw that look in her eyes, I realized Thanksgiving was going to have trouble sitting down that year.

> (*They start setting up plates of food. This process should take a while—the meal they're setting up is epic. In fact, the audience can actually smell how epic it is.*)

You should have seen the food at this thing. Sweet corn from my cousin Tom's farm, slathered in homemade honey butter. My aunt Judy's raspberry walnut salad. Our neighbor Paul's pesto risotto. And the desserts. Bourbon pecan pie—a family recipe. Red velvet cupcakes from the neighborhood bakery, brought personally by the neighborhood baker. My grandma's banana pudding. I mean, this was an embarrassing amount of first-world excess, all topped off with the most indulgent touch of all—an entire pig, splayed across the grill, lacking only an apple in its mouth to make the picture complete.

> (*People start to arrive. Some bring food, some don't.*)

This must have been what the harvest was like in olden days—serfs taking the smallest of breaks from their unsatisfying lives to congratulate themselves with more food than they could ever consume. If only they had had barbecue sauce in the middle ages.

> (*The party's getting bigger.*)

But as disgusting as I wanted to find it, there was something about all those people being in one place that sounded...lovely. If you couldn't tell by now, my mother had invited anyone she had ever met to partake. Distant cousins, old grade school teachers, acquaintances she hadn't seen in years and didn't like even when she knew them. Janet must have wracked her brain trying to get every last person there. And the thing is, it worked. Everybody came.

Everybody but me. I was in a studio apartment in Anchorage, Alaska, eating my third straight day of reheated spaghetti.

(SALLY *looks at her watch, then at an unseen monitor overhead. She's worried. Meanwhile, everyone's on stage by now. They mingle, say hi, sample the food. They're having a great time.*)

I did see the pictures. Janet was helpful enough to email them, six at a time. No text in the message. Just attachments. The subject line? "Whitley Family Feast (Minus One)." Subtle, Mom.

And I knew why she planned the stupid thing in the first place. I mean, I told her I was going to give Alaska six months before I would even <u>think</u> about moving back, and she schedules it for seven months after I go? She wants it her way, and I...don't. Maybe I was trying to punish her. And when the second Family Feast happened and Janet <u>didn't</u> send any pictures, I thought, "Okay. She got the message."

But I haven't been home in almost three years. And I guess after this one, we can only have the Feast every other year, because of the economy. And because Dad is sick.

So I decided to travel the 3,110 miles home. Which isn't really an accurate number, because that's if you go in a straight line, which I've never been good at. And I haven't told anyone I'm coming, though I think my sister Mary has guessed.

(*She looks again at the monitor.*)

But the flights are all delayed.

And I just wanna get home for dinner.

ARTISANAL FOODS ANONYMOUS
by Steve Moulds

A circle of chairs, set up like any typical Al-Anon meeting. Half a dozen or more attendees. DOROTHY *is standing and finishing up her time.*

DOROTHY. That's when it became clear that I'm not even allowed to go into Whole Foods anymore.

(CHARLES, *the leader of the group, leans forward.*)

CHARLES. Remember, Dorothy: put it in active terms.

DOROTHY. (*Frustrated with herself.*) That's when I decided I won't <u>allow</u> <u>myself</u> to go into Whole Foods anymore.

CHARLES. Excellent. Just excellent progress.

(*The group claps half-heartedly.* DOROTHY *sits while* CHARLES *stands.*)

I have to say, Whole Foods has never been a big problem for me—I personally think their bread selection is substandard. But I get why it can be a temptation. And not to impede anyone's progress, but it's actually a pretty fabulous place to score a neti pot. Sorry, Dorothy.

DOROTHY. No, I know it is.

CHARLES. Okay, who wants to share next? Perhaps one of our first-time visitors?

(CHARLES's *eyes land not so subtly on* JACK.)

JACK. Oh…me?

CHARLES. You didn't come in here just to listen, did you? Why don't you tell us your name?

(CHARLES *cedes the floor to* JACK.)

JACK. Hi, my name is… I'm Jack.

(*"Hi, Jack."*)

I was a little nervous about coming here tonight. I've never been to a support group before. But I hear these things can help, so—

CHARLES. Progress begins with the first bite, Jack.

JACK. …yeah. I wouldn't say my relationship to food is tortured or anything.

CHARLES. Well, from the inside, it wouldn't look that way, would it?

JACK. I definitely get worse when I'm stressed out. I had to look for work recently, and I could <u>not quit</u> with the snacks.

CHARLES. It's a familiar story.

JACK. Do you always…talk during?

CHARLES. You're right. Sorry.

(CHARLES *makes a passive-aggressive mouth-zipping gesture.*)

JACK. But as far as I can tell, it seems like my biggest problem—and listening to all of you, maybe the problem we all have—is impulse control.

(*Murmurs of assent and agreement.*)

Late at night is the worst.

(*People _really_ agree with this.*)

If I'm working late, I have a hard time not stopping for a bite. I know it's gross, but something about a Burger King chicken sandwich…

(*Silence from the group.*)

CHARLES. I'm sorry. Did you say…Burger King?

JACK. Yeah. Sometimes it's Wendy's. I try not to go to Taco Bell, but you know.

CHARLES. Oh…oh Jack. I think you found the wrong support group.

JACK. This isn't for food addicts?

CHARLES. It's for artisanal food addicts.

JACK. I don't get it.

CHARLES. We're people who can't resist the finest in foods, Jack. Eating isn't our problem. Money is.

JACK. Oh.

CHARLES. Maybe you should try Overeaters Anonymous.

JACK. But I don't have a weight problem.

CHARLES. None of us does, Jack.

(*Looking at the audience.*)

I think you'll agree, we're all incredibly fit, attractive professionals in our twenties who are both talented and employable.

(*Back to Jack.*)

No, Jack, the real tragedy here is that the financial crisis has made our lifestyles unsustainable.

DOROTHY. What'd you pay for that chicken sandwich, anyway? Five bucks?

JACK. $7.28, with the combo meal.

DOROTHY. I made a grilled cheese the other day with fontina, sweet butter, and black winter truffles on freshly sliced boule. I spent $74 on that sandwich.

RANDOM ATTENDEE. Can you send me that recipe?

DOROTHY. I will. It's amazing.

JACK. This isn't a support group. This is a food club.

CHARLES. It most certainly is not. And frankly, I'm a little insulted that you'd equate your struggles with ours. The only thing uniting you and me is that, like those burgers you're so fond of, I measure my produce by the quarter pound.

JACK. Nobody said you can't love food. Just…buy it cheaper.

CHARLES. If only we could. But once you've tasted Iranian caviar, I'm afraid Imperial Russian won't do.

DOROTHY. I have to go to the market.

(DOROTHY *grabs her purse and heads for the door.*)

CHARLES. Look at this, Jack, you're encouraging backsliding. Before you know it, she'll be hoarding crostini again. You need to leave.

(*Dejected,* JACK *starts to leave. But something stops him.*)

JACK. The other day, I stopped at Panera for lunch… Anybody ever been there?

RANDOM ATTENDEE. (*As if he were trying an alien language.*) Puh… Pa-*ne*-ra?

JACK. Anyway, they've got this stone-milled rye that's pretty fantastic. Only cost me six dollars.

CHARLES. Was that loaf, or miche?

JACK. I…don't know that second word.

CHARLES. Go on.

JACK. And I know it's not a steak, but…McDonald's has Angus burgers now. And wraps. Plus, they've started offering lattes and mochas alongside their regular coffee.

RANDOM ATTENDEE. Do they have a frappuccino?

JACK. You know, I think they do.

(CHARLES *offers him a chair.*)

CHARLES. Why don't you rejoin the circle, Jack?

(JACK *goes back and sits down.*)

JACK. Has anyone tried the natural-cut sea salt fries at Wendy's?

(*Somebody nods.*)

They're good, right?

(*As he keeps talking, the lights fade.*)

CODE FRIES

by Tanya Saracho

> GRRL *(who is a boi) has entered the kitchen with grocery bags.* ROOMMATE, *in her PJs, comes to help put them away.*

GRRL. I can gauge her mood—

ROOMMATE. Hey, did you get the paper towels?

GRRL. *(Nods.)* By what she's eating. And how she's eating it.

ROOMMATE. How about the Fritos? Did you...oh, yes you did. Thank you, girl!

> *(She eats some Fritos and continues taking out groceries from the bags.)*

GRRL. *(To audience.)* Something like plain yogurt is nothing. She's just eating yogurt. But flavored yogurt out of the family-size container while she stands by the kitchen window looking at the brick wall that is our panoramic view? That's her worrying about her bank account. She's not good at budgeting. Flavored yogurt means she's trying to tell me she might not make rent this month.

ROOMMATE. Did you look on Facebook today?

GRRL. I did earlier. These the Pop Tarts you wanted?

> *(* Denotes overlapping.)*

ROOMMATE. *(She attacks the box.)* Ah, you are my everything!* Yes! Thank you!

GRRL. *(To audience.)* A baked potato means she's missing her dad; macaroni and cheese, she misses her mom. They're divorced. They don't get along.

ROOMMATE. Did you see Kevin's update?

GRRL. I haven't. Why? What does he say?

ROOMMATE. Not what he posted. He just said he was having a good day.

GRRL. Soup means she's missing her ex. He just got engaged. They're having a June wedding. This is a source of anxiety as of late.

ROOMMATE. But that Marisa girl with the frizzy hair—you know who I'm talking about?

GRRL. Kevin's not the ex by the way.* Kevin's a new...

ROOMMATE. That fucking tacky-ass girl writes on Kevin's thread, "Yeah, and a great night if I do say so myself." Winky smiley face. All suggestively! Winky smiley face?! Like what is that supposed to mean, you know?

GRRL. And steak—strangely enough—steak means she's feeling fat. It means she's going to start dieting the next day. Steak means she's going to be running the blender at 6 a.m.

ROOMMATE. "And a GREAT night if I do SAYSOMYSELF?" Like, shut up. Frizzy-haired bitch.

(*Looking at the bag of chips.*)

Five bucks for BBQ chips?!

GRRL. Those are the ones you wanted, right?

ROOMMATE. That's like criminal. Yeah, these are great. Thanks, girl. (*Beat.*) Can you believe that? "If I do say so myself?"

GRRL. Pure trash.

ROOMMATE. Kevin hasn't texted me since yesterday morning. Do you think they... I wonder if they were like... You think they hung out last night?

(GRRL *shrugs his shoulders.*)

GRRL. But right now we must note and recognize that she's on to the Chips. She had me run and get her three kinds of chips, and what you have to understand is that the consumption of Chips is Code Orange. Not quite Code Red—that would Fries—but getting to Code Red if I don't do some damage control. If I don't navigate the codes.

GRRL. That's like so fucking tacky, if you think about it. Putting him on blast on Facebook like that? I mean, if they did happen to... Skank. So gross.

ROOMMATE. If we do reach the Fries State, that's... Well, that will be bad news. She'll concoct all sorts of abominations with fries involving different cheeses and chili. Buttermilk ranch dressing and even pasta sauce if she gets desperate. It won't be pretty. Usually Tequila will follow Fries and then I know we're in for a long weekend.

ROOMMATE. I just wish he would like text back, you know?

GRRL. But right now, we're just on Chips so the situation is still manageable.

ROOMMATE. I wasn't even going to sign onto Facebook tonight because I actually had some shit to do that I didn't finish at work. I was so over it today at work, girl. My new supervisor is... Ever have one of those days where you don't feel like doing anything?

GRRL. Totally.

ROOMMATE. I just signed on for five minutes and his update just happened to pop up on my feed.

GRRL. His update didn't just pop up on her feed. She's a compulsive Facebooker and refreshes her browser like a nervous tick. (*To* ROOMMATE.) Whose feed?

ROOMMATE. Kevin's, grrl!

GRRL. Oh, right. (*To audience.*) Kevin is our new fixation. And when I say "our" I mean my roommate's new all-consuming obsession. Like clinical. Like those people that wash their hands and have to retrace their steps? Like that... And she only just met dude like three weeks ago at our friend's house. After she met him, she didn't eat anything for three days and that's when I knew that we could be in for some trouble. Because...

ROOMMATE. You know, when he and I are like just alone together, it's so absolutely amazing.

GRRL. They've never technically been alone together. She's counting texting and the phone as being alone together, but I try not to engage. I'm just here to manage the codes.

ROOMMATE. Like, people don't really see that side of him, you know?* He's like actually really gentle and he like, listens when... I don't know. You know how you just know when you have a connection with somebody? That's how it was for me. That day at Marty's house it was like BAM! I know you. That's how it felt. Like we knew each other from a past life, you know? Like we were meant to meet at Marty's. I mean, you know I almost didn't go that night. But something told me... Something MADE me get my ass into those jeans and put on some damn makeup and... I mean, it was like destiny. It wasn't like destiny, it WAS destiny. God, I like him so much, you know?

GRRL. Because if I do let this escalate to a Red, I won't get to watch cable the whole fucking weekend and you know, I pay my share of cable! I pay to take up half the space in this apartment but if she goes on one of her binges, she will be occupying the damn couch until she has to go to work Monday morning and we can't have that, now can we?! My favorite thing about Saturdays are the all-day *Kardashian* marathons on E! *The Real Housewiveathons* on Bravo. I fucking love Bravo! I want to take these Cheetos, if there are any left, and sit and watch Bravo all fucking day. I deserve to watch it after the week I've had. But now this girl is tweakin' out over some guy that... Seriously, he's not into her. She's not his type!

(GRRL *turns his attention to* ROOMMATE. *She's started crying. Mess of chips all over her.*)

TRUST ME. He's a douche. He was stepping up to me that night while nobody else was looking and sorry, but homey don't play that. I don't do the D.L. thing. I just don't. Asshole. He's actually been texting me all fucking day.

What's the matter, Booboo?

ROOMMATE. Nothing, I just... nothing, girl. I just...

GRRL. Baby, this guy is not worth* your...

ROOMMATE. I just like him so much, you know? I've never liked anyone this fucking much, this fucking fast. I'm serious, there's like something really different about him.

(*Pause.*)

GRRL. Come on, why don't you…have a Cheeto.

ROOMMATE. Thanks. You're my girl, you know that? Thank you.

> (*They have a moment.* GRRL *turns on the TV. They watch for a little bit.*)

You know what I just got a taste for? Fries.

THE GAME

by Carson Kreitzer

Part One

Three people. Sitting, or slouching. Maybe on beanbag chairs. Probably wearing hoodies.
A moment, then:

ONE. Mung Bean Incident.

TWO. Nice.

THREE. Killer Chef.

TWO. Uh-huh.

ONE. TGIFriday Drive-By.

THREE. Band?

ONE. Suburban punks.

THREE. Fair enough.

> (*Beat. A smile…*
> *"Heavy metal" voice:*)

Octopus.

> (FOUR *enters.*)

ONE. Nice one!

> (TWO *has not yet contributed.* ONE *and* THREE *look at* TWO, *expectantly. A moment. He looks around, desperate. Suddenly shouts:*)

TWO. BERLIN ALEXANDERPLATZ.

> (*Beat.*)

THREE. That makes no sense on any level.

TWO. I panicked.

FOUR. What are you playing?

ONE. Band Name, or Cause of Death.
Restaurant-related.

> (FOUR *thinks for a moment, contributes:*)

FOUR. Bad Sushi.

THREE. Nice.

ORDERING: Memories
by Michael Golamco

> RICK, ZELDA, POE, *and* HERB *are sitting at a table at a restaurant with menus.*

ZELDA. Hey, what are you guys gonna order?

POE. Oh, I don't know—I was thinking about having The Valentine's Day My Ex Dumped Me.

RICK. Of course you are.

ZELDA. (*To* HERB.) Oh—how's the Valentine's Day here?

HERB. S'ok. I've had better.

POE. Well what are you gonna get?

HERB. I'm probably gonna have The Thanksgiving My Cousin Gave Us Food Poisoning.

ZELDA. Eating light?

HERB. I'm not that hungry.

RICK. He has Manorexia.

POE. Maybe I'll get The Breakfast My Parents Announced They Were Getting a Divorce.

RICK. Right before we go see a movie?

POE. I'll have something else.

RICK. I'm going to get The Night I Had That Random Hookup in Manhattan.

POE. Of course you are.

ZELDA. (*Playfully.*) Asshole.

RICK. What?—I've had it here before, it's great.

POE. (*To* ZELDA.) What are you gonna get?

ZELDA. Either The Day My Cat Died or My First Makeout Session at Summer Camp.

POE. I'd totally do the Makeout. Dwayne had the Cat before, and he said it was really dry.

HERB. Hey how's the Little League Championship Game My Dad Missed?

RICK. Oh, it's good. It comes with a Belated, Rushed I'm Sorry Card—you should really try it.

HERB. I think I shall…

POE. Okay, you know what? I'm going to try something new: The Sudden Outburst of Joy. BOOM.

ZELDA. Excellent!

> (*A* WAITER *arrives.*)

WAITER. Hey there, friends. Before I take your order, a quick announcement: Today's special is That Accidental Racist Comment I Made at the Persian Restaurant.

EVERYONE. (*Various manifestations of the following:*) Oh no / Not interested / No thanks / I'll have something else

RICK. Okay, well, let's just order already. Zelda—you're having The Makeout?

ZELDA. Actually, I'm going to take a risk and do the Dead Cat.

WAITER. (*As he writes.*) Meow! Aw, kitty!

POE. Well, I'm going to play it safe and go with the Unwarranted Moment of Self-Criticism.

WAITER. That comes with either a Panic Attack or a Bout of Insomnia.

POE. Let's go with the Panic Attack.

HERB. I'm getting the Little League Championship Game My Dad Missed.

WAITER. Just to warn you, we're all out of "I'm Sorry" cards; you okay with a Cheaply-Made Mall Photographer Baseball Card with Your Picture On It From, Like, Two Years Ago?

HERB. Yeah, yeah, sure.

RICK. Okay, and I'm going to get The Christmas My Grandma Was Diagnosed with Alzheimer's.

WAITER. But wasn't she just so much easier to shop for afterwards? I mean, you could just re-gift her the same...

(*He pauses as no one appreciates that joke.*)

I'll put that in.

All righty, and would you like to order something to start?

EVERYONE. PUBERTY.

TASTES LIKE HOME
by Matt Schatz

A WOMAN, *alone, sings to the audience.*

WOMAN. I WON'T HAVE CREAM CHEESE
I WON'T EAT CHEESE AND I WON'T HAVE CREAM
I WON'T EAT GREEN PEAS
I WON'T EAT ANYTHING THAT'S GREEN

I WON'T EAT BACON
AND I'M NOT BAKIN' ANYMORE
AND I STOPPED MAKIN'
SPECIAL TRIPS TO OUR SPECIAL STORE

I STILL HAVE COFFEE EV'RY DAY
BUT NO MORE LATTES EXTRA FOAM
CUZ I WON'T HAVE ANYTHING WE LIKE
UNTIL YOU'RE HOME

(*A* MAN *enters wearing a military uniform.*)

MAN. DON'T THINK WE GOT CREAM CHEESE
BUT WE GOT CHEESE AND WE ALSO GOT CREAM
I SAW SOME GREEN PEAS
BUT THEY WERE THE LEAST GREEN PEAS I'VE SEEN

YOU HAD TO SAY BACON
BABY YOU'RE MAKIN' ME INSANE
MY HEART HAS BEEN ACHIN'
AND NOW I GOT BACON ON THE BRAIN

ALL OF THOSE THINGS WE LIKE THE MOST
I HOPE YOU'LL SEND THEM HERE BY POST
CUZ I WILL EAT ANYTHING AT ALL
THAT TASTES LIKE HOME

I WILL EAT ANYTHING AT ALL THAT TASTES LIKE HOME

WOMAN. I WON'T EAT ANYTHING

MAN. I WILL EAT ANYTHING AT ALL

WOMAN. THAT TASTES LIKE HOME

MAN. THAT TAKES ME HOME

WOMAN. I WON'T EAT ANYTHING WE LOVE
UNTIL YOU'RE HOME

(*Blackout.*)

IN THE LINE

by Tanya Saracho

Sounds of revelry in the next room; it's some kind of dinner party. ANNIE *enters the room on the verge of tears,* IAN *(her fiancé) follows. Please observe the overlapping denoted by the *.*

IAN. Annie, she was joking.* My mother was joking about that… Of course she knows that you know how to use a fork. She was just being cheeky. She's had like three glasses of wine, Annie, which for her is like having three bottles. She's a lightweight. Oh, come on, don't get like that.

ANNIE. No, I don't think that was a joke, Ian. Your mom… You know what, let me stop. She's your mom and this is her house and although she thinks I have no manners, that I don't know how to use eating utensils and that I was raised by wolves, I'm going to stop before I make this into… Ian, could I just have a moment to… Could you please give me a sec?

(Beat.)

Please?

IAN. Annie. Don't get like this. It was a joke. A stupid joke. I'll make her apologize.

ANNIE. God, no! Please! Could you, could you please just let me chill out for a little bit? I'll go in there in a second. I promise.

IAN. Alright, sweetheart. I'll go back in there and make something up if you want. I'll tell them something about you powdering your nose. Just don't be too long, alright?

ANNIE. I'll be right in.

IAN. I love you, you know?

> (ANNIE *smiles for the first time. He kisses her. She softens. He starts to go but right before he exits he says:*)

Oh, and it's really easy; you just go from the outside in. Salad fork first, dinner second. Easy.

ANNIE. Are you fucking serious?! Did you just school me in fucking fork etiquette?! It's not enough that your mom just publicly shamed me in front of your family with her* "Annie, we use the butter knife to butter our bread and NOT the dinner knife," and you're still going to stand here and prep me so what? So I won't embarrass you in front of your guests? What's so shitty is that you just sat there, Ian. You didn't say a word. You let her just take me to town and you let everybody just chuckle it away.

(Beat.)

I knew it.

IAN. No, Annie… sshhwaitaminute. What are you…? I was just saying. No, Annie. She didn't say it, she didn't mean it that way. God, I think you're taking this a little too—Annie, of course I'm not embarrassed of you. Jesus. You're blowing this way out of proportion.

(*Beat.*)

Ssshhh, wait. Let's… Sweetheart, could we just—

(*Pause.*)

ANNIE. I shouldn't have come.

IAN. Whoa.

(*Pause.*)

ANNIE. No, actually, I'm glad you brought me Ian. I'm glad I saw.

IAN. You're glad you saw what, exactly?

ANNIE. Listen to me, because we've never talked about this and I just think it's time. You kind of tiptoe around it when I bring it up but we need to take it out right now and talk about this shit or it's just going to fester and blow up on us: I grew up poor, Ian. I grew up hungry. Really hungry. Not like stomach growling hungry; stomach burning, hand shaking hungry. Hungry like you thought a giant was crushing your forehead with his thumbs. Hungry like you thought your knees would give out on you on your walk home cuz you were so weak because you knew there would be no relief that night. Not until the morning when you headed to school early for the free breakfast. For the runny eggs and microwaved English muffins that were bricks. Hey, but it was breakfast, right? There were days when we had nothing, Ian. You will never understand that kind of nothing. I don't want to throw the word privileged around, but you will never understand that kind of poverty. And it's not like my mom didn't try, it's not like she didn't work. She did the best she could. But shit, if there was no money, there was no food and more times than not, there was no money so it was a simple equation.

IAN. Annie…

ANNIE. Your fiancée grew up on food stamps, Ian. FOOD. Stamps. What's your mom going to say about that?

(*Pause.*)

It's something that you don't ever shake. The knowledge that yeah, you could be doing okay, but you're always two paychecks away from being back in the food bank line.

IAN. Baby, with me you'll never have to worry about something like that happening.

ANNIE. See, Ian?! That is not a noble thing you just said to me. You might think you just said some romantic-ass shit that I'm supposed to swoon over but actually, it's kind of gross. Because you didn't listen to a word I just said and I know that when we go back in there and the fucking dessert comes out and your mom reminds me to use the dessert fork, you're just going to stay quiet, or shit, you might even crack a smile. I don't know!

(IAN *is silent. Long pause. The following is labored.*)

IAN. Annie. I am going back to the table. If you'd like to join us, please do. I'd love it if you came back to join us, but I'll completely understand if you don't.

(*He starts to go.*)

ANNIE. That's what you're going to say to me?

(*He stops before exiting and stares at* ANNIE.)

That's what you're going to say.

(*He finally exits.*)

Okay.

(ANNIE's *been left alone. Is she going to go back in there? Lights down.*)

FEAR AND LOATHING AT THE FOOD TRUCK

by Carson Kreitzer

Part Two: A Little Later

>*We return to the Food Truck area.*

LANA. Microgreens.

Micro micro micro greens.

What did they want to be when they grew up?

We don't know! We harvested them with a scissors at 23 days!

Yes, from one perspective it's tragic.

But from another…it's delicious!

And full of micronutrients!

>(DAVE *approaches her.*)

DAVE. Are these sprouts?

LANA. (*Scandalized.*) No, they're Microgreens.

DAVE. What's the—

LANA. If they were sprouts, it would say *sprouts.*

>(*Points.*)

He's got sprouts.

DAVE. Oh, uh, never mind, I—

>(*He retreats in confusion, heads towards the ice cream truck.*)

ADRIAN. Okay, this one.

>(DAVE *looks up. He sees* JEANNINE. *In all her radiance. It is like seeing his own destiny open up before him. About five different expressions cross his face. He becomes utterly paralyzed with shyness.*)

JEANNINE. Can I help you?

>(DAVE *is mute.*)

All our ingredients are locally sourced…

>(ADRIAN *clears her throat.* JEANNINE *snaps to attention.*)

Except the Tropical Nuts. And the nibs. And Vanilla. Which is ethically sourced from Madagascar.

>(ADRIAN *shakes her head. Oh, the new recruits.*
>DAVE *is still standing there. It is becoming more awkward by the nanosecond. He gives it his all, launches into one overly formal sentence:*)

DAVE. Can you describe the Tropical Nut Brittle?

>(*A tense moment.* JEANNINE *looks at* ADRIAN, *panicked. Stiff:*)

JEANNINE. It's a nut brittle.
In a… Madagascaran Vanilla.

> (*Almost under her breath, desperately trying to communicate something without going overboard:*)

It's heavenly…

DAVE. With specks?

JEANNINE. Yeah.

DAVE. I love the specks.

JEANNINE. It's got specks.

DAVE. Okay.

> (*Whew! Got through that.*)

JEANNINE. Cup or cone?

DAVE. Oh, uh…

JEANNINE. (*Cheerful.*) The waffle cones are locally sourced, made fresh daily and

DAVE. (*Too loud.*) OKAY.

JEANNINE. Just a single, or—?

DAVE. (*Hearing "are you single?"*) Yes, I— (*am*)

JEANNINE. Did you want to try another of our scrumptious flavors?

DAVE. Oh, I—
no, I'll just start with—

JEANNINE. Great!

> (*She enthusiastically scoops ice cream. You know what that looks like, right? Dave becomes a little weak in the knees.*)

DAVE. Oh, I—

JEANNINE. Would you like anything else?

DAVE. (*Under his breath.*) *to wake up with you next to me*

JEANNINE. Pardon me?

DAVE. No, no, that's great.

> (*She hands him the cone. He just stands there.*)

JEANNINE. Four dollars, please.

> (*DAVE reaches for his wallet, with the cone hand. The gorgeous scoop of ice cream falls to the ground.*)

ADRIAN. Aaaaaand *that's* why you ask for the money first. And then hand them the cone.

JEANNINE. (*Panicking.*) I'm sorry—

DAVE. (*Mortified to have gotten her in trouble.*) I'm sorry—

ADRIAN. Don't worry about it.

    (*Gives them both a smile.*)

Training Day.

Let's try it again.

    (DAVE *holds out his four dollars, as* JEANNINE *says:*)

JEANNINE. Four dollars please—

oh, thank you!

    (*She rings up the sale. Re-scoops the ice cream. It is once again a beautiful experience. She hands* DAVE *the cone. He tries to brush her fingers with his, but it's hard to distinguish this from just awkward grabbing for the cone.*)

DAVE. Thank you.

    (*He stands there staring at her. Makes no move to eat the ice cream.*)

ADRIAN. All right, you got this for fifteen? I need a goddamn cigarette.

JEANNINE. Sure! (*To the frozen* DAVE.) Your ice cream is gonna melt.

DAVE. Oh. (*He tries the ice cream.*) It's really good.

JEANNINE. I know, isn't it?

    (DAVE *stands there. Just barely keeping up with the ice cream melt. He's about to speak, when— his courage fails. He turns away.*)

JEANNINE. Ice cream! Creamery-fresh, five flavors today!

DAVE. (*Under his breath.*) *Talk to her, you idiot.*

JEANNINE. Ice cream!

THE MIX

by Steve Moulds

The MASTER BAKER *watches the* APPRENTICE *whisk a bowl with an electric mixer. When the mixer stops, the* MASTER BAKER *speaks.*

MASTER BAKER. What made you want to apprentice with me, anyway?

(*Brief pause, then the* APPRENTICE *starts the mixer again. The* MASTER BAKER *speaks over the sound.*)

Come on. You can tell me <u>that</u> much.

… No, that's smart. People talk too much about what they're <u>gonna</u> do, they feel like they've accomplished something. Let your food speak for you. I always do.

(*The mixer stops. The* APPRENTICE *thinks about saying something, but doesn't. The mixer resumes.*)

Don't be too aggressive with that. You're trying to <u>coax</u> it. Think of the mix as an invitation. You're asking your ingredients to get along.

(*Even the* APPRENTICE *thinks this metaphor is questionable.*)

Which brings me to the subject of harmony and balance. You'd think you'd want a perfectly even consistency, but there's a reason God invented the mint swirl. Or hell, the chocolate chip. People like to find the unexpected in their brownie. And no, I'm not talking about mary jane, though I can tell you were about to make that joke.

(*The* APPRENTICE *smiles and stops the mixer. She picks up another bowl and pours it into the first.*)

Next time, maybe don't let the chocolate cool so much. But I'm quibbling. You know what you're doing.

(*The* APPRENTICE *begins beating to combine the two mixtures.*)

I realized this morning, I'm gonna miss our sessions.

(*The* APPRENTICE *stops the mixer. This is sad.*)

<u>You're</u> probably overjoyed. Don't have to hear me yapping atcha anymore. I know that's what you're doing over there. You're judging me.

(*The* APPRENTICE *looks at him, exasperated, but he's just kidding.*)

Seriously, though, you're… You're gonna make a great baker.

(*Mixing again.*)

I'm kinda glad we saved brownies for last. You never go wrong with the basics. Don't get me wrong, a great layer cake is like nothing else, but if you woke up tomorrow and all you ever made was cupcakes and brownies, you'd still have a future in this business.

(*The* APPRENTICE *combines a third bowl's contents into the mixture.*)

The key to long-term happiness is to find the thing <u>you</u> love to bake. The dessert that expresses something. Brings you back to yourself. For me, it's tres leches cake. Something about it's too much—too much milk, too much flavor, too much sweetness. Just like me.

What do you think yours is?

> (*The* APPRENTICE *thinks, but doesn't want to say.*)

You don't have to know now. You'll find it. Hey, maybe it's those brownies.

> (*The* APPRENTICE *starts to pour the final mix, but the* MASTER BAKER *stops her.*)

You make one hell of a dessert, girl. It's been a pleasure.

> (*The* APPRENTICE *nods thank you, then pours the brownie mix. It looks creamy, and delicious, and perfect.*)

Time to put it in the oven.

MY MOM WON'T LET ME EAT THAT

by Michael Golamco

BILLY *and his teacher,* MRS. SHRIVER, *alone in a classroom at lunch.*

MRS. SHRIVER. I'm sorry that we can't find your lunch, Billy.

BILLY. It was in a purple Doctor Who lunch box.

MRS. SHRIVER. Well, Mr. Samson is looking for it. So hopefully it'll turn up—

BILLY. Did you tell him that it's purple.

MRS. SHRIVER. Yes.

BILLY. Actually we should let him know that it's kind of dark violet and it has a Dalek on it.

MRS. SHRIVER. Okay, I'll let Mr. Samson know. But in the meantime, I can share my lunch with you.

(*She takes out her lunch, splits a PB&J in half. Offers it to him.
He looks at it like she's holding a wad of puke in her hand.*)

BILLY. My mom won't let me eat that.

MRS. SHRIVER. Oh. Are you allergic to peanuts?

BILLY. No.

MRS. SHRIVER. Strawberry jelly?

BILLY. No.

MRS. SHRIVER. This is whole wheat bread—

BILLY. It has glutens.
My mom won't let me eat anything with glutens.
Because I could develop a spastic colon.

(*Re: the jam:*)

And I can't eat anything processed.

(*Re: the peanut butter:*)

Or anything that's not organic.

MRS. SHRIVER. Oh.

BILLY. I'm hungry.

MRS. SHRIVER. Well, I have an orange—

(*She produces an orange.*)

BILLY. Yeah, my mom won't let me eat that.

MRS. SHRIVER. It's just an orange—

BILLY. She won't let me eat anything that's harvested by oppressed migrant workers.

MRS. SHRIVER. Oh.

BILLY. Because supporting large-scale farming on that level is basically like supporting murder.

Of people.

MRS. SHRIVER. Okay.

BILLY. Of brown people.

MRS. SHRIVER. I understand.

BILLY. So it's evil.

MRS. SHRIVER. I have a hardboiled egg—

BILLY. My mom won't let me eat anything that comes from an animal raised in a cage—

MRS. SHRIVER. They're from free-range chickens—

BILLY. Or an animal that is injected with steroids—

MRS. SHRIVER. They're a hundred percent organic—

BILLY. Or an animal.

MRS. SHRIVER. I see.

BILLY. It's okay.

I'll just sit here.

And be hungry.

>   (*A long pause.*)

MRS. SHRIVER. Do you mind if I—

>   (*She makes a motion to indicate that she's hungry and she wants to eat her lunch.*)

BILLY. Sure, go ahead.

>   (MRS. SHRIVER *begins to eat her lunch.*
>   BILLY *stares straight ahead, hungry and depressed.*
>   *After a moment,* MRS. SHRIVER *begins to feel guilty.*)

MRS. SHRIVER. Would you like some water at least?

BILLY. Yeah, my mom won't let me drink water from a tap.

MRS. SHRIVER. I can go down to the vending machine and buy you a bottle of—

BILLY. Or anything that comes in a plastic bottle. Because they last forever and seagulls get their heads stuck in them and then they die.

They die.

>   (*She studies him.*)

MRS. SHRIVER. So Billy, what can you eat?

BILLY. An uncooked paste made from sprouts that my mom grows in our backyard and crushes herself with a mortar and a pestle.

>   (*A long, awkward pause.*)

MRS. SHRIVER. Oh. Well you know what? I have some of that.

BILLY. What.

MRS. SHRIVER. Sprout paste. That I grow myself and crush with a mortar and pestle.

I have some of that right here—

(*She breaks off a piece of her sandwich.*)

MRS. SHRIVER. I used my Dr. Who sonic screwdriver to change the sprout paste on a molecular level so that it looks and tastes like a peanut butter and jelly sandwich.

(*Re: the sandwich.*)

Eat it, it's good for you.

(*He tentatively takes it, takes a bite.
For Billy, the moment is transcendent.*)

BILLY. (*Sincerely.*) It's good!

MRS. SHRIVER. I know.

BANANA GIRL
by Tanya Saracho

A young woman is sitting at her desk. She takes out a banana and slowly starts to peel it. JAY *is sitting by his desk, on a swivel chair, watching the young woman. His* CO-WORKER *has just entered, she doesn't notice right away that* JAY *is looking at the* BANANA GIRL.

CO-WORKER. Hey did you get my emails? If you don't send me those by three, I can't turn them around by five to send them with this release, Jay.

>   *(Beat.)*

We can't leave here today without sending this press release.

>   *(Beat.)*

Hey, are you listening? We're up shit creek if we don't send by five.

>   (BANANA GIRL *has taken her first scrumptious bite.*)

JAY. Do you think she practices at home?

CO-WORKER. Come on, because then we have to proof it and I don't want to be here all night.

>   (BANANA GIRL *takes an even deeper bite.*)

JAY. It's an art form, what she does.

CO-WORKER. Jay…

JAY. It is. It's art.

CO-WORKER. You know…it's kind of creepy how you're obsessed with this girl.

JAY. I'm not obsessed with the girl. Just with how she eats a banana. Hey, I admire good technique.

CO-WORKER. You're gross, you know that?

JAY. Don't drink the Haterade now. Not my fault you're not this gifted.

>   (BANANA GIRL *is now looking at* JAY, *only* CO-WORKER *doesn't see it.* BANANA GIRL *is basically fellating the banana.* JAY *is getting all worked up.*)

CO-WORKER. She's just sitting there, minding her own business, Jay. This is how we keep losing receptionists.

JAY. Oh, Banana girl…

CO-WORKER. This is so… On like so many levels…

JAY. You do it on purpose, don't you Banana girl? Yes you do!

CO-WORKER. She's just eating a banana! It's just a fucking banana, Jay!

>   (BANANA GIRL *takes out a whole damn bouquet of bananas. She starts on another one. She consumes it, the whole thing is animalistic.*)

JAY. Not in her hands, it's not. It is a vessel. A conduit. A channel to the divine.

(BANANA GIRL *attacks the banana in a messy frenzy of banananess.* CO-WORKER #2 *enters with a stack of papers.*)

CO-WORKER #2. You all heard we have to send this thing by five, right? Oh, no. Are we in banana land right now?

CO-WORKER. Every time he gets like this, half of me thinks I should go straight to Joan in HR but then I don't like want to be THAT person, you know?

CO-WORKER #2. Yeah, you don't want to be that person.

CO-WORKER. But it's a little ridiculous.

(*Beat.*)

JAY! Don't make this girl uncomfortable and let her eat her damn banana!

(CO-WORKER *exits.*)

CO-WORKER #2. Pig.

(CO-WORKER #2 *exits.* MALE CO-WORKER *enters.*)

MALE CO-WORKER. Hey, Jay did they tell you that we have to send this shit by… Oooh. Banana girl. Look at that mess all over her pretty face. Eatthatbanana, Bananagirl!

(*They're making sounds. They shudder and keep staring her way. She's a savage wild mess of bananation. Then, calmly, she returns to her typing. Sounds of an office. Everything back to normal. Including BANANA GIRL, as if she didn't have mess all over her face.*)

A NUMBERS GAME
by Tanya Saracho

> ONE *(female)*, TWO *(female)*, THREE *(male) speak to the audience, never each other. Who knows if in an esoteric way they are aware of each other, but for our intents and purposes, they won't interact. The live sound in this piece is very important: the song of the marbles. There is a fishbowl in front of* ONE; *she holds a bag of marbles in her hands. Every time she says a number, she drops a marble in the bowl. It makes a loud clinking sound.* TWO *holds a bag of marbles in her hand as well. There is a bucket with water in front of her; she also drops a marble every time she counts.* THREE *holds another bag of marbles and is standing over a tin tub. The clanky kind. The counting and the sound will serve as the drive and metronome of the piece. The whole thing unravels a bit at the end, but they have to get to a climax before* ONE *breaks away from the other two with her narrative. (Something to play with is additional clinking with the marbles. Do they keep going, like keeping count, when others are speaking, even though they are not saying numbers? Just something to play with.)*

ONE. The very first one, you don't notice.

(ONE *drops a marble in the fishbowl.*)

TWO. Water weight.

THREE. Please, who are these people who notice gaining just one?

TWO. (*Dropping marbles in her water bucket.*) 2,3

ONE. In fact, the first five go pretty much undetected.

THREE. (*Dropping marbles in his tin tub.*) 4,5

TWO. Every month, I go up and down.* It's water weight.

THREE. Scales are evil.

ONE. But then I notice.

THREE. That's why you should only weigh yourself like once a week—

TWO. 6, 7,* 8

THREE. —wearing the same thing.

ONE. 9, 10

THREE. Or shit, don't weigh yourself at all.

ONE. And then others start to notice. People start saying little things.

TWO. 11,12

THREE. It's like your own fucking obsession anyway, nobody else cares what you look like.

ONE. Your face looks different. You start to feel a little different.

TWO. I start to be aware of skinny girls. Is that awful?

ONE. 13

TWO. I start to be really annoyed at them.

THREE. 14

TWO. Like I want to fucking—

ALL. 15

>   (*Pause.*)

TWO. Shit. That's a pant size.

ONE. I start a diet, a cleanse. There's cayenne pepper involved.

TWO. My sister's a stick, and out of the blue I start being a bitch for no reason. Which is just like…

ONE. 16, 17

THREE. I know! We're "obsessed because the media feeds us images of…" * blah blahZzzzzz… (*Snoring.*)

ONE. 18, 19

TWO. But it's not her freakin' fault she's a size 2, you know? And I'm here stuffing my freakin'…

ONE. I buy Zumba. I hear it works. I buy a bunch of crap. Because I hear it works.

THREE. We should all like fucking love ourselves!

ALL. 20

ONE. But nothing works.

THREE. It's such a first world problem, you know?

ONE. In fact, now I feel like if I even breathe; I gain weight.

TWO. 21, 22, 23

ONE. I'm starting to move differently.

TWO. 24

ONE. To wear more sweatshirts.

TWO. 25

ONE. I look at myself in the mirror and I'm… Who is this person?

TWO. 26

THREE. People in Sierra Leone, Liberia, they're not signing up for fucking Weight Watchers* to count DOWN their intake of food, for God's sake. I mean, that shit is ridiculous.

ONE & TWO. 27, 28, 29

ONE. I stop wanting to have sex. I mean, like I want to, but I feel so fucking ugly.

TWO. I walk around so pissed at everybody.

ONE. So disgusting.

TWO & THREE. 30

ONE. My boyfriend,* he doesn't know what to do with me, because even though he tells me that I look fine to him, fine is not enough to me. Do you know what fine means? Fine means, I'll fucking tolerate you. That's what fine means.

TWO & THREE. 31, 32, 33, 34, 35, 36

(TWO *and* THREE *keep clinking marbles into their respective containers.*)

ONE. Fine means, "Sure, but could we please turn the lights off so I don't have to look at you?" Fine means "Our days are counted, baby unless you do something about your weight." Fine is people looking at you when you put anything in your mouth because all of a sudden you've turned into a social pariah. I sat there yesterday at a restaurant, and these two assholes were having some kind of a ball over at their table as I was trying to eat my freakin' lunch.

(TWO *and* THREE *stop. They turn to look at her for the first time.* ONE *is breaking down.*)

The two actually sat there staring at me, as I put the sandwich in my mouth. It was so embarrassing. I'm sitting there alone, which I hate in the first place, and these two douchebags are like whispering something—I notice cuz they're giggling like little girls over there. So I look and they don't really stop. I try to ignore them but I mean, I have to freakin' eat my food, right? I have 45 minutes for lunch, I have to eat this thing. And I can feel their freakin' eyes on me, like burning across the restaurant and I say fuck it and take another bite and they... These two jerks make this noise. Like...

(*Beat.*)

And I know what that noise is. I know what it means.

(*Silence.*

More silence.)

How did I let it get this bad?

HOW DO YOU KNOW?

by Matt Schatz

A girl enters and sits at a piano. She accompanies herself as she sings to the audience (like she's performing in a recital).

GIRL. WHEN I WAS SIX
IT HIT ME THAT TURKEY ON THE TABLE
WAS THE SAME THING AS TURKEY ON A FARM
AND SO WHEN I WAS SIX
I STOPPED EATING TURKEY
MY MOM CALLED ME "QUIRKY"
BUT SHE SAID: "WHAT'S THE HARM?"

AND THEN WHEN I WAS SIX AND A HALF
I WAS TAKING A BATH (BAFF)
AND WAS PLAYING WITH MY TOY KOI NAMED ROY
AND IT HIT ME THAT KOI IS A FISH
AND THAT FISH IS A DISH
AND THAT ROY WAS A KOI AND OH BOY...

AND THEN LATER THAT YEAR
WHILE EATING A FRANKFURTER
I SCREAMED BLOODY MURDER
AT A GAME WITH MY DAD
AND BY EIGHT ALL I'D PUT ON MY PLATE
WAS JUST VEGETABLES
I ATE ONLY VEGTABLES
THEY WERE ALL THAT I HAD

(*Pause.*)

AND TODAY I TURNED NINE

(*Beat.*)

Thank you.

AND LIFE IS JUST FINE
BUT THERE'S A BOY THAT I KNOW
NOT MY FRIEND JUST A BOY
AND HE'S NOT EVEN COOL
BUT HE GOES TO MY SCHOOL
AND HE KNOWS I THINK MEAT
IS DISGUSTING AND CRUEL
HE SAID: "PLANTS ARE ALIVE
CUZ THEY BREATHE AND THEY GROW"
AND I SAID: " DUH, UM, I KNOW,

BUT UM VEGGIES DON'T FEEL"
I WENT BACK TO MY MEAL
AND THIS KID, WHO'S NAME'S JOE
HE JUST SMILED AND ASKED ME:
"WELL, HOW DO YOU KNOW?"

AND I SAID: "OH…"

(She bows and exits.)

ORDERING: Eat What You Kill

by Michael Golamco

CHLOE *and* ZACK *are seated at a table looking at menus.*
A WAITER *arrives—*

WAITER. Hello friends! Do you need to take another minute, or—

CHLOE. I have a question. How's the beef short rib?

WAITER. Oh, it's excellent. They're from a highly marbleized short rib cut, coated in our house dry rub and smoked overnight until absolutely tender.

ZACK. Wow, that sounds great—

WAITER. They're fantastic. They come from a heifer named Betsy. She had a cream-colored, dappled coat and big brown eyes that trusted deeply. She often dreamed of wide open spaces that she would never look upon, because her very short life was spent in tiny corrals and ended in tremendous agony—

CHLOE. Um… How's the chicken?

WAITER. Why, it's fantastic of course! It's marinated overnight in a blend of olive oil, garlic, and herbs we grow ourselves on our terrace. Then it's roasted and basted.

CHLOE. And it's free-range chicken?

WAITER. Of course it is—we're not monsters here!

ZACK. Let's get that, then—

WAITER. Excellent! Your chicken's name was Bella. She was the pet of a small girl who saved her, just like in *Charlotte's Web*—

ZACK & CHLOE. Uh huh—

WAITER. BUT unlike the book, there wasn't a spider around that could speak English.
So the girl's father took Bella away. Bella was injected with hormones until she couldn't walk, the tip of her beak was chopped off, and the father made the girl watch because she needed to know that THIS IS HOW THE WORLD WORKS—

CHLOE. LET'S GET THE SALAD.

WAITER. Our house salad tonight is sourced from local organic farms who take pride in their work—

ZACK. Sure—

WAITER. Despite the fact that they're always juggling crushing debt and an insanely fickle market. And the farmer who grew your lettuce recently had his hand crushed in a harvester and now has an addiction to painkillers—

ZACK. What.

WAITER. Oxycontin. He crushes it with a rusty spoon and snorts it—

CHLOE. So you're saying that everything on your menu is the product of suffering and death?

WAITER. (*Proudly:*) Of course!

(ZACK *and* CHLOE *look at each other.*)

ZACK. I'm going to do the short ribs.

CHLOE. I'll have the chicken.

WAITER. I'll put those right in.

THE GAME

by Carson Kreitzer

Part Two

Four people. Sitting. Maybe on beanbag chairs.
Silence.
Finally:

ONE. The Naked and the Bread.

(*All nod.*)

TWO. The *Bun* Also Rises.

(*Ad libs— "Ah hah." "Good one."*
THREE *starts to say something. Then stops. Then starts again.*)

THREE. (*Quickly.*) Yeast of Eden.

(*More ad libs of approval.*
Silence.)

FOUR. Ham On Rye.

TWO. No!

ONE. What?

THREE. Maybe…

TWO. No! We're playing Novels and Baked Goods! Not Poetry that already has bread in the title!!!

ONE. What?

THREE. (*Explaining.*) Bukowski…

FOUR. (*Calm.*) It's a novel.

TWO. No! Bukowski's a poet

FOUR. It's a novel. *Bildungsroman.*

ONE. What?

THREE. (*Explaining.*) Coming of age novel.

TWO. GODDAMMIT. You gotta do something to it, you can't just find it *lying* there.

FOUR. (*Quite pleased with self.*) Found art.
I am Marcel Duchamp.

TWO. Come on…

THREE. I believe the round is to Marcel.

ONE. Catcher in the Rye? Bread?

TWO. I'm hungry.
Let's order a pizza.

TOMATOES

by Carson Kreitzer

Light on a farmer. Young. Kinda Little House on the Prairie, *kinda Seattle/rock and roll. Sexy in a confident, low-key way.*

FARMER. This land
has been my family's farm for seven generations
and this one...
I knew my sister didn't want to do it, she'd moved away already, and
my brother didn't want to do it, he was in Law School
and
I was going to school for MB&B, uh, microbiology and biochemistry
but I realized that if I didn't do it
none of us were gonna do it
and it would be gone.
my grandfather's farm.
And his father's. And his father's.
Seven generations of our family putting their hands in this dirt.
So I quit school and started to learn.
Apprenticed myself to a farmer who grew other things than we did. Wanted
to bring something back to the farm,
something new.
We were mostly dairy cows, meat cows, with a little kitchen garden.
Now we've got heirloom lettuces, redleaf, Greenleaf, oakleaf, tatsoi, mizuna,
we've got kale, kohlrabi, cabbage, brussel sprouts
summer squash, zucchini, Patti-pan, butternut, buttercup
One of my favorite things, now that we're branching out, is the heirloom
*tomatoes

     (WOMAN *appears, overlapping at* *.)

WOMAN. *Tomatoes!
I grow them in the backyard... Started out with just a few plants, but every
summer now we plant more and more. Early Girl, Brandywine, Cherokee
Purple, and of course you've got to plant some *cherry tomatoes

     (GIRL *becomes visible, overlapping at* *.)

GIRL. *Cherry tomatoes!

WOMAN. for that not-quite-instant, but constant, ongoing gratification.
First to ripen up, and then a steady stream all season.

GIRL. I grow them in a pot up on my roof—these crazy tiny little things.
So sweet! I got the pot at the greenmarket on 14th Street, I thought, I can do
this. I don't care if I'm in Manhattan. I've got roof access!

WOMAN. We started with just a little patch—

GIRL. There's great sun up there. We're up pretty high.

FARMER. They're tough, you know, take a lot of love. Tomatoes. Hard to transport.

Have to be very gentle with them. They bruise easy.

GIRL. It *bakes* though. You've got to make sure you're up there every other day, every day if it's one of those crazy New York heat waves.

WOMAN. ...We had a couple of scrubby little mulberries by the side of the house, we ripped those out and added some bags of topsoil and compost we got from the Home Depot.

GIRL. Me, lugging a watering can up in the elevator, up those last two flights to the roof.

And then you're up. Out. In the baking hot sun, on the baking hot tar roof.

FARMER. There used to be things I liked, and things I didn't... Picking the squash, the prickers on the leaves, your arms get all scratched up, I hated when it was time to pick the squash, but now

WOMAN. And now we're just hooked!

FARMER. I just love it all.

Every day. I just love to get out here. Whatever it is that needs to be done.

WOMAN. We've got three raised beds, my husband rigged up a watering system from those rain barrels over there by the garage, all the way over to here...

GIRL. Seems like you can see the whole world from up here. For once, the city is quiet.

Tiny people, getting into taxicabs, kissing on the street corner, going into the deli for a carton of milk...

WOMAN. They're trellised, which is great for a smaller amount of space, but they get heavy like that and they can just snap the twine—

GIRL. Birds, swooping close. The sun on my skin.

(*Beat. A moment.*)

FARMER. You pick something. Something to do. Some little corner of the world.

To make better.

To make it grow.

And feed people.

And sustain

us.

Right?

I mean, I don't want to get all...

but I kind of do.

That's what we're doing, here.

Putting our hands in the dirt.

Giving back to the dirt. Not just taking, any more. Not depleting—practicing the old ways, crop rotation, bringing the nitrogen back to the soil the way they used to, legumes, using the manure to enrich the soil, keeping it healthy and full of worms and bacteria the breakdown of plant matter into dirt

good, black dirt.

Bury me in it, man.

That's our land.

It's the dirt.

I'm taking care

of the dirt.

     (Beat. The energy picks back up.)

It's not a big farm. Just a few acres for the vegetables.

WOMAN. It's just my backyard. And this bit on the side, where it gets the good sun—

GIRL. It's not much. Just a plastic bucket. Maybe ten pounds of dirt. Felt like my arms were gonna fall off, carrying it home on the subway, but it's not that much.

But it's *my* dirt.

WOMAN. My favorites this year are these striped romas…

FARMER. Next week we're getting in the first of the heirloom tomatoes. Brandywine. Cherokee Purple. They're *almost* there.

WOMAN. I mean, I love the eating tomatoes. The fresh slicers. But there's just something about the romas, the way you can have a great big pot full of 'em, bubbling, and the smell of garlic and oregano all through the house.

FARMER. I love this time of year. BLT time…

GIRL. And I get to sit on my roof. Looking out over the city. Eating cherry tomatoes, warm from the sun.

FARMER. Fresh sourdough bread—

WOMAN. This year I think we've finally got enough. We'll put 'em up. Freeze 'em when it's too hot to cook. And they'll be waiting there, when the days get shorter, and the chill sets in.

FARMER. Bacon crisp and cracking. Whatever lettuce came in that day. Hellman's from the jar.

All you need.

WOMAN. We're gonna have sauce all winter long.

GIRL. It's gonna be winter. And slush. And getting freezing slush splashed all over you by a taxi as you're on your way to an audition, and you're halfway to pneumonia when you show up looking like a freezing drowned rat…

But you know what? I will have stood on my roof in the asphalt heat with cherry tomatoes that I grew
bursting in my mouth.
And that's gonna make it a better year. This year
      (*Smiles.*)
is gonna be better.

C.S.A. BATTLE
by Matt Schatz

We're at a farmers market. A FEMALE FARMER *is at her C.S.A. booth talking to two farmers market* PATRONS. *She is trying to sell them on her C.S.A.*

PATRON 1. What is a C.S.A. again?

FEMALE FARMER. Community-supported agriculture, people pledge support to a farm where the growers and consumers share the risks and benefits of food production.

    (Beat.)

So basically you pay once and you get a box of vegetables and fruit every week. You interested?

PATRON 2. Maybe? But why should we join your vegetable thing over someone else's?

    (A hip hop beat kicks in.)

FEMALE FARMER. Oh well, I'll tell ya.

WHEN I WAS A LITTLE GIRL I WENT TO A FARM
THIS LADY WHO WAS EIGHTY CAME AND TOOK ME BY THE ARM
SHE SHOWED ME WHAT SHE DID AND EVER SINCE I ALWAYS KNEW THAT
I WAS JUST A KID BUT I SAID SHIT I WANNA DO THAT
MY MOTHER IS A DOCTOR AND MY FATHER IS A LAWYER
I COME FROM A PLANET WHERE THERE'S GRANITE IN THE FOYER
MY PARENTS THEY WERE SKEPTICAL BUT NOW I'M
AN EMPLOYER
EVEN THOUGH I DRESS LIKE TOM SAWYER

SIGN UP FOR MY C.S.A.
THERE'S ONLY ONE PRICE YA PAY
WE EVEN GOT A ONE DAY SALE
AND NEXT WEEK WE GOT KALE
SIGN UP, SIGN UP

    (MALE FARMER *enters and takes position at a C.S.A. booth near* FEMALE FARMER.
    He gets the attention of the PATRONS.)

MALE FARMER. THIS IS NOT THE KIND OF WORK THAT I THOUGHT I WOULD DO

BUT MY FATHER WAS A FARMER SO NOW I'M A FARMER TOO
THERE IS NOT A FREAKIN' LOT THAT I WOULD LIKE TO ADD
DO YOU LIKE MY SHIRT?
IT'S PLAID.

SIGN UP FOR MY C.S.A.
THAT IS ALL I HAVE TO SAY...

    (FEMALE FARMER *sees* MALE FARMER *as competition and goes at him.*)

FEMALE FARMER. LOOKY LOOKY HERE LOOKS
LIKE SOMEONE GREW A CROP
THIS LITTLE SKITTISH KID IS LIKE A BRITTLE BRITTISH FOP
MY BEETS ARE RED AND MEATY YO
HIS BEETS ARE PINK AND PALLID
I WOULDN'T TAKE A LEEK FROM HIM
LET ALONE A SALAD
BABY DON'T YOU KNOW NOW THAT MY SHIT IS
SELF-SUSTAINABLE?
MY EXPERTISE AND KNOWHOW IS MAD CRAZY
UNATTAINABLE
I'M A VEGETARIAN BUT BABY I'M A CAIN-NIBAL
BECAUSE I'LL EAT A FARMER LIKE A AIN-IMAL

SIGN UP FOR MY C.S.A.

    (*The* PATRONS *are tug-of-warring between the two C.S.A.'s.*)

MALE FARMER. SIGN UP FOR MY C.S.A.

FEMALE FARMER. SIGN UP FOR MY C.S.A.

MALE FARMER. SIGN UP FOR MY C.S.A.

FEMALE FARMER. I'M THE BOMBEST FARMER THAT YOU'D
EVER WANNA KNOW
I DRIVE TRACTORS PAST THE ACTORS WHEN I'M GOIN' TO A
SHOW
I'M AN ARTIST WHEN I HARVEST AND I PLANT BEYOND
BELIEF
AND SUDDENLY HE'S GOT BEEF?

MALE FARMER. I do have beef actually.

PATRON 2. Your C.S.A. has beef?

MALE FARMER. We do!

FEMALE FARMER. You do?

PATRON 1. I like beef.

    (*The* PATRONS *sign up at* MALE FARMER'*s booth.*)

MALE FARMER. THEY SIGNED UP FOR MY C.S.A.
THEY SIGNED UP FOR MY C.S.A.
THEY SIGNED UP FOR MY C.S.A.
THEY SIGNED UP FOR MY C.S.A.
YAY!

ORDERING: Free Lunch

by Michael Golamco

> MACK *and* DENNIS *are sitting at a table getting ready to order lunch.*
> MACK *puts down his menu.*

MACK. I'm gonna get the burger.

DENNIS. Cool. By the way, I got this.

MACK. (*Jovially annoyed, like they're an old married couple.*) "You've got this?" Why are you getting this?

DENNIS. Well, I actually have an ulterior motive in buying you lunch.

MACK. (*Playfully peeved.*) Oh, I see.

DENNIS. Yeah… I have a favor to ask you.

MACK. I give you a favor and you give me a burger.

DENNIS. (*Laughing.*) Yes please.

MACK. You need my truck, don't you?

DENNIS. …Maybe.

MACK. Damn. I hate owning a truck.

DENNIS. Too bad, Truck Buddy!

MACK. You know what? I'm changing my order.

DENNIS. But I haven't told you what the favor is yet.

MACK. I don't care. I'm gettin' a steak.

DENNIS. This favor is not worthy of a steak. It is at or beneath the burger level.

MACK. Shouldn't I be the judge of that?

DENNIS. Okay, well what if I want you to give me a ride to the airport?

MACK. Now that's worth a burger.

DENNIS. Help me move my TV?

MACK. Worth a double burger.

DENNIS. Help me move my bed?

MACK. Triple burger. It's a quarter pound of beef per 50 pounds of weight to be moved.

DENNIS. That sounds fair.

Catsit my cat?

MACK. A steak.

DENNIS. What?!

MACK. I hate your cat.

DENNIS. Gee, what a way to find out.
What if I want you to give me a hug?

MACK. That's worth one chicken nugget.

DENNIS. Oh, that's nice.
Gently caress my face?

MACK. Chicken sandwich.

DENNIS. A full body massage?

MACK. Chicken sandwich.

DENNIS. (*Amazed at the possibilities.*) Whoa.
Go on a date with my newly divorced Mom?

MACK. Your Mom's lasagna.

DENNIS. Be my Pretend Internet Supermodel Girlfriend to make people think I'm cool?

MACK. One French fry per Tweet.

DENNIS. Loudly sing in public?

MACK. (*Sings.*) I'LL DO THAT FOR FREE…!

DENNIS. You have a really nice singing voice.

MACK. Thank you.

DENNIS. Strike down my enemies and all who oppose me?

MACK. Spaghetti and meatballs.

DENNIS. Slowly descend into madness?

MACK. A pizza.

DENNIS. Burn my house down and make it look like an accident so I can collect the insurance?

MACK. Steaks for a month.

DENNIS. Kill Steve?

MACK. Steaks for life.

> (DENNIS *pauses, thinking.*
> The WAITER *arrives.*)

WAITER. Hey there, friends. What'll you have?

> (MACK *looks expectantly at* DENNIS.
> DENNIS *leans in, whispers into* MACK's *ear.* MACK *reacts.*)

MACK. I'll have a lobster.

FEAR AND LOATHING AT THE FOOD TRUCK

by Carson Kreitzer .

Part Three: A Minute After That

ADRIAN *exits the truck. Takes pity on* JIMMY.

ADRIAN. Hey—

(*Jerks her head toward* LANA.)

Over there.

JIMMY. Are you serious?

ADRIAN. Ask if she's got any big, fat greens.

(LANA *giggles.*)

JIMMY. Thank you!

ADRIAN. (*On her way out.*) yeah yeah

(JIMMY *approaches* LANA. *More confident, but still as though in a spy movie.*)

JIMMY. Do you have any *big, fat greens?*

LANA. I don't know what you're talking about.

(JIMMY's *face falls.* LANA *cracks up.*)

Oh, so sad! I'm kidding!

(*He looks up. Is she messing with him?*)

Big. Sticky. Greens.

JIMMY. This is a good day.

LANA. It is.

You should get some microgreens, too. They're really good. Have you ever seen a tinier shiso leaf?

JIMMY. I've never seen a shiso leaf.

LANA. Oh, you have to try—here.

(*She places a tiny shiso leaf on his tongue.*)

JIMMY. Wow—that's

LANA. I know, isn't it?

JIMMY. I'll take…whatever the Greens Mistress recommends.

LANA. A package of our finest, coming right up.

NOT ALWAYS SO GOOD

by Matt Schatz

We hear music. A riff similar to the opening number ("I Am Good At Eating A Lot"), but slower, sadder.
Spotlight on COMPETITOR 1. *He or she is holding a trophy.*

COMPETITOR 1. IN DENVER
I ATE TOO MANY OMELETS
IN EVERY CONTEST
SOMEBODY VOMITS
AT A DAY'S INN IN DAYTON
SPENT TWO DAYS ON THE POT
I WOULD STOP IF I COULD
CUZ WHILE I'VE ALWAYS BEEN GOOD AT EATING A LOT
EATING A LOT IS NOT ALWAYS GOOD
I SAY THAT EATING A LOT IS NOT ALWAYS SO GOOD

I SAY THAT EATING A LOT
IS NOT ALWAYS SO GOOD

LAST SUPPER

by Michael Golamco

SAMANTHA, *20s, seated at a kitchen table.*
She is extremely ill. Maybe wearing a head scarf. Weak. But content. Still very much alive inside.
GIL, *20s, her brother, comes out of the kitchen wearing an apron. He's been cooking—a lot.*

GIL. All right Sam: Everything's cooking. All of your absolute favorite things.

SAMANTHA. Yay!

GIL. Peach cobbler's in the oven, made with canned peaches.

SAMANTHA. Mom's recipe!

GIL. Yep, Mom's recipe.

SAMANTHA. Just like she'd make whenever one of us got sick.

GIL. Yeah.
And I'm mixing the waffle batter in fifteen minutes; finished wrapping the hot dogs in bacon, and the gravy's going to be done in five.

SAMANTHA. (*Like Billy Bob Thornton in* Sling Blade.) With MASHED POTATERS.

GIL. Yes, with mashed potatoes. And then I've got McDonalds' French fries that need to go into the toaster oven.

SAMANTHA. You didn't need to do all that.

GIL. It's no problem. It's for you.

SAMANTHA. I know, but.

GIL. Anything for my little sister.
And then tomorrow.

SAMANTHA. Gil.

GIL. (*Strangely distant.*) Everything's all laid out, all set for tomorrow.

SAMANTHA. Gil, can we not talk about—

GIL. (*Hurt.*) I'm sorry.

SAMANTHA. It's okay. I'd rather not.
Let's just enjoy ourselves right now.

> (*He pulls out a chair for her. She sits.*)

GIL. Hey, you know what? I found Mom's old photo album.

SAMANTHA. ...Yeah?

GIL. Yeah, it's got a bunch of old pictures of you and me, and later I thought that we could—

(*The doorbell rings. GIL looks at* SAMANTHA *quizzically.* SAMANTHA *smiles, shrugs. GIL goes to get the door—and returns with* CHRIS, *20s. He's bearing a meatloaf.*)

CHRIS. WASSUP SAMMICH.

SAMANTHA. CHRIS P.!

(*They hug. Perhaps a little too much.*)

GIL. Have we met?

(SAM *hangs off of* CHRIS.)

SAMANTHA. Gil—you remember Chris!

(CHRIS *extends his hand.*)

CHRIS. We met three years ago!

GIL. We did?

CHRIS. (*Trying to jog* GIL's *memory.*) I was the guy at Dan Chung's party...

SAMANTHA. He was in Dan's bedroom...

CHRIS. Rolling the spliffs...

GIL. (*Vaguely remembering.*) Oh, right... (*Suddenly remembering.*) Wait, you're Chris Preston.

CHRIS. (*Cheerful.*) I so totally am!

GIL. You burned down our high school's gym!

CHRIS. (*Still cheerful.*) That was so totally unintentional!

GIL. I...didn't know you were coming.

CHRIS. Your sister called me!

SAMANTHA. I called him!

GIL. (*Trying to remember.*) Wait—did the two of you ever...

SAMANTHA. Yeah—we used to / date—

CHRIS. Yeah, I used to

(*Makes a hand gesture indicating sex.*)

your sister.

(SAM *cracks up.*)

SAMANTHA. Yeah, he used to

(*Makes the same hand gesture.*)

me.

(CHRIS *and* SAM *both crack up.* GIL *doesn't.*)

CHRIS. Oh! I BROUGHT IT.

(CHRIS *proudly presents the meatloaf.*)

SAMANTHA. (*More thrilled than we've ever seen her.*) OH MY GOD!!!

GIL. What is that.

SAMANTHA. It's Chris's meatloaf.

CHRIS. I make a really good meatloaf, bro.

SAMANTHA. It should begin with a capital M, this Meatloaf.

CHRIS. I'm kind of a prodigy at making Meatloaves.

SAMANTHA. HIS MEATLOAVES ARE MAGIC.

CHRIS. You've heard of First World Problems? My Meatloaves are First World Awesomes.

SAMANTHA. They are Awesomes!!

GIL. I'm sure they are. (*To* SAMANTHA:) Can I talk to you for a sec?

SAMANTHA. What's up?

GIL. Can I talk to you alone for a sec?

SAMANTHA. You can say whatever you want—Chris doesn't mind.

CHRIS. I don't mind, bro.

SAMANTHA. Look at him, he totally doesn't.

GIL. Okay: I thought that we were gonna take tonight for ourselves.

SAMANTHA. It is for ourselves.

GIL. Just for ourselves.

SAMANTHA. Change of plans.

GIL. Yeah, well, I wasn't informed of the—

SAMANTHA. I declare a change of plans.
I haven't seen Chris in a really long time and I remembered how f'ing good his Meatloaf is.

CHRIS. You almost have to use the f-word when you describe my meatloaf, bro.

SAMANTHA. It's soooo good, and I wanted to taste it again.

GIL. I know but—

SAMANTHA. Just one last time.
One last little taste.

CHRIS. So your sister called me and let me know what's going on—

GIL. (*Uncertain, betrayed.*) Sam—

CHRIS. She told me about your guys' plan. And I'm all for it. It's a person's right.

GIL. Okay, I appreciate that, but this is a private moment.

CHRIS. And so, I made this just for her.

SAMANTHA. It's made with bacon.

CHRIS. And love.

SAMANTHA. It's to die for.

GIL. Okay—

CHRIS. TOTALLY TO DIE FOR!

> (*The moment is extremely awkward.*
> SAMANTHA *is amused.* GIL *is not.*)

GIL. Well if this was any other night I'd say okay, fine—

SAMANTHA. But—

GIL. But it's tonight, so—

SAMANTHA. Well I don't see why you need to be so—

GIL. Not tonight. Okay?

Because I'm cooking for you—everything that you love, all your favorite things plus French fries from McDonalds, so thank you Chris for the meatloaf, but tonight is just for—

SAMANTHA. He's staying.

GIL. Tonight is just for family—

SAMANTHA. He's staying Gil, because I asked him to make me a Meatloaf and he made it and he's going to eat it with us—

CHRIS. (*Relenting.*) Sam—

SAMANTHA. No, Chris—

CHRIS. I should just go, Sammich.

SAMANTHA. Hold on.

CHRIS. Your bro's right.

You're right, bro: This is a family moment, you guys are family, I'm going.

GIL. Thank you Chris for being polite.

> (CHRIS *gives the Meatloaf to* SAMANTHA.)

SAMANTHA. No—wait—STOP, stay right where you are. (*To* GIL.) I want us to all eat together.

GIL. Sam: This isn't part of the plan—

SAMANTHA. F THE PLAN! (*To* CHRIS.) You: Don't go. (*To* GIL.) You: Do something for me.

> (*She grabs a fork, shoves it into* GIL's *hand. Re: The Meatloaf.*)

Taste it.

GIL. You want me to—

SAMANTHA. Taste the F'in Meatloaf, Gil.

> (GIL *pauses.*)

DO IT.

> (GIL *tentatively places a fork in the Meatloaf, draws out a nugget of it, and eats it.*)

GIL. It's...
Really average.

> (*Chris laughs.*)

SAMANTHA. Shut up.

GIL. Okay, it's really good.
Really really good.

> (*Surprised at how sincere he is in this moment:*)

It's actually the best Meatloaf I've ever tasted.

CHRIS. It's the last Meatloaf you should ever eat, man.
It ruins you for all other meatloaves.

GIL. It does.
It really, really does.

> (*To* CHRIS:)

You want a beer?

CHRIS. You got a Pabst?

GIL. No.

CHRIS. (*Ceremoniously.*) Then I shall have whatever!!

GIL. I'll set another place.

> (SAM *hugs him, hangs off of him.*)

SAMANTHA. Thank you, Gil.

GIL. You're welcome.
Chris... Have a seat.

CHRIS. Let's eat.

> (*Lights going down. Suddenly realizing:*)

Bro—we just made a rhyme!

FIRST TASTE

by Steve Moulds

The APPRENTICE *and the* MASTER BAKER *sit. The kitchen is clean, the oven is working, and the brownies are still baking. Nothing to do but wait. That, and bust the* APPRENTICE's *chops.*

MASTER BAKER. Have you always been this quiet?

(*The* APPRENTICE *makes a noncommittal gesture.*)

Didn't you ever raise your hand in class? Say a prayer at the dinner table?

(*The* APPRENTICE *nods. Of course she did those things.*)

I mean, I know it's nice to be a good listener, but this is ridiculous. You're actively <u>trying</u> not to speak. And that's just…well, it's rude is what it is.

(*The* APPRENTICE *shrugs. Maybe it is, maybe it isn't.*)

You're not mute, are you?

(*No, she's not.*)

You got secrets you're not telling me, and that sorta thing drives me crazy. You can keep secrets from <u>other</u> people. But you gotta tell <u>me</u>. That's the rule in my kitchen. I get to know things.

(*The* APPRENTICE *opens her mouth as if to speak, then reconsiders.*)

Then I'm just gonna guess. I'm gonna make up all sorts of things about you.

(*She gestures—go ahead.*)

You have guilt you're carrying around. You had a friend in elementary school, she would buy two desserts every day for lunch. And you never told her that was a bad idea. So when you make cookies now, or cupcakes, you think about her, and how she probably has diabetes, and how you're contributing to the same industry that killed your childhood best friend.

(*Killed? What the hell is he talking about?*)

If I'm wrong, speak up.

(*She holds his gaze. The* MASTER BAKER *suddenly has an epiphany.*)

No, I've got it. This is an act of rebellion. You're acting out against your mother's wishes. No, that's too easy. Your father. And he always hated desserts. Never saw the need for a sweet tooth. Felt it was indulgent.

But he <u>did</u> like to drink. He even had a saying—"The bitter, the better."

(*What does that even mean?*)

Don't look at me. He's <u>your</u> father.

And your dad, he'd get to the end of a long week, and he'd come home from work and his little girl—that'd be you—she'd have already poured him a cocktail. And he would think, "What a weird daughter I have." Let's see. What did he drink?

(It hits him. Of course.)

Bourbon. Maker's on the rocks.

Is that why you put bourbon in your brownies? You want to make Dad happy?

(She stares at him. This is an absurd notion.)

This is fun. Maybe we can tie in your high school crush somehow.

(But before he can continue, the APPRENTICE *shushes him loudly. It's the first sound she's made.*

He stops talking, stunned, and looks at her. But she's looking at the oven. Which now dings.

The APPRENTICE *opens the oven, and pulls out a pan of the most delicious brownies you've ever smelled.*

She places them on the counter and raises a knife to cut.)

MASTER BAKER. Aren't you gonna let them— (cool first) ?

(But she silences him with one upraised finger.

She takes a taste of the brownie. Hard to tell if she likes it. She's awfully circumspect.

Then she cuts a slightly larger piece, puts it on a plate, and carries it over to a member of the audience.

She hands it to them and gestures for them to eat.

Presumably, they do.

And when they've finished taking their first bite:)

APPRENTICE. ...I think they're pretty good.

(The MASTER BAKER *smiles. So does the* APPRENTICE.

Everyone should feel happy now.)

THE GAME
by Carson Kreitzer

Part Three

> *The gang. Hangin' around. Beanbag chairs? Ad libs of varying degrees of approval.*

ONE. Much Ado About Nu—
tella?

> *(Eh…)*

TWO. Julius Caesar Salad.

> *(That's more like it…)*

THREE. Anchovy and Cleopatra.

> *(Good one!)*

FOUR. The Taming of the Shrimp.

FIVE. Love's Lobster's Lost.

TWO. A Midsummer Night's Bream?

ONE. What?

TWO. 's a fish.
fergeddit.

FOUR. Romeo and Junior Mints?

TWO. As You Pike It?

ONE. What?

TWO. 's a fish.
fergeddit.

ONE. Henry the Fifth of Bourbon!

> *(Yeah!)*

TWO. HENRY THE FISH!

ONE. QUIT IT WITH THE FISH!

FOUR. Oh, Jello!

FIVE. The Merchant of Venison.

> *(Nice…)*

TWO. *(Can't resist…)* All's Whelk that Ends Whelk…

ONE. whatthehell is—

TWO. *(Dying.)* 's a mollusk!

ONE. I SAID QUIT

FIVE. Coriander-olanus?

TWO. *Romeo and Jellyfish!*

ONE. *(Gritted teeth.)* I will rip you limb from limb...

THREE. Troilus and Cress...

>   *(hmmm)*

ONE. Huh. subtle.

>   *(Enough of that...)*

FOUR. Much Ado About Pork.

FIVE. All's Pork that Ends Pork.

THREE. The Merry Wives of...Pork!

>   *(A sudden group realization... They rush and overlap:)*

ONE & TWO. *Ham*-let!

FIVE. Omelet!

THREE & FOUR. HAMLET ON RYE!

FEAR AND LOATHING AT THE FOOD TRUCK
by Carson Kreitzer

Part Four: Much Later. Now.

LANA and JIMMY *have been tasting the greens. Of all sorts.*
They are baked and giggling.
Giggling and baked.
DAVE has somehow found his way into the inner sanctum of the food truck.

DAVE. You really think it's okay for me to be in here?

JEANNINE. I think so.

DAVE. I mean, I don't want to get you in trouble.

JEANNINE. (*Flirty.*) Yeah. We wouldn't want that.

DAVE. I just...didn't wanna...

JEANNINE. Uh-huh?

DAVE. Go home without
at least trying to
(Damn, I'm—
so bad at this)

JEANNINE. Actually, I think you're doing okay.

DAVE. Really?

JEANNINE. You're in the truck, aren't you?

　　　(*Outside,* LANA *and* JIMMY:)

LANA. I love grass.

JIMMY. Me, too. (*Giggling.*) "Grass"...

LANA. No...the grass! That we're sitting on!

JIMMY. (*Giggling some more.*) Oh, yeah...that's pretty great, too!

LANA. Grass? Who says "grass"? That's like—

JIMMY. My uncle says "grass"

LANA. history book stuff. Really?

　　　(*He nods.*)

How old is your uncle?

JIMMY. OLD!!!

　　　(*They hysteric about this for a bit. Meanwhile, in the Food Truck:*)

DAVE. I really don't... I know, this is your first day of work and everything.
I wouldn't want—
I mean, if I should just leave

JEANNINE. do you want to leave?

DAVE. No, I don't want to leave—

>   (LANA *looks over at them.*)

LANA. Uh-oh. Lover's spat.

JIMMY. (*Instantly in hysterics.*) SPAT!

LANA. (*Laughing.*) Yeah, like a…
like they're having a…

JIMMY. SPAT!

JEANNINE. Yeah, I'm risking my job, here

DAVE. I knew it. I'll just—

JEANNINE. Would you think about that for a second? What kind of—

DAVE. I'm trying not to do the wrong thing, is all, I just—

JEANNINE. Well you're about to.

DAVE. You don't want me to—?

JEANNINE. No.
I don't.
Okay?

>   (*He finally stops fidgeting and fussing, trying to leave. Looks at her. Smiles.*)

JIMMY. Like a THING
that goes on your
SHOE

LANA. What on earth are you

JIMMY. SPATS COLUMBO!
The gangster—
So named because he used to ARGUE WITH HIS GIRLFRIEND IN PUBLIC ALL THE TIME!

LANA. Oh, SPATS!
Yeah.

>   (DAVE *moves toward* JEANNINE. *Brushes her hair back from her face.*)

You never just have a spat.

JIMMY. Unless you lost one!

>   (DAVE *leans in.* JEANNINE *leans in. They are kissing. Sweet.*)

Then you would have a spat.
Singular.

LANA. A singular spat.
I think it's over, anyway.

>   (*They look over at the kissing couple.* JEANNINE *pulls down the grate, or a roll-top shade. It says "CLOSED."*)

JIMMY. Uh-oh.

Closed for business.

You think that truck's gonna start a-rockin'?

LANA. I would not be surprised.

You see all kinds of things at the Farmers Market. All kinds of humanity. Birth. Death.

JIMMY. Grass.

LANA. Grass!

LANA & JIMMY. Spats!

> (*Romantic music begins to emanate from the Food Truck. Perhaps "Strangers in the Night."*)

JIMMY. (*Suddenly standing and extending a hand.*) Madame, would you care to dance?

LANA. (*Surprised to realize this.*) You know, I would.

> (*She takes his proffered hand, rises. They sway, surprisingly elegantly, there in the grass.*
> *Elsewhere,* ADRIAN *surveys the scene. She's talking to the* FARMER.)

ADRIAN. How was your day?

FARMER. Pretty good. How 'bout you?

ADRIAN. Well, I think my new trainee has a boyfriend.

FARMER. That's nice.

ADRIAN. I guess.

As long as she's not crying into the register tape this time next week.

FARMER. How come you gotta have that dark outlook all the time?

ADRIAN. Cos you got the sunny disposition taken care of.

> (*She leans in for a kiss.*)

FARMER. You wanna go home?

ADRIAN. Yeah.

Whaddaya think, should I lock 'em in?

FARMER. See if they want a Mutsu.

> (ADRIAN *approaches the Food Truck. Knocks.*)

JEANNINE. We're closed!

ADRIAN. A little ahead of schedule.

> (*There is a flurry of activity behind the shade. Soft cursing, clothing being rearranged.*
> *The* FARMER *calls to* LANA *and* JIMMY.)

FARMER. Hey—you want a Mutsu?

LANA. Hey Frank! Yeah!

(*He throws her an apple. And one to* JIMMY.
The shade flies up. JEANNINE *and* DAVE, *hair messed up, breathless.*)

JEANNINE. Oh god, am I fired?

ADRIAN. Are the receipts totaled up?

JEANNINE. Yeah, they're all right here—

ADRIAN. And the drawer balanced?

JEANNINE. Yes, it's fine, I put the money in the envelope, and the bank is ready to go—

ADRIAN. All right then.
See you tomorrow.

      (*They stare at her.*)

Outta the truck or I'm lockin' you in.

DAVE. Sorry—

JEANNINE. Sorry—

      (*They stumble out.* ADRIAN *locks up.*)

See you tomorrow?

ADRIAN. Yeah.

      (DAVE *and* JEANNINE *head off together, hand in hand, smiling.*
      ADRIAN *and the* FARMER *head to their car.*
      LANA *and* JIMMY *bite into their apples.*
      Crunch.)

LANA & JIMMY. Goddamn.

LANA. That's a good apple.

THE FAMILY FEAST
by Steve Moulds

Part Two

The meal is in full swing now. People are on their second or third plates, making sure to pick out the dishes they didn't have room for before, with perhaps a forkful or two of an earlier favorite.
MARY *steps aside from all of it to talk to us.*

MARY. I think this might be Mom's best feast yet.

I should give Dad some credit too. He <u>was</u> the one who roasted the pig. But let's be honest. This is Mom's victory.

(She surveys the feast. People really are having a good time.)

I mean, Andrea and Susan haven't spoken since their boys got into that scrap at the St. Joe's picnic last year. But there they are smiling at each other while Susan eats Andrea's cheese grits. If that's not forgiveness…

And check out Aunt Jocelyn talking up her French silk so she can get investors in that pie shop she's always wanted.

Oh my god, and little Johnny, sucking on that pig's eye socket like a lollipop? That's… the future of Kentucky basketball right there.

I know this is technically a family picnic, but as far as I'm concerned, this might as well be the state fair. I feel like this is what the harvest was like back in the old days—more food than you could ever save, and a place at the table for everyone.

I just wish Sally could've made it. She and Mom need to stand in the same room and… I don't know, scream? Hug it out? Punch each other? Something different from the last three years.

Those two could teach a master class in overreacting to an argument. The way Mom blanched when Sally decided to track down her birth parents was just stupid. And she definitely never understood the Alaska thing. I don't think <u>Sally</u> understands the Alaska thing.

But deciding that the Family Feast was Mom's elaborate scheme to get her to come home? That's a stretch, even for Sally. And yeah, we get it, you're vegetarian. But the roast pig is for our <u>guests</u>.

Last week, I dropped some hints on Facebook that if she was going to finally make it to one of these, this would be the year. And not just 'cause Dad's feeling worse. But after a message or two, she dropped off the face of the earth. Again.

I guess what pisses me off the most about my sister is that she's never understood herself. She likes to believe that she's the family outcast, because she's adopted, and liberal, and…well-traveled, or something. But you find two women more similarly stubborn than Sally and Mom, and I will pay you a thousand dollars.

(MARY *doesn't notice it, but* SALLY, *carrying her backpack and suitcase and wearing her winter coat, stumbles into the celebration.*
MARY *looks down at the plate of food in her hand.*)

Ah well. It was a great day. I should start cleaning up.

(*And then she catches sight of* SALLY *across the way.* SALLY's *saying hi to a few people, looking for a good place to put her stuff down, generally out of sorts. Then, before* SALLY *even sees it coming,* MARY *is hugging her. It lasts a long time.*
Finally, MARY *breaks the hug, and with a big smile on her face:*)

MARY. You want something to eat?

DO YOU WANT SOMETHING TO EAT
by Matt Schatz

Someone in the band begins to play. The same familiar riff. BAND MEMBER 1 begins to sing in a melody reminiscent of the bridge to "I Am Good At Eating A Lot."

BAND MEMBER 1. *(To SALLY.)*
SO, DO YOU WANT SOMETHING TO EAT?
THERE'S PLENTY OF STUFF WITHOUT MEAT
SO, COME AND HAVE SOMETHING TO EAT
WE ALWAYS SAVE YOU A SEAT
WE ALWAYS SAVE YOU A SEAT
WE ALWAYS SAVE YOU A SEAT

(The rest of the band joins in. The music builds.)

BAND MEMBER 2. *(To the FEASTERS.)*
SO, DO YOU WANT SOMETHING TO EAT?

(To SOMEONE specific.)

WE HEARD YOU'RE ALLERGIC TO WHEAT
STILL, WE'LL FIND YOU SOMETHING TO EAT
WE ALWAYS SAVE YOU A SEAT

(EVERYBODY joins in. Banging on dishes with silverware, stomping on the floor, that kind of thing.)

EVERYBODY. *(To the audience.)*
SO, DO YOU WANT SOMETHING TO EAT?
WITHOUT YOU, THE MEAL'S INCOMPLETE
COME AND HAVE SOMETHING TO EAT
WE'LL ALWAYS SAVE YOU A TREAT
WHETHER IT'S SAV'RY OR SWEET
WE'LL ALWAYS SAVE YOU A SEAT
WE'LL ALWAYS SAVE YOU A SEAT
WE'LL ALWAYS SAVE YOU A SEAT

(The music stops. In the clear.)
WE'LL ALWAYS SAVE YOU A SEAT

End of Play